The Foreign Policy of the European Union

Stephan Keukeleire
and
Jennifer MacNaughtan

palgrave
macmillan

First published 2008 by
PALGRAVE MACMILLAN
Houndmills, Basingstoke, Hampshire RG21 6XS and
175 Fifth Avenue, New York, N.Y. 10010
Companies and representatives throughout the world

PALGRAVE MACMILLAN is the global academic imprint of the Palgrave Macmillan division of St. Martin's Press, LLC and of Palgrave Macmillan Ltd. Macmillan® is a registered trademark in the United States, United Kingdom and other countries. Palgrave is a registered trademark in the European Union and other countries.

ISBN-13: 978–1–4039–4721–5   hardback
ISBN-10: 1–4039–4721–X   hardback
ISBN-13: 978–1–4039–4722–2   paperback
ISBN-10: 1–4039–4722–8   paperback

This book is printed on paper suitable for recycling and made from fully managed and sustained forest sources. Logging, pulping and manufacturing processes are expected to conform to the environmental regulations of the country of origin.

A catalogue record for this book is available from the British Library.

A catalog record for this book is available from the Library of Congress.

10   9   8   7   6   5   4   3
17   16   15   14   13   12   11   10   09   08

Printed and bound by The Cromwell Press, Trowbridge, Wiltshire.

To Klaartje, Camille and Soetkin

To Adam

Contents

List of Tables and Figures

Tables

Figures

List of Abbreviations

ACP	African, Caribbean and Pacific
AFSJ	Area of Freedom, Security and Justice
AIDCO	EuropeAid Cooperation Office
AMIS	African Union Mission in Darfur
APF	African Peace Facility
ASEM	Asia-Europe Meeting
AU	African Union
BAM	Border Assistance Mission
BiH	Bosnia and Herzegovina
CAP	Common Agricultural Policy
CARDS	Community Assistance for Reconstruction, Development and Stabilization (Balkans)
CCP	Common Commercial Policy
CEECs	Central and Eastern European countries
CFSP	Common Foreign and Security Policy
CIS	Commonwealth of Independent States
CIVCOM	Committee for Civilian Aspects of Crisis Management
COREPER	Committee of Permanent Representatives
COREU	Correspondance européenne
COTER	Council Working Party on Terrorism
CSCE	Conference on Security and Cooperation in Europe
DCI	Development Cooperation Instrument
DDR	disarmament, demobilization and reintegration
DG	Directorate General
DG E	Directorate General E – External Economic Relations, Politico-Military Affairs (Council of the EU)
DG ECHO	Directorate General Humanitarian Aid (European Commission)
DG RELEX	Directorate General External Relations (European Commission)

DRC	Democratic Republic of Congo
EAR	Emergency Aid Reserve
EBA	'Everything but Arms'
EBRD	European Bank for Reconstruction and Development
EC	European Community
ECAP	European Capabilities Action Plan
ECJ	European Court of Justice
ECOFIN	Economic and Financial Affairs Council
ECOWAS	Economic Community of West African States
ECSC	European Coal and Steel Community
EDA	European Defence Agency
EDC	European Defence Community
EDEM	European Defence Equipment Market
EDF	European Development Fund
EDR	energy dependence rate
EDTIB	European Defence, Technological and Industrial Base
EEAS	European External Action Service
EEC	European Economic Community
EIDHR	European Initiative/Instrument for Democracy and Human Rights
EMP	Euro-Mediterranean Partnership
EMU	European Monetary Union
ENP	European Neighbourhood Policy
ENPI	European Neighbourhood and Partnership Instrument
EP	European Parliament
EPA	Economic Partnership Agreement
EPC	European Political Cooperation
ESA	European Space Agency
ESDP	European Security and Defence Policy
ESS	European Security Strategy
EU	European Union
EU15	European Union (with 15 member states)
EU25	European Union (with 25 member states)
EU27	European Union (with 27 member states)
EU BAM Rafah	European Union Border Assistance Mission for Rafah Crossing Point
EU COPPS	European Union Co-ordinating Office for Palestinian Police Support

EUMC	European Union Military Committee
EUMS	European Union Military Staff
EUPT	European Union Planning Team
Euratom	European Atomic Energy Community
EUSC	European Union Satellite Centre
EUSR	EU Special Representative
FAO	Food and Agriculture Organization
FYROM	Former Yugoslav Republic of Macedonia
GAERC	General Affairs and External Relations Council
GMES	Global Monitoring for Environment and Security
GNI	Gross National Income
GPS	Global Positioning System
GSP	Generalized System of Preferences
IAEA	International Atomic Energy Agency
ICC	International Criminal Court
ICTY	International Criminal Tribunal for the former Yugoslavia
IFI	international financial institution
IFS	Instrument for Stability
IGC	Intergovernmental Conference
IPA	Instrument for Pre-Accession Assistance
IMF	International Monetary Fund
IPTF	International Police Task Force
IPU	Integrated Police Units
JHA	Justice and Home Affairs
KFOR	Kosovo Force
LDC	Least Developed Countries
MDGs	Millennium Development Goals
MEDA	Mesures d'Accompagnement
MEP	Member of the European Parliament
MFA	Macro-Financial Assistance
MONUC	United Nations Mission in the DRC
NATO	North Atlantic Treaty Organisation
NGOs	non-governmental organizations
NIS	Newly Independent States (former Soviet republics)
NPT	Non-Proliferation Treaty
OCCAR	Organization for Joint Armaments Cooperation
ODA	Overseas Development Aid

OECD	Organisation for Economic Co-operation and Development
OJ	Official Journal of the European Union
OOPEC	Office for Official Publications of the European Communities
OSCE	Organization for Security and Co-operation in Europe
PCA	Partnership and Cooperation Agreements
PJCC	Police and Judicial Cooperation in Criminal Matters
PNR	Passenger Name Records
PSC	Political and Security Committee
QMV	qualified majority vote
RRM	Rapid Reaction Mechanism
SAA	Stabilization and Association Agreement
SALW	small arms and light weapons
SAP	Stabilization and Association Process
SARS	severe acute respiratory syndrome
SEA	Single European Act
SFOR	Stabilization Force in Bosnia and Herzegovina
SSR	security sector reform
TACIS	Technical Aid to the Commonwealth of Independent States
TEC	Treaty establishing the European Community
TEU	Treaty on European Union
TRIPS	World Trade Organization's Agreement on Intellectual Property
UNDP	United Nations Development Programme
UNFCCC	United Nations Framework Convention on Climate Change
UNMIK	United Nations Interim Administration Mission in Kosovo
UNRWA	United Nations Relief and Works Agency for Palestine Refugees in the Near East
UNSC	United Nations Security Council
UNSCR	United Nations Security Council Resolution
WEAG/O	Western European Armaments Group/Organization
WEU	Western European Union
WMD	weapons of mass destruction
WTO	World Trade Organization

Preface

This book is the culmination of a long journey, and has proved both interesting and challenging to write. Not only is the EU foreign policy field vast and complex, it is also a moving target. This work has evolved through different manifestations, spanning several years and locations, and we would like to take this opportunity to say some much deserved thank yous.

We would like to express our gratitude to our publisher at Palgrave, Steven Kennedy; the 'European Union Series' editors, Neill Nugent and William Paterson; and anonymous reviewers for their constructive comments and patience.

Stephan Keukeleire would like to thank the Directors of the European University College Brussels (HUB/EHSAL) and its Master of European Business programme for providing the necessary time to start this book whilst teaching in Brussels. Thanks also to colleagues at the Institute for International and European Policy and the Leuven Centre for Global Governance Studies of the University of Leuven (K.U.Leuven) for their encouragement and useful insights. Stephan would also like to express his gratitude to those who, in the 1980s and 1990s, contributed to the genesis of his thoughts on international relations and European foreign policy, notably Paul Van de Meerssche, Luc Reychler, Hugo Paemen, Karel De Gucht and Simon Nuttall. Jennifer MacNaughtan is particularly grateful for the support over the last years of Neil Winn and Dieter Mahncke. She would also like to thank Alexandra Cupsan-Catalin for her contribution. We are grateful to the team of brilliant young researchers that provided us with relevant data, critical comments and practical assistance. We would particularly like to thank Arnout Justaert of the University of Leuven for his untiring support, dedication and assistance, as well as Edith Drieskens, Tom Delreux, Sue Basu, Simon Schunz, Rouba Al-Fattal, Justine Sys and Tom Corthaut. Thanks also to Alejandro Ribo Labastida, Ruth Seitz and Daniele Marchesi, former assistants at the College of Europe.

Gaining a deeper insight into the marvels of EU foreign policy was only possible through the talks and discussions with many diplomats and civil servants over the last couple of years. Stephan's experience at the Belgian foreign office, as well as Jennifer's experiences at the Commission's DG Development and in the European Parliament, were critical in allowing us to look beyond the EU's facade, documents and institutional arrangements. Thanks to all the practitioners, particularly from the Belgian foreign office, for their time, insights and knowledge. We would also like to thank colleagues from other universities and research institutes who, through our discussions and their constructive remarks, indirectly contributed to this book.

Stephan is grateful to the students who over the last ten years have followed his European Foreign Policy courses: at the College of Europe in Bruges and in the Master's in European Studies and European Politics and Policies at the University of Leuven. They were a stimulating sounding board and excelled in continuously challenging ideas and approaches.

In embarking on this book, we inevitably underestimated the time that would be required to accomplish such an endeavour, and took too lightly the sacrifices that family and friends would also have to make. Their sustained support, comprehension and love have been the crucial ingredients for keeping this project moving along its winding path. Stephan would like to express his warm gratitude to the Keukeleire and Proesmans families for their untiring encouragement; to Vera, Jan, Jo, Bart, Marijke, Stratton and the 'play group' friends for support during the highs and lows of this project; and most of all to Klaartje, Camille and Soetkin who day after day shared this book adventure. Jennifer would like to say a massive thank you to Peter, Jean, Stephen, Hannele and Iain for their support and untiring encouragement; to Amber, Emily, Al, Yael, Phoebe, Tara, Marie-Claire, Jo and Katherine – an endless well of inspiration; and to Adam. After several years, both our families and friends will be as relieved as we are that the writing of this book has finally come to a happy end.

Leuven   STEPHAN KEUKELEIRE
London   JENNIFER MACNAUGHTAN

A range of supporting materials for this book, including an internet guide to EU foreign policy, suggestions for further reading and update articles on important new developments in EU foreign policy, is available on the associated website: www.palgrave.com/politics/keukeleire

Introduction

In 1993, in the midst of the Bosnian war, the Treaty of Maastricht came into force. With it came the creation of the European Union (EU) and its *Common Foreign and Security Policy* (CFSP), which was established as a distinct intergovernmental *second pillar* of the EU. CFSP was explicitly foreseen by member states and perceived by the international press, the academic world and the global arena at large as the site for the future elaboration of the EU's foreign policy. This new second pillar was distinct from its fellow fledgling, the *third pillar*, which was to deal with *provisions on cooperation in the fields of justice and home affairs*, and in particular from the by now familiar policy fields of the first pillar. The *first pillar* comprised the *European Community* (EC) with its internal market, common agricultural policy, trade and development policies.

The very name 'Common Foreign and Security Policy' aroused major expectations, both in terms of the intensity of integration and the scope of policy. It suggested a qualitative difference from CFSP's modest predecessor, European Political Cooperation (EPC), which was launched in the early 1970s as the member states' first attempt to coordinate their foreign policies. Expectations continued to grow when, in the late 1990s, the Amsterdam Treaty mandated the establishment of a High Representative for the CFSP and member states subsequently agreed to give the EU a *European Security and Defence Policy* (ESDP) within the second pillar. This ESDP included the creation of new permanent political and military structures. It also led to a commitment to strengthen military capabilities, enabling the EU to deploy up to 60,000 troops capable of carrying out peacekeeping and crisis management tasks.

Evaluating the foreign policy of the EU since the launch of its CFSP leads to rather mixed, even contradictory, conclusions. On the negative side of the balance we can identify an impressive list of failures in defining a common European foreign policy towards international crises including those in, but not limited

1

to, Rwanda, Darfur, Sierra Leone, Bosnia, Kosovo, Chechnya and Iraq. In each of these cases, EU attempts to forge a united foreign policy have been thrown into complete disarray. The consequences of this have ranged from impotence and inaction *vis-à-vis* Chechnya, to a failure to move beyond providing money and low-level diplomacy in the face of genocide in Darfur, and to member states adopting contradictory policy positions on, and activities during, the Iraq war.

The EU's troubled record has not been limited to highly publicized failures with regard to crises in specific countries, but also extends to difficulties in formulating effective common policies on the major 'thematic' issues of the day. For example, the fight against the proliferation of weapons of mass destruction (WMD) gained a new salience in the post-September 11 geopolitical environment and the EU duly developed a Strategy and Action Plan providing for a range of initiatives. However, this policy does not conceal enduring differences between the EU's member states which implied, for example, that at the 2005 Non-Proliferation Treaty Review Conference, the EU was unable to table a common stance on the most pertinent issues under discussion.

However, the picture is not clear-cut. While in 2003 the world focused on EU member states' quarrels over Iraq, this year also marked the launch of the EU's first military operations, in the former Yugoslav Republic of Macedonia (FYROM) and in the Democratic Republic of Congo (DRC). These were to be followed, between 2003 and 2007, by over 15 further military and civilian crisis management operations in Bosnia-Herzegovina, Kosovo, FYROM, Palestine, Iraq, the DRC, Sudan, Georgia, Indonesia and Afghanistan. Many operations launched under the EU's ESDP are modest in scope and design. Nevertheless, they symbolize remarkable progress in the development of an EU foreign policy, not least considering that until the mid-1990s it was inconceivable for many member states that the EU might embark on military operations. These crisis-management operations demonstrated that the EU was willing, as well as able, to match words with action. The operation in FYROM, for example, followed successful but barely noticed diplomatic efforts aimed at preventing tensions escalating into a new Balkan war. These CFSP actions were part of broader and equally undervalued efforts on the EU's part to structurally reorganize and stabilize the Balkans. These efforts were not only based on the CFSP and ESDP (the second pillar), but also developed through various policies of the EU's first pillar: the European Community (EC), with its powerful instruments of trade, aid and long-term contractual agreements.

Casting the net a little wider still, the 2004 and 2007 enlargements of the EU to include ten Central and Eastern European countries (CEECs) can be considered one of the major successes of EU foreign policy. This was the final step in nearly two decades of EC/EU policy aimed at supporting the process of political and economic transformation in the region during and following the break-up of the Soviet bloc, at tackling the conflicts and tensions between and within these countries, and at stabilizing the region on the basis of new structures and norms. The EC/EU's quiet long-term policy aimed at stabilizing and restructuring the CEECs should be considered as at least as central to the long-term security of European citizens as the US-led military operations in Bosnia and Kosovo of the late 1990s. Yet this policy is not considered a success of EU foreign policy in the way that the rather more dramatic interventions of the US and NATO were acknowledged as foreign policy successes.

The approach

This book has two major objectives. The first is to provide an overview and analysis of EU foreign policy. For purposes of clarity, the book is organized in a rather conventional way, including a historical chapter, three chapters on policy-making, two on the second pillar, two on the first pillar, and two on the EU's foreign policy towards other parts of the world. This also implies that in its basic organization, the book follows the basic pillar structure which member states used to construct the EU's foreign policy framework. The second objective is to reappraise the nature of EU foreign policy and of foreign policy more generally, looking beyond the narrow focus of conventional foreign policy analysis on states, crises and conflicts by focusing also on what we term structural foreign policy. This conceptual approach (elaborated in Chapter 1 and returned to in the assessment of theoretical approaches in Chapter 12) enables us to consider dimensions of EU foreign policy which dominant analyses have tended to overlook. In particular, it provides a vehicle to understand how foreign policy seeks to shape and influence structures and long-term processes.

Before moving on to the contents of the chapters themselves, it is useful to clarify two further points of departure in the book. We do not restrict EU foreign policy to CFSP and ESDP. Some of the most important sites of EU foreign policy are to be found outside this limited realm in policies such as trade, development, the environment or energy. This book also takes more of an 'inside-out' than an 'outside-in' approach. While we do evaluate the outputs of EU foreign policy, not least by taking a geographical perspective in Chapters 10 and 11, we can only provide a snapshot of the actual impact of EU foreign policy. Likewise, although the majority of relevant issues and geographical locations are discussed to some extent, we cannot consider the EU's policy *vis-à-vis* every region of the world or every issue on the international agenda.

Outline of chapters

Chapter 1 points to the main themes and questions to be tackled by focusing in particular on the changing context in which EU foreign policy operates beyond the 20th-century conception of the international system and within today's globalized world. This changed context implies that we must in turn update the concept of foreign policy, for which we offer a structural foreign policy–conventional foreign policy framework as an alternative approach. Having explored the context in which foreign policy operates and a generic understanding of what 'foreign policy' is, we turn to analyse the rather particular nature of EU foreign policy.

Chapter 2 gives a historical overview of the ambiguous relationship between European integration and foreign policy from the end of World War II to the present day. It demonstrates how the roots of current discussions on European foreign and security policy are to be found in early debates and policy choices.

The EU's foreign policy-making system is the focus of Chapter 3. We explore the divergence between a single institutional framework on paper, and the practice of different policy-making regimes and competences. The longest section of the chapter provides an in-depth analysis of the actors and procedures of EU foreign policy. It examines who or what is behind the facade of each of these actors.

After considering the competences and actors of the EU's foreign policy system, we proceed to analyse the policy-making process itself. Chapter 4 provides an overview of the various formal decision-making procedures in order to focus next on the broader policy-making processes. Both are essential to understand the nature, possibilities and constraints of EU foreign policy as well as the complex web of intra-institutional, inter-institutional and inter-state interaction and bargaining that it involves.

Within each of the policy-making regimes analysed in Chapter 4, national foreign policy actors play an important role. The purpose of Chapter 5 is to analyse the national level of foreign policy-making and its relationship and interaction with the European level. In the multilevel foreign policy system, member states position themselves in terms of power and capabilities, interests, worldviews and special relationships, which has significant ramifications on policy at the EU level. Meanwhile, membership of the EU has had a fundamental though varying impact on national foreign policies. This chapter also offers a critical assessment of arguments that are traditionally evoked to explain the limits of EU foreign policy, particularly 'the different interests' and 'the lack of political will'.

Chapter 6 focuses on the Union's self-proclaimed primary instrument of foreign policy: CFSP. A preliminary legal and political assessment of CFSP's basic principles and instruments provides the grounding for analysis. It becomes apparent that all too often, non-cooperation and member states' unilateral actions have continued to prevail. The chapter analyses CFSP's main instruments and provides a succinct overview of its thematic priorities.

ESDP is one of the most rapidly advancing fields of EU foreign policy. Chapter 7 takes stock of these new yet remarkably successful efforts to provide the EU with military and civilian capabilities and to strengthen its crisis management capacities. Given the alacrity with which developments in this field occur and new operations are launched, this chapter offers analytical axes along which future developments in ESDP can be measured. Attempts to strengthen the industrial and technological basis of the European defence sector are also analysed, including the development of an autonomous space capability, before ESDP's political dimension is considered.

Chapter 8 focuses on policy fields developed within the framework of the European Community but which are essential for the foreign policy of the EU since they provide its major instruments, have shaped the formation of EU foreign policy, yet paradoxically can hinder the achievement of some of its objectives. We look particularly at trade, association and cooperation agreements, development, conflict prevention, and human rights and democracy-promotion policies. This chapter argues that particularly through its association and cooperation agreements and long-term contractual relationships, the EU has attempted to shape and influence external political, economic and security structures, with varying degrees of intensity and success.

Building on this analysis, Chapter 9 draws on some equally relevant 'internal' policy fields. We consider freedom, security and justice policies and counter-terrorism, which have had a marked impact on the EU's foreign policy as well as the way in which it is perceived by third countries and regions. In recognition of their impotence in the face of globalization, member states have vested in the EU competence to try to shape certain external developments which ultimately have major repercussions for the EU internally. In this light we consider environment, energy, health and demographic policies.

Using the concepts developed throughout the preceding chapters, Chapter 10 gives an overview and assessment of EU foreign policy in its main arenas of international action: Central and Eastern Europe, the Balkans, the Commonwealth of Independent States, the Mediterranean, the Middle East and Africa. For each, we assess the extent to which the EU has moved beyond trade and contractual relations to developing a conventional and structural foreign policy.

Chapter 11 focuses on the EU's relationship with two sets of what we term global 'structural powers'. We first look at the EU's self-proclaimed 'choice of multilateralism' and how it interacts with the main international financial and political institutions. We then turn to the structural power of three states – the United States, Russia and China – and the increasingly influential structures under the umbrella term of 'Islamism'.

Finally, in Chapter 12, we consider the implications of our findings with regard to both International Relations theories and European Integration theories, and we assess the use of the 'structural foreign policy–conventional foreign policy' framework.

Chapter 1

The Context and Nature of EU Foreign Policy

This book takes three questions as its point of departure. At the start of the 21st century, the international system is a very different place to a 20th century shaped by two World Wars and Cold War bipolarity. Add to this the increasing scope, depth and impact of globalization and we come to our first question: *what is the context in which EU foreign policy operates?* The conceptualization and study of foreign policy needs to evolve in-line with our understanding of the context in which foreign policy operates. If the world is a different place, it is clear that analysis of foreign policy can no longer be based on the conventional state and (military) power-centred concept of foreign policy inherited from a previous era. Any analysis of EU foreign policy must then tackle a second question: *what is foreign policy?* Once we have understood the context which shapes foreign policy and what foreign policy thus looks like today, we can then turn to the particular case of the EU. The third question is: *what is the nature of EU foreign policy?* This chapter formulates an answer to these preliminary questions, points to the major themes of the book and develops a conceptual framework to facilitate the analysis of EU foreign policy in its 21st-century setting.

The changing context of EU foreign policy

The 20th-century context

Traditionally, foreign policy is considered to be one of the central tasks, prerogatives and even *raisons d'être* of sovereign states. Through their foreign policy, states define and manage their relationships with each other, defend their security and territorial integrity, and promote their national interests. This conventional

8

Figure 1.1   Areas of tension in EU foreign policy

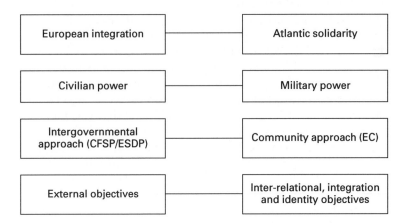

view, based on the Westphalian order, was shaped by the 'hard' security context of the 20th century. Military confrontation with Germany in the first half of the century and the Cold War with the Soviet Union in the second were at the heart of the foreign policy of the day. The consequence of this continuous struggle for survival was an image of foreign policy rooted in the role of strong states, the existence of military threats from other states and the consequent need to maintain a robust military capability as the core foreign policy instrument. The touchstone of foreign policy became the ability to prevail in military conflict and to use military power to safeguard interests and security.

This context and dominant foreign policy concept heavily influenced European integration and the position of foreign policy therein. It also gave rise to a number of areas of tension which are crucial to understanding the evolution and nature of EU foreign policy. Presented schematically in Figure 1.1 and explained in detail below, these different loci of tension have a major impact not only on the macropicture of EU foreign policy's evolution but also on the micropicture of responses to specific foreign policy dossiers.

European integration versus Atlantic solidarity
The Soviet threat, Western European military weakness and American military superiority meant that for most member

states, the Atlantic Alliance and the American security guarantee were the essential prerequisites for security after World War II. The logic of such a choice was confirmed in the early 1950s and 1960s by the failure of French proposals to bring defence within the scope of European integration (the European Defence Community and the Fouchet plans). Initial attempts to develop a European foreign policy through the European Community (EC) and European Political Cooperation (EPC) seemed largely irrelevant next to NATO, since it was NATO that was tackling the main foreign policy concern of the time: the Cold War. It also explains why, when the EC member states cautiously stepped towards developing common foreign policy initiatives in the 1970s, the EC/EPC was conceived and defined as a civilian actor.

East–West confrontation and military dependence on the US not only determined defence policy, but also largely defined the parameters of member states' national foreign policies and EPC. Until the end of the Cold War, foreign policy actions were largely to remain within the constraints of a world structured around the dividing lines of this contest. As has continued to be the case after 1989, depending on an external actor for military security carries a fairly sizeable price tag since the demands of that protector must be taken into account when taking a stand on foreign policy issues. Practically every proposal for a common foreign policy initiative was, and is, reviewed by several member states against what we might call the 'what do the Americans think?' test. The appropriateness and feasibility of an EU foreign policy initiative became measured not solely, or not in the first place, in terms of the EU's potential impact on the issue at hand, but rather in terms of its impact on transatlantic relations. The extent to which the 'Atlantic factor' had to be taken into account would prove to be one of the most divisive issues in the development of a common EU foreign policy. This tension of 'Atlantic solidarity versus European integration' is a first recurrent theme in this book.

Civilian power versus military power
The EC/EPC developed from the early 1970s as a civilian power. The concept of 'civilian power' (Duchêne 1972, 1973) was one of the first and most influential attempts to conceptualize (Western) Europe's status and role in the world and has since

been widely elaborated. Duchêne's conception revolved around three principal hypotheses. Firstly, it referred to the transformation of interstate relations within Europe from war and indirect violence towards 'civilized' politics. The EU's recent enlargements demonstrate the ongoing relevance of this point, which also provides an interesting formula for troubled interstate relations elsewhere. Secondly, the civilian power concept focused on the possibility of an actor being a 'power' whilst not possessing military instruments. It is this part of Duchêne's thesis which has received widest attention. From a normative perspective, this enabled the EU's endeavours on the international stage to be conceived in a non-threatening (and thus positive) light. Thirdly, Duchêne considered the role a civilian power could aspire to play. He noted that in a world where security policies were increasingly concerned with interdependence and shaping the international milieu, a civilian power's potential for constructive intervention was significant.

The dominance of the US in the military security arena left the EC/EPC with little other option than to maximize its potential impact as a civilian power. Any contemplation of branching into the 'hard' domain of military power lost relevance when measured against the American military goliath. However, the constraints of being a civilian power in a distinctly uncivil world became painfully obvious during and since the conflicts in the former Yugoslavia of the 1990s. This tension of 'civilian power versus military power' is a second recurrent theme in this book.

Intergovernmental versus Community approaches
Since foreign policy was understood to be a core task of the state, EPC was launched in the 1970s as a purely intergovernmental affair. Intergovernmentalism would equally become one of the defining features of the CFSP, as confirmed in the creation of a separate intergovernmental pillar in the Maastricht Treaty. Member states retained control over decision-making through the dominant unanimity rule in this second pillar. EPC/CFSP were thus formally separated from the EC framework and its Community method, based on an institutional equilibrium between the Council of Ministers, the Commission, the European Parliament and the Court of Justice, and on majority voting for a range of decisions in the Council. The Community method would itself be confined to the first pillar by the

Maastricht Treaty's institutional construct. The price member states paid for ensuring that the EC's institutions in Brussels would not meddle in EPC/CFSP was that these policies would not be supported by established institutional mechanisms or by common instruments.

This weakness of EPC/CFSP was made more explicit as its development was paralleled by the growing foreign policy relevance of EC policies (in particular trade policy, development cooperation and association and cooperation agreements) and of the EC mechanism and Community method (with a well-elaborated institutional set-up, significant competences and extensive instruments). EPC/CFSP was often forced to rely on the EC to flesh out or implement its decisions. However, more fundamentally, the EC through its various 'external policies' was gradually developing its own unspoken foreign policy dynamic.

Member states differ on where they envisage the appropriate balance between intergovernmentalism and the Community method to lie in foreign policy. This depends not in the first place on considerations of efficiency or cost–benefit analysis but rather on their overarching view of the nature and *finalité* of European integration. Member states also assess the viability of a potential EU foreign policy initiative in terms of whether it fits within their own conception of European integration. Foreign policy debates in the EU are thus likely to focus beyond the issue at hand, to broader questions of defining policy competences between the EU institutions and between the national and the EU levels. This tension 'EPC/CFSP versus EC' and 'intergovernmental versus Community approach' is a third recurrent theme in this book.

External objectives versus interrelational, integration and identity objectives
Following the harrowing experiences of two World Wars, France, West Germany, Italy and the Benelux countries launched the European integration process as a radically new method to definitively tackle long-standing enmity between Germany and its Western European neighbours. European integration provided the answer to the security dilemma posed by a European order shaped by the Westphalian system of sovereign, and thus unrestrained, states. Member states were offered a new framework in which to define and manage their mutual relationships and to defend and promote national interests in a less

threatening way. Mutual oversight was designed to resolve, or at least contain, the tensions and conflicts arising between member states, enhancing the predictability of behaviour and promoting mutual understanding. In short, European integration was also created to serve as an instrument of interrelational foreign policy, a function which remains essential to the present day.

The interrelational dimension of European integration has important, but underplayed, implications for the analysis of EU foreign policy. It implies that the EU's foreign policy and specific foreign policy actions do not always aim to influence the external world (external objectives), but could have the management of internal EU relations as their principal goal. Conversely, it can also imply that member states agree *not* to handle a foreign policy issue within the EU framework out of fear that this would revive mutual tensions and augment internal disagreement and distrust. Thus, in some instances, member states do not measure the effectiveness of an EU foreign policy initiative against its *external* impact, but rather against its *internal* impact.

In addition to interrelational objectives, foreign policy initiatives can stem from two further types of objective over and above external goals. Firstly, member states can promote or adopt new foreign policy initiatives which primarily aim to strengthen European integration or influence the nature of the European project (integration objectives). Secondly, member states' main goal can be to emphasise the specificity of the European approach to international politics, to differentiate the EU from other actors (particularly the US) and to strengthen European identity (identity objectives).

To sum up, in order to understand EU foreign policy we must appreciate that decisions on EU foreign policy are often not only steered by *external objectives* (aimed at influencing the external environment), but also by various *internal objectives*: *interrelational objectives* (aimed at managing member states' mutual relations), *integration objectives* (aimed at strengthening or influencing European integration) and *identity objectives* (aimed at asserting the identity of the EU). The extent to which a member state will give different weight to these types of interest will vary over time and according to the issue at hand. These different types of objective also help to explain divergences in the levels of expectation of political leaders, the general public and the rest of the world: the general public and external actors evaluate EU foreign policy in terms of its external impact whereas political leaders may be operating according to an entirely different agenda. This tension between the external objectives and the various internal objectives of EU foreign policy is a fourth recurrent theme in this book.

The post-Cold War context

With the conclusion of the all-encompassing global contest between the US and the USSR, and between capitalism and Communism, a period of East–West geopolitical 'order' also came to its end. During the Cold War, both superpowers controlled those parts of the world within their respective spheres of influence. This order was achieved through the containment or suppression of latent or manifest conflicts and destabilizing factors. Support was provided to allied governments to maintain order within their territory. A stabilizing impact was even exerted on neutral or non-aligned countries. With the end of the Soviet empire and the East–West confrontation, this 'stabilizing' influence disappeared and previously ignored conflicts came to the fore. The world became characterized by the emergence, or re-emergence, of regional or intrastate conflicts between ethnic, religious, political or (para)military groups as they struggled for power, territory, wealth, independence or recognition (SIPRI 2002). The consequences of this new context for EU foreign policy and for foreign policy in general are several. The need to structure and stabilize other regions in the world moved up the agenda and the nature of conflicts and threats changed. New types of military capability became necessary, as did a wider range of non-military instruments.

The need to create new structures

For EU foreign policy, a first implication of the changed context was its new responsibility for supporting and steering an alternative order in Central and Eastern Europe by developing new political, legal, economic and security structures (with the military security structure being tackled by NATO). On a less ambitious level, the EU also sought to elaborate upon or introduce new rules of the game and new structures in other regions of the world through its association and cooperation agreements and development policies, and through an increased use of conditionality and support measures.

That foreign policy needed to focus more on structures became clear in the aftermath of war in Bosnia, Kosovo, Afghanistan and Iraq. These crises demonstrated that wielding military force alone would result in neither lasting peace nor long-term stability. Rather, in the post-war stage, the creation of viable and sustainable political, legal, socio-economic and security structures within states and in the relationships between states was of equal importance. Chapters 8 and 10 assess the mixed results of these policies.

At the start of the new millennium, the need to rethink existing structures also emerged on a global level. Non-Western countries no longer uncritically accepted the international economic order. The status quo of an almost exclusively Western-determined international financial architecture was increasingly challenged by a coalition of developing countries finding, and exercising, their voice. Meanwhile, the dominance of Western values and the almost unbounded expression of Western norms were confronted by anti-Western fundamentalist movements. The EU and its member states, to a greater extent than the US, emphasized the need to respond to demands from southern countries and to tackle the so-called 'root-causes' of terrorism and extremist fundamentalism. However, as we show in Chapter 11, the EU has been reluctant actually to use its power to transform criticized international structures. The extent to which it has focused on shaping national, regional and global structures in the conduct of foreign policy is a fifth recurrent theme in this book.

The EU's struggle with power

The EU's civilian power status was seriously challenged in the period following the end of the Cold War. The need to promote and support new political, legal and socio-economic structures in other regions of the world compelled the EU to make more active use of its various non-military foreign policy instruments, most of which fell under the EC pillar. More significantly, it also increased pressure on the EU to behave as a civilian *power*, willing to exert itself purposefully to achieve foreign policy objectives. But, engagement in Central and Eastern Europe aside, the EU proved reluctant to use its instruments to enforce desired changes or attitudes. The EU, it seemed, was unable to fulfil the expectations of a civilian power at the same time that the disadvantages of being limited to civilian power alone were becoming very apparent. In two stages, from 1991, particularly in the Balkan wars, and again from 2001, through the effects of September 11, the EU was forced to gradually depart from the familiarity of its status as a non-military power.

The dissolution of Yugoslavia confronted the EU with a typical post-Cold War crisis – war within countries and between different ethnic groups – for which new types of 'lower-scale' military operation and capabilities were required. Conflict in the Balkans demonstrated that the EU and its member states were unable to respond adequately as they did not possess the requisite military capabilities for conflict prevention, crisis management or peacekeeping. This was particularly dramatic for European countries because the traditional military security providers (NATO and the US) were initially reluctant to intervene. It was not a coincidence that from 1999, efforts within the ESDP to endow the EU with its own military capabilities focused on peacekeeping and crisis management tasks (see Chapter 7).

The terrorist attacks in the US, Madrid, London and other parts of the world, the wars in Afghanistan and Iraq and the fear of the proliferation of WMD forced EU countries to focus on yet another level of military challenge. For the first time since the height of the Cold War, threats went to the core of a nation's survival, thus touching the most sensitive foreign policy decisions of national political leaders. Whilst these challenges demonstrated the sharply divisive character of the 'Atlantic solidarity versus European integration' dilemma, they also provided the impetus behind developing a common anti-terrorism policy and an EU 'Strategy against Proliferation of WMD'. In this way, external events centred the EU debate on issues that just two years previously had been completely taboo (see Chapters 6 and 9).

To summarize, the end of the East–West order had a dual effect on the EU's civilian power status. On the one hand, confrontation with this new world challenged the EU to behave much more as a civilian *power*. On the other hand, the EU was forced to transform itself from a civilian power into a civilian *and* military power. This points to the following fundamental question: to what extent does the EU have or want to become a power? The EU's struggle with power is a sixth recurrent theme of this book.

Globalization

A further major contextual change of foreign policy is the increasing scope, depth and impact of globalization. This process both reinforces the effects of the end of the East–West 'order' and carries implications which are fundamental, yet not always acknowledged. Globalization essentially refers to the expanding scale, growing magnitude, speeding up and deepening impact of patterns of social interaction and interregional flows of people, trade, capital, information, technological knowledge, ideas, values and norms. Indeed, few areas of social life escape its reach. These increasingly intensive flows are facilitated by different kinds of physical infrastructure (such as transport networks and communication and banking systems), but also by immaterial, normative and symbolic factors (such as trade rules, the spread of Western values and customs, and of English as the lingua franca) (Held and McGrew 2000: 3–4).

As globalization constrains and empowers actors, its impact is profoundly uneven, reflecting and strengthening existing patterns of inequality and hierarchy while also generating new patterns of inclusion and exclusion, new winners and losers (Held *et al.* 1999: 27). The positive effects of globalization and increasing interdependence are matched by a growing vulnerability in a burgeoning number of interrelated policy areas. This is not only the case in the military field (proliferation of WMD and sensitive military technology, threat of 'low-scale' terrorist attacks with large-scale effects) and in the economic field (including energy provision or the vulnerability of information networks). It also extends to policy fields that used to receive less attention: the environment (ecological change, unsafe nuclear plants), public health (HIV/AIDS, avian influenza, TB) and societal security (the preservation of a society's essential features). Threats are no longer solely posed by states, but increasingly by a wide range of non-state actors, anonymous and diffuse networks and incremental developments that cannot be associated with a specific actor.

Linking globalization to foreign policy leads to a dual paradox. Firstly, globalization reflects a growing predominance of economics over politics and of foreign economic relations over foreign policy. Yet at the same time, the implications of globalization and the vulnerabilities it causes make foreign policy more essential than ever. So, secondly, there is a need for more foreign policy and for a different kind of foreign policy. Yet national governments find themselves increasingly irrelevant in addressing the challenges as their traditional foreign policy is impotent in the face of multiplying vulnerabilities.

There is a rather ambiguous relationship between European integration and globalization, with the European Union acting both as a shield against, and an agent of, globalization (Wallace 2000: 48–9). The EU functions as an instrument to protect its member states from the negative consequences of globalization and to try to contain, manage and order this process. Increasingly helpless, member states' governments turn to the EU to respond to questions they are incapable of answering. The EU's rich cross-border legal mechanisms and the Europeanization of an increasing number of 'internal' policy fields within the framework of the first pillar, helped member states to control some of the repercussions of globalization and to protect themselves from turbulent global events. Vulnerability in traditionally 'domestic' or 'internal' policy fields, such as health, the environment, energy or communication networks, explains the pressure to gradually elaborate an EU foreign policy in these fields (see Chapter 9).

However, the EU also functions as an agent of globalization. It promotes multilateralism in an attempt to protect itself from globalization. But, in so doing, it acts as an agent of this very process. More fundamentally, the EU contributes to globalization through its trade policy and its support for a global free-market economy and neo-liberal international order (including through the World Trade Organization (WTO), the International Monetary Fund (IMF) and the World Bank, and through its initiatives to create free trade areas with other regions of the world). The EU has not sufficiently considered the consequences of its policies: it contributes to international structures that, whilst positive in many ways, also reproduce and reinforce patterns of exclusion, alienation and uncertainty (see Chapter 10).

In terms of foreign policy, globalization has several implications. The interrelatedness of the international system means distant occurrences can have a serious impact domestically, while local developments can in turn engender significant global repercussions (Held and McGrew 2002: 3). Furthermore, while globalization generates or emphasizes new patterns of inclusion and exclusion, expanding communication networks and a proliferation of arms provide the 'losers' with easy channels to strike back.

Updating the concept of foreign policy

We define foreign policy as that area of politics which is directed at the external environment with the objective of influencing that environment and the behaviour of other actors within it, in order to pursue interests, values and goals. Foreign policy thus differs from external relations since the former is about influencing the environment and external actors while the latter is about maintaining relations with external actors.

It is archaic to assess the foreign policy of the EU, or any other actor, using a conventional understanding of foreign policy as strictly centred on state and military security. Today, we require a more comprehensive understanding of foreign policy (see Kubálková 2001; Carlsnaes 2002; Cooper 2003; Hill 2003). This might seem self-evident to most scholars of international relations. However, despite the fact that scholars readily acknowledge the complexity of *international relations*, when it comes to assessing the *foreign policy* of an actor, a one-sided understanding of foreign policy is still often used as the main or only benchmark against which foreign policy is measured and as the main lense through which foreign policy is conceptualized and 'recognized'.

The purpose of the next two sections is to present tools through which we can analyse those dimensions of foreign policy that tend not to be central to either the study, or the conduct, of foreign policy. The first tool presented here is a checklist of both dominant and other dimensions of foreign policy, which links relevant concepts from various approaches in International Relations research to the study of foreign policy. The second tool is a conceptual framework that ties these concepts together, encompassing both dominant and other dimensions of foreign policy. This framework is based on comparing a conventional understanding of foreign policy to what we call a structural foreign policy.

Table 1.1 provides a short (and non-exhaustive) checklist of both the traditionally dominant and the other dimensions of foreign policy. The 'dominant dimensions' refer to those aspects

Table 1.1   Dominant and other dimensions of foreign policy

	Dominant dimensions of foreign policy	Other dimensions of foreign policy

Actors	States
	Elites
	Heads of state/
	    government,
	    Ministry of Foreign
	    Affairs/Defence
	Governmental actors
		Non-state actors, networks
		Population/society
		
		Other governmental
		    actors
		
		Non-governmental actors

Interests and objectives	Self-regarding interests Myopic self-interests Possession goals	Collective interests Other-regarding interests Far-sighted self-interests Milieu goals Global public goods
Security	Military security Territorial/National security Securitization	Non-military security Global security Societal security Human security Desecuritization
Power and capabilities	Military instruments Material instruments Hard power Relational power	Non-military instruments Immaterial instruments Soft power Structural power

Focus	Actors, events, crises
	    and conflicts
	Material aspects
	    (economy, military
	    security)
		Structures, processes,
		    contexts
		Immaterial aspects (identity,
		    culture, beliefs,
		    legitimacy)

of foreign policy which are emphasized in a conventional understanding of foreign policy. The 'other dimensions' refer to those aspects of foreign policy that are increasingly important in international relations (and International Relations research) and have significant consequences for the nature, contents and conduct of foreign policy, but that tend to receive less attention in the analysis and conduct of foreign policy or are in some cases neglected completely.

Actors

The nature of actors in international relations has evolved. State actors do not cease to be relevant. However, other governmental actors, such as ministers of finance or interior affairs become relevant in addition to the traditionally central actors of foreign policy (Heads of State or Government, foreign ministry, defence ministry). More importantly, taking states as the sole actors in foreign policy is no longer tenable. The state is not the sole reference point for foreign policy because a wider spectrum of subnational and transnational actors and entities, including religious and ethnic groups, societies, multinationals, international organizations, non-governmental organizations (NGOs) and criminal organizations are increasingly relevant foreign policy actors (Josselin and Wallace 2001). Diffuse and ambiguous entities, perceived more as networks than as concrete and well-defined actors, should also be understood as actors in foreign policy. Financial networks or al-Qaeda terrorist networks are examples (see Castells 2000). Such a change in focus also implies that foreign policy should no longer be a solely elite-centred activity, but should become more population- or society-orientated.

Interests and objectives

To defend and promote an entity's own interests and achieve its foreign policy objectives, protecting *global public goods* (for example the environment and health) (Kaul *et al.* 1999) and acknowledging or even promoting the basic interests of other states and non-state actors (for example ethnic and religious groups) becomes essential. George and Keohane (1980: 221) make a useful distinction between, on the one hand, the usually promoted and emphasized *self-regarding interests* (where the state in question is first and foremost the interested party), the less emphasized *collective interests* (where several states and actors enjoy advantages in common) and the usually ignored *other-regarding interests* (where the interests of other actors are dominant, but where the state in question can derive indirect benefit from the improved situation of other actors).

In a 21st-century context of mutual dependence and vulnerability, factoring collective interests and other-regarding interests into foreign policy choices is more a question of efficacy and *far-sighted self-interest* (Keohane 1984: 122) than of idealistic, naïve altruism. However, pursuing collective and other-regarding interests is a task of such magnitude that most national governments are incapable of doing so. As national governments struggle to justify such interventions to parliament or their electorate, the relevance of international organizations, such as the EU, increases.

In terms of objectives, 'milieu goals' as well as the more traditionally emphasized 'possession goals' are increasingly relevant to foreign policy. Following Wolfers' formulation, *milieu goals* aim to shape the conditions beyond a state's national boundaries, that is the international environment in which a state operates, while *possession goals* refer to the realization of objectives that directly benefit the state concerned (1962: 73–6).

Security

The state's principal foreign policy objective remains to guarantee its security. However, this is complicated by a security agenda which has become both deeper and broader. Focussing solely on military security is insufficient. Survival becomes equally dependent on fields such as environmental security and health security (Buzan *et al.* 1998; Kaul *et al.* 1999). Security can no longer be defined solely at a state level. Globalization and the end of the East–West order compel foreign policy to look beyond national territorial security and towards both the global level (collective interests) and the societal and individual levels. The following points explain the less well-known security concepts presented in Table 1.1 that complement the (territorial/national/military) security concepts which conventionally prevail:

- *Global security* refers to issues such as the uncontrolled proliferation of military technology and WMD. 'National' security cannot be assured without tackling such elements of global security.
- *Societal insecurity* refers to the ability of a society (largely defined on an ethnic or religious basis) to persist in its essential character. It is about the sustainability, allowing for an acceptable level of evolution, of traditional patterns of language, culture, association, values and religious, ethnic or

national identity (Waever 1993: 23). Societal insecurity can be the result of internal pressure within a state or of direct external pressure from other states or societies. It can flow from indirect external pressure in the international system, for instance through the homogenizing impact of globalization, Westernization and capitalism (Buzan 1993; Latouche 1996).

- *Human security* refers to the security situation of individuals. It encompasses both the freedom from fear (of violence, violations of human rights, crime) and the freedom from want (of hunger, poverty, disease, environmental degradation) (UNDP 1994). Peace, stability, democracy and economic development cannot be achieved unless individuals have human security.

- *Desecuritization* refers to the process through which an issue is no longer considered or 'felt' to be a security problem and is gradually moved from the security agenda into the ordinary realm of politics. The concept of desecuritization indicates that in addition to developing measures to fight a particular threat, foreign policy will only be successful if this threat not only disappears, but if it is also *perceived* to have disappeared. Policies can also aim at keeping issues desecuritized – that is keeping an issue off the security agenda and ensuring that it is not considered or defined as a security problem. An example of desecuritization is the Franco-German relationship after World War II (see Chapter 2). The opposite of desecuritization is *securitization* – bringing a relationship or an issue into the realm of 'security' and considering or presenting it as a threat, which thus requires emergency measures (Waever 1995; Buzan *et al.* 1998: 21–47). Migration, health or drugs are all examples of issues which have been securitized.

Power and capabilities

The challenges evoked by the 21st-century context mean that military and diplomatic power and instruments are essential, but are also insufficient to achieve foreign policy goals. Military power and military instruments must be complemented by economic and financial power and instruments. And hard power needs to be complemented by soft power. *Hard power* is essentially based on coercion. It can rest on both inducements and threats ('carrots' and 'sticks') and can involve the use of military, economic or other instruments. *Soft power* rests on the ability to shape the preferences of others and to get others to want the outcomes that you want. It arises from the attractiveness of an entity's culture, values, political ideals and policies, or from the perception that these are legitimate (Nye 2004).

Less utilized but arguably even more useful concepts are relational and structural power, which are to be seen as two sides of a continuum. *Relational power* refers to the power of one actor to get another actor to do something it would not otherwise do. Elaborating on the description provided by Holsti (1995: 69), *structural power* refers to the authority and capacity to set or shape the organizing principles and rules of the game and to determine how others will play that game. Structural power involves more than coercive capacity as it includes unstated assumptions about standards and rules. The possessor of structural power can 'change the range of choices open to others, without apparently putting pressure directly on them to take one decision or to make one choice rather than others' (Strange 1994: 31). The range of options available for an entity could be extended through the development of new opportunities, or restricted through the imposition of costs or risks, rendering some choices more attractive, and others more difficult. In altering the context in which other actors operate, the use of structural power can lead to fundamental and enduring changes in the actions, behaviour and identity of actors.

Focus

Being effective in the changed 21st-century context requires that an 'actor', 'conflict' and 'event'-orientated foreign policy approach be complemented by a 'process', 'structure' and 'context'-orientated approach. To explain: the focus of foreign policy should not only rest on events and actors or on conflicts between those actors. It should also consider the underlying structures and processes which are at the root of conflicts or solutions, or which provide the context in which problems and conflicts multiply or opportunities arise. Structures (such as the Western-dominated international financial system) and processes (such as climate change, democratization, the transition to an open market economy, or the rise of anti-Western sentiments) have an impact on an actor's behaviour and provide the framework in which it operates.

In addition, foreign policy must look beyond the material realm of military security or economic well-being towards immaterial issues such as culture, beliefs, identity and legitimacy (see Goldstein and Keohane 1993; Katzenstein 1996; Hudson 1997). Culture, beliefs and identity shape the perception and behaviour of actors, influence how they define their interests and what kind of role they want to play in the international system. As Pritzel (1998: 19) argues, identity 'serves not only as the primary link between the individual and society, but between a society and the world'. These factors, combined with legitimacy, also determine the potential impact of a foreign policy. For example, while in objective terms a foreign policy may succeed in removing a specific military threat, states, societies or individuals might continue to act as if this threat remained and continue to feel insecure until the less tangible immaterial aspects have also been tackled. This dimension points to the importance in foreign policy of 'winning the hearts and minds'.

Conventional and structural foreign policy

Having identified various dominant and other dimensions of foreign policy, we now reconceptualize foreign policy to incorporate some of the generally overlooked 'other' dimensions and to take into account the challenges posed by globalization and post-Cold War instability. Comparing a conventional conception of foreign policy with a 'structural foreign policy' allows us to broaden what we understand as foreign policy (Keukeleire 1998, 2002, 2003, 2008):

- *Conventional foreign policy* is orientated towards states, military security, crises and conflicts (including most, though not necessarily all, of the 'dominant' dimensions in the left column of Table 1.1).
- *Structural foreign policy* refers to a foreign policy which, conducted over the long-term, seeks to influence or shape sustainable political, legal, socio-economic, security and mental structures. These structures characterize not only

states and interstate relations, but also societies, the position of individuals, relations between states and societies, and the international system as a whole.

Both conceptualizations of foreign policy are relevant in today's international system. The breakdown of the Westphalian and East–West orders has undermined the structures which supported these orders. This process can encourage states to strengthen their own (military) capabilities in order to try to survive in this increasingly dangerous and unpredictable world. The result is a renewed emphasis on foreign policy as it is conventionally understood, and particularly on the need for military instruments. However, the breakdown of the old structures also implies that foreign policy must try to reorder or restructure the international arena to diminish vulnerability and uncertainties. This process takes into account new or emerging actors, processes, challenges, dangers and opportunities. The capacity to 'structure' the global environment and influence long-term developments becomes critical.

Comparing a conventional understanding of foreign policy with a structural foreign policy concept is a useful lens through which to analyse past as well as current foreign policy. An example of a successful structural foreign policy is American foreign policy in the decade following World War II which aimed to establish new structures in Western Europe and definitively resolve Franco-German hostility (see Chapter 2). Other examples are the EC/EU's policy *vis-à-vis* Central and Eastern Europe as well as the Stabilisation and Association Process aimed at restructuring and stabilizing the Balkans following conflict in the 1990s. Examples of failed structural foreign policies are the policy of the EU towards the Palestinian Territories and towards the Mediterranean (see Chapter 10) and the policy of the US in the early 2000s to spread freedom and democracy to the Middle East.

Structural foreign policy and conventional foreign policy are not mutually contradictory and can even be complementary and mutually dependent. For example, structural foreign policy towards the Balkans became possible only after successful conventional foreign policy actions (including military operations and diplomatic initiatives). However, that this success would be enduring was only assured through the creation of a comprehensive set of new structures to make peace sustainable in the long term.

Before we go any further, it is useful to explain the basic features of a structural foreign policy: the focus on structures, sustainability, comprehensiveness and the importance of mental structures.

Structures consist of relatively permanent organizing principles and rules of the game that shape and order the political, legal, socio-economic and security fields. Structures are made operational through a complex organizational and/or institutional set-up that can vary from country to country, from society to society, and from region to region. For example, 'democracy' is an organizing principle that shapes politics in many states. However, the way in which it is made operational differs between, for example, the US, Germany and Japan.

The objective of a structural foreign policy is to influence, shape or create structures that are not only viable in the short term, but that are equally *sustainable* in the long term, including when external pressure or support has disappeared. In view of their relatively permanent quality, influencing or changing the structures within which actors operate can be harder and take more time than influencing or changing the behaviour of actors in specific crises. However, if successful, the impact of these efforts can be both more profound and more enduring.

A structural foreign policy can generally only be effective and sustainable if it is *comprehensive* and if it simultaneously focuses on the various relevant interrelated structures (political, legal, socio-economic and security) and levels (individual, state, societal, relations between states and societies, interregional and global). Neglecting one or more relevant levels or structures can undermine the foreign policy achievements at other levels and structures. Being comprehensive necessitates the use of a wide variety of instruments. Combined with the fact that sustained effort is required over the long term, this explains why a structural foreign policy is beyond the capacity of most individual states – and why the EU is a potentially interesting locus for member states to develop such a policy. Figure 1.2 presents the dimensions of a comprehensive structural foreign policy, also offering a useful checklist to analyse the structural foreign policy of an international actor.

Figure 1.2   Structural foreign policy: structures and levels

		STRUCTURES				
		Political	Legal	Socio-economic	Security	Mental
L	Individual					
E	State					
V	Societal*					
	Inter-state					
E	Inter-societal*					
L	(Inter)-regional					
S	Global					

* Societies can be situated within one state or can be transnational.

Whether changes to structures are sustainable depends on the extent to which they are seen as legitimate and are (or are becoming) part of the mindset, belief systems or *mental structure* of the people concerned (population as well as elites). Changes to structures will be more enduring when they are seen as desirable and legitimate, and not just as the result of external pressure or of a purely rational cost–benefit calculation (acquiescing in order to gain economic support, for example) (see Wendt 1999: 266–78). This explains why a structural foreign policy is more likely to be successful if the promoted structures take into account, or are embedded within, endogenous traditions or processes in the target country, society or region. Where the elite and population share the same values, and view the structures being promoted as desirable, these will be more readily internalized. Acting on other-regarding interests and possessing soft power can also help increase the legitimacy of the policy and the prospects of the promoted structures being accepted and internalized.

The nature of EU foreign policy

Having explored the generic concept of foreign policy, we now use this analysis to help us examine the nature of EU foreign policy. We understand the foreign policy of the EU as being the multipillar and multilevel foreign policy of the EU as a whole. It thus includes the foreign policy developed across all three EU pillars, through interaction between those pillars, as well as through interaction with the foreign policies of member states. As such, in this book, EU foreign policy is not considered as being the same as:

- *CFSP/ESDP*: the preceding sections indicated that it is untenable to narrow down foreign policy to the decisions and actions adopted in the EU's second pillar.
- *European foreign policy*: as the EU does not include all European states and is only one of the various 'European' multilateral frameworks through which foreign policy is developed, the EU cannot be equated with 'Europe'.
- *The sum of the national foreign policies of EU member states*: the foreign policy of the EU is neither all encompassing nor exclusive. This implies that member states maintain their own national foreign policies, which may in part be defined and developed with no or minimal involvement from the EU. The label 'EU foreign policy' only includes national foreign policies in so far as these are developed at least to some extent through interaction with the EU mechanism.

Having clarified these basic conceptual choices, it is useful to point to their consequences for the analysis of EU foreign policy in this book, to situate this within the broader debate on European integration, and to point to some major recurrent themes that will be tackled throughout.

Multipillar foreign policy

As noted in the Introduction, the Maastricht Treaty gave the EU a three-pillar system: the CFSP as a distinct intergovernmental second pillar; a third pillar, which was to deal with provisions on cooperation in the fields of justice and home affairs; and a first pillar – the EC – which brought together policies including the internal market, common agricultural policy, trade and development policies. The precise attribution of policy fields among the three pillars has gradually evolved, with CFSP for example being complemented by ESDP and the third pillar being refocused on police and judicial cooperation in criminal matters. However, this

Figure 1.3   EU foreign policy: formal set-up, policy-making methods and actors

EUROPEAN UNION		
First pillar *EC*	Second pillar *CFSP/ESDP*	Third pillar *PJCC*
External trade; EMU; trade, cooperation and association agreements; economic sanctions; development policy; asylum and immigration; conflict prevention; internal policies; etc.	Foreign and security policy; peace-keeping, crisis management; etc.	Police and judicial cooperation in criminal matters; internal security matters; etc.
Community method	*Intergovernmental method*	
Council (majority voting or unanimity), EP, Commission, Court of Justice	Council (dominance unanimity), High Representative for the CFSP, ESDP bodies	Council (dominance unanimity), Europol, Eurojust and related bodies

basic structure (see Figure 1.3) was not fundamentally overhauled until the Reform Treaty, which while retaining a distinct second pillar for CFSP and ESDP collapsed what was left of the third pillar into the first (IGC 2007).

The intergovernmental method which characterizes the second and third pillars implies that member states retain complete control over the development of foreign policy within these pillars through the dominant position of the Council of Ministers and unanimity in decision-making. This is in contrast to the first pillar's 'Community method', which is based on an institutional equilibrium between the Council of Ministers, the Commission, the European Parliament and the Court of Justice, and on majority voting for most decisions in the Council.

EU foreign policy is developed through the three pillars of the EU and through the interaction between those pillars, although the main emphasis is on the EC (first) pillar and CFSP/ESDP (second) pillar. The pillar system has far-reaching consequences for the nature and outcome of EU foreign policy. However, the formal division between EC and CFSP/ESDP is also misleading and the practice of EU foreign policy does not always follow the formal categorization of the treaties.

Within the individual pillars, there are major variations in competence and policy-making method (see, for example, the substantial differences between trade and development policy). This points to the much larger complexity of, and diversity within, the EU's foreign policy mechanism than the simplistic categorizations 'EC versus CFSP/ESDP' and 'Community method versus intergovernmental method' indicates. It might be more accurate to characterize EU foreign policy as existing on a continuum, going from various degrees of supranational integration, over various degrees of intergovernmental integration, to purely intergovernmental cooperation. Although there is a clear boundary between the three pillars (which has significant repercussions for EU foreign policy), in practice there is also a strong interaction and sometimes even symbiosis between them, which can make the pillar system sometimes less relevant. As Stetter (2004: 720–1) argues, the functional indivisibility of foreign policy led to a gradual and partial erosion of the pillar structure and to the rise of cross-pillar politics. In any case, we should question a one-sided emphasis on CFSP/ESDP in assessments of EU foreign policy. Depending on the foreign policy issue at hand and the time period under discussion, the centre of gravity in terms of the site of policy elaboration will differ. Whilst CFSP is formally considered the motor of foreign policy-making, on several major issues the political and operational heart of EU foreign policy is the EC and not CFSP.

Multilevel and multilocation foreign policy

Characteristic of EU foreign policy is the interaction between the national and EU levels, with the centre of gravity and the nature of this interaction varying according to the issue at hand. However, EU foreign policy is not a simple two-level game. The national and EU levels are not neatly separated from each other and policy-making also occurs on other levels (see below). To a large extent, EU foreign policy can be conceptualized as a complex *multilevel foreign policy*, with actors that are linked to each other through formal or informal relationships. Depending on the policy issue and policy framework these actors have different competences, legitimacy, obligations and resources. EU foreign policy can thus be characterized as an example of multi-level governance, including a range of mutually dependent actors across different policy levels, with multiple powers and interests, complementary functions and overlapping competences (see Schimmelfennig and Wagner 2004).

Understanding EU foreign policy as being multilevel also has wider dimensions. Although we may focus on the EU, we must avoid the trap of EU-centrism, giving the false impression that for member states the EU is the only, or even the main, international framework in which to develop foreign policy, promote foreign policy goals or fulfil commitments. As Krahmann (2003) rightly emphasizes, EU foreign policy is in turn embedded within a wider set of multilevel foreign policy networks, including other multilateral settings such as NATO, the Organization for Security and Co-operation in Europe (OSCE), the Council of Europe and the UN (see also Knodt 2004). Nearly all foreign policy actions undertaken by the EU are developed either in cooperation with other international organizations (and sometimes also on their initiative or at their request) or in parallel to (and sometimes also in competition with) the actions of these organizations. Following Wallace (2005: 78), it may be more accurate to speak of a *multilocation foreign policy*, to avoid the notion of hierarchy often implied by the multilevel concept and to indicate that the EU is only one among the various relevant locations for foreign policy-making. This implies that the member states perpetually weigh up the pros and cons of developing foreign policy in the EU rather than in another foreign policy forum.

Zero-sum and positive-sum games

Many studies of the EU's external relations or foreign policy focus on the EU's capabilities as an international actor and its capacity 'to mimic the features of a nation-state within the international system' (Rosamond 2002: 175). This becomes obvious in the plethora of publications about the famous 'capability-expectations gap' (Hill 1993) and about the EU's 'actorness' or 'presence' (Sjøstedt 1977; Allen and Smith 1990; Caporaso and Jupille 1998; Bretherton and Vogler 2006).

This book questions the tendency to evaluate EU foreign policy mainly or exclusively against the yardstick of the foreign policy of individual states. It can be useful or even necessary for EU foreign policy to gain some of the capabilities and characteristics of states' foreign policy. However, it is questionable whether EU foreign policy must automatically, and on all levels, be seen as a substitute or as a transposition to the European level of individual member states' foreign policies. The specificity and added value of an EU foreign policy can be precisely that it varies on certain points, tackling different sorts of problems, pursuing different objectives through alternative methods, and ultimately assuming a form and content which differs from the foreign policy of its individual states. At a time when globalization is demonstrating the limitations of nation states and conventional foreign policies, it seems odd that we would look to the EU to develop a foreign policy equivalent to that of a state.

This book thus also questions the tendency to automatically perceive the relationship between the foreign policy of the EU and that of its member states as a zero-sum game. Such a perspective implies that a fully fledged European foreign policy can only emerge to the extent that it takes the place of member states' policies, which are to disappear in the process. Or, conversely, that as long as national foreign policies continue to exist, there can be no true European foreign policy (see Allen 1998). This book's point of departure is that the relationship between the foreign policies of the member states and the EU can be a zero-sum game (with a stronger EU foreign policy leading to weaker national foreign policies), but that in other cases it can be a positive-sum game (with EU foreign policy complementing and even strengthening national foreign policies and foreign policies developed in other international fora). The question of whether, and under what conditions, the relationship between EU and national foreign policies is to be seen in either this negative or positive light is one of the most essential and sensitive aspects of EU foreign policy.

Conclusion

Today's world is a markedly different place to that of a 20th century defined by two World Wars and subsequent bipolarity. Today, the Cold War is in the past, and the increasing impact of globalization throws up new sets of opportunities and challenges.

The context in which (EU) foreign policy is designed and operates has thus changed. Foreign policy has had to evolve in line with this changed environment and our understanding of what constitutes foreign policy must make a similar journey. We propose a conceptual approach – conventional foreign policy and structural foreign policy – on which we base our analysis of EU foreign policy in the chapters which follow. These concepts are complementary, not contradictory – they help us understand more dimensions of foreign policy challenges and how these are being, and could be, addressed. Building on this understanding of the context and definition of foreign policy, this chapter has begun an exploration of what constitutes EU foreign policy specifically. We understand EU foreign policy as multipillar and multilevel, operating within a complex multilocational web of interlocking actors and processes. These ideas form the conceptual backbone on which the rest of this book is based.

European Integration and Foreign Policy: Historical Overview

The relationship between European integration and the development of a European foreign policy has remained ambiguous from the end of World War II to the present day. Nevertheless, over the last half a century, European integration has evolved from a primarily economic endeavour to one with a substantive political and foreign policy dimension. This chapter charts this progress. In providing a historical overview, it quickly becomes clear that many of the obstacles that were highly problematic in the earliest stages of the process continue to be the stumbling blocks of EU foreign policy today.

European integration: the product of a structural foreign policy (1945–52)

The Marshall Plan of 1947 and the Schuman Declaration of 1950 launched a highly successful structural foreign policy towards post-war Western Europe, in which the process of European integration played a crucial role. To use today's terminology, the Marshall Plan and Schuman Declaration proposed to tackle the 'root causes' of the wars and economic and political crises that had characterized Europe in the first half of the 20th century by creating new structures to govern both the new (West) German state and its relations with its neighbours. This policy towards West Germany was one of the greatest successes of post-war American and French policy, precisely because it deviated from both the conventional concept of a foreign policy and the traditional approach to defeated nations.

The Marshall Plan

In his speech at Harvard University, the then American Secretary of State, General George Marshall, outlined the main features of a long-term American assistance programme for Europe (Marshall 1947; Hogan 1987). This speech came at a moment when the humanitarian, economic, political and security situation in Europe was in a pitiful state. Washington feared the further spread of communist ideology in the West, fuelled by the dire economic and humanitarian situation in Western European countries. Through the Marshall Plan, the US provided $20 billion for economic relief, $13 billion of which had already been pumped into Europe by 1953. Washington aimed to improve the socio-economic context, to restore order and stability in Western European societies and to obtain rapid improvements in living conditions. American policy was not only elite-focused, but also concentrated on the population (improving their economic situation) as well as on society (weakening the impact of communist ideology). Today we would call this 'winning the hearts and minds' of Western Europeans in the face of an increasingly popular communist ideology. The Marshall Plan was thus more than an impressive economic assistance programme. It was also aimed at influencing and shaping the ideas, norms and values that would govern Western Europe. The US used its Marshall Plan as an instrument to shape and/or consolidate a whole set of political, economic and societal structures based on the principles of democracy, rule of law and a free market economy, which affected not only individual states, but also the relationship between states.

One of the major features of the Marshall Plan was that it was based on the principle of European 'ownership', which paved the way for future European integration. Washington put pressure on Western European states to cooperate in economic reconstruction and to accept one another – including the two former enemies, Germany and Italy – as partners in the framework of the Marshall Plan and the Organisation for European Economic Cooperation (the predecessor of the Organisation for Economic Co-operation and Development (OECD)). Psychologically and politically, the American approach was critical because it forced political and economic leaders, diplomats and civil servants from across Western Europe to work together. And in so doing, it laid

Table 2.1 Key dates in the development of European foreign policy

Year	Treaty/Document	Event/Development
1947	Marshall Plan	US assistance for Western Europe
1949	Treaty of Washington	North Atlantic Treaty
1950		Creation of NATO
1951	Treaty of Paris	Creation of ECSC
1952		Signing of EDC Treaty
1954		Non-ratification of the EDC Treaty
	Modified Brussels Treaty	Creation of the WEU
1957	Treaty of Rome	Creation of the EEC
1963		Yaoundé Treaty with former African colonies
1964		Failure of the Fouchet Plans
1970	Luxembourg Report	Start of EPC (and Helsinki Process)
1975		First Lomé Agreement with the ACP countries
1986	Single European Act	EPC gains treaty basis
1988		Start of a policy towards reformist CEECs
1989		Fall of the communist regimes in CEECs
1991		Start of Balkan wars
1992	Treaty of Maastricht	Creation of the EU and CFSP
1993		Copenhagen criteria for the CEECs
1995	European Council in Madrid	Start Euro-Mediterranean Process Set of strategies/partnerships towards main regions in world
1997	Treaty of Amsterdam	Creation of position of High Representative for the CFSP
1998		End of Balkan wars Franco-British Saint Malo Agreement
1999	European Councils in Cologne and Helsinki	Establishment of ESDP
2000		Cotonou Agreement with ACP countries
2003		Iraq war First ESDP operations European Security Strategy
2004		Enlargement to 25 member states Start of European Neighbourhood Policy
	Treaty Establishing a Constitution for Europe	Constitution for Europe (not ratified)
2007		Enlargement to 27 member states
	Lisbon/Reform Treaty	Amendment of the Treaties

the psychological foundations for the later European Coal and Steel Community (ECSC) negotiations, which would also be strongly supported by the US. The Marshall Plan contributed to the necessary restoration of self-confidence and responsibility in Western European countries and West Germany in particular, as well as to the redefinition of Germany as a full partner in the West and in the Western European integration process. However, as much as the Marshall Plan contributed to the process of *Western European* integration and reconciliation, it also strengthened *European* disintegration and confrontation, as, on Soviet insistence, the Central and Eastern European countries were not able to participate in its assistance programme.

The Schuman Declaration and the ECSC

It is not coincidental that it was Jean Monnet, one of the driving forces behind the implementation of the Marshall Plan in France, who became the intellectual father of France's new policy towards West Germany. It was Monnet's preparatory work that allowed the French Minister of Foreign Affairs, Robert Schuman, to present in 1950 the first positive French policy towards its enemy. Schuman proposed placing French and German coal and steel production under a common High Authority. Control over these two major industrial sectors (that were also the basis of the military industry) would be transferred from both France and West Germany to a supranational entity. While this proposal had a major economic component, it also went to the heart of foreign policy:

> The pooling of coal and steel production should immediately provide for the setting up of common foundations for economic development as a first step in the federation of Europe, and will change the destinies of those regions which have long been devoted to the manufacture of munitions of war, of which they have been the most constant victims. The solidarity in production thus established will make it plain that any war between France and Germany becomes not merely unthinkable, but materially impossible. (Schuman 1950)

Less than one year later, France, West Germany, Italy, the Netherlands, Belgium and Luxembourg signed the Paris Treaty establishing the European Coal and Steel Community (ECSC). The Schuman Plan and the creation of the ECSC presented European integration as a revolutionary new method to resolve hostility between states and, more generally, to organize interstate relations on the basis of equality as well as mutual solidarity and control. As Monnet noted in 1962, 'we adapted to our situation the methods which have allowed individuals to live together in society: common rules which each member is committed to respect, and common institutions to watch over the application of these rules' (Monnet 2003: 23). With the Schuman Declaration and the ECSC, the belief in a rules-based international order and multilateralism was born. This would become a constant theme in European foreign policy and a major element in the *European Security Strategy* adopted half a century later.

Crucial to the Schuman Plan and the ECSC was that they also affected the immaterial dimension of interstate and intersocietal relations. As Duchêne (1994: 224) emphasized, the Schuman Plan was 'about turning around the psychology of relations between states and peoples'. The process of integration that it launched contributed to a gradual change in the mental structures of both the elite and the people: 'national' identities and interests were gradually no longer articulated in opposition to each other, but were redefined by an inclusion of 'Europe' and of 'the other' (i.e. the other member states) (Waever 2000). It is this redefinition of the identity of the EU's founding member states that contributed to the desecuritization of the Franco-German relationship, the lasting transformation of Germany from an enemy into a partner and the transformation of Western Europe into a 'security community' (see Adler and Barnett 1998).

European integration and foreign policy: a long-standing taboo (1952–70)

In April 1949, in the face of a perceived growing threat from the Soviet Union, the signing of the North Atlantic Treaty sealed America's commitment to providing a security guarantee for its Western European allies. However, it was not at all clear what kind of military structures would be established to organize Western Europe's collective defence and what the position of West Germany would be therein.

NATO and the transatlantic imbalance

It was not the US but the Europeans (including France) that pushed for greater American leadership and the continued presence of American soldiers to defend their territories. Initially, the US expected Western European countries themselves to assume responsibility for managing Europe's defence and viewed the new Atlantic Alliance rather like 'a military Marshall Plan, to help the Europeans pull up their own socks and take the future in their own hands' (Cook 1989: 225). The outbreak of the Korean War in June 1950 transformed this context, and half a year later the North Atlantic Treaty was upgraded to a North Atlantic Treaty Organization. At the top of an integrated military alliance (including a heavy commitment of American troops), an American Supreme Allied Commander directed the territorial defence of Western Europe. As Calleo has underlined, with NATO, 'America's European policy moved out of its Marshall Plan phase, which had emphasized economic recovery and European initiative, and into a new phase that featured massive rearmament and direct American leadership' (1987: 28). 'Along with militarization came a different style in transatlantic political relations, a move from a "two pillars" pattern, emphasizing a European unity distinct from American ties, towards a hegemonic pattern, emphasizing America's direct role in managing European affairs' (Calleo 1983: 8).

The repercussions of transferring primary responsibility for the security and defence of Western Europe to America were to be felt for the next half a century. The parameters set by the globalization of America's military presence, by the globalization of the East–West confrontation and by the highly confrontational approach of the US, implied that in addition to structuring Western Europe's security and defence policies, America also structured its foreign policy. Given that the US bore the burden of the West's military efforts, Washington understandably expected at least a political return from its NATO allies through their active support for American foreign policy objectives and actions. Thus, the scope for Western Europe to pursue or even formulate its own foreign policy interests, to take its own foreign policy initiatives and to approach foreign policy issues in a different way was dramatically reduced. During the decades which followed, Washington often exploited this imbalance, pulling the plug on Western European positions on matters such as improving relations with Eastern European countries, developing a balanced approach to conflict in the Middle East and particularly creating an autonomous European foreign, security and defence policy. Remarkably, this pattern of transatlantic relations survived the disappearance of the Soviet threat with the effect of the Cold War prism being replaced by the 'war on terror' prism since 2001.

From European Defence Community to Western European Union

Incorporating German military power into the West's defence brought the most sensitive aspect of the German issue to the top of the political agenda: German rearmament. The US was prepared to strengthen American forces in Europe on the condition that European countries increased their defence efforts, including using West German military potential to defend against possible attack from the east. However, barely five years after being victims of German aggression, the idea of a new German army was a step too far for France and the rest of Western Europe.

The methodology developed some months earlier in the Schuman Declaration seemed to provide the solution. Following the ECSC's example, creating a supranational European Defence Community (EDC) would mean German soldiers could operate within a European army, without having to create a new German army. In October 1950, the French launched the Pleven Plan under which military units from the member states would be integrated to create a European army controlled by a European Minister for Defence, who would operate under the direction of a Council of member states' ministers (see Fursdon 1980). In May 1952, the EDC Treaty was signed by the six ECSC states and submitted to national parliaments for ratification (Hill and Smith 2000: 16–32). The opening article of the Treaty announced that the High Contracting Parties 'set up amongst themselves a European Defence Community, supra-national in character, comprising common institutions, common Armed Forces, and a common budget'. On closer inspection, the Treaty was actually less 'common' or European than suggested. Under pressure from the other ECSC states and the US, the French had been forced to

accept that the project become more Atlantic and intergovernmental than originally anticipated. By mid-1954, improvements
in the East–West relationship had lessened the urgency and the
original motivation for creating a European army. Amidst growing concerns of the loss of national sovereignty in security and
defence, the French Assembly refused to ratify the EDC Treaty,
which effectively killed it off.

Creating the Western European Union (WEU) provided an
alternative solution to the question of German rearmament. The
Modified Brussels Treaty of October 1954 allowed West
Germany and Italy to enter a six-year-old military assistance pact
(originally elaborated against Germany!) between France, Great
Britain and the Benelux countries (Hill and Smith 2000: 40–1).
The Treaty's Article IV stated that: 'Recognising the undesirabil-
ity of duplicating the military staffs of NATO, the Council [of the
WEU] and its Agency will rely on the appropriate military
authorities of NATO for information and advice on military
matters.' Responsibility for military affairs was de facto passed
to NATO – with West Germany thus being militarily integrated
into NATO through a back door opened by the WEU. Stripped
of its potential as a site for European defence cooperation, the
Europeans lost the opportunity to use their own military capabilities to pursue their own foreign policy choices. European
military impotence at the outbreak of the Yugoslav war 40 years
later would be the painful consequence of the choice made in the
early 1950s.

The failure of the Pleven Plan and EDC project and the subsequent creation of the WEU implied that from then on military
security structures would be Atlantic not European, intergovernmental not supranational. These fault lines became more
pronounced after the failure of the second French attempt to get
the Six to act as one in foreign policy and defence. With the
Fouchet plans of 1960 and 1962, Paris proposed creating a
Union with a European foreign and defence policy outside the
EEC framework on the basis of purely intergovernmental cooperation. The negotiations eventually came to nothing as most
EEC partners feared that President de Gaulle's plans were aimed
at undermining the Atlantic Alliance, as well as the EEC and its
Community method. Overcoming these fault lines became ever
more problematic when in 1965 France withdrew from the mili-
tary structures of NATO after America and Britain rejected its

request to be on an equal footing with the UK in NATO's military command structure. The French withdrawal and decision to follow its own military and nuclear doctrine provoked a fundamental breach between France and the other EEC countries, making cooperation or integration in security and defence virtually impossible, that is until Paris and London launched the ESDP process in 1998.

The EEC's external dimension

With the Rome Treaties of 1957, the European Economic Community (EEC) and European Community for Atomic Energy (Euratom) were established. European integration was assuming a primarily economic path, with no foreign policy, security or defence dimension foreseeable. However, with the Rome Treaty, the EEC was granted competences in external trade and the conclusion of agreements with third states which allowed it to evolve gradually into an international actor. By 1963, the EEC had already established and organized relations with member states' former African colonies within the framework of the Yaoundé Treaty, predecessor to the Lomé and now Cotonou agreements with the African, Caribbean and Pacific (ACP) countries. In 1966–67, in an unambiguous confirmation of a distinct European identity in terms of external trade, the European Commission acted on behalf of the six member states in the Kennedy Round negotiations of the General Agreement on Tariffs and Trade (predecessor to the WTO).

The EEC's external competences forced the Europeans to define their relations with the rest of the world and created external expectations about the role of the EU as a major power – which also entailed foreign policy related choices. The growing international 'presence' of the EEC was so significant, that it was compelled to also further develop its 'actorness' (see Sjøstedt 1977; Allen and Smith 1990). This goes to the heart of the EU foreign policy problematic: the EEC gradually and quietly became a foreign policy actor despite the fact that it did not possess clear foreign policy competences, that this had not originally been foreseen by the member states and that it certainly did not have the wholehearted support of all member states.

European Political Cooperation (1970–93): setting the stage

At their 1969 summit meeting in The Hague, the EEC member states relaunched the European integration process in a changing international and domestic context: détente in East–West relations; a question mark over America's commitment to Europe; a new West German Chancellor, Willy Brandt, whose foreign policy priority was rapprochement with the Eastern European countries; and the end of Charles de Gaulle's rule and thus the removal of a major obstacle to new European initiatives. In addition to decisions to strengthen the EC and to begin accession negotiations with the UK, Ireland, Denmark and Norway, the Heads of State and Government of the six EEC countries also instructed their Ministers of Foreign Affairs 'to study the best way of achieving progress in the matter of political unification' (for this, The Hague Summit Declaration, and all other European Political Cooperation (EPC) declarations, see Hill and Smith 2000: 71–119).

The resulting Luxembourg Report, adopted in 1970 by the Ministers of Foreign Affairs, signified the start of what was termed European Political Cooperation. The report emphasized 'the need to intensify political cooperation' and, in an initial phase, to 'concentrate specifically on the co-ordination of foreign policies in order to show the whole world that Europe has a political mission'. This mission was to play a role 'in promoting the relaxation of international tension and the rapprochement among all peoples, and first and foremost among those of the entire European continent'. More precisely, the objectives of this foreign policy cooperation were defined as follows (Hill and Smith 2000: 77):

- to ensure, through regular exchanges of information and consultations, a better mutual understanding on the great international problems
- to strengthen their solidarity by promoting the harmonisation of their views, the co-ordination of their positions, and, where it appears possible and desirable
- common action

To meet these objectives, the following mechanisms were established: biannual meetings of the six Ministers of Foreign Affairs, quarterly meetings of a Political Committee consisting of member states' Directors of Political Affairs, specialist working parties, and the designation within Foreign Ministries of an official to correspond with his/her counterpart in other member states.

As the first experience with EPC proved positive, the Heads of State and Government in 1973 adopted the Copenhagen Report and, later on that year, a Declaration on a European Identity. The Copenhagen Report proposed to formalize practices developed in the previous years, including an increase in the number of meetings. It also specified that in the foreign policy questions selected by the Foreign Ministers, 'each state undertakes as a general rule not to take up final positions without prior consultation with its partners'.

As M. Smith (2001: 86–8) indicates, from these basic EPC texts a whole set of procedural and behavioural norms were incrementally developed. The London Report of 1981 and the Single European Act (SEA) of 1986, in which EPC gained treaty status, largely confirmed these foreign policy habits rather than launching major new commitments or mechanisms, and without making any attempt to solve the problems that had arisen in practice (Hill and Smith 2000: 139–45) (for an in-depth analysis of EPC, see Pijpers *et al.* 1988; Nuttall 1992, 1997a).

Basic features

Like CFSP until the late 1990s, EPC was based on purely intergovernmental arrangements between member states' Foreign Ministries, with consensus required for every decision, no transfer of competences to the European level and no formal role for common institutions. Member states agreed to foster consultation, coordination and possibly joint action in a number of foreign policy areas. But, they retained full control over their foreign policy. EPC relied entirely on interministerial arrangements and particularly on the rotating Presidency. This became a major handicap when the number of member states and the scope of EPC activities increased. The creation of a small EPC secretariat in the 1980s aside, EPC's lack of common actors was not to be thoroughly addressed until the creation of a High Representative for the CFSP in the 1997 Amsterdam Treaty.

EPC was also rigidly separated from the legal and institutional framework of the EC. As a legacy of the Fouchet Plan debacle, the French wanted to avoid any involvement of common institutions or the Community method, while the other member states wanted to avoid intergovernmental arrangements contaminating the EC. This implied that the Commission, the European Parliament and the Court of Justice had no formal role in EPC. Although the 1986 Single European Act linked EPC to the EC Treaties, the provisions on EPC did not form part of Title II concerning the 'Provisions amending the Treaties establishing the European Communities', but were included in a separate Title III concerning 'Treaty provisions on European cooperation in the sphere of foreign policy'. This of course foreshadowed the development of a pillar system with the Maastricht Treaty.

In practice, the formal separation of EPC and EC was not sustainable. Although they functioned according to their own logic, interaction between EPC and the EC in both institutional and policy matters was unavoidable. As an unforeseen consequence of EPC's lack of common institutions and instruments, EPC often had to rely on the EC to give substance to its declarations and initiatives. EPC needed the EC's economic instruments for sanctions (against Poland in 1982, Argentina during the Falklands crisis in 1982, and South Africa from the mid-1980s) and for economic support (for Central American countries' peace initiatives in the mid-1980s) (Nuttall 1997a). Furthermore, the Nine and later Twelve were increasingly faced with questions from the outside world which required a joint economic and political response. The EC's successful internal market project, launched in 1985, increased external expectations about not only its economic but also its political power (see Redmond 1992).

Objectives and policies

During the first years of its existence, EPC established some basic patterns in its objectives and policies that by and large remained valid over the following decades. EPC not only aimed at pursuing *external* objectives (influencing the external environment), but also at achieving *integration* objectives, *interrelational* objectives and *identity* objectives (see Chapter 1). Integration objectives dominated the start of EPC, which became one element of efforts to relaunch European integration. Interrelational objectives were prominent in the goals of cooperation defined in the Luxembourg Report: regular information and consultation was a method to ensure 'a better mutual understanding' while harmonizing views and coordinating positions was a way to 'strengthen their solidarity'. EPC provided a gentle way to keep an eye on West Germany's emerging *Ostpolitik* and to embed it in a larger European setting, while for West Germany EPC provided a tool to lever support for its new foreign policy orientation. Identity objectives were prominent in the 1970 Luxembourg Report and the 1973 Declaration on European Identity. But also more generally, EPC allowed the member states to elaborate a specific 'European' position to the world and to step back from the US at a time when that country was losing international support due to the Vietnam war.

Rather than developing a 'common' foreign policy, EPC aimed at shaping foreign policy through consultation, coordination and cooperation between member states' foreign policies. As the list of objectives enumerated in the Luxembourg Report had already made clear, joint action – where 'possible and desirable' – was only one of the options. In any case, EPC did not tackle the whole spectrum of foreign policy. The number of foreign policy issues discussed among EPC states was initially rather limited. For example, foreign policy towards the former colonies and the military dimension were both excluded from debate. However, EPC did play an important role both in the negotiations with the Eastern Bloc countries in the Conference on Security and Cooperation in Europe (CSCE or 'Helsinki Process') and in discussions on the Middle East and the Palestinian question (see Chapter 10). Experience was to prove encouraging with the former, but discouraging with the latter – one of the determining factors being whether Washington allowed the Europeans to take the lead and pursue a policy of their own.

By the early 1980s, EPC had already established the general trends that European foreign policy would follow over the decades to come. There was a clear focus on promoting structural changes in other regions over the longer term. However, EPC proved ineffective in formulating a policy on the crises of the time, including the Middle East conflict, Afghanistan and Poland. From 1988 onwards, even before the fall of the Berlin

Wall, the EC/EPC had shifted its focus on structural changes up a gear by supporting the reforms on which some Eastern European countries were embarking. After the fall of the communist regimes in late 1989, Central and Eastern Europe became the subject of the first comprehensive structural foreign policy of the EC/EU (see Chapter 10).

The Maastricht Treaty (1992) and the illusive CFSP

Motivations and geostrategic context

The member states' rationale in creating CFSP is the key to understanding its nature. Their motivations were closely linked to the geostrategic changes that had preceded and acted as a catalyst for the Maastricht Treaty: the fall of the communist regimes in 1988–91, the reunification of Germany in 1990, military conflict in the Gulf following the Iraqi invasion of Kuwait in 1990 and the start of the Yugoslav crisis in 1991.

Firstly, CFSP was about strengthening European integration and particularly about member states managing their interstate relations in an unstable geopolitical environment. In conjunction with establishing the EU and Economic and Monetary Union (EMU), CFSP was part of a greater diplomatic operation and balance of power exercise in which the member states sought to firmly embed an enlarged German state in a stronger European entity whilst Germany gained support for its unification process.

Secondly, CFSP was about managing inter-institutional relations and the relations between member states and the Commission. For most member states, creating CFSP in a separate intergovernmental second pillar was deemed necessary to contain the EU as a foreign policy actor and to ensure member states' full control. Under President Delors, the Commission had become increasingly assertive in foreign affairs, taking full advantage of its potential to back up nice declarations with concrete operational measures. The foreign policy potential and aspirations of the EC needed to be curtailed, and CFSP was to serve as a filter to stop the substance of foreign policy entering the EC machinery.

Thirdly, CFSP was about identity and public relations management. In this period of major geopolitical change, in which 'Europe' had suffered a loss of face during the Gulf and

Yugoslav crises, CFSP was seen as a tool to strengthen European identity. Hence, one of the new objectives of the Treaty on European Union (TEU) was 'to assert its identity on the international scene, in particular through the implementation of a common foreign and security policy' (art. 2 TEU). Finally, for some of the original member states, CFSP was about creating an effective and credible European foreign policy – although for others, such as the UK and Denmark, the opposite was true. For some member states, the disappearance of the old East–West order made it imperative that the new EU become a stronger and more coherent foreign policy actor. The Gulf and Yugoslav crises demonstrated the EU needed new tools to cope with new external challenges. However, for other member states, these crises were a stark reminder that the EU should not aim to tackle such events if only because member states differed so fundamentally on the role of the US and the use of military force.

It is clear that from CFSP's inception, interrelational, integration and identity objectives were for many member states as important, if not more important, than external objectives. Although all member states accepted CFSP for the reasons outlined above, some were firmly opposed to a CFSP that would be able to make true its name. And for other member states, CFSP had already fulfilled its main function at the moment of its creation.

The Maastricht Treaty: debates and results

In sharp contrast to the Intergovernmental Conference (IGC) on EMU, which had been thoroughly prepared since 1988 by the Delors committee, the parallel IGC on European Political Union, in which the CFSP was negotiated, suffered from a lack of serious preparatory discussion. This was an indication that rather than resulting from a well-considered initiative, creating CFSP was a panicked response to turbulent geopolitics. Foreshadowing the future of treaty negotiations, the position of foreign policy in the new treaty framework, the decision-making system and the military dimension of security dominated the IGC (for a detailed analysis, see Laursen and Vanhoonacker 1992; Nuttall 2000).

The first major issue was how to position foreign policy in the new treaty. In the final stage of the IGC, the Dutch presidency proposed establishing a unitary institutional framework, integrating the political, economic and security dimensions of foreign policy. For the Dutch, this was vital to ensure the efficiency and coherence of EU foreign policy. However, this unitary system was rejected by most other member states and negotiators returned to the three-pillar approach that had been discussed earlier in the IGC. The Union's competences in the various dimensions of external relations and foreign policy were organized through distinctive policy-making regimes enshrined in different titles of the treaty, including the titles on the European Community (the 'first pillar') and Title V on the CFSP (the 'second pillar'), with the latter replacing the provisions on EPC of the 1986 Single European Act. Title VI (the 'third pillar') was to deal with provisions on cooperation in the fields of justice and home affairs. The member states deprived CFSP of a direct link to either essential foreign policy instruments or the EU's strongest policy domains: trade policy, the network of trade and cooperation agreements, development cooperation, and the external dimensions of internal policy fields. This was all the more remarkable as member states did not endow the second pillar with its own policy instruments or financial resources to allow it to deliver.

The second issue to be tackled in the run-up to Maastricht was decision-making. One of the main rationales behind the pillar system was to avoid features of the EC decision-making system applying to CFSP. Policy-making in CFSP would be an intergovernmental affair – monopolized by the Council of Ministers with unanimous voting almost across the board and with member states also dominating the initiation and implementation stages.

The third issue that dominated the IGC was the military dimension of security. It was here that divergences between member states were starkest with one group of member states led by France and Germany pleading for a 'common defence', and the neutrals and Atlantic-orientated states maintaining their opposition. Regardless, the pressure on the EC to play its part in the aftermath of the Gulf War made it impossible for member states to continue to ignore the military dimension of security. They developed two formulae to overcome this paralysing situation. They negotiated a treaty text that a year previous would have been unacceptable. By being deliberately ambiguous in its formulation and incorporating safeguards for neutral and

NATO-orientated states, they managed to agree that, 'the common foreign and security policy shall include all questions related to the security of the Union, including the *eventual framing* of a common defence policy, which *might in time* lead to a common defence' (art. J.4(1) TEU, our emphasis). And, since it could serve as both the military arm of the EU and the European arm of NATO, member states agreed to use the WEU as a bridge between both camps. The major innovation, on paper, was that the Council could request the WEU 'to elaborate and implement decisions and actions of the Union which have defence implications' (art. J.4(2) TEU).

In the aftermath of the Maastricht European Council that adopted the TEU it appeared that there was something for everyone. The French, Germans and like-minded states achieved the grandiose phrases and symbolic changes they had asked for (i.e. 'common foreign and security policy', 'all aspects of security', 'common defence'); but a closer reading of the text made it clear that the UK and other member states had conceded much on words and symbols, but nothing on substance and practice. Nevertheless, this was too much for Danish public opinion. After initially rejecting the new treaty outright, Denmark obtained an opt-out from Maastricht's defence provisions. As such, even now Denmark cannot contribute to military EU crisis management operations, either financially or in terms of military assets (see Olsen and Pilegaard 2005).

Irrespective of the member states' underlying motivations and arm-wrestling, the creation of CFSP and the very name 'common foreign and security policy' created major expectations. European leaders presented the CFSP to the public as a fully fledged foreign policy that would allow the EU to act cohesively and effectively on the international stage. In the following years, CFSP was thus tested against the standards of the conventional foreign policy it had been proclaimed to be. But, of course the EU was doomed to fail this test. The member states were not committed to the success of CFSP and had not provided it with the necessary instruments or institutional framework (see Chapter 6). Meanwhile, the more intensive cooperation with the WEU proved illusive.

European impotence and disarray in the Balkan wars in the two years between the signing and the entry into force of the Maastricht Treaty in November 1993 further discredited the whole project from its very inception (see Chapter 10). To make things worse, CFSP's first Presidency fell to a Greece that was completely isolated on the most important foreign policy dossiers of the day: the Balkan crisis and the recognition of 'Macedonia' in particular. This also contributed to the further decline of member states' interest in CFSP. Quite paradoxically, at the moment when scholars were becoming increasingly fixated by the development of the second pillar, and thereby often equating 'EU foreign policy' with 'CFSP', the member states themselves were losing interest in their new creation (for the CFSP's first years, see Holland 1997; Regelsberger *et al.* 1997).

Strategies and partnerships beyond CFSP

From 1994 on, member states and the EU institutions shifted their attention from elaborating CFSP to outlining general EU strategies and partnerships towards other regions in the world (Keukeleire 1998: 367–459). These strategies and partnerships encompassed the EU's three pillars, but were based essentially on the EC pillar. At the heart of this move lay two issues. Firstly, the need to counterbalance the EU's dominant focus on the CEECs with more attention to the Mediterranean and other parts of the world. Secondly, the ambition to apply at least partially the EU's comprehensive approach towards the CEECs, with its focus on support for structural reforms, to other regions in the world.

In well coordinated efforts, the German, French and Spanish Presidencies between July 1994 and the end of 1995 gained support from their partners for this balancing exercise and reorientation of EU foreign policy. For the five-year period to follow, 6.6 billion and 4.4 billon ecu/euros were allocated to Central and Eastern Europe and the Mediterranean respectively, while the 8th European Development Fund (EDF) for the ACP countries would receive 13.3 billion ecu/euro. This amounted to a serious increase in expenditure for the EC's external policies and contrasted markedly with the CFSP's lack of financial resources.

By the end of 1995, with the active support of the Commission, the EU had mapped out the major lines of its policy towards most regions in the world. This was reflected in the extensive *Conclusions of the Presidency* after the European Council of Madrid in December 1995 – Conclusions which an insider labelled euphorically, but not undeservedly, as 'a strategy paper for European foreign policy for the coming 20 years' (Rhein 1996: 58). While these Presidency Conclusions covered CFSP in barely a few lines, they dealt extensively with the strategies and partnerships that would determine EU policy for the following decade. In addition to a report on relations with the CEECs, the Presidency Conclusions included: the Barcelona Declaration adopted at the first Euro-Mediterranean Conference, the New Transatlantic Agenda adopted during the EU–US summit meeting, the EU's position for the first Euro-Asian Summit (ASEM), the 'European Union's Strategy for Future EU/Russia Relations', Council guidelines for cooperation between the Community and Latin America, as well as references to the Regional Framework Agreement with Mercosur. Breaking from the mode of the previous five years, with their quasi-exclusive focus on the CEECs and the Balkans, a literal globalization of the EU's external attentions was occurring.

A detailed analysis of the EU's strategic papers *vis-à-vis* other regions shows that several of these were, to a greater or lesser extent, manifestations of a structural foreign policy. They aimed to promote a more favourable international environment by pursuing and supporting long-term structural changes in the internal situation of third countries, in interstate relations and the overall situation of third regions. They aimed at transfering, in varying degrees, the political, societal, economic and interstate structures that characterized the EU itself: democracy and good governance, human rights, the principles of a free market economy, regional cooperation and integration, and the 'Helsinki' or OSCE principles (such as the peaceful resolution of conflicts). The strategic papers focussed on support for political and economic reforms as well as for economic development as a necessary condition to stabilize a region. To a large extent, the strategic papers aimed at what we labelled in the first chapter milieu goals, other-regarding interests or far-sighted self-interests. Interestingly, many of these strategic documents adopted the format developed in the early EPC days with the three 'baskets' of the Helsinki negotiations with the Eastern Bloc – a political and security dimension, an economic dimension and a human dialogue dimension.

The intensity and scope of the EU's structural foreign policy varied considerably from region to region. In some cases (such as

Latin America and Asia) the structural foreign policy dimension appeared on paper but not in practice, as it was not supported by considerable financial resources or other Community instruments. The structural foreign policy dimension was very clear in policies towards the CEECs, the Mediterranean, the Palestinian Territories and, from the late 1990s, the Balkans, even if over the longer term the results of policies towards the Mediterranean and Palestine were disappointing (see Chapter 10).

In short, with its intensified partnerships towards the rest of the world and its structural foreign policy towards the surrounding regions, in the second half of the 1990s the EU did have a foreign policy. But, this was neither the foreign policy conceived by the Treaty of Maastricht through the CFSP, nor a foreign policy as might be conventionally understood.

The Amsterdam Treaty (1997) and ESDP: moving towards action

The late 1990s saw two major attempts to tackle the lack of common actors and common instruments that had undermined both EPC and CFSP. These qualitative changes only partially resulted from treaty reforms brought about by the 1997 Amsterdam Treaty itself (see also Monar 1997). In fact, as ESDP's early development outside the treaties testifies, changes to the treaties proved again to be a poor instigator or indicator of real change in EU foreign policy.

The Amsterdam Treaty

The main qualitative change of the Amsterdam Treaty was the creation of the function of 'Secretary General/High Representative of the CFSP'. The High Representative was to assist the Council and the Presidency in the formulation, preparation and implementation of policy decisions, and would be supported by a newly created 'policy planning and early warning unit' (or 'Policy Unit'). This change was fundamental. For the first time, CFSP would be supported by a permanent actor and would also have a 'face'. The impact of this innovation was not initially clear as several member states thought a rather low-key figure would be suitable for the new job. However, following the

EU's most recent Balkans debacle in Kosovo, the 1999 Cologne European Council opted for the high-profile political figure of Javier Solana, who as Secretary General had just led NATO through its military operations against Serbia. By appointing Solana, the member states indicated they were indeed serious about strengthening the EU's foreign policy and security capabilities.

A second innovation of the Amsterdam Treaty was the creation of a new 'common strategies' instrument. In 1999–2000, three 'common strategies' were adopted – towards Russia, Ukraine and the Mediterranean. However, this instrument's design reflected the need to reconcile incompatible negotiating positions rather than any particular desire to strengthen CFSP (Nuttall 1997b). As they offered no real added-value to the partnerships and strategies which the EU had been developing since the mid-1990s, this new instrument was quickly dropped. A third treaty change had even less effect – a slight relaxation of the voting requirements in the Council. However, as was the case before the Amsterdam Treaty, the Council never voted, making the new decision-making provisions as insignificant as they were complex.

Finally, the Amsterdam Treaty strengthened the relationship between the EU and the WEU. The EU gained access to the WEU's operational capability for humanitarian and rescue tasks, peacekeeping tasks and tasks of combat forces in crisis management, including peacemaking (the 'Petersberg tasks'). The EU was also to 'foster closer institutional relations with the WEU with a view to the possibility of the integration of the WEU into the EU'. However, the new provisions on EU–WEU relations were quickly overtaken by a new dynamic – the European Security and Defence Policy.

The European Security and Defence Policy (ESDP)

In the space of a few years, the military dimension, which had for decades been taboo in the European integration process (see Duke 1999) became one of the spearheads of EU foreign policy. This was made possible because for the first time in some 50 years of European integration, the member states managed to sufficiently overcome two areas of tension that had paralysed EU foreign policy: 'European integration versus Atlantic solidarity' and 'civilian power versus military power'. The first area of tension was tackled through intensive high-level negotiations among Paris, London and Berlin, while the second was overcome by carefully balancing NATO states and the EU's neutral states and by complementing new *military* crisis management tools with *civilian* crisis management tools (Howorth 2000; Ojanen 2000).

Such new found flexibility in member sates' traditional mindsets was triggered by the Kosovo crisis which increased frustration in London, Paris and Berlin – but also Washington – over Europe's military impotence and dependence on the US (Howorth 2000, 2001). Further conflict in the Balkans convinced Germany that it would have to start participating in external military operations, reversing its post-World War II doctrine. The British government, under the new Prime Minister Tony Blair, adopted a more pro-European attitude than previous British governments, for the first time seeing the strengthening of Europe's military capacities as essential to rebalance transatlantic relations and thus safeguard the future of NATO. French political leaders in turn assumed a more pro-Atlantic attitude and demonstrated a greater willingness to cooperate with NATO. America's military superiority in the Balkans was a humbling experience for Paris while good cooperation with British forces on the ground had laid the foundations for a Franco-British entente.

These moves were sealed in several bilateral agreements, most importantly the Franco-British Saint Malo Declaration of December 1998. At Saint Malo, Jacques Chirac and Tony Blair agreed the EU must have 'the capacity for autonomous action, backed up by credible military forces, the means to decide to use them, and a readiness to do so, in order to respond to international crises'. The Cologne European Council of June 1999 duly adopted the goal to establish the ESDP, repeating crucial elements of the Franco-British text. This set a pattern that would be followed in other important ESDP steps, with London, Paris and Berlin effectively pre-cooking decisions.

That the member states were serious about ESDP was quickly confirmed. Merely half a year after the Cologne summit, the European Council in Helsinki took two major decisions. It adopted a commitment to being able to deploy military forces (the Helsinki Headline Goal) and agreed to create a standing Political and Security Committee, a Military Committee and a Military Staff within the framework of the Council. The same year, on the initiative of Sweden and Finland, the EU agreed to develop civilian crisis management capabilities – police and rule of law missions. After difficult debate with the US, the thorny issue of EU access to NATO military assets and command structures was resolved by the December 2002 'Berlin-Plus Agreement' and a mere three months later, the EU took over the NATO operation in Macedonia and began its first-ever military operation, Operation Concordia. This was followed in fairly rapid succession by military and civilian operations in the Balkans, Africa, the Middle East and even Asia (see Chapter 7). In short, less than three years after its decision to establish an ESDP and to break the 45-year-old taboo, the EU had not only established the necessary institutional and instrumental apparatus, but had also launched its first crisis management operations. This was rapid progress indeed for an organization infamous for its mainly declaratory nature, its slow and problematic decision-making and its paralysing internal divisions.

ESDP qualitatively changed the nature of CFSP. It allowed CFSP to move from a declaratory foreign policy focused on diplomacy to a more action-orientated foreign policy focused on more proactive crisis management. For the first time, the member states succeeded in developing a framework to effectively pool national resources within CFSP. And although still limited in scope, the EU finally had boots on the ground. This strengthened both the credibility of the EU and the potential effectiveness of CFSP in tackling conventional foreign policy issues.

EU foreign policy beyond September 11, enlargement and the Lisbon/Reform Treaty

The geostrategic shock waves of terrorist attacks against the US in September 2001 and EU enlargement in May 2004 forced the EU to upgrade its foreign policy set-up with regard to objectives and approaches (leading to the *European Security Strategy*) and with regard to institutional provisions (leading to the 'Reform Treaty').

September 11, Iraq and beyond

The 2001 terrorist attacks in the US, the wars in Afghanistan (2001) and Iraq (2003), the terrorist attacks in Madrid (2004) and London (2005), and renewed fears about the proliferation of WMD all forced EU countries to focus on yet another level of military challenge. For the first time since the height of the Cold War, security threats went to the heart of the survival of a nation's population – which had its impact on EU foreign policy. These events had both a divisive and an invigorating effect on EU foreign policy (see also Bono 2006).

The divisive element revealed itself in two ways. Firstly, it further widened the gap between the three largest member states on the one hand and the rest of the member states on the other, also throwing doubt on the relevance of the EU as a site for foreign policy cooperation. This resulted from member states' varying military capabilities, the American preference for only dealing with the largest states and the real need for a more restricted and confidential format to discuss sensitive foreign policy issues. The cleavage was most visibly reflected in the British, French and German leaders organizing a separate meeting before the extraordinary informal European Council convened in the aftermath of September 11 (see Duke 2002a). Despite criticism from the other states, the trilateral format would grow in relevance, both for ESDP issues and for tackling sensitive matters such as policy towards Iran's quest for nuclear power in 2004–06. Secondly, the Atlantic factor came to the fore more sharply than ever particularly during the Iraq crisis in 2002–03 (see Van Ham 2004). The public spats between member states seriously undermined the credibility of the EU as an international actor. One group of member states including the UK, Spain and Italy actively participated in the military invasion and occupation of Iraq. Meanwhile a second group led by France and Germany actively opposed the war which they considered both illegitimate and detrimental to global and Western security. The customary area of tension between Atlantic solidarity and European integration was further strengthened as the candidate member states joined the Atlantic camp.

The dramatic events also had a revitalizing impact on EU foreign policy – providing a new impetus to ESDP and broadening the number of issues on the EU foreign policy agenda to

include strategies on the proliferation of WMD and anti-terrorism. The wars in Afghanistan and Iraq painfully demonstrated
the limitations of European military capabilities, leading to new
commitments within ESDP to tackle these shortfalls. Moreover,
with its new military engagements in Iraq and Afghanistan, it
became clear that the US would be unable and unwilling to maintain its extensive military presence in the Balkans, implying that
the Europeans should prepare to assume these responsibilities.

The European Security Strategy

External and internal shock waves forced the EU in 2003 to
reconsider the basic principles and objectives of its foreign policy
in order to incorporate new security threats and challenges, to
formulate an approach to tackle these and to articulate a specific
position within this new geostrategic context. This exercise took
the form of Javier Solana's *European Security Strategy*, adopted
by the European Council in December 2003 (see Quille 2004;
Biscop 2005; Whitman 2006). The EU's first ever security strategy was not just important as a point of reference for future
foreign policy action. It was at least as important in terms of
interrelational objectives (contributing to overcoming divergence and mutual distrust) and identity objectives (highlighting
the specificity of the EU foreign policy approach).

Its threat-driven approach made the Strategy already quite
remarkable, particularly since actually addressing these threats
was the first of three EU strategic objectives. This was an innovation, as EU foreign policy texts had been traditionally filled with
'positive' approaches and concepts – the word 'threat' fitting
awkwardly within the EU's civilian discourse. The second strategic objective was to build security in the EU's neighbourhood. It
aimed to 'promote a ring of well governed countries to the East of
the European Union and on the borders of the Mediterranean'
with whom it could 'enjoy close and cooperative relations',
reflecting the partnerships and common strategies the EU had
already developed towards its neighbouring regions, and particularly the new European Neighbourhood Policy (ENP). The third
strategic objective was an 'international order based on effective
multilateralism'. Aiming to develop 'well functioning international institutions and a rule-based international order', this was
generally considered to be the most important distinction to

American foreign policy and indeed reflected the EU's active role in promoting international organizations and treaties. The Strategy also stated that the EU 'must be ready to act when their rules are broken' – an implicit reference to the EU's disarray when Iraq breached UN Security Council resolutions (and an indication of its future tougher stance towards Iran in 2006). The final section of the Strategy was an attempt to translate the threat assessment and objectives into policy priorities for the EU. It emphasized the role of multilateral cooperation and partnerships with key actors in achieving EU goals, which indeed reflected the reality of EU foreign policy. However, the Strategy also emphasized the need to adopt a more active approach, to undertake preventive engagement, and 'to develop a strategic culture that fosters early, rapid, and when necessary, robust intervention'.

Enlargement

At the same time that it was attempting to adapt to a changing geostrategic environment, the EU concluded its most significant foreign policy act to date: the accession of ten Central and Eastern European countries (CEECs) plus Cyprus and Malta. These enlargements in 2004 and 2007 and the prospect of further enlargement to include Turkey and the Balkan countries had multiple foreign policy relevance (see also Chapter 10).

The EU's enlargement process *was* and *is* foreign policy. The conditions set by the EU, as well as the goal of membership for the former communist countries, turned the enlargement process into the most successful structural foreign policy of the EU. Despite ambiguities and hesitations, since the first signs of reform in 1988 the EC/EU had played a crucial role in reshaping the political, legal, socio-economic and mental structures in Central and Eastern Europe. By contributing to the stabilization and transformation of this region, the EU strengthened the security situation of the entire continent – an achievement which is all too often underestimated.

Enlargement forced the EU to broaden and intensify its foreign policy towards its new (and prospective) neighbourhood. The 2004 enlargement turned Belarus, Ukraine and Moldova into immediate neighbours. Enlargement brought distant conflicts suddenly very close to home, forcing the EU into more action. Hence the EU launched in 2003–04 the ENP, became an active player during the political revolution in Ukraine in late 2004, and appointed EU Special Representatives for the South Caucasus, Central Asia and Moldova. The new member states also had an impact on the debate on EU policy towards Russia and other former Soviet countries and on the importance of democracy and human rights considerations in the EU's policy stance. The accession of ten CEECs affected the 'European integration versus Atlantic solidarity' tension, with the balance in crucial debates tilting more towards the Atlantic solidarity end of the spectrum. For the new EU member states that had also joined NATO, the security guarantee provided by that organization, and particularly the US, was essential in light of what they considered to be Russia's unpredictable future behaviour (on the effects of enlargement for EU foreign policy, see Edwards 2006; Müller-Brandeck-Bocquet 2006).

At the same time, the sheer rise in the number of member states, the proportional growth in the number of small states, and the growing divide between large and small member states had a serious impact on the EU's foreign policy system. With their more limited diplomatic services and foreign policy tradition, many new member states remained conspicuously quiet in EU meetings. The growth in numbers also contributed to the tendency of the largest states to shape EU foreign policy in more restricted settings to which only the largest or most relevant states were issued an invite.

From the Constitutional Treaty to the Lisbon/Reform Treaty

As had been the norm with previous enlargements, the 2004 enlargement was preceded by negotiations on adapting the treaties in order to first strengthen the EU before the new member states joined the club. The shock waves caused by September 11 and the Iraq and Afghanistan wars provided a further incentive to strengthen the European project generally, as well as its foreign policy capacities. That the member states had been so quick to translate their fine ESDP intentions into concrete steps indicated that the time was ripe to codify developments and to move forwards in this field. Remarkably, the schism caused by the 2003 Iraq War did not discourage member states from strengthening the EU's external capabilities. Rather, this episode was a catalyst to dismantling some of the hurdles that EU attempts at international action faced. The preparatory negotiations in the framework of the Convention on the Future of Europe, with representatives from governments, national parliaments, the European Parliament and the Commission, indicated that this time everyone was prepared to slaughter some sacred cows (Cremona 2003; European Convention 2003; Everts and Keohane 2003). This was confirmed by some major innovations included in the Treaty Establishing a Constitution for Europe, which was signed by the 25 member states in October 2004 (Duke 2004; Forsberg 2004).

A first innovation was that the EU's pillar system was formally buried. The Constitutional Treaty achieved what Maastricht had deemed impossible: bringing all dimensions of the Union's external action under one treaty title (Title V, 'The Union's External Action'). In parallel, the Union as a whole was granted legal personality (which had previously only been granted to the European Community). But, old habits die hard, and although the Constitutional Treaty abolished the pillar system in terms of presentation, it retained the division between the policy-making regimes for CFSP/ESDP and the EU's other external activities. The various actors were to continue playing different roles, and different decision-making methods were maintained.

A second, more significant innovation was the creation of the function of Union Minister of Foreign Affairs, of a European Council President, and of a European External Action Service (EEAS). The new EU Foreign Minister would combine the positions of the High Representative for the CFSP and the Commissioner for External Relations, and preside over the Foreign Affairs Council. The Minister would be assisted by an EEAS made up of officials from the Council's Secretariat, the Commission and staff seconded from member states' diplomatic services. The new European Council President would not only chair European Council meetings and drive forward its work, but also, at his or her level, ensure the external representation of the Union on issues concerning CFSP.

A third set of innovations was to be found in the chapter on ESDP. The Constitutional Treaty significantly broadened the original Petersberg tasks, introduced several provisions allowing for flexibility in developing and implementing ESDP, a solidarity clause and new institutional developments in the form of a European Defence Agency (EDA).

The Constitutional Treaty was less innovative in the other (formerly first pillar) chapters on the EU's external action. The Constitution did not strengthen the EU's capacity to act as a coherent force in international organizations and other fora, such as the UN, G8, IMF or the World Bank, thereby disregarding one of the major weaknesses of the EU's international actorness. However, it did include provisions on some 'internal' policy matters with potentially important foreign policy implications. For instance, ensuring security of supply became one of the three objectives of energy policy. And, as part of the EU's research and technological development policy, the EU gained competence to develop a European space policy.

The rejection of the Constitutional Treaty in the French and Dutch referenda of 2005, and the refusal of other member states to defend the treaty, sparked something of an existential crisis in the EU and seemed to put much of the treaty's innovation back to square one. The first main casualty was the attempt to strengthen leadership and coherence in EU foreign policy. The second main casualty was the EU's further enlargement as both a tool and substantive component of its foreign policy. Scepticism and outright hostility *vis-à-vis* the Constitution was interpreted in some quarters as a rejection of the EU's further enlargement and immediately translated into greater reluctance to absorb the Balkan countries and particularly Turkey (see Chapter 10). However, not all policy areas were victim. ESDP suffered very little. New ESDP operations were launched and the European Defence Agency was established regardless. This testifies to the fact that member states do not always need treaty provisions if they are serious in their intention to move something forward.

During their European Council meeting of June 2007, the member states' Heads of State and Government agreed on the contours of a new treaty to come into force before the European Parliament's elections of June 2009, replacing the Constitutional Treaty. They convened an IGC to prepare a 'Reform Treaty' on the basis of the detailed mandate agreed upon during this meeting (European Council 2007b). The European Council, during its informal meeting in Lisbon in October 2007, adopted the Reform Treaty to be signed in Lisbon in December 2007. In fact, in the foreign policy field the Lisbon or Reform Treaty retains the majority of innovations which had been foreseen by the Constitutional Treaty, albeit banishing the 'constitutional' symbols and terminology which had provoked concern in several member states. Hence, the title 'Union Minister for Foreign Affairs' is swapped for 'High Representative of the Union for Foreign Affairs and Security Policy' even though, beyond the new label, this function is practically identical to that anticipated by the Constitutional Treaty. The Lisbon/Reform Treaty also includes several provisions which emphasizes the specificity of CFSP and clarifies the status of the member states' foreign policy. Declarations annexed to the treaty underline that, despite the partial burial of the pillar system, CFSP and ESDP will retain their separate policy-making regime and that member states' capacity to conduct national foreign policies will not be curtailed.

Conclusion

This brief historical overview provides a stark demonstration of the remarkable progress that has been made, particularly over the last decade, in developing EU foreign policy. It also demonstrates that the roots of today's discussions on European foreign policy, as well as its basic features, are to be found in the earliest debates and policy choices. Firstly, in the first two decades after World War II, foreign policy was at the basis and at the heart of European integration; yet from 1954 onwards it was also one of its principal taboos. Since the early 1970s, incorporating foreign policy in European integration has been an incremental process of trial and error to try to circumvent this taboo. Secondly, foreign policy cooperation and integration has largely focused on structural foreign policy objectives; yet it has generally been presented and perceived through the conceptual lens of a conventional foreign policy, even though it has only been since the late 1990s that this conventional foreign policy component has received more substantial attention from the member states. Thirdly, the gradual development of cooperation and integration in foreign and security policy has been as much aimed at pursuing interrelational objectives, integration objectives and identity objectives than at pursuing external objectives. Hence, member states have not always accepted new treaty amendments relating to foreign policy because they wanted the EU to become a stronger international actor, but because they wanted to fulfil one of these other objectives.

Particularly since the Treaty on European Union (Maastricht Treaty) of 1992, foreign policy cooperation has been gradually institutionalized and formalized. However, the subsequent treaty changes and institutional build-up present only one picture of EU foreign policy. In general, incremental changes in beliefs, norms and practices of member states' behaviour have been at least as influential as the 'history making decisions' of treaty reform (see also M. E. Smith 2004).

Chapter 3

The EU's Foreign Policy System: Actors

Single by name, dual by regime, multiple by nature – this is the Union's institutional framework in a nutshell. An overarching 'single institutional framework' exists on paper and in its broad outline, but the practice is of different policy-making regimes through which the competences of the EU's foreign policy actors are determined. Painting the actors and procedures in broad strokes is quite easy. In CFSP/ESDP, the Council, under the strategic leadership of the European Council, dominates all stages of policy-making, with the growing support of central actors (the High Representative and his staff). In EC areas, the Commission proposes, the Council decides (alone, after consultation with the European Parliament (EP) or in co-decision with the EP) and the Commission implements, controls and manages budgets. In this case, acts are legally binding on the member states, and the European Court of Justice (ECJ) provides judicial oversight. This chapter focuses on political actors. It examines who or what is behind the façade of each of these actors as well as their varying strengths and weaknesses in delivering policy.

One framework, two regimes, or a continuum?

Despite the creation of three distinct pillars at Maastricht, the treaties emphasize that the Union is to be served by a single institutional framework. The same institutions serve the Community and CFSP (as well as the third pillar), irrespective of the area of action or the degree of competences in these areas, in order to ensure the consistency and continuity of that action (Art. 3 TEU). However, despite this single institutional framework, the Union's foreign policy system is governed by two different policy-making regimes. This was made explicit through

Maastricht's pillar system which organized the Union's competences into distinct regimes under separate titles: the 'first pillar'
(EC) and the 'second pillar' (CFSP).

The first policy-making regime is the '*Community method*'.
This works on the principle of a common interest, which actors
define, defend, promote and represent. The Community method is
not synonymous with supranationalism, which would imply that
member states lose complete control over policy-making. Rather,
it is operationalized through a system designed to maintain institutional equilibrium between a supranational Commission which
has a key role in defining and defending common interests; a
Council of Ministers with representatives of the member states
which decides by majority voting on a wide range of decisions; a
directly elected EP; and a supranational ECJ. The Community
method applies to trade, development cooperation, humanitarian
aid and other competences that fall under the EC.

The second policy-making regime is the '*intergovernmental
method*'. The basic principle of this method is that governments
retain control over policy-making. This is achieved in two ways.
Through *intergovernmental cooperation* governments do not
transfer competences to the EU but, within the EU framework,
cooperate in the elaboration of foreign policy and coordinate
their national foreign policies. *Intergovernmental integration*, on
the other hand, implies that member states have transferred
competences to the EU, but that, within the Union's institutional
framework, governments retain strict control over policy-making
through the dominant position of the Council and the application
of the unanimity rule in its decision-making. The intergovernmental method is predominant in CFSP, ESDP and in police and
judicial cooperation in criminal matters (the 'third pillar').

However, foreign policy decisions are not easily divided
between the pillars. In many foreign policy dossiers, both policy-
making regimes are involved, with competences, actors, procedures and instruments from both pillars being used. There are
also gradations within each pillar and within each policy-making
regime in terms of the role of the various institutions and of the
member states, the decision-making procedures, the available
instruments, and so on. In other words, there is a whole range of
methods on the continuum between intergovernmentalism and
supranationalism. Both formally and in practice, pillars and
methods are blurred.

The European Council: strategic leadership?

The European Council has a pivotal role in the strategic direction, scope and main decisions of the Union's foreign policy. It brings together the Heads of State and Government of the member states accompanied by their Foreign Ministers, the President of the European Commission and one Commissioner, and the High Representative for the CFSP. The European Council is thus the locus of power within the European Union – if not legally, then at least politically and symbolically – with policy-making lines from all EU pillars and from national foreign policies coming together in this forum. The Lisbon/Reform Treaty foresees that the European Council will be chaired by the newly created function of a 'President of the European Council'. The incumbent of this new position is to ensure the external representation of the Union on CFSP issues 'at his or her level'.

The European Council is to 'provide the Union with the necessary impetus for its development' and to 'define the general political guidelines thereof' (Art. 4 TEU). With regard to CFSP, the European Council defines 'the principles' and 'general guidelines' and decides 'on common strategies to be implemented by the Union' (Art. 13 TEU). Although it does not have a formal role in the first pillar foreign policy legislative process, it is clear that no strategic decision can be adopted in the first pillar without the (at least tacit) consent of the European Council.

The European Council has led EU foreign policy in new directions, such as adopting new strategies towards other regions or developing ESDP from 1999 onwards. However, it is its role as an 'organe d'impulsion' (Cloos *et al.* 1993: 486) rather than as a decision-making actor that is most important. For most issues on the agenda of its meetings, the European Council 'confirms', 'welcomes' or 'endorses' decisions and documents that have either been previously agreed by the General Affairs and External Relations Council, or have been developed by the High Representative, the Presidency or the Commission – with the European Council subsequently 'inviting' or 'asking' other actors to further elaborate on these measures. These European Council meetings are important: pushing decision-making forward from the highest political level; making crucial intergovernmental and inter-institutional bargains on the most sensitive issues; and conferring the legitimacy and visibility on decisions and policy documents essential for both the internal and external audience.

However, normally meeting only four times a year, the European Council cannot provide the permanent strategic leadership needed for many foreign policy dossiers, particularly the most sensitive and urgent. Paradoxically, the concentration of the highest authorities from all member states in the European Council is also its Achilles heel. Heads of State and Government first and foremost defend their national foreign policy and act according to their domestic concerns and personal agendas.

Given the high external visibility of European Council meetings, their main purpose often relates to interrelational and identity objectives rather than external objectives (see Chapter 1). Even where member sates are divided on an issue, being *seen* to have a united and 'European' approach is often prioritized above formulating guidelines that actually provide a basis for action. Consequently, conclusions adopted tend to be purposefully vague and declaratory so that they can be interpreted in different ways and used for all kinds of future action. There is some considerable distance between defining general foreign policy principles and guidelines and putting these into practice. The majority of European Council decisions require further political follow-up, operational implementation and/or legal translation by the Council, Commission, High Representative and/or member states – which implies that further hurdles must be overcome before the European Council's deliberations can have any effect.

The Council of Ministers: losing control

Its composition, competences and frequent meetings make the Council of the European Union the main foreign policy decision-making body in the EU, both in political and legal terms. The primary Council configuration for foreign policy is the General Affairs and External Relations Council (GAERC) which covers foreign trade, development cooperation, humanitarian aid, international agreements, CFSP and ESDP. It brings together member states' Foreign Ministers, the High Representative and members of the European Commission. Depending on the issues on the agenda, Ministers of Defence, of Development or of Trade also participate. Additional relevant Council configurations include the Economic and Financial Affairs Council (ECOFIN), the Justice and Home Affairs Council (JHA), and other sectoral Council configurations (such as Agriculture or Environment).

In addition to the generally monthly GAERC meetings, Foreign Ministers also meet in informal 'Gymnich' meetings, in the margins of European Council meetings, in the margins of international conferences, and where urgent international developments necessitate an unforeseen meeting. Defence, Development and Trade Ministers have their own informal meetings and sometimes meet in parallel or together with the GAERC. Although formal decisions cannot be adopted during 'informal' meetings, they do contribute to steering the course of EU foreign policy.

Ministers discuss and adopt external relations and foreign policy decisions based on both Community and CFSP/ESDP procedures. The agenda does not differentiate between decision-making modes or competences. In functional terms, policy-making is thus cross-pillar, reflecting the Council's responsibility for ensuring the unity and consistency of the Union's action (Art. 13 TEU). However, although the Council is the Union's key decision-making institution for all foreign policy issues and lumps these together in Council meetings, its role and power are quite different in both pillars:

- *CFSP/ESDP competences*: the Council is the sole decision-making body of CFSP/ESDP and formally reigns over all stages of policy-making: from issue definition to decision-making, implementation and control. In conjunction with the European Council, this ensures that the evolution and actions of CFSP and ESDP remain under member-state control and supervision. The Council also plays a central role in strengthening systematic cooperation and coordination between member states' foreign policies: member states have to inform and consult one another within the Council on any matter of foreign and security policy of general interest (Art. 16 TEU). The Council is also responsible for ensuring that the member states comply with the principles of CFSP and support the Union's policy (Art. 11(2) TEU).
- *Community competences*: again the Council is the main decision-making institution, but it is embedded in a broader

institutional set-up incorporating the Commission, the EP and the ECJ. The Council can ask the Commission to take initiatives and propose legislation, but cannot legislate without a formal Commission proposal. The Council is involved in the adoption of all decisions, but in some major fields – such as budgetary decisions and association agreements – can only decide together with, or with the assent of, the Parliament. While the Council can make major decisions about the EU's relations with other regions and countries, it depends on the Commission for their implementation.

One of the paradoxes of the Council's position is that, as an *institution*, it is at the heart of EU foreign policy-making since it is involved in the full spectrum of EU foreign policy initiatives. However, as a *meeting of Foreign Ministers*, it decides precious little and is struggling to live up to expectations of it as the EU's main foreign policy decision-making forum. In fact, most decisions are not actually taken in the Council – they will already have been taken at a lower level in the Council's substructures (see below). And, the current set-up of the Council, with too many issues on the agenda and too many ministers sitting at the table, impedes decision-making and problem-solving on precisely those issues where its capacity to cut through divergence is required.

The expansion of the EU's foreign policy competences, activities and instruments mean that Foreign Ministers now face an impossibly overloaded agenda. Gomez and Peterson (2001) aptly named their study of the Council: 'The EU's Impossibly Busy Foreign Ministers: No One is in Control'. The agenda of the GAERC meeting of 22 January 2007 is illustrative (Council 2007a). The Ministers debated relations with Ukraine, the European Neighbourhood Policy, Sudan, Somalia, Iran, the energy problematic (and tensions with Russia), the Western Balkans, the Middle East Peace Process, Lebanon, Libya, the campaign against the death penalty, and free trade negotiations with the Gulf countries. At the start of their formal session they also adopted without discussion a long list of (often quite important) A-points, that is the 'Agreed Points' that had been agreed upon at a lower level in the Committee of Permanent Representatives in the European Union (COREPER), in the Political and Security Committee (PSC) or in the working groups (see below). Obviously, even with a system of A-points, too many important issues remain on the agenda, making it impossible to tackle them seriously. In practice, this often implies that debates focus only on the most pressing or controversial themes, with no time left for equally significant but less urgent or media-attractive issues.

Debate is not only hampered by the number of issues on the agenda, but also by the number of Ministers. In an EU of 27 member states, the Presidency must keep a tight hand on deliberations. Debates have become a succession of interventions and a genuine exchange of views and arguments is quite rare. The setting of the meeting room is far from conducive to discussion on sensitive issues. Some 150 people attend: one or two Ministers for each member state, plus their representatives to COREPER and the PSC, one or two other senior diplomats or advisors, seats for the Presidency, the Commission, the High Representative and the Council's Secretariat. The informal lunch meeting attended by Ministers has become particularly important insofar as it provides a restricted 'safe' setting to debate sensitive issues and openly discuss disagreements. Iraq, Iran, Russia, the Western Balkans, the Middle East and relations with the US regularly feature on the Ministers' lunch menu. With most sensitive issues scheduled for that part of the day, lunch in fact often lasts longer than the formal 'external relations' session in the afternoon.

However, since the EU enlarged to 27 member states, even the lunch format and informal Gymnich meetings no longer permit a sufficiently intimate gathering. The consequences are several. As its decision-making and problem-solving capabilities come under strain, to avoid deadlock other actors or fora have partially taken over the role of Council meetings. More important decisions are being taken at COREPER, at the PSC and even at working-group levels. 'Common' actors (High Representative, Council administration, Commission) and smaller groupings of member states are playing a larger role. In other words, some are in control – but it is not necessarily the Foreign Ministers, many of whom feel increasingly irrelevant during Council meetings.

Ministers lose interest in Council meetings that offer little scope for either real decision-making or personal interventions. Ministers from the largest member states, although, increasingly also others, attend only a short part of the Council meeting. They arrive in Brussels in the late morning, leave after lunch, and use the gatherings there for bilateral or other restricted meetings with their most relevant counterparts in the corridors of or even outside the Council's Justus Lipsius building. It is not unusual for Council of Ministers meetings to end without any Ministers present, and with only the member state's Permanent Representatives around the table. As Council meetings start to be perceived as irrelevant, the basic legitimacy of the Council, as the main forum for the expression of national interest, risks being undermined. Besides the diminished *output legitimacy* (because of its diminished problem-solving capacity), the Council meeting is thus also faced with a diminished *input legitimacy*.

However, none of the above is to suggest that Council meetings are unimportant for EU foreign policy-making. They are important, but in most cases not only for what is decided or confirmed by Ministers during the meeting, but because (like European Council meetings) they lead to a monthly culmination point of consultations, meetings and decisions on lower, diplomatic and bureaucratic levels. Preparing for monthly Council meetings necessitates an intensive negotiation process that in turn pushes EU foreign policy-making forward.

The Council's substructure: representing the member states

The Council's functions have been partially taken over by diplomatic, bureaucratic and military actors within the Council's system. As discussed in this section, there are various preparatory committees composed of national representatives which mirror the Council's composition and its involvement in both pillars. Then, as discussed in the next section, there are central bodies in Brussels under the authority of the Council's Secretary General/High Representative which serve the CFSP/ESDP (see also Duke and Vanhoonacker 2006).

GAERC meetings do not make a strict division between first and second pillar competences. However, the committees which prepare the work of GAERC – COREPER and PSC (or 'COPS' from the French acronym) – do make this distinction.

COREPER (*Committee of Permanent Representatives*) is the most senior preparatory body of the Council. 'COREPER II' is composed of the member states' Permanent Representatives to the EU (at ambassador level) plus a representative from the Commission. It meets at least once a week to prepare GAERC, ECOFIN and JHA Council meetings ('COREPER I' prepares most other Council configurations). A traditionally 'Community' body, its work is concentrated on the first pillar's external relations and foreign policy as well as on the horizontal institutional, legal and financial cross-pillar dimensions of foreign policy. As the central clearing house for all preparatory work for the GAERC meetings, COREPER II also determines GAERC's final agenda and oversees the work of all other preparatory committees. However, a proliferation of other committees and the growing importance of the PSC have somewhat undermined COREPER's general authority and its ability to supervise all Council activities. This implies, for instance, that COREPER does not in principle change positions adopted by the PSC.

The PSC (*Political and Security Committee*) is the lynchpin of CFSP/ESDP. The PSC is composed of national representatives at ambassador level from member states' Permanent Representations in Brussels, plus a representative of the Commission. It meets in principle two times a week. It monitors the international situation in areas covered by CFSP/ESDP, prepares the CFSP/ESDP aspects of Council meetings, deals with the day-to-day running of CFSP/ESDP and monitors the implementation of agreed policies. It also exercises, under the responsibility of the Council, the 'political control and strategic direction' of the EU's military and civilian crisis management operations. It is particularly this operational role in an expanding ESDP which explains its growing workload and status (see Duke 2005; Juncos and Reynolds 2007). The PSC is supported by two specialized committees: the European Union Military Committee (EUMC), which provides military advice and exercises military direction, and the Committee for Civilian Aspects of Crisis Management (CIVCOM), which advises the PSC and COREPER and assures the follow-up of civilian crisis management capabilities and operations.

Four additional specialized committees prepare Council deliberations: the Article 36 Committee (cooperation in police and judicial matters), the Economic and Financial Committee

(Economic and Monetary Union), the Special Committee on Agriculture (common agricultural policy) and the Article 133 Committee (common commercial policy). These committees also affect the EU's position in the world and can have an indirect impact on its foreign policy. COREPER and the PSC rely on a large network of working groups and on the European Correspondents that manage the COREU telex network:

- *Working groups* are staffed by experts from national capitals or from the member states' Permanent Representations and by a Commission representative. Around ten working groups have a geographical focus (and are both Brussels and national-capital based), and a further 15 work on thematic issues such as human rights, non-proliferation or relations with the various international organizations. While in theory working groups deal with both the EC and CFSP issues which fall under their remit, in practice this is generally not the case. The 'geographical' working groups generally meet in different constellations for EC issues (with staff from the Permanent Representations) and CFSP issues (with experts from the Ministries of Foreign Affairs) and they report to COREPER and the PSC respectively. The 'thematic' working groups are in fact pure CFSP working groups, reporting to the PSC. Although they do not have authority to take decisions in their own right, a great mass of work is done in these working groups. They exchange views, ensure mutual consultation, further cooperation between specialized national diplomats, and identify options for consideration and decision at a higher level. However, in a CFSP that increasingly requires operational action, the system of non-Brussels-based CFSP working groups, with nearly 30 actors around the negotiating table, is reaching its limits (see Juncos and Pomorska 2007).

- The Brussels-based *Working Party of Foreign Relations Counsellors* (RELEX or CFSP Counsellors) is composed of diplomats from the member states' Permanent Representations in Brussels and representatives from the Council's Secretariat and the Commission. It is responsible for coordinating the agendas of COREPER and the PSC, and for the horizontal institutional, legal and financial aspects of foreign policy activities (including the formal preparation of joint actions). It plays an important role in bridging, first, the pillar-reflecting divisions between the PSC and COREPER; and, second, the world of national diplomats in the working parties and the world of the Brussels institutions.

- The network of *European Correspondents* is composed of capital-based officials responsible for coordinating CFSP/ESDP within their national Foreign Ministries. They provide the permanent liaison between Foreign Ministries (and the Commission), coordinate daily CFSP business, deal with work coming up from the working groups, and prepare the meetings of the PSC and the CFSP points of the Council and European Council.

- The *Coreu* ('Correspondance européenne') telex network allows for an ongoing exchange of encrypted messages and is the EU's foreign policy central nervous system. It provides for a permanent linkage between all the thousands of diplomats and other officials in the member states, the Council and the Commission involved in EU foreign policy-making. Hundreds of 'Coreus' are exchanged daily and vary widely in substance and importance: from practical arrangements, to clarifications of a member states' position, to proposals for joint action forwarded for final approval.

These diplomatic and bureaucratic substructures of the Council play a crucial role in the continuous process of information exchange and consultation, coordination of national policies, intergovernmental bargaining and developing common approaches. In the preparation of decisions by the Council of Ministers, each level plays its part in identifying points of special interest, highlighting in advance the main issues of contention and concern, detecting the windows of opportunity and the bottlenecks. Dossiers that are ripe for formal decision-making, as well as those that are important but need further high-level deliberation, bubble up the organizational hierarchy.

However, several issues hamper the effectiveness of this system. The dual character of EU foreign policy has been strengthened by the development of the PSC into an actor independent of COREPER. Although by the time they reach the Council agenda there is no differentiation between issues from the first and second pillars, the limited interaction between

COREPER and the PSC, and between EC and CFSP working groups, results in parallel policy-making processes which does not facilitate a comprehensive pillar-transcending approach towards the issue at hand.

Further, these structures are staffed by national representatives, whose primary commitment and responsibility naturally lies in promoting the national interest, despite whatever socialization effects may occur (see Chapter 5). Consequently, although they may play an important role in overcoming divergent national positions, this does not imply that common European interests are sufficiently promoted in policy-making. As such, policy-making can be more about striking a balance between competing national interests in the short-term than developing long-term approaches better suited to achieving 'European goals' or actually meeting the challenges of a specific dossier.

Finally, the Council substructures suffer from the same problems as the Council of Ministers itself: too many issues, too many diplomats – and too many *coreus*. And although the enlargement of the EU did not lead to the anticipated deadlock, it has had an impact on the negotiations.

The Council's 'common' actors: representing the EU

Because national representatives from official level upwards are overburdened by the weight of the EU foreign policy agenda and because institutional dynamics have been altered by ESDP's development, the Council's common actors have become increasingly influential. By common actors we mean the Presidency, and particularly the High Representative and his staff. Indeed, it is under the institutional umbrella of the Council's Secretariat that major foreign policy institutional innovations have been occurring. Developments have not been confined to the process of 'Brusselization', but also extend to the more important processes of 'operationalization' and 'commonization' of the EU's CFSP/ESDP (see below). This leads to the question of whether the central actors in the CFSP/ESDP framework now play a role similar to that of the Commission in the first pillar, that is identifying and operationalizing the common 'European interest'.

The Presidency

The Presidency of the Council rotates between member states on a six-monthly basis. It plays a key role in CFSP: it represents the Union in matters within the CFSP remit; is responsible for the implementation of decisions; expresses the Union's position in international organizations and conferences; conducts political dialogue with third countries on behalf of the Union; and consults and informs the EP. The country holding the Presidency chairs all meetings of the European Council, Council, COREPER, the PSC and working groups, as well as the meetings of the diplomatic missions of member states in third countries and of their permanent representations to international organizations. Proposals for joint actions, common positions, démarches and other initiatives are often formulated or at least submitted to the other member states via the Presidency.

In its contacts with third parties, the Presidency will often work under the *troika* format. The troika is made up of the Presidency, the next member state to hold the Presidency and the High Representative, operating with the Commission. An *open troika* format means that other member states also participate in the troika, allowing those with special interests and expertise to become involved.

Obvious problems of continuity result from the rotating Presidency. The negative effects are particularly felt in implementing policies and conducting negotiations with third parties. Whilst the troika formation is designed to mitigate this, its success in bridging continuity gaps is marginal. Too often, the troika's main impact is to add yet another layer of confusion for the EU's interlocutors. Continuity issues aside, the Presidency suffers from several structural problems which undermine the credibility and efficiency of CFSP. Presiding over all meetings at all levels and on all policy dossiers, as well as being the external face of the EU, is a heavy workload. Perhaps with the exception of the largest, the diplomatic structures and networks of most member states struggle. As such, the Presidency will often have to act *vis-à-vis* a third country or on a particular issue about which it has scant experience. Compounding this, the Presidency often lacks the necessary authority to act because a specific action rests on a delicate agreement or little more than the tacit consent of the Council. Where it is acting on the basis of a mandate which is too strict or too weak, the Presidency cannot offer the leadership necessary for effective diplomacy. This is particularly problematic in acute crises requiring a rapid and firm response.

The Presidency also has an ambivalent 'European' statute. It is in essence a national actor even if it does temporarily assume a European role. Although the member state holding the Presidency is expected to promote and defend common European interests, it inevitably relies on its established relationships to do so, and will still be influenced by national interests and preferences. This is not necessarily disadvantageous if it creates new dynamics at the EU level for policy with regard to a specific region or issue. For instance, the Swedish Presidency in 2001 successfully brought civilian crisis management, a national priority, onto the ESDP agenda. However, it can undermine both the internal and external credibility of the Presidency if actions are seen to stem from a national rather than European perspective.

The High Representative

It was partially in response to some of these problems that the member states in the Amsterdam Treaty created the new position of *Secretary General/High Representative for the CFSP*, and that other permanent common bodies were created under the Council's institutional architecture. The new common bodies provided the CFSP with a degree of visibility and permanence which had previously been entirely absent. In addition to 'assisting' the Presidency (Art. 18(3) TEU), the High Representative for the CFSP is to

> assist the Council in matters coming within the scope of the common foreign and security policy, in particular through contributing to the formulation, preparation and implementation of policy decisions, and, when appropriate and acting on behalf of the Council at the request of the Presidency, through conducting political dialogue with third parties. (Art. 26 TEU)

By nominating then NATO Secretary General Javier Solana as the first incumbent of this role, member states opted for a high profile political figure able to draw on a network of contacts and a high level of respect in European capitals as well as in Washington and NATO. Javier Solana has successfully increased the visibility and effectiveness of the CFSP on key occasions including in the Balkans and in Ukraine in late 2004. However, his status and diplomatic skills alone are not always sufficient to overcome the limited policy-making capabilities of the Presidency, Council and Council substructures. The High Representative's credibility and effectiveness are conditioned by two further factors: the mandate received from the Council and the availability of instruments to shore up his diplomatic activities. The strength of mandate and support from member states directly correlates with the High Representative's capacity to negotiate with third actors. Even where the mandate is strong, the success of his actions also depends on whether diplomatic activities are backed up by the necessary economic, financial, military or other instruments which are not under his control.

The Constitutional Treaty proposed to create a new function of Union Minister for Foreign Affairs – a function renamed by the Lisbon/Reform Treaty as *High Representative of the Union for Foreign Affairs and Security Policy*. This new position is an important innovation, not least because it bestows on one individual the existing functions of High Representative for the CFSP, the Commissioner for External Relations and the current functions of the Presidency with regard to EU foreign policy. It is because of this culmination of tasks that there is real potential to strengthen EU foreign policy by breaking down institutional barriers, providing oversight of the different decision-making regimes and instruments, and countering the weaknesses of a six-monthly rotating Presidency (see Crowe 2005; De Ruyt 2005).

However, this High Representative of the Union for Foreign Affairs and Security Policy could also create new problems, new disappointments and new turf wars. As Crowe remarks, the future incumbent 'runs the risk of schizophrenia in triple-hatted accountability to the Council which he chairs and leads; to the Commission of which he will be the Vice-President responsible for external affairs; and to the President of the European Council who will represent the EU abroad "at his level"' (2005: 2). Indeed, the High Representative of the Union for Foreign Affairs and Security Policy will have to manage a potentially challenging relationship with the new President of the European Council. In addition to chairing the European Council, the President 'shall, at his or her level and in that capacity, ensure the external representation of the Union on issues concerning its common foreign and security policy, without prejudice to the powers of the Union Minister for Foreign Affairs'. Potentially yet another source of tension, these two new functions also imply that an answer to the famous request of former US secretary of state Henry Kissinger that there be one single telephone number to call 'Europe' might remain as elusive as ever.

In any case, the High Representative of the Union for Foreign Affairs and Security Policy is unlikely to provide the magical solution to all the EU's foreign policy woes – several of the obstacles defined in the previous sections are likely to remain. Principally, while the new function might facilitate policy-making and the ability to employ the whole range of EU instruments, his or her capacity to act will still hinge on the mandate he or she receives from the Council, and on the ability of the Council to adopt decisions. Moreover, it is unclear how the different institutional logics of the Council and Commission can be combined. This new figure will have to carry out CFSP/ESDP as mandated by the Council, but as a member of the Commission will have to act independently in the general interest of the Union and will not be allowed to take instructions from any body.

In addition to creating two new functions, the Lisbon/Reform Treaty foresees the creation of an *External Action Service* to assist the new High Representative in fulfilling his or her mandate. This service is to work in cooperation with the diplomatic services of the member states and be composed of officials from relevant departments of the General Secretariat, the Commission and staff seconded from member states' diplomatic services.

The High Representative's staff

The High Representative relies on the central services situated within the Council's Secretariat (formally 'General Secretariat'). This consists of entities attached to the High Representative (his Cabinet, the Policy Unit, the Joint Situation Centre and the Military Staff) and the Directorate General E – External Economic Relations – Politico-Military Affairs (DG E) within the regular services of the Secretariat. In addition, the High

Representative can rely on 'Special Representatives' on the ground in key geographic areas and three Personal Representatives. Combined, this amounts to slightly more than 400 people, including 200 military personnel in the Military Staff.

*   Together with his personal office or 'Cabinet', the *Policy Unit* (formally the 'Policy Planning and Early Warning Unit') is at the heart of the High Representative's staff. Composed of around 35 officials mainly from the Council Secretariat and the member states, it is charged with the monitoring, analysis and assessment of international developments and events and, importantly, with assessing the EU's interests therein. The Policy Unit contributes to policy-making through the preparation of policy options. It also plays an increasingly important role in informal contacts and foreign policy cooperation with third countries.
*   Institutionally located within the Policy Unit, the *Joint Situation Centre (SITCEN)* provides early-warning, monitoring and intelligence for potential crisis management operations. It facilitates the exchange of sensitive information with member states and provides a secure communications network. Since the 2004 terrorist attacks in Madrid, SITCEN also examines threats within the EU, on the basis of intelligence analysis provided by member states. In this latter role, it also serves the Justice and Home Affairs Council.
*   *Directorate General E – External Economic Relations – Politico-Military Affairs (DG E)* of the Council's Secretariat has gradually mutated from a primarily bureaucratic body (supporting the Presidency and preparing Council decision-making) into a more operational entity that under the High Representative's authority has worked more closely with the Policy Unit and become a motor of CFSP/ESDP.
*   *The European Union Military Staff (EUMS)*, which works first and foremost for the EU Military Committee, is formally attached to the Council's Secretariat. It provides military expertise and support to the ESDP, particularly in the conduct of military crisis management operations.

Combined, these structures represent an increasingly influential foreign policy machinery. The Policy Unit/DG E network in particular not only administers the High Representative's actions and Council meetings, but also plays an important conceptual and operational role in preparing, steering and ensuring follow-up of decisions in working groups, the PSC, COREPER and the Council. The Policy Unit and DG E network has thus become crucial in shaping EU foreign policy actions from a common European perspective and has increased the High Representative's capacity for autonomous operational action, reducing his dependence on cooperation from the member states and the Commission. It has also heightened links with, and hence support from, key member states through the appointment of senior diplomats from particularly the largest member states to key positions. Javier Solana's staffing has been strategic – senior diplomats from smaller member states have also been appointed to key positions, but mainly where their expertise and their link to national decision-makers could contribute to the High Representative's operational capacities in the specific areas that these countries' contributions can provide added value.

The High Representative can also rely on a growing number of *EU Special Representatives (EUSR)* that form a more permanent EU presence on the ground. The Special Representatives are given strategic guidance and political input by the PSC, but act under the authority and operational direction of the High Representative. Appointed through a Council joint action, they are specifically second pillar actors, with no first pillar competences. The only exception to this rule is the Special Representative in FYROM who, since late 2005, is both an EU Special Representative and the Head of the European Commission delegation. This 'personal union' of the Council and the Commission in FYROM reflects the member states' awareness that EU foreign policy must absolutely succeed in this country as well as the fact that FYROM is a candidate country. In mid-2007, the EU had nine Special Representatives, covering the following regions and issues: Afghanistan, the Great Lakes region of Africa, Bosnia-Herzegovina, Central Asia, FYROM, the Middle East peace process, Moldova, South Caucasus and Sudan. In addition, the EU was preparing to appoint an EUSR to Kosovo as part of the post-status arrangements. There are significant differences between EU Special Representatives in terms of mandate, staff and importance – with the Representatives in the

Balkans having the most important operational roles. In addition to Special Representatives, Solana has appointed three *Personal Representatives* for Human Rights, Non-Proliferation of Weapons of Mass Destruction, and Parliamentary Affairs in the area of CFSP.

'Operationalization', 'Brusselization' and 'commonization'

Institutional innovations since the Amsterdam Treaty and the launch of ESDP proper are testimony to three processes which have been occurring in CFSP since the late 1990s: operationalization, Brusselization and commonization.

CFSP has become more operational because of the new bodies and actors within the Secretariat of the Council. This *operationalization* is now sufficiently developed for CFSP to go beyond mere declaratory diplomacy to actually undertaking concrete action. However, caveats do remain. The operationalization process is significant, but is constrained by the fact that relative to the Commission, large member states or international organizations, the CFSP/ESDP's instruments and institutional set-up remain limited. Moreover, this operationalization has been much more significant *vis-à-vis* the Balkans than other parts of the world. Brussels-based CFSP/ESDP actors today play a critical role in preparing decisions and making CFSP happen. This process of *Brusselization* stands in contrast to a past in which CFSP (and EPC) were completely steered from national capitals. More important than the Brusselization process, however, is a related process, which we suggest terming *commonization*: the establishment and increasing importance of central common actors that define, defend, promote and represent common EU interests, and that develop and implement common policies from this European perspective.

That this process of commonization could begin was the main significance of creating a High Representative and a Policy Unit in the Amsterdam Treaty. For the first time, the 'common' foreign and security policy was granted 'common' actors to make true its adjective. The central CFSP/ESDP bodies and actors are now more able to feed the Council, COREPER, the PSC and working group meetings with analysis and policy options based both on common European interests and on a problem-solving approach – which is in contrast to a mere aggregation of national interests and statement-producing approach. It is this action- and common-interest-orientated approach of the common Council bodies which has contributed to changing debates in the Council and which allowed CFSP/ESDP to move beyond the limitations of its purely inter-governmental set-up.

With common actors that promote a common interest, CFSP/ESDP to some extent now reflects one of the basic principles behind the Community method, in which the Commission fulfils this role. However, commonization is not the same as communitarization and does not imply that Community actors or procedures are gaining ground in CFSP/ESDP. There remain fundamental differences between the position of common central actors in CFSP/ESDP and the position of the Commission in the first pillar.

These differences point to limitations in the extent to which commonization has occurred in CFSP/ESDP. The Council's common actors have what could be called a partial capacity of initiative, but not the exclusive right of initiative enjoyed by the Commission in the first pillar. Despite the growth in common CFSP/ESDP bodies, their staffing levels are far too limited to provide all working groups with policy option papers or common analysis for every issue on the agenda. Moreover, the common CFSP/ESDP bodies still need the Presidency's agreement to present a common EU analysis and common policy recommendations. This implies that not all discussions in the Council are based on documents from the High Representative or Policy Unit/DG E network. Furthermore, the Council's common bodies cannot take on the role of mediator between member states across all levels of Council meetings (as the Commission does in the first pillar). The High Representative and his staff do not have the leverage of legal procedure or the time and people to adopt such a role. The difference between the Commission in the first pillar and the common actors in the second pillar is particularly evident at the implementation stage: the High Representative and his staff have neither the broad set of competences, legal, financial or other instruments, nor the extensive bureaucratic framework or network of external delegations. This also explains the continued dependence of CFSP/ESDP's central bodies on both the member states and the first pillar.

The Commission: a foreign policy actor by stealth?

As the EU's supranational political actor, the European Commission finds itself awkwardly straddling EU foreign policy. It plays a critical role in defining, defending, promoting and representing the common interests in EC external policies where it is granted strong competences by the treaties and can rely on a robust administrative and budgetary apparatus to make full use of these competences. However, the Commission is largely sidelined in the EU's CFSP and ESDP.

More than any other actor, the Commission has struggled with the major boundary problem between EC and CFSP/ESDP competences, and thus also between being centre stage, backstage, or not on the stage at all. This issue is closely related to other 'boundary problems' (M. Smith 1997): between external economic relations and external political relations; between 'development' and 'foreign policy' or 'security' issues; between 'domestic/internal' policy issues and 'external' policy issues. These boundary problems have led to a succession of 'border conflicts' or outright 'war', not only between the Commission and the Council or member states, but also within the Commission's own internal structures.

Internal organization

The increase in the Commission's external policy responsibilities and its difficult quest since 1993 to find a way to align itself with CFSP has made the division of labour within both the College of Commissioners and its administration problematic. The policy portfolios of the Commissioners responsible for external relations, as well as their Directorates General (DGs), have been regularly reshuffled, each bringing their own turf wars (Nugent and Saurugger 2002). The Barroso Commission from late 2004 divided the portfolios as follows: External Relations and European Neighbourhood Policy, External Trade, Development and Humanitarian Aid, and Enlargement, with the Commission President chairing the Group of External Relations' Commissioners.

The Commissioners most directly involved in foreign policy rely on five DGs and an agency. With a combined staff of around 2,300, these structures play an essential role in the EU's foreign policy-making system. The external relations DGs each have their own philosophy, set of objectives, legal bases for policy initiatives, and different types of instruments. This explains why, beyond the normal turf battles, coherent action is not always straightforward.

- *DG External Relations* (or DG RELEX, after its French acronym) is responsible for programmes and relations with every region of the world (except the ACP countries), for the general coordination of external relations within the Commission, and for Commission contributions to CFSP/ESDP. It has developed policies on specific issues such as conflict prevention, election monitoring, human rights and democratization, non-proliferation and disarmament. DG RELEX has an ambiguous position, crushed between DGs Trade and Development on one side (with their clear treaty-based competences, their more orthodox 'communitarian view' and their distrust of DG RELEX) and the Council's CFSP actors on the other (who see DG RELEX as a competitor). Its contractual relations and budget lines can sometimes make it easier for DG RELEX to react to external demands than for CFSP actors, which contributes to the animosity between both.
- *DG Trade* is in a very strong position given the EC's exclusive competences in many trade issues and its central role representing the largest trade bloc in international trade negotiations. Despite the gradual introduction of political conditionality in trade and other agreements, the basic philosophy and overarching goals of DG Trade are the defence of EU trade interests and the liberalization of world trade, which do not always coincide with foreign policy and development goals.
- *DG Development* works exclusively on development policy in the framework of the Cotonou Agreement with the 77 ACP countries and the Overseas Countries and Territories. Although EC development competences are concurrent with those of the member states, DG Development gains its strength from its two main instruments: contractual relations through the Cotonou framework and the considerable development aid budget (EDF). Its goals and philosophy focus on poverty reduction and development, with the latter

incorporating a range of conditionalities, such as good governance and respect for human rights.

- *DG Enlargement* seemed to have lost a major part of its importance following the accession of ten new member states in 2004. However, the debate surrounding the accession of Turkey and the Balkan countries, and the EU's decision to be firmer in terms of compliance with all conditions, indicates that DG Enlargement's role is far from redundant.

- *DG for Humanitarian Aid (ECHO)* (until 2005 the European Community Humanitarian Aid Office) manages the EC's humanitarian aid. With an annual budget of more than €500 million, it is one of the largest humanitarian aid donors and supports people in more than 60 countries worldwide.

- The *EuropeAid Cooperation Office* (widely known as AIDCO) is the implementing agency for the first pillar cooperation programmes with third countries developed by DGs RELEX and Development. Every year, it translates over €7 billion in external assistance into projects in more than 150 countries and territories. These projects include activities which are closely related to, but formally distinct from, CFSP activities such as EU Election Observation Missions and the African Peace Facility.

Other sectoral DGs can also play an important role in specific dimensions of foreign policy. Some DGs are directly or indirectly involved in key strategic areas of the EU's development into a global actor, such as DGs Environment, Agriculture and Rural Development, Competition, Research, and Transport and Energy. High levels of interaction between external and internal policy issues imply that today almost every DG has some relevance for external policy.

Finally, the European Commission's strength in EU foreign policy also relates to its extensive network of delegations, rivalling in number all except those member states with the most global reach (see Table 5.2 in Chapter 5) (Bruter 1999; Duke 2002b). It has delegations in over 120 countries worldwide, as well as offices to international organizations. The delegations are the Commission's eyes and ears on the ground and act as mouthpiece *vis-à-vis* the authorities and other actors in their host countries. Depending on the host country, the focus of activities of these 'embassies without a state' is rather more trade-orientated or development-orientated (Bruter 1999). In the latter case, they are closely involved in policy programming and the implementation of EC policies.

This short overview makes it clear that the Commission should not be understood as a unitary body, but as a creature with both multiple heads (various Commissioners) and multiple bodies (various DGs and agencies).

Community competences

The Commission is at the heart of the EC's external action, involved in all stages of policy-making. As the Council and EP can only adopt legislative acts and international agreements on the basis of a formal proposal from the Commission, its exclusive right of initiative is powerful. However, the Commission does have to take into account the specific interests of individual member states if it wants to see its proposals accepted in the Council. Beyond this strictly legislative task, the Commission plays a broader role in furthering EU policy through non-binding recommendations, opinions or other forms of 'soft law'. The Commission has made efficient use of this competence to assert itself as a relevant foreign policy actor and, sometimes, to voice an opinion on issues over which it had no direct authority.

The Commission conducts negotiations with third states and international organizations on trade and other agreements (Art. 300 TEC). It interacts with committees of national representatives in its negotiations, and acts on the basis of a Council mandate. It not only negotiates agreements, but will be the main implementing body. The scope of this competence has gradually broadened as agreements have incorporated more foreign policy elements such as political dialogue and conditionality clauses regarding democracy, human rights, and so on (see Chapter 9). The Commission represents the EU externally in areas of Community competence and is responsible for establishing cooperation with international organizations.

The Commission also has an important budgetary function, drawing up the draft budget, and implementing the budget, in accordance with the provisions of the financial regulations made by the Council (Arts. 272, 274 TEC). This gives a formidable power to the Commission, as it administers an external relations budget of (in 2007) €6.4 billion and as Council or EP decisions which have implications for the EC budget cannot be implemented without the Commission's involvement. In the management of EU funds the Commission has some considerable latitude. This is related to its executive function (Art. 211 TEC) which varies from pure administrative and financial management to clear-cut foreign policy tasks. The Commission is in continuous interaction with the third parties (NGOs, UN agencies, etc.) that implement EC policies on the ground. When delegating implementation powers to the Commission, the Council of Ministers maintains some control through the comitology procedures and the related committees of national representatives. Nevertheless, the Commission does have the scope to react to external developments and can take foreign policy choices which might diverge from those of the member states and CFSP actors (see Chapter 8).

How can we evaluate the Commission's foreign policy actions within its EC competences? On the positive side, the Commission has been highly active in developing and implementing long-term policies and strategies with regard to third countries/regions. On the basis of its implementation, management and budgetary powers, the Commission has also often reacted more quickly to crises or changes in the international environment than CFSP actors – particularly until CFSP/ESDP's operational capabilities were strengthened in the early 2000s. Several of the Commission's hundreds of Communications and other documents have been important in developing the EU's foreign policy, and particularly its structural foreign policy. As a stream of often thorough conceptual and operational preparatory work, they have allowed the Commission to quickly deliver at those moments when the policy context was ripe for concrete policy actions. They have also contributed in terms of agenda setting, and putting 'external policy' actions in a clear strategic 'foreign policy' perspective. Examples include the Communications on *Conflict Prevention*, *The Choice of Multilateralism*, *European Neighbourhood Policy* and the Green Papers on a European energy strategy (Commission 2000, 2001a, 2003b, 2004f, 2006b) (see Chapters 8, 9 and 10). In important policy fields like conflict prevention, civilian crisis management and energy the Commission preceded Council actors in formulating new foreign policy orientations.

On the negative side, the Commission too often 'administers' its various external programmes, losing sight of their foreign policy dimension. The Commission (and the EU) depends to a large extent on other actors to implement its policies on the ground. It risks becoming more focussed on disbursing funds and supervising the adherence to budgetary and other procedures than the actual foreign policy output. Similarly, the Commission is also involved in the regular political dialogue which is foreseen in its agreements with third countries/regions, but this dialogue is often more bureaucratic than political, and more a formality than a real dialogue. As such, this instrument is not always used to its full potential of exerting leverage to promote EU foreign policy goals.

One of the paradoxes of the Commission's stance towards foreign policy is thus that it has promoted new foreign policy tools and a more strategic approach towards the EU's external relations, yet in practice has not ensured foreign policy objectives are pursued and external partners live up to their commitments. This paradox can be partially explained by the dislocation between those parts of the Commission involved in strategic policy-making (with clear foreign policy goals) and those responsible for the subsequent policy implementation and day-to-day management (where the respect of budgetary and other rules prevail).

Finally, although it understandably defends its first pillar competences, the Commission's obsession with a strict delineation between EC and CFSP activities sometimes undermines the effectiveness and coherence of EU foreign policy actions as a whole and leads to conflict with the Council. This particularly arises where the Commission adopts implementation and budgetary decisions which are significant in terms of EU foreign policy *vis-à-vis* specific countries or crises, but are taken without any consultation or consideration of member states' views.

Second pillar

The European Commission is the subject of the shortest article in the TEU's CFSP chapter. Article 27 of the TEU mysteriously says that 'The Commission shall be fully *associated with the work carried out* in the common foreign and security policy *field*' (our emphasis) – instead of simply asserting that the Commission shall fully participate in the CFSP. This formulation aptly summarizes the Commission's ambiguous position in the second pillar. Further treaty articles provide additional clues to the Commission's potential role. The Commission does not have an exclusive right of initiative in the second pillar – it may, like any member state, 'refer to the Council any question relating to CFSP and may submit proposals to the Council' (Art. 22 TEU). The articles relating to the Presidency's role indicate that the Commission shall be 'fully associated' in the Presidency's tasks of representing the Union in CFSP matters and implementing CFSP decisions (Art. 18(4) TEU). This indicates that the level of Commission involvement is highly dependent on the extent to which the Presidency is willing to accord the Commission a role.

Although the Commission's role in CFSP is quite distinct from its role in the EC, it is not as powerless as CFSP's intergovernmental nature might at first suggest. The Commission enters the CFSP game when the implementation of CFSP decisions requires the use of EC instruments (such as sanctions or the provision of aid) or financing through the CFSP budget which, as one part of the general EU budget, falls within the scope of Commission competence. The Council also often relies on the Commission's expertise, be that on developments within a specific country or regional organization, or on thematic issues, which empowers the Commission.

However, the Commission will be largely sidelined in other instances, particularly when diplomatic instruments and ESDP measures are used to give substance to CFSP decisions. The creation of the function of High Representative for the CFSP, the strengthening of his staff and particularly the creation of civilian and military crisis management capabilities within ESDP was thus fundamental. By endowing the Council with its own operational executive capacities, the Council could sideline the Commission (and the EC framework). However, the effectiveness of independent CFSP or ESDP measures often depends on the adoption of parallel measures, which fall within the EC's competence, to tackle other aspects of a crisis. This again brings the Commission to the fore.

In general, an orthodox and defensive view of the EC relationship with the second pillar dominates the Commission's administration. According to this view, the Commission should focus on its clear, strong and extensive competences in the first pillar, fiercely defend its independence and competences granted by the treaties, and should not undermine its own position by supporting the CFSP too much. From the outset, the Commission refused to make formal use of its non-exclusive right of initiative in CFSP affairs. It has also contested the view that CFSP provisions could apply to first pillar issues and that the Commission could be reduced to an implementing body for CFSP policies (Nuttall 2000: 264). This explains why, for instance, it has denied EU Special Representatives political control or an automatic right to Commission instruments and assistance programmes in their countries, even if this would be logical from a practical point of view and would increase the effectiveness and coherence of EU action. This is not to say that the Commission does not provide support for CFSP actions, but rather that the Commission itself wants to take the initiative for such support.

The European Parliament

As is the case for many member states' national parliaments in foreign policy, the role of the EP in EU foreign policy is rather limited. However, the EP has organized itself in such a way as to maximize its involvement. The main actors are the EP's Committee on Foreign Affairs, its subcommittees on Human Rights and on Security and Defence, and for institutional matters also its Committee on Constitutional Affairs. For reasons that will become clear later, the Budget Committee and Budgetary Control Committee have also played an interesting role, adding potential leverage to the EP's involvement in EU foreign policy.

In addition to these Committees, the EP has nearly 40 Interparliamentary Delegations, Joint Parliamentary Committees and Parliamentary Cooperation Committees with assemblies from other regions and third countries. Interparliamentary dialogue is foreseen in, for instance, the Association Agreements and the Partnership and Cooperation Agreements. These Delegations and Committees are useful tools in the EP's parliamentary diplomacy. They provide the EP with a vehicle through which to try to influence the views and attitudes of parliamentarians from third countries and, particularly, to push its position on human rights and democracy issues. They also give the EP an insight into specific foreign policy dossiers, which in turn strengthens its position in dialogue with the Council and Commission (see Corbett *et al.* 2005: 149–59).

The limited power of the EP in EU foreign policy is particularly apparent in the CFSP framework, where it has been granted only a (very limited) consultative role. The Presidency consults the Parliament on 'the main aspects and the basic choices' of the CFSP and ensures that its views are 'duly taken into consideration'. The Presidency and the Commission are to keep the Parliament 'regularly informed' of developments in the CFSP. The Parliament can 'ask questions of the Council or make recommendations to it' and holds an annual debate on progress in the CFSP's implementation (Art. 21 TEU). But, the EP is not involved in appointing the High Representative for the CFSP.

The EP tries to voice its position on foreign policy issues through a constant stream of own-initiative reports, resolutions and parliamentary questions. It has managed to obtain regular formal and informal dialogue with the High Representative, members of his staff, the Presidency and the Commission. Through inter-institutional agreements, the EP has gradually managed to get some concessions from the Council and Commission to allow it a slightly more significant position in foreign policy affairs (see Maurer *et al.* 2005). Unsurprisingly, the Parliament has consistently lamented its role in CFSP proceedings, particularly since the Council and Presidency tend to adopt a minimalist interpretation of their duty to consult and inform (see Diedrichs 2004: 34–7; Crum 2006).

Within the EC framework, the EP has two major instruments to influence EU foreign policy: the assent procedure, which gives it veto power over some categories of international agreements, and its position in the budgetary process. The EP must give its assent to Association Agreements; to other agreements establishing a specific institutional framework; to agreements with important budgetary implications for the Community; and to agreements which entail amending an act adopted under the co-decision procedure (Art. 300(3) TEC). This means that the EP not only has a veto power over association and cooperation agreements with third countries/regions, but also over the financial protocols with third countries and over significant amendments to agreements.

The major limitation of this instrument is that it is a blunt tool, and in most cases the threat of actually rejecting an agreement is simply not credible. However, the EP has on a limited number of occasions refused its assent, delayed its assent, or threatened to refuse or delay its assent, in protest against specific (mostly human rights) problems in third countries. Examples include the Partnership and Cooperation Agreements with Kazakhstan and Uzbekistan in the late 1990s and earlier agreements with Israel, Turkey, Syria and Morocco (see Corbett *et al.* 2005: 152, 227–8). A further limitation to the assent procedure is that it does not foresee formal parliamentary involvement in either the definition of the Commission's negotiating mandate or the conduct of negotiations, although through inter-institutional agreements it has been agreed that MEPs can ask to be part of the EC delegation during negotiations as observers. Quite painfully for the EP, it is given no role at all in the EC's most important external policy competence – the common commercial policy. The EP is notified about trade agreements and the Commission discusses trade issues with the EP, but it does not have to be formally consulted.

The EP's second major foreign policy instrument is its role as one of the two budgetary arms of the EU (together with the Council). As the EC's expenses for external relations and development fall under the category of non-compulsory expenditures where the EP has the final say, it has used this budgetary power to gain indirect leverage over the EU's foreign policy. The most obvious example of this was the EP's initiative in 1994 to create a chapter in the EU budget entitled the 'European Initiative for Democracy and Human Rights' and the subsequent gradual increase in funds under this chapter (for further examples see Corbett *et al.* 2005; Lord 2005). The EP has also sought to counter the Council's propensity to enter into new political (and thus often also financial) engagements without having a priori identified a financial basis for this.

The Council and member states have been highly critical of the EP for improper use of its first pillar powers to try to gain a foothold in CFSP. The funding of EU foreign policy has become a main arena of EP–Council struggle, with the former trying to compensate for the absence of formal influence in the second pillar, and the latter remaining adamant that the EP should not use (or, in the Council's view, abuse) its budgetary powers (Thym 2006: 113–17).

What has been the impact of the EP's foreign policy actions? It has clearly been successful in pressuring the other institutions to take human rights and democracy dimensions more seriously. The EP has achieved this by consistently focusing on these dimensions in resolutions and questions to the Council, in its *Annual Report on Human Rights in the World*, its yearly Sakharov Prize and the European Initiative for Democracy and Human Rights programme. In more general terms, the EP has played a role in pushing forward the boundaries of debate on EU foreign policy and bringing neglected dimensions to the fore. It has also scored some goals in specific foreign policy dossiers. But, cumulatively, its impact has been rather limited and it remains on the whole a marginal player in the shaping of EU foreign policy.

This brings us to the question of whether EU foreign policy is indeed suffering from a 'democratic deficit' (see also Koenig-Archibugi 2002; Lord 2005; Wagner 2006). As Barbé (2004: 49, 54–5) argues, the principles of coherence, visibility and continuity were the leitmotiv of successive reforms of the CFSP's institutional framework, while 'accountability' has been largely overlooked. Barbé presents several reasons why for many governments the limited role of the EP is part of the game. A first argument is that too much parliamentary involvement would damage the need for secrecy, speed, coherence and efficiency in foreign policy. This is related to a second argument, that is member states' understanding 'that the EP's capacity and willingness to control foreign policy would be greater than those of national parliaments' and belief that the EP's strong emphasis on human rights and democracy would interfere. A third argument is that 'given the primarily intergovernmental nature of CFSP, its source of legitimacy still resides in national sovereignty'. Ministers in the Council are in first place politically accountable to their national parliaments. From this perspective, there is no democratic deficit at the European level and no argument for EP involvement since national parliaments should be the locus of democratic control. However, this last argument disregards the diminished role of individual Foreign Ministers in shaping EU foreign policy. National governments – and certainly national parliaments – are no longer in a position to closely follow developments in all domains of EU foreign policy.

Conclusion

It is clear from this chapter that the overarching idea of a 'single institutional framework' belies a much more complex reality. The structure of the EU's foreign policy system has been determined by the extent to which member states were prepared to hand over control of this policy area to other actors. However, at the same time as the number of member states sitting around the policy-making table has grown, so has the sheer breadth of issues to be debated. These two developments have meant that even in those areas member states wished to retain full control, they have been forced to delegate responsibilities to central actors and smaller configurations of member states. Considering the complexity of the system – the different roles each actor plays depending on the policy regime in question and the institutions' competing agendas and turf wars – it is quite impressive that the EU manages to develop any foreign policy at all. The methods developed to circumvent this complexity are the subject of the next chapter.

Chapter 4

The EU's Foreign Policy System: Policy-making

The treaties set the boundaries and framework of the EU's foreign policy actors by conferring upon the institutions specific competences and by detailing the decision-making process. This chapter first reveals the utter complexity of competences, decision-making, voting procedures and the limits of intervention under which the institutions labour. Viewed in this light, it is impressive that the EU manages to achieve the foreign policy output that it does. By adopting a policy-making perspective, a view from the ground as it were, the dynamics which drive EU foreign policy onwards become apparent – revealing how the EU manages to overcome its institutional and procedural hurdles. We go on to assess an additional layer of complexity in shaping and implementing policy – the financing of EU foreign policy – before finally turning to the difficulties of ensuring consistency and coherence between the various policy-making regimes and institutions.

Competences

The distribution of the EU's formal competences is crucial to explain the nature of its foreign policy and the relationship between EU foreign policy and that of the member states (for a detailed analysis, see Eeckhout 2004; Lenaerts and Van Nuffel 2005: 828–99). As seen in Chapter 2, the competences in external policies have evolved considerably, moving from a clear cut situation in the 1957 Treaty of Rome to a very complex distribution of competences half a century later.

According to the principle of *conferral of powers* which underpins the EU's competences framework, the EU must act within the limits of the competences conferred upon it by the member states in the treaties, in order to attain the objectives set out within the treaties. This implies that competences not conferred upon the EU remain with the member states, and that competences conferred upon the EU have to be seen in function of objectives as stated within the treaties. This principle is crucial to understanding the nature of EU foreign policy. It implies that the Union has no general legal basis authorizing it to act *vis-à-vis* the external environment. Hence, when we evaluate EU foreign policy, we should never expect the EU to have an exclusive or all-encompassing foreign policy. In fact, given its restricted competences, the expectation should rather be that the EU would not act in certain aspects of foreign, security and defence policy. This, however, often runs counter to expectations of the public, press and politicians.

With its direct impact on state sovereignty, the distribution of competences between the EU and the member states is of course highly sensitive. It is also far from clear cut. Until the Lisbon/Reform Treaty, there was no list stating which competences are reserved for the federal entity and which for its component states. The distribution of competences varies depending on the policy field, but can be understood in terms of general categories of competence, which was confirmed by the Lisbon/Reform Treaty. The following paragraphs first focus on EC competences, to evaluate next how CFSP and ESDP fit within this categorization.

In areas of *exclusive competence* only the EC has the power to legislate and adopt legally binding acts. The common commercial policy, which is highly relevant for foreign policy, is one of the very few areas of exclusive competence. Another area of exclusive competence is monetary policy for member states in the eurozone. Moreover, through its jurisprudence, and particularly the AETR case, the European Court of Justice (ECJ) has established that where the EC has competence to regulate on a matter internally, it also has competence to act externally, even if this is not explicitly mentioned in the treaties. This principle of the 'parallelism' of internal and external competences means that by exercising its internal law-making powers, the EC is taken to have the exclusive power to negotiate and conclude international agreements in the same area, even if this capacity is not explicitly foreseen by the treaties.

In areas of *shared competence* between the EC and the member states, the exercise of competence by the member states is subject to what is called the pre-emption principle (Lenaerts and Van Nuffel 2005: 96–7). This implies that both the EC and the member states can legislate and adopt legally binding acts in a specific area, but that the member states can only exercise their competence to the extent that the EC has not yet exercised its competence. Member states can thus only act where the Community's own action has left them space to do so. This category applies to a whole range of policy areas, including some that are relevant for the EU's foreign policy such as environment, internal market and agriculture.

In other areas, the principle of *parallel competences* applies. In these cases, the pre-emption principle does not come into play: the EC is competent to carry out activities and conduct a common policy, but in so doing it does not prevent member states from also carrying out activities and conducting a national policy. This category applies to several domains of importance to EU foreign policy including development cooperation, humanitarian aid, research and technology. In some policy areas, the EC has competence merely to carry out actions to *support, coordinate or supplement* the actions of the member states, without superseding their competence in these areas. This includes various fields that can be part of the EC's contractual relations with third parties, such as culture and education.

The distribution of competences is in practice even more complex than the above would indicate. Within one policy field, there can be further variations and gradations in the competences attributed to the EC, and thus also in the scope of action which rests under member state control. In more complex policy initiatives, the use of multiple legal bases is nearly always necessary (see below), which adds to the complexity of policy-making.

However, the delineation of competences within the treaties is not as rigid as it may at first appear. Article 308 of the EC Treaty is a flexibility clause under which the EC can undertake action in areas not included explicitly in the treaties (see below). This clause has been used for several prominent initiatives, including support programmes for Central and Eastern Europe, the former Soviet republics and the Mediterranean area (PHARE, TACIS and MEDA), support for individual countries (such as Bosnia-Herzegovina) and horizontal programmes (promoting democracy and human rights in third countries other than developing countries).

How does the EU's second pillar fit within this categorization? Generally speaking, CFSP can be understood as falling within the category of parallel competences. Member states have always rejected the idea of drawing up a list of foreign policy matters that would fall under exclusive EU competence, not least because in so doing they could be prohibited from acting when a foreign policy decision had been adopted at the EU level. This is not to imply that CFSP decisions do not commit the member states in terms of the positions they adopt and the conduct of their activity (see Chapter 6). Even if we do categorize CFSP as being an area of parallel competence in principle, given the different institutional and legal set-up of both pillars, this parallel competence is of a different order than the parallel competences in the first pillar.

The availability and choice of legal base is crucial, not only because it determines the extent to which the EU can act, but also because it has major implications for the actors involved, the decision-making and voting procedures used, the budgetary consequences and the possibility of recourse to the ECJ. This also explains why specific policy actions and their legal bases are not always adopted in function of the requirements of the foreign policy issue, but also in function of their repercussions for the inter-institutional balance of power. Member states can prefer to rely on a specific treaty article, not because it is seen as the most effective to tackle the problem at hand, but because it ensures, for instance, that the Community budget can be used or that the EP can be excluded from policy-making.

The fact that the distribution of competences is not particularly clear and that foreign policy matters can often be tackled from different policy perspectives results in inconsistencies and turf battles between the EU's actors. This is particularly true for the many grey areas that fall between Community and CFSP competences (Duke 2006). For example, in 2005 the Commission sought from the ECJ the annulment of the Council's (second pillar) decision to support an initiative of the West African regional organization ECOWAS to tackle the spread of small arms and light weapons, which the Commission considered to be part of Community powers in the field of development (Case C-91/05). A further example was the Commission's use of development money to combat terrorism in the Philippines – brought before the Court in 2005 by the EP which claimed that the Commission had exceeded its powers (Case C-403/05). Interestingly, it is in this grey zone that the ECJ – which was excluded from CFSP – is called upon to play the role of arbitrator (see Corthaut 2005; Lenaerts and Van Nuffel 2005: 54, 808). In mid-2007, the Court's judgement was still pending in both cases, and it was also unclear whether the ECJ would be willing to formulate judgements with the potential to have far-reaching impact on the sensitive issue of the division of competences in foreign policy matters.

Decision-making

This section first gives an overview of the various formal *decision*-making procedures, in order to focus in the next section on the broader *policy*-making process. Both are essential to understand the nature, possibilities and constraints of EU foreign policy as well as the complex web of intra-institutional, inter-institutional and interstate interaction it involves.

Community decision-making

Decision-making in the European Community belies the homogeneity generally associated with the 'Community method'. Indeed, whilst the basic tenets of the process stand, the power balance between and within the institutions varies depending on the policy area. The main procedures for first pillar policies are:

- *Decision-making in trade policy* (Art. 133 TEC): this is the simplest procedure. The Council acts by a qualified majority vote (QMV) on a proposal of the Commission. There is no treaty obligation to consult the EP.
- *Decision-making in development cooperation* (Art. 179(1) TEC): measures to advance development cooperation objectives are decided through the co-decision procedure, under which the EP decides together with the Council, on the basis of a proposal from the Commission.
- *Decision-making in economic, financial and technical cooperation with third countries* (Art. 181a TEC): measures are adopted by the Council, acting by QMV on a proposal from the Commission and after consulting the EP.

The main procedures with regard to the negotiation and conclusion of international agreements are less straightforward. Confusion surrounding the precise delineation of competences makes Article 133, in particular, extremely complex (for a detailed analysis, see Eeckhout 2004: 49–53, 169–89):

- *Decision-making on trade agreements* (Arts 133 and 300 TEC): on the Commission's recommendation, the Council authorises it to open negotiations. The Commission then negotiates the agreement, in constant coordination with the special committee appointed by the Council (the 'Article 133 Committee') and in line with the negotiating mandate issued by the Council. At the conclusion of negotiations, the Council decides on the signing and conclusion of the agreement, on a proposal from the Commission. The EP has no formal right to be consulted before, during, or at the conclusion of negotiations, although in practice it is generally kept informed of proceedings. The Council decides by QMV, except for on those issues enumerated in Art. 133(5).
- *Decision-making on international agreements with regard to development cooperation and economic, financial and technical cooperation* (Arts 181, 181a, 300 TEC): the conclusion of cooperation agreements follows the same decision-making process as outlined above for trade agreements. Again, the Council acts by QMV, unless the agreement covers a field for which unanimity is used for the adoption of internal policies. The major difference is related to the role of the EP – the Council can only conclude agreements after consulting the EP. In three cases, an agreement can only be concluded once the assent of the EP is secured: entering into an agreement that entails the establishment of a specific institutional framework, that has important budgetary implications, or that would necessitate the amendment of an act adopted under the co-decision procedure.
- *Decision-making on association agreements* (Arts 310, 300(2–3) TEC): the process largely follows the principles outlined above for the negotiation of trade and cooperation agreements. However, the Council acts unanimously, and the association agreement can only be concluded after the assent of the EP has been obtained.

- *Decision-making on agreements in other policy fields*: the EC has the competence to enter into agreements with third parties in specific policy fields (such as environment or research). The legal basis for the agreement will then be the article on the specific policy area (which provides the substantive legal basis) combined with Art. 300 TEC (which deals with decision-making procedures for international agreements). For example, if the agreement relates to environmental policy, Art. 175 TEC (on environmental policy) in combination with Art. 300 TEC will provide the legal basis and determine the decision-making process (see Delreux 2006).

Two further factors make decision-making even more complex. Agreements can have several legal bases. For instance, if an agreement includes not only trade issues but also elements of environmental policy, it will be based on Articles 133, 175 and 300 TEC. Association Agreements in particular are based on several treaty articles, as they tend to cover a broader range of policy areas. This also implies that the decision-making procedures of the various treaty bases can differ. In these cases, a complex set of implicit and explicit rules (including ECJ judgements) then determine what decision-making procedure will be used.

The second complicating factor is that most agreements are 'mixed agreements': agreements which cover policy areas that fall under both EC and member states' competences (see Leal-Arcas 2001; Eeckhout 2004: 191–9). This is logical because the number of exclusive EC competences is actually rather limited. The decision-making rules already outlined are also valid for mixed agreements. But, in addition to being agreed upon by the EC, member states must also submit the parts of the agreement which fall under their competence to national ratification processes. The fact that most agreements are mixed also explains why, independent of whether unanimity or QMV is foreseen in the formal procedures, there is a significant pressure to adopt agreements by consensus, or else endanger national ratification processes.

Two further procedures deserve special mention. Art. 301 TEC touches upon decision-making with regard to the *interruption or reduction of economic relations with one or more third countries* (sanctions). This is the only article in the EC Treaty

Figure 4.1   Decision-making procedures in the first pillar

	Commission	Council	European Parliament	Treaty basis (TEC)
Trade policy	Proposal	QMV	No role	Art. 133
Development cooperation			Co-decision	Art. 179(1)
Cooperation with third countries			Consultation	Art. 181a(2)
Trade agreements	Recommendation to open negotiation; proposal for signing and concluding an agreement	QMV (with exceptions)	No role	Arts 133, 300
International (development and cooperation) agreements		QMV (with exceptions)	Consultation or EP assent	Arts 181, 181a, 300
Association agreements		Unanimity	EP assent	Arts 300, 310
Interruption or reduction of economic relations	Proposal (on basis of a CFSP common position or joint action)	QMV	No role	Art. 301
Action when treaty does not provide powers	Proposal	Unanimity	Consultation	Art. 308

which includes an explicit link to decision-making in CFSP and makes a Community decision subject to a preliminary decision in the CFSP framework. According to this article, if a CFSP common position or joint action states that the EC should interrupt or reduce economic relations with a third country, the Council decides by QMV on a Commission proposal. The consequence of this article is that the Commission's exclusive right of initiative – one of the basic features of the first pillar's Community method – is undermined since it is pre-empted by the preceding decision of the Council in the CFSP framework.

Finally, Article 308 TEC outlines the procedure for *actions where the treaty does not provide the necessary powers*. If action is required to attain one of the objectives of the Community but the treaty has not provided for the necessary powers, the Council can take the 'appropriate measures' acting unanimously on a Commission proposal (and following consultation of the EP). As seen above, this article has enabled the EU to undertake some essential foreign policy initiatives.

Decision-making in CFSP/ESDP

Decision-making in CFSP/ESDP follows the intergovernmental method: the Council is centre stage and decision-making is by unanimity. However, the treaty text gives the (misleading) impression that some aspects of the Community method are creeping into CFSP decision-making. Formally speaking, member states and the Commission share the right of initiative: any member state or the Commission may refer to the Council any question relating to the CFSP and may submit proposals to the Council (Art. 22 TEU). To date, the Commission has not formally made use of its shared right of initiative in the CFSP context, although at working-group level it has contributed to CFSP deliberations. In practice, most proposals come from one or more member states and are voiced through the Presidency, which plays a major role in formulating and tabling (or 'COREU-ing') proposals. As discussed in Chapter 3, over recent years the High Representative has played an increasingly important role in formulating policy initiatives.

The treaty foresees several procedures for decision-making within CFSP. The overriding characteristic of these is that all decision-making power is concentrated in the European Council and the Council (Arts 13, 23 and 24 TEU). It is important to bear in mind from the outset that the provisions of treaty texts can be misleading, and that the provisions on majority voting (QMV), common strategies and enhanced cooperation, in particular, are not reflected in the practice of decision-making.

The main procedures foreseen in the Treaty are:

- *Principles of and general guidelines for the CFSP*, including for matters with defence implications, are defined by the European Council by unanimity.

- *Common strategies* in areas where the member states have important interests in common are decided by the European Council by unanimity, on the basis of a recommendation from the Council (acting by unanimity). The Council is to then take decisions to implement these common strategies, in particular by adopting joint actions and common positions, by QMV.

- *Decisions necessary for defining and implementing the CFSP* (including decisions on *joint actions* and *common positions*) are taken by the Council on the basis of the European Council's general guidelines. The basic rule is that the Council acts unanimously, with abstentions not preventing the adoption of decisions. By way of derogation, QMV applies in three cases: when appointing a special representative, when adopting a decision implementing a joint action or common position, and when taking a decision (including a joint action or common position) on the basis of a common strategy. When QMV does apply, member states' votes are weighted in the same way as in the first pillar, although with additional requirements regarding the minimum number of favourable votes required.

- *International agreements* with one or more states or international organizations under the CFSP rubric (Art. 24 TEU): the Council authorizes the Presidency, assisted by the Commission as appropriate, to open negotiations. The Council concludes the international agreement on a recommendation from the Presidency. The Council acts unanimously, except when the agreement foresees implementing a joint action or common position, in which case QMV applies.

- *Procedural questions*: the Council acts by a simple majority of its members.

Whereas the responsibility for taking decisions is clear-cut (the European Council and Council decide), the treaty provisions on voting procedures in the Council are more complex (Art. 23 TEU). Beyond the already intricate voting arrangements outlined above, with a basic rule (unanimity) and derogation (QMV), there are some additional complications:

- *Constructive abstention*: when the Council acts unanimously, abstentions by member states do not prevent the adoption of decisions. However, if a member state qualifies its abstention by making a formal declaration, it is not obliged to apply the decision which otherwise binds the Union, although 'in a spirit of mutual solidarity, the member state concerned shall refrain from any action likely to conflict with or impede Union action'. But, if the members of the Council qualifying their abstention in this way represent more than one third of the votes, the decision cannot be adopted.
- *Limitations to QMV derogations*: QMV does not apply to decisions with military or defence implications. Furthermore, when QMV applies but a member state declares that 'for important and stated reasons of national policy' it intends to oppose the adoption of a decision taken by a qualified majority, then the Council does not vote. In such cases, the Council may, acting by a qualified majority, request that the matter be referred to the European Council for decision by unanimity.

It is clear from the previous overview that decision-making in the second pillar is highly constrained. The limitations on the use of QMV imply that member states can block any decision, regardless of the gradually broadened scope for majority voting introduced by the Amsterdam and Nice Treaties. This is also one of the reasons why the Nice Treaty foresaw an additional procedural device, designed to facilitate policy-making in cases where the EU cannot proceed as a whole: *enhanced cooperation* (see Jaeger 2002; Stubb 2002). These provisions (Arts 27a–e, 43–45 TEU) allow eight or more member states to establish enhanced cooperation between themselves and to make use of the institutions, procedures and mechanisms laid down by the EU and EC treaties. This mechanism can only be used to implement a joint action or a common position – issues with military or defence implications are excluded. Establishing enhanced cooperation is subject to a range of conditions and safeguards. However, treaty provisions can be misleading and, in some cases, utterly irrelevant. Enhanced cooperation is one such example. Because of its heavy procedures and strict requirements, these provisions have never been used. In a similar vein, after the adoption of three 'common strategies' in 1999–2000, this instrument was effectively dropped (see Chapter 6). As such, the treaty provisions on the implementation of common strategies and the related use of QMV are also irrelevant. In practice, consensual decision-making has remained the norm in CFSP. And, since the Council in fact does not vote on CFSP issues, the provisions on constructive abstention are not used either.

However, while many treaty provisions are irrelevant for the practice of decision-making, one procedure not provided for by the treaties, but in article 12 of the Council's internal 'Rules of Procedure', plays a central role. On the Presidency's initiative, the Council can use the *simplified written procedure* (or *silence procedure*) under which a proposal is deemed adopted at the end of a specified time period, unless a member of the Council objects. The silence procedure through the COREU network, which can delimit reactions to 24 or 48 hours, allows the EU to take urgent or less important decisions without having to convene a meeting. In practice, this procedure is also of crucial importance in overcoming, or at least putting to one side, divergent views. Major divisions cannot be overcome in this way, but the silence procedure can help overcome less significant disagreements or allow isolated member states to 'silently' drop their resistance without losing face publicly. Countries can thus clearly formulate their critical remarks and objections to a proposed decision during a Council meeting, without having either to block the decision or to be seen as publicly climbing down.

This reflects a general tendency to avoid formal voting. Instead, the Presidency is responsible for 'feeling' during the meetings (and in the corridors of Justus Lipsius) when key member states, despite remaining critical or even opposed, will no longer formally object to the proposed initiative, document or decision. In such circumstances, at the end of the debate, the Presidency will formulate its conclusions and announce to participants that a consensus is presumed to be crystallizing and that the initiative, document or decision can be deemed to be adopted (with the absence of a formal vote allowing member states to disagree without explicitly having to block a decision).

The absence of formal voting, together with the large number of issues on the agenda and the fact that many member states are not really interested in a considerable number of these issues, begins to explain why EU foreign policy-making, in contrast to what is often asserted, is not necessarily subject to the lowest common denominator, even in unanimity-ruled CFSP. The following section provides some additional arguments for this conclusion.

Policy-making in practice

What do we learn about EU foreign policy if we adopt a *policy*-making perspective rather than a *decision*-making perspective? How can it be explained that the EU manages to develop foreign policy at all given the many potential blockages built into its decision-making systems? This section sheds light on some basic features of EU foreign policy and on the underlying dynamics that push EU foreign policy forward.

Basic features

EU foreign policy towards most issues is *pillar-transcending*, with policy-makers using the whole range of instruments on the EU menu. When ministers, diplomats and civil servants really want to deliver action *vis-à-vis* a specific country or crisis, their priority is not whether procedures or instruments from the first or second pillar are used. In Council debates, separation is rarely made between policy instruments and measures from the different pillars. Although on paper the second pillar would seem to be the locus for EU foreign policy, in practice the greater availability of instruments and useful budget lines in the first pillar, and the relative autonomy and flexibility of the Commission in implementing EC policies and budgets, means the first pillar is more involved in foreign policy actions than one would expect from a purely institutional standpoint.

EU foreign policy-making is not only based on EU decisions, but also on *systematic cooperation between member states*, on their active support and on member states adopting complementary actions (see Chapter 6). In CFSP, 'strengthening systematic cooperation between Member States in the conduct of policy' (Art. 12 TEU) is one of the central methods of EU foreign policy-making. The statement that 'Member states shall support the Union's external and security policy actively' (Art. 11 TEU) is more than an optimistic treaty article. Support, particularly from those member states that can make a difference in specific policy dossiers, is often essential for EU action and success. And a lack of support can also explain the lack of success of EU foreign policy initiatives. Cooperation and coordination are also important components in first pillar policy domains such as development cooperation. Provisions on development cooperation explicitly state that the EC and member states shall coordinate their policies, shall consult each other on their programmes and may undertake joint action (Art. 180 TEC).

EU foreign policy-making is part of a broader *multilevel foreign policy-making process*. Involvement in EU foreign policy-making entails numerous policy-making processes within the member states. These involve different sets of national actors and different procedures leading to the usual tug-of-wars, requirements to coordinate, discussions about responsibilities and budgetary consequences of policy-making. EU policy-making is also part of policy-making processes within a broader set of interlocking international organizations. A narrow focus on the EU's decision-making process might lead the observer to conclude that it is EU actors taking the initiative, setting the agenda and implementing the decisions. A policy perspective demonstrates that other actors (governmental and non-governmental, international organizations and third states) are often at the root of the EU's policy actions and sometimes also take responsibility for the implementation of its policies. Moreover, to be effective, EU action will often require support or complementary actions from international organizations. Within this multilevel and multilocation foreign policy-making process, the dividing lines between the national level, EU level and other international organizations are not always evident as political leaders, diplomats and civil servants take part in the processes in different institutional settings.

Underlying dynamics

Given the complexity of decision-making procedures, the unanimity requirement in CFSP/ESDP, and the problems of a Council weighed down by too many participants and too many policy issues, the real question is how the EU manages to make any foreign policy at all. The argument presented in this text is that three different political dynamics and related operational mechanisms provide the necessary steering to allow the EU to translate declaratory policy into action: the Community dynamic (communitarization), the Council Secretariat dynamic (commonization) and the core-groups dynamic (segmentation). These three mechanisms can appear to be contradictory and they indeed regularly clash with each other. However, it is because of these three complementary and often mutually reinforcing mechanisms that in many concrete issues the EU has been able to develop a substantive foreign policy. Some explanation of these three dynamics and mechanisms is useful:

- *Commission-steered foreign policy*: the European Community (EC) and the Commission in particular have become increasingly involved in foreign policy issues through the EC's new and deeper contractual relations with third countries or regions, budgetary instruments and horizontal foreign policy initiatives (such as human rights and democracy, conflict prevention and institution-building). The Commission's position in EU foreign policy came under pressure with the rise of new CFSP/ESDP actors and instruments. Nevertheless, the first pillar's comprehensive foreign policy toolbox, together with the activism and relative autonomy of the Commission, explain the importance of Commission-steered foreign policy and of the Community as a locus of and dynamic in EU foreign policy-making. This refers to a *communitarization* of EU foreign policy.
- *Council Secretariat-steered foreign policy*: the gradual qualitative and quantitative reinforcement of common CFSP actors in the Council Secretariat (the High Representative, Special Representatives, Policy Unit, DG E and ESDP bodies), and the growth of ESDP instruments, has led to a new mechanism for providing political steering and operational action in foreign policy dossiers. These central common bodies are increasingly

able to contribute to and promote the definition of a common European interest and policy. This Council Secretariat-steered foreign policy is related to the *commonization* process discussed in Chapter 3.

- *Core-groups-steered foreign policy*: in many foreign policy issues, political steering and operational action is provided by an informal self-selected group of member states that take the lead in EU policy-making towards specific issues in which they have a particular interest and/or value added. They provide both the necessary impetus to EU policy and essential complementary actions (for instance, in other international organizations or with regard to dimensions that fall outside the realm of EU foreign policy). The growing role of informal core groups mirrors a broader process of specialization and division of labour between member states in an EU of 27. The result is a partial *segmentation* of EU foreign policy, with EU foreign policy-making towards specific issues being based on a set of specialized policy networks where some member states together with the Commission and/or the Council Secretariat are at the driving seat of EU foreign policy (see Keukeleire 2006a).

It is important to note that this last dynamic is about more than 'directoire' style groups of large member states such as the Contact Group for the Balkans (Keukeleire 2001; Gegout 2002; Hill 2006a). Core groups or contact groups can include smaller and medium-sized member states as well as the largest. The nature of such groups and of their relationship with EU actors and policies can be very diverse. They can operate temporarily or permanently, they can be firmly embedded within the EU framework or only loosely related to it, they can operate informally and have a low profile, or work in a very structured way and be highly visible. Examples of such groups include: the EU Core Group on Somalia (particularly the UK, Italy, Sweden and the Commission), the contact group on the Democratic Republic of Congo (particularly France, the UK, Belgium and the Council Secretariat), the EU3 on Iran (the UK, France, Germany and the High Representative) or more temporary forms of cooperation such as between the High Representative and the Polish and Lithuanian Presidents during the Orange Revolution in Ukraine (see Borda 2005; Delpech 2005a, 2005b; Keukeleire 2006a).

Figure 4.2 presents these three dynamics schematically. The large circle represents the general framework of EU foreign policy towards a specific issue. This EU policy is defined, supported and followed by all member states and is developed through the decision-making processes previously discussed. The three smaller circles represent the mechanisms that can provide the necessary political and operational steering to EU foreign policy. Depending on the issue, there can be variations in this figure: the three smaller circles can be larger or smaller (depending on the relative importance of each of the three mechanisms in the case at hand), they can be more or less interwoven (depending on the degree of interaction and mutual reinforcement), and the 'core group' circle can be situated to a greater or lesser extent inside or outside the large circle (depending on the extent to which the core group's work is embedded in the EU foreign policy framework or proceeds autonomously). The figure can also change over time, mirroring the subsequent stages in policy towards the issue at hand.

Figure 4.2   Political and operational steering in EU foreign policy

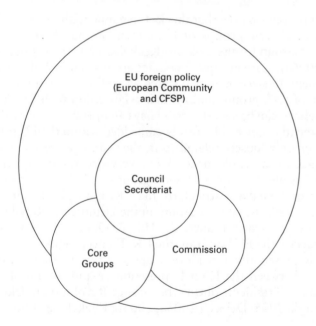

The dynamic provided by the three policy-steering mechanisms further supports the conclusion that EU foreign policy-making is not necessarily subject to the lowest common denominator despite the unanimity rule, but that it has developed methods to overcome divergent views and interests. These methods also help overcome a hurdle which all too often hampers the development of a more active EU policy: the lack of interest of member states towards a specific issue (see Chapter 5).

Financing EU foreign policy

The complex system of competences, procedures and policy processes with regard to the *substance* of EU foreign policy is interrelated with an equally complex system of competences, procedures and processes with regard to the *funding* of EU foreign policy. Analysing these financial arrangements explains some of the restrictions the EU faces as a global actor and provides insight into the nature, scope and priorities of EU foreign policy.

The difficult debate on financing EU foreign policy is closely related to inter-institutional and inter-pillar tensions. In certain fields, member states do want an EU foreign policy underpinned financially by the EC budget. But, they also want to retain control and protect the second pillar from unwanted Community interference. Both the Commission and the EP attempt to use their budgetary powers in the first pillar as a lever to gain influence in the second pillar. Thus, it is not the effectiveness of the EU's foreign policy but the ramifications on the actors' power positions which often prevail in decisions on financing EU foreign policy.

The financing of EU foreign policy extends beyond the budgetary provisions analysed below. It is part of a complex multilevel and multilocation system. This implies that the funding of EU foreign policy activities not only occurs through the EU budget but also through national budgets, through common arrangements outside the EU budget (such as the European Development Fund for the ACP countries, or the Athena mechanism for ESDP operations with a military dimension), and through funding for other international organizations (such as the UN, the World Bank and NGOs).

Financial Framework 2007–13

In the EU's Financial Framework for the period 2007–13, funding for the various strands of the EU's external action is brought together in 'Heading 4: European Union as a Global Partner', although appropriations under other headings (such as the €1 billion foreseen for the Galileo satellite system) can also have potential foreign policy significance.

For the 2007–13 period, €53.3 billion or 5.7 per cent of the EU budget has been devoted to the 'EU as a Global Partner'. There is a steady annual increase in allocations over this seven-year period, from €6.396 billion in 2007 up to €9.066 billion in 2013 (Commission 2004a–d, 2007a; EP, Council and Commission 2006a). This represents an increase of 8 per cent on the 2000–06 allocation, which is significant, but is also meagre compared to the growth in foreign policy ambitions, new initiatives such as the European Neighbourhood Policy (ENP), the growing number of ESDP operations, and the appointment of EU Special Representatives in more and more regions.

As can be seen in Table 4.1, the Financial Framework provides for a set of geographic and thematic instruments. With the exception of the CFSP budget, all of these financial instruments are aimed at supporting first pillar decisions. This clearly indicates that at least the power of the purse lies in the first and not the second pillar.

The following three geographic instruments receive the lion's share of funds (nearly €40 of the €53.3 billion) and are also the financial basis of the EU's structural foreign policy:

- *The Instrument for Pre-Accession (IPA)* covers the candidate countries and potential candidate countries. It provides wide-ranging economic and financial assistance, and supports the countries in fulfilling the political and economic requirements of accession. In the Balkans it also supports confidence-building programmes, stabilization, regional cooperation and institution-building. The Instrument for Pre-Accession has replaced various long-standing regional instruments, such as CARDS, which until 2006 regulated the EC's support to the Balkans.
- *The European Neighbourhood and Partnership Instrument (ENPI)* covers countries targeted by the European

Table 4.1 Financial Framework 2007–13 – 'Heading 4: EU as a global partner' (in € million)

Financial Instruments	2007	2008	2009	2010	2011	2012	2013	Total 2007–2013
Instrument for Pre-Accession (IPA)	1,263	1,383	1,480	1,621	1,782	1,929	2,014	11,476
European Neighbourhood and Partnership Instrument (ENPI)	1,420	1,417	1,481	1,543	1,637	1,798	1,922	11,222
Development Cooperation Instrument (DCI)	2,186	2,202	2,310	2,419	2,497	2,596	2,746	16,958
Instrument for Cooperation with Industrialized Countries	22	23	24	24	24	26	26	172
European Instrument for Democracy and Human Rights (EIDHR)	140	147	152	156	163	168	175	1,104
Instrument for Stability (IFS)	139	179	258	291	340	382	471	2,062
Instrument for Nuclear Safety Cooperation	70	72	74	75	75	77	78	524
Humanitarian Aid	732	754	777	800	824	849	875	5,614
Macro-Financial Assistance	58	92	99	107	114	123	137	732
Rapid response instrument for major emergencies	5	6	8	8	9	9	11	56
Common Foreign and Security Policy (CFSP)	159	200	242	281	327	363	406	1,981
Emergency Aid Reserve	234	239	244	248	253	258	264	1,744
Loan Guarantee Reserve	200	200	200	200	200	200	200	1,400
Total	6,396	6,678	7,108	7,529	7,997	8,524	9,066	53,300

Notes: January 2007 figures. The table does not include decimal places hence the 'Total' column can diverge from the sum of annual amounts for each instrument.
Source: Commission (2007a).

Neighbourhood Policy: the former Soviet republics in Eastern Europe and the Southern Caucasus, and the Mediterranean. It also covers the EU's partnership with Russia. The ENPI provides the financial backing for activities under the EC's bilateral agreements with these countries and focuses in particular on supporting the implementation of ENP Action Plans. The ENPI replaced TACIS and MEDA that until 2006 regulated the support for the Commonwealth of Independent States and the Mediterranean regions respectively.

- *The Development Cooperation Instrument (DCI)* covers developing countries, territories and regions that are not eligible for assistance under the two previous instruments. It supports development cooperation, economic and financial cooperation, and has poverty reduction as one of its main objectives. The DCI replaces 15 long-standing regional and thematic financial instruments, such as those for developing countries in Asia and Latin America, development cooperation with South Africa, rehabilitation and reconstruction operations in developing countries, or the fight against poverty-related diseases such as HIV/AIDS and malaria.

It is important to note that cooperation under the Cotonou Agreement with the ACP countries is funded mainly through the European Development Fund (EDF), which does not fall under the Financial Perspectives. The EDF is funded through separate contributions by member states, with the 10th EDF for the period 2008–13 amounting to €22.7 billion (Representatives of the Governments 2006). This is as much as the IPA and the ENPI combined and more than the DCI that finances development aid for the rest of the world. The inclusion of the EDF in the Financial Framework would have contributed to the coherence of the EC's external action and would have partially removed a historically defined discrimination between developing countries. However, its 'budgetization' was rejected by the member states, which wanted to keep their control over the EDF's purse strings.

The major thematic financial instruments foreseen in the Financial Perspectives – receiving one fifth of funds for 2007–13 – have a global reach and are mainly designed to respond to crisis situations, whether political, humanitarian or financial: the Humanitarian Aid instrument, Emergency Aid Reserve, Macro-

Financial Assistance instrument, the Loan Guarantee Reserve, the Nuclear Safety Instrument, the European Instrument for Democracy and Human Rights (EIDHR), the Instrument for Stability (IFS), and the CFSP. As analysed in Chapter 9, the EIDHR and the Instrument for Stability in particular are used for foreign policy activities closely related to, or overlapping with, CFSP actions.

The CFSP budget

CFSP and ESDP policies are funded through two different mechanisms, depending on whether they are civilian or military in nature (see Art. 28 TEU). CFSP actions and ESDP operations of a civilian nature are generally financed through the CFSP budget, with the exception of the salaries of personnel seconded by member states to the operation, which are borne by those member states. The Financial Framework for 2007–13 foresees €1,981 million for the CFSP, which amounts to 4 per cent of appropriations for 'Heading 4: EU as a global partner' and 0.2 per cent of the total EU budget. This is a significant increase compared to the 2000–06 period. However, when compared to the growing number and scope of CFSP initiatives and ESDP operations to be financed by the CFSP budget as well as the other allocations in the Financial Framework, this sum begins to look fairly paltry. It is quite symbolic that the Financial Framework foresees nearly as much for the new External Borders Fund (€1,820 million), which provides for upgrading infrastructure along the EU's external borders, as for the whole of the CFSP (Commission 2007a).

The CFSP chapter in the general budget for 2007 (Commission 2007b) organises appropriations under seven headings: monitoring and implementation of peace and security processes (€21 million), non-proliferation and disarmament initiatives (€25 million), conflict resolution and other stabilization measures (€15 million), emergency measures (€23 million), preparatory and follow-up measures (€3 million), EU Special Representatives (€14 million), and police missions (€55 million). The budgetary constraints are severe. For example, with €92 million from three of these headings, 14 civilian operations are to be financed in the Balkans, Georgia/South Ossetia, Iraq, the Palestinian Territories, the DRC, Sudan and Indonesia. Thus, the financial basis of many of these operations is extremely limited and their scope and impact will probably be likewise.

The limited budgetary allocation for CFSP points to one of the main paradoxes in several member states' attitudes towards EU foreign policy. They cherish the second pillar as an arena through which to develop EU foreign policy, yet they are reluctant to endow the CFSP budget with the necessary resources for serious foreign policy action. One explanation for this paradox relates to the fact that the CFSP budget is subject to the general budgetary procedures of the Community. Hence, political decisions on CFSP actions and civilian ESDP operations are adopted by the Council as absolute sovereign in the second pillar, but their budgetary dimension is determined through the EC's normal budgetary procedure in which the Council must take heed of the budgetary powers of the Commission and EP. For the Council, this has two implications. Firstly, the Council must always reach agreement with the EP to adopt the Financial Framework and the yearly CFSP budget (with the CFSP falling under the 'non-compulsory expenditures' of the EU budget). Secondly, if appropriations in the CFSP budget are insufficient to finance Council decisions – which proves to be a recurrent problem – the EP's agreement is required to obtain a supplementary budget or to transfer appropriations from other sections of the EC budget (on a Commission proposal). This procedure is not only time consuming, but also systematically leads to inter-institutional bickering as the EP tries to manipulate this situation to influence decisions adopted in the second pillar. As member states try to avoid what they consider inappropriate parliamentary interference in CFSP, they generally opt for ad hoc solutions to finance CFSP actions, or launch these actions with insufficient funding. That these normal budgetary procedures apply to CFSP/ESDP decisions also makes CFSP/ESDP subject to rather heavy procedures and ill-equipped for crisis management operations which require rapid and flexible action (see also Bendiek 2006).

A different financial mechanism applies for ESDP operations with military or defence implications. These are completely financed by member states, with the main burden falling on those countries participating in the military operation in question. Participating member states pay the costs of their operational contribution to an ESDP mission, with a limited number of common costs financed through the *Athena mechanism* (see

Missiroli 2003; Scannell 2004; EU Council Secretariat 2007a). This mechanism is separate to the EU budget and is under the authority of a Special Committee composed of member state representatives. Although this system allows for swift funding once an agreement is reached, its major disadvantage is that each operation requires new ad hoc arrangements between participating member states. Whether the EU can act thus hinges on whether a sufficient number of member states are willing to provide operational support.

EU foreign policy and consistency

The EU's complex system of competences, institutions, decision-making procedures, policy-making processes and funding mechanisms cannot but lead to significant problems with regard to consistency. However, a lack of consistency in EU external policies is detrimental to the EU's capacity to 'speak with one voice' in international politics and undermines its credibility as an international actor as well as its ability to achieve specific foreign policy goals. In fact, the issue of consistency does not relate to one problem, but a series of problems (for a systematic overview see Nuttall 2005):

- *Horizontal inconsistency*: refers to a lack of consistency between policies formulated across the EU's policy-making machine and particularly across policies developed through the various pillars. Horizontal inconsistency can also occur intra-pillar – across the policies elaborated in CFSP/ESDP and, particularly, across EC policies (trade, development, human rights and democracy promotion).
- *Institutional inconsistency*: refers to areas of inconsistency in the two different sites of elaboration of external policies, that is the Council and its substructures on the one hand and the Commission on the other. It can also occur intra-institutionally: within institutions, policy-making communities work towards different goals, under different mandates and with different philosophies (cf. DG Trade and DG Development in the Commission).
- *Vertical inconsistency*: refers to inconsistencies arising between policies agreed at the EU level and those pursued by

member states nationally. The EU's foreign policy capabilities are limited, reliant on member states not undermining agreed foreign policy positions and indeed requiring member states' active support (diplomatically and operationally) to give substance to those positions. Of particular importance is that the most relevant member states (relevant because of their economic leverage or their special relationship with a third country, for example), in any given foreign policy issue, buy into and propagate the EU's position.

- *Interstate inconsistency*: this refers to inconsistency between the member states' different national foreign policies irrespective of whether a policy line has been agreed a priori at the EU level. The highly publicized disputes – Britain vs France and Germany, and 'old Europe' vs 'new Europe' – prior to the 2003 Iraq war is a prime example. Although a policy had not yet been agreed on the EU level (and was unlikely to be, given the vehemence of divisions) these disagreements were highly damaging to the EU's credibility as a uniting force in member states' foreign policies as well as a potential actor in Iraq.

Remedying this multi-dimensional consistency issue is complicated by the fact that solving one part of the problem often aggravates the next. The EU has, however, taken some measures. Beginning with legal instruments and practices, Article 3 TEU contains a general prescription for consistency:

> The Union shall in particular ensure the consistency of its external activities as a whole in the context of its external relations, security, economic and development policies. The Council and the Commission shall be responsible for ensuring such consistency, and shall cooperate to this end. They shall ensure the implementation of these policies, each in accordance with its respective powers.

In Article 13(3) TEU, falling under the provisions on CFSP, we learn that 'The Council shall ensure the unity, consistency and effectiveness of action by the Union'. Not only is there a lack of concrete mechanisms to translate these provisions into practice, but by emphasizing in Article 3 TEU that the Council and Commission are to act 'each in accordance with its respective powers', Article 3 TEU actually emphasizes the inter-institutional turf battles at play.

In terms of institutional innovation to further the consistency cause, the results have been mixed. In creating a function of High Representative for the CFSP and establishing new CFSP/ESDP bodies, for example, inter-institutional inconsistency was built into the EU's system. Moreover, this was not paralleled by the creation of mechanisms to ensure the consistency between, for instance, an ESDP operation in a third country and Commission activities using instruments such as the Instrument for Pre-Accession or the Instrument for Stability. However, because of its structure, incoherence is built into the EU's foreign policy system and, ultimately, there is little prospect of the consistency problem being solved without amalgamating the various areas of EU external policy.

Conclusion

Foreign policy is a highly complex policy field and it is extremely difficult to clarify or subdivide its various elements. Nevertheless, it is precisely this which the EU has sought to do. Understanding the distribution of competences between the different institutions in the EU's foreign policy-making system is crucial to understanding not only the processes at play in any particular foreign policy dossier but also broader themes. These include repeated battles between first and second pillar actors and between the EU level and the member-state level. On paper the decision-making processes appear unworkable. In practice, the EU's various foreign policy actors have developed methods to overcome the complexity and the bottlenecks. But this also implies that the practice of foreign policy-making is rather different to that which might appear from reading the treaties.

Chapter 5

EU Foreign Policy and National Foreign Policies

EU foreign policy is a complex multilevel policy network in which policy is not only developed within and across all three pillars, but also through interaction with the foreign policies of member states. EU-member state interaction is not a simple two-level game, with the national and EU levels remaining neatly separated. Rather, EU and national foreign policies are interconnected and mutually influencing. To understand EU foreign policy then, we must also examine national foreign policies and national foreign policy actors since they play an important and varied role in the EU's policy-making regimes. It is useful to consider what the impact of a specific national foreign policy system and style will be on a member state's foreign policy-making in the EU.

In the framework of this book, it is not possible to analyse the foreign policies of member states in turn (see Hill 1996; Soetendorp 1999; Manners and Whitman 2000a). Rather, the focus here is on patterns, categories, problems and issues. We also give more attention to the 'Big 3' – France, Britain and Germany – since, as will become clear, these countries play a special role in EU foreign policy. This chapter is divided into three sections. Firstly, we consider the impact of the nature of member state foreign policy-making mechanisms on the EU level. Secondly, we consider the constitutive elements of national foreign policy: power, interests and identity. This provides a more sophisticated understanding of two issues often considered to be major obstacles for EU foreign policy, member states' different interests and 'lack of political will', as well as the other obstacles: differences in power, in world views and role definitions, and in identity. Finally, we evaluate the various dimensions of the 'Europeanization' of national foreign policies.

Foreign policy-making in the member states

This section examines the design and functioning of member states' foreign policy-making systems and considers how this influences policy-making at the EU level. At the base of this analysis lies the presumption that member states are not the 'billiard ball' unitary actors that realists would have us believe.

The member states' constitutional design

In their comparative analysis of EU member states' foreign policies, Manners and Whitman (2000c: 252–7) demonstrate that the constitutional design of member states influences the foreign policy process in the EU. Constitutional design determines the nature of government; the relationship between the Head of State or Government and other governmental actors (and particularly the Minister of Foreign Affairs); and the role of political parties, parliaments, as well as subnational entities.

With the exception of the UK and France (at least for its Presidential elections), all member states have a governmental system based on proportional representation electoral systems. The majority of member states also have coalition governments. As such, two, three or more political parties concurrently share power. In these countries, policy formation will be more complex, particularly when the Head of State or Government and Foreign Minister (and other relevant ministers) belong to different parties. Coordination and consultation between the various members of government is difficult enough. In coalition governments, this is further complicated by the fact that the different political parties might not only have diverging views on foreign policy, but are also in continuous competition to strengthen their positions *vis-à-vis* their party political rivals. This can have a negative effect on national foreign policy-making and the position and consistency of that member state in the EU framework.

The way in which foreign policy-making is organized and the relationship between Heads of State or Government, Foreign Ministers and other members of government is very diverse (see Hocking and Spence 2005, and Manners and Whitman 2000a for an analysis of the 15 'old' member states). The distinctive position of the UK and France deserves special attention.

Although the constitutional set-up in Britain and France is very different, both countries have similar patterns of strong leadership and clear hierarchy, with the French President and British Prime Minister (supported by their own cabinets and diplomatic advisers) reigning over foreign policy. Combined with strong horizontal coordination between and within ministries, and with the extensive foreign policy instruments and capabilities of both countries, this strong hierarchical pattern explains why Britain and France are key players in the EU's foreign policy process.

In the British one-party government system, the Prime Minister is firmly at the head of foreign policy, with the Prime Minister's Cabinet Office, rather than the Foreign Office, being the lead institution in coordinating foreign policy. As Forster (2000) argues, British foreign policy-making is characterized by a very informal but highly effective system of coordination between ministries and officials, which generates a unity of purpose in terms of objectives, and which is capable of rapid decision-making. The coordination system ensures that 'on routine matters, whenever the UK needs a policy on a foreign policy issue it has one, and that the policy is advanced consistently by ministers and officials in the various fora of the Union' as well as in NATO, the UN, bilateral relations and other contexts. Further, 'the speed with which officials operate also ensures the British are one of the first to set out a position', which delivers important negotiating benefits by establishing 'a posture which other member states must accommodate if an EU policy is to be acceptable to London' (Forster 2000: 50–1). What would normally be the disadvantage of the British mechanism – its lack of flexibility – is rather an advantage in the EU foreign policy context.

In the French presidential system, the President exercises a hierarchical form of authority, particularly pronounced when French vital interests are perceived to be at stake. But presidential domination of foreign policy can be challenged, particularly during periods of cohabitation when the President and Prime Minister come from different political parties. There is a close and permanent interaction between all relevant foreign policy actors. As Blunden (2000: 28) puts it:

Foreign policy is defined and conducted in almost permanent symbiosis between the Elysée and the Quai d'Orsay [the residences of the President and the Minister of Foreign Affairs]. It

> is not accurate to see the Presidency, the Prime Minister's Office, the Quai d'Orsay, the Ministry of Defence, the Ministry of Finance, as separate entities . . . In practice, the leaders of these institutions – ministers, secretaries general, directeurs de cabinet, counsellors, in all twenty or thirty people – are in uninterrupted contact between themselves.

Such levels of interaction combined with its extensive and strong administration, allow France to be always among the first member states to define in detail its position in EU negotiations.

This pattern of a highly centralized system and 'tightly focussed horizontal coordination' distinguishes France and Britain from the other EU member states, including Germany (Manners and Whitman 2000c: 259). Although the overall coordination of German foreign policy is in the hands of the Chancellor (Aggestam 2000: 68), German foreign and security policy is characterized by a fragmented, less hierarchical system in which the Chancellor does not wield the same power as his or her counterparts in London and Paris. The Foreign Minister generally comes from another political party, implying that he or she has both the opportunity and inclination to take a slightly more autonomous path. The relatively high autonomy of the German Foreign Ministry combined with the absence of Franco-British style strict coordination mechanisms explains why German diplomats often appear less organized in EU meetings than their British and French colleagues. Together with their tendency to adopt a more legalistic approach, to the detriment of a more strategic negotiation style, this puts German diplomats at a disadvantage.

In most member states, the Foreign Minister is squeezed between a dominant Head of State and an increasingly important set of 'internal' foreign policy actors. This mirrors the blurred distinction between the internal and the external in 'foreign policy'. On the one hand, the President, Chancellor or Prime Minister are increasingly involved in the EU framework, since the European Council now meets on average four times per year, increasing their exposure to EU foreign policy decision-making. On the other hand, the Foreign Minister relies on specialized ministers to implement (and gradually also to adopt) EU foreign policy decisions. For example, the growing number of ESDP operations has made EU foreign policy more relevant on the international stage. But, for a Foreign Minister, this has the drawback of increasing his or her dependence on other ministers and ministries to implement and plan the operational components of these foreign policies: the Minister of Defence for military crisis management operations; of Internal Affairs and of Justice for civilian crisis management operations (where the intervention of police officers or lawyers is needed); and of Finance and/or Budget for both of the above. A Foreign Minister can promise a national contribution in the EU context. But to deliver, he or she requires the cooperation of colleagues in government. This can become problematic if these colleagues are not from the same party, if they have different priorities or approaches (not only in terms of substance, but also on the question of whether to use the EU framework) and particularly when the inevitable discussion as to who will foot the bill arises.

Finally, the constitutional set-up of a country also determines whether and to what extent other actors, such as subnational governments and parliaments, play a role in foreign policy-making. Subnational government in those countries with a federal state system (such as Germany, Belgium and Spain) can play a role in specific dossiers where the regions have clear economic interests to defend, or where there are different sensitivities and approaches in the regions. However, even in these countries federal government remains the central actor in national foreign policy-making.

Parliamentary oversight of foreign policy is rather weak in most member states, as the formal role foreseen for parliamentarians is constitutionally limited, and as government whips and party headquarters seek to maintain tight control. The main exception to this rule is the Nordic member states (Sweden, Denmark and Finland) where specialized parliamentary committees on foreign policy and EU affairs have a real impact. In other countries, such as the UK, Parliament becomes important where foreign policy decisions touch on fundamental issues of geostrategic positioning and identity in the world (for example, whether or not to use power, or whether the Atlantic, UN or EU framework is preferable).

The diplomatic and bureaucratic level

There are major differences in the structure of foreign policy-making bureaucracies across member states. These cleavages include: centralization or autonomy in decision-making/implementation; levels of efficiency in functioning of lines of command; the role of presidential and/or ministerial staff and their cabinets; efficiency of horizontal coordination; and, amount of autonomy of ministries and of representatives in institutions (Manners and Whitman 2000c: 258–60).

The divisions within Foreign Ministries between 'Europe', 'Bilateral relations' and 'Multilateral relations' departments can directly effect a member state's input into the EU foreign policy system. Where the pillar division of the EU is reflected in national bureaucratic systems, CFSP/ESDP issues are often tackled by 'Multilateral relations' departments and first pillar issues by 'Europe' departments. This does not facilitate a coherent or consistent policy at the EU level. Such divisions also have an influence on the extent to which decisions and consultations within EU meetings penetrate the member state's bureaucratic system – for example, whether national diplomats' interventions in the PSC or COREPER reflect the general views and commitments of all departments in a ministry, or mainly of those specifically dealing with the EU dossier.

While Foreign Ministers are becoming less prominent in EU foreign policy, their Foreign Ministries are being crowded out by the growing role of other ministries in foreign policy-making. The Foreign Ministry is no longer the 'gatekeeper' controlling domestic–international transactions, but more like a 'boundary spanner' managing coordination or facilitating policy-making over permeable issue boundaries and multilayered policy arenas. In some cases, even this role is being challenged (Hocking 2002: 9–11, 285).

Quantitative and organizational differences have a substantial impact on the contribution member states make to EU policy-making, with the large countries (particularly France and Britain) having a major advantage over other member states. The sheer quantity of issues discussed in EU meetings, as well as their increasingly operational character, prevents the bureaucracies of many member states from keeping up. For the predominantly small countries that joined the EU in 2004, the challenge has been to reorganize their Foreign Ministries to ensure that they can at least cover most issues on the foreign policy agenda and can participate effectively in the EU's foreign policy mechanism. This has in large part been achieved, even if the coverage tends to be patchy and if further adaptation to the 'Brussels game' is still required (Edwards 2006: 156; Juncos and Pomorska 2007: 14–24).

Particularly in the case of intensive negotiations on a specific foreign policy decision with major operational implications, meetings are called in rapid succession and national delegations are expected to react quickly to new proposals. In these cases, it is often only the diplomatic services of the largest member states that can scrutinize all documents completely and prepare concrete amendments to these texts, providing them with a major advantage in the ensuing debate. This reinforces the tendency towards segmentation in EU policy-making (see Chapter 4).

Power, interests and identity

The constitutional set-up and foreign policy making mechanisms of member states are a first set of factors determining a member state's position and input into the EU's foreign policy-making system. A second set of factors are the constituent parts of national foreign policy: power, interests, world view and identity.

Power and capabilities

The basic ingredients of power are geography, demography, economic power, military power and diplomatic power (Cline 1980). These factors are further qualified by less tangible components such as will and strategic culture. Table 5.1 provides a general overview of some of the basic ingredients of power.

One of the most interesting characteristics of the EU is the enormous diversity in terms of the power of the 27 member states and, particularly, the cleavage between the UK and France on the one hand and the rest of the member states on the other. This has major implications for foreign policy-making in the EU. To put it bluntly, member states that have nuclear weapons, hundreds of combat-capable aircraft, a fleet with strategic submarines, aircraft carriers, destroyers, frigates, military bases and personnel on other continents, veto power in the UN Security Council, and a major share in the world economy behave in a different way in international relations and react differently to international crises than member states that cannot rely on such components of power (see details in IISS 2006: 61–134). These differences in power and capabilities give rise to a different status in the world and, in the EU, to different foreign policy interests, objectives and ambitions, to different possible routes of intervention and to different 'responsibilities' and expectations both within the country in question and in third countries. Combined, these differences constitute a major obstacle to developing a common foreign policy within the EU.

Member states' diplomatic representations in third countries (Council 2007b: 10–21) are a further example of member states' diverging capabilities. As Table 5.2 demonstrates, the number of embassies a member state has varies from less than ten (Malta and Luxembourg) to around 50 (countries like Hungary, Denmark and Portugal) and more than 100 (only the UK, Germany and France). It is noteworthy that the European Commission also belongs in the 100+ league. Member states' levels of representation in countries which are prominent on the international foreign policy agenda illustrates the problem quite well: only eleven member states are represented in Kabul (Afghanistan), only nine in Chisinau (Moldova) and only seven in Khartoum (Sudan). Such variation in the number of embassies is particularly important when we consider the role of the Presidency as a central actor in the second pillar. As Table 5.2 illustrates, when most EU member states hold the Presidency of the Council, they do not have the extensive diplomatic network necessary to support EU foreign policy action with intensive and systematic diplomatic contacts in all relevant third countries, nor to feed deliberations in Brussels with input and expertise from diplomats in the field.

Cleavages in power and capabilities partially explain why the EU is not a natural arena for foreign policy-making for the member states. The smaller and medium-sized member states fear that they will be dragged along in the largest member states' power games. Meanwhile, the largest states doubt the relevance of an EU composed of powerless member states with little capabilities to offer, yet which expect to have their say in the decision-making process. This is one of the reasons the largest member states have a tendency to act unilaterally or in other bilateral or multilateral settings. The power position of the largest member states also implies that they have different interests to defend

Table 5.1 Ingredients of power

Country (in order of population size)	Population (millions 2005)[1]	GDP (in € billion, 2005)[1]	Exports (in € billion, 2004)[1]	Development and humanitarian aid (€ million, 2004)[2]	Military expenditure (€ million, 2005)[3]	Total active armed forces (2006)[4]
Germany	82.501	2,247	725.1	5,740.5	30,435	284,500
France	60.561	1,710	338.7	6,456.0	42,502	254,895
UK	60.035	1,791	281.2	6,007.2	46,738	216,890
Italy	58.462	1,417	283.3	1,876.1	25,107	191,152
Spain	43.038	904	149.0	1,857.1	9,330	147,255
Poland	38.174	243	65.9	89.9	4,500	141,500
Romania	21.659	79	18.9	–	1,797	97,200
Netherlands	16.306	502	253.4	3,203.0	7,957	53,130
Greece	11.076	181	12.7	354.2	8,120	163,850
Portugal	10.529	147	29.9	785.5	3,164	44,900
Belgium	10.446	298	197.4	1,114.8	3,696	36,950
Czech Republic	10.221	98	54.1	82.2	1,868	22,272
Hungary	10.098	88	45.1	41.9	1,147	32,300
Sweden	9.011	288	99.2	2,074.1	4,515	27,600
Austria	8.207	245	90.1	516.4	1,810	39,900
Bulgaria	7.761	21	8.0	–	514	51,000

Denmark	5.411	208	60.2	1,551.7	2,859	21,180
Slovakia	5.385	38	22.4	21.3	744	20,195
Finland	5.237	155	49.1	498.9	1,887	28,300
Ireland	4.109	160	80.5	462.3	923	10,460
Lithuania	3.425	21	7.5	6.8	371	13,510
Latvia	2.306	13	3.4	6.0	218	5,238
Slovenia	1.998	27	12.9	23.6	460	6,550
Estonia	1.347	11	4.8	3.8	164	4,934
Cyprus	0.749	13	0.9	3.8	158	10,000
Luxembourg	0.455	29	11.0	179.7	273	900
Malta	0.403	4	2.1	7.6	33	2,237
TOTAL	490.718	10,917	2,906.8	32,956.4	201,290	1,928,798

Sources: 1 Commission (2007c: 51, 152–3, 171); 2 Commission and OECD (2006); 3 SIPRI (2006); 4 ISIS (2006: 61–134).

Table 5.2   Member states' embassies and Commission
delegations in third countries (2007)

France	132	Belgium	63	Slovakia	32
Commission	123	Sweden	59	Ireland	31
Germany	122	Greece	57	Slovenia	20
UK	112	Austria	56	Lithuania	18
Italy	96	Portugal	50	Cyprus	17
Netherlands	84	Denmark	49	Latvia	13
Spain	80	Hungary	48	Estonia	10
Poland	74	Finland	47	Malta	8
Romania	68	Bulgaria	42	Luxembourg	7
Czech Rep.	66				

Source: Council (2007b: 10–21).

than other member states. These include, inter alia, permanent
seats in the UN Security Council (UNSC) and nuclear status (for
the UK and France); their position in the world; their privileged
political, economic and military relationships with third countries; and their privileged access to third markets, energy sources
and raw materials. Larger member states' interest in maintaining
or maximizing their power can make it more difficult and sometimes impossible to develop a common EU policy on related
issues, such as the reform of the UN, the relationship with other
permanent members of the UNSC, nuclear non-proliferation, or
the use of pressure to force third countries to respect human
rights.

The impact of the difference in power of the member states on
EU foreign policy-making should however be qualified. Firstly,
the EU sometimes relies on this greater power of its largest
member states to act on the international scene. In the case of the
ESDP, the largest member states are even indispensable – the UK
and France are the only member states with military bases and a
considerable number of troops in overseas territories or third
countries in the framework of bilateral agreements (outside the
context of UN, EU or NATO operations). Combined with their
fleet and military cooperation agreements with third countries,
this military presence facilitates autonomous French and British

foreign policy action. Their external military reach proved essential for the EU to launch several crisis management operations, including in the DRC, Darfur and Aceh/Indonesia. However, their relative military power also explains why France and Britain do not always share the view of other member states that a multilateral framework and legitimation is necessary for military action.

Secondly, while the power gap between the largest and smallest EU member states may be glaring, the power gap between on the one hand the UK, France and Germany and on the other the US, Russia and increasingly China is equally glaring. And, in terms of both relational and structural power, even the largest member states are not sufficiently powerful to unilaterally exert major influence. It is thus clear that even the largest EU member states need partnership and support from other international actors to overcome their limitations. Furthermore, even if the largest member states shoulder most of the burden, they sometimes need the wider label of EU foreign policy and the partnership of other EU countries to make external actions acceptable domestically and internationally.

Thirdly, other member states may have specific assets to offer. For geographical or historical reasons, some member states have privileged contacts (political, economic and/or military) with specific countries in the world, which can be essential for EU initiatives. For example, the mediatory role played by the Polish and Lithuanian Presidents, in tandem with the High Representative, was pivotal in the peaceful resolution of the 2004 Ukrainian Orange Revolution. Likewise, for countries such as Spain, Italy, the Netherlands, Portugal or Belgium this is a major component of their power. Some smaller or medium-sized countries rely on less visible but nevertheless equally important immaterial power assets. These can include a country's reputation and the credibility which it has earned with diplomatic skills in peace negotiations or through its position as a major donor of development aid, provider of neutral monitors or peacekeepers. The power of Sweden and Finland, for example, is in part built on such immaterial power assets. This means that despite their small populations of barely nine and five million, these countries can punch far above their weight on some foreign policy dossiers.

Interests

Interests, like power, shape member states' foreign policy. They also determine the input and position of a member state in the EU's foreign policy system. The divergence between member states' interests and the limited number of 'common interests' are often portrayed as major obstacles for EU foreign policy. However, these arguments frequently mask a more complex pattern of converging and diverging interests, as the following categorization demonstrates:

- *Collective interests*: member states share a set of fundamental and overarching interests, such as their interest in peace, stability and welfare in Europe and its environs, and the development of a rule- and institution-based international order in which principles like democracy and human rights, free market economy and peaceful resolution of conflicts are accepted and respected. There are two main characteristics of collective interests – no single country can pursue them alone and a country can profit from their realization without actively contributing or sharing the costs (the free-rider problem). Both features explain why working through the EU can be useful, or even necessary, for member states.
- *Common interests*: member states' interests converge with regard to specific issues, such as solving a conflict or promoting good governance in a specific country.
- *Interests converge but member states are competitors*: member states can have the same interests such as developing privileged political relations or military cooperation with a third country, or obtaining commercial contracts for national businesses. However, in pursuing these interests, member states compete for a limited number of opportunities. For example, one member state obtaining a commercial contract for its companies to supply military aircraft to China might be at the expense of the commercial or geostrategic interests of another member state.
- *Interests diverge and are incompatible*: examples include the promotion of human rights and democracy in a third country such as Russia (combined with the willingness to put pressure on that country and to use sanctions) versus the economic interest of obtaining energy contracts in Russia

and the geostrategic interest of obtaining its support in the UN Security Council.

- *Absence of interest*: although largely underestimated, in many cases it is not that member states' interests are opposed, but rather that they simply lack interest in the foreign policy priorities of the other member states. This in turn impedes the development of the EU's foreign policy. The vast majority of member states are only interested in a limited range of countries, regions or issues and are just not interested in the rest of the world or the rest of the issues. Consequently, they do not feel the need for an EU foreign policy *vis-à-vis* those regions or aspects.

Finally, in many cases where member states' opinions diverge on a specific foreign policy issue, the main obstacle is not a divergence in interests per se. Rather, it is a divergence in issues such as timing, prioritization of interests, choice of the most appropriate organizational setting (EU and/or NATO, for example), choice of methods and instruments to pursue interests, and determining acceptable costs and risks in pursuing interests.

World view, role conception and identity

In addition to power and interests, a country's world view and role conception also play a role in determining its input and position in the EU's foreign policy system. These issues are more difficult to grasp and define, but are closely tied up in a state's identity.

A *world view* is the specific conception of 'the world' which a state holds. It incorporates all the general assumptions about the nature of the international system and interhuman relations that act as a set of lenses through which the external environment is perceived. World views are shaped by a variety of factors, such as historical experience, geographic position and security situation. World views provide a key to answering a range of fundamental questions: for example, the nature of the external environment and interstate relations, the use of violence in international relations (and the conditions under which this is legitimate), the preferred world order and security architecture, or the relative importance of general principles and values (such as human rights and democracy) compared to the pursuit of economic profit and geostrategic gain. Hence, the eight CEECs which joined the EU in 2004 prioritize a tough line on respect for human rights and democracy in Russia over currying its geostrategic favour. Likewise, their more recent experience of regional military conflict makes them more concerned about territorial and regional security than less tangible global security threats (Edwards 2006: 152). A member state's specific world view also has an impact on where it will stand with regard to the main areas of tension in the development of EU foreign policy: Atlantic versus European integration, civilian versus military power, intergovernmental versus Community approach (see Chapter 1).

Closely linked to a country's world view is its understanding of its particular role within this context: its *role conception*. Role conceptions are self-defined by policy-makers, and more generally by a nation or population. They refer to 'the general kinds of decisions, commitments, rules and actions suitable to their state, and of the functions, if any, their state should perform on a continuing basis in the international system or in subordinate regional systems' (Holsti, 1970: 245–6). In conjunction with its world view, a country's role conception indicates whether it identifies with specific values and objectives and whether it sees itself playing a particular role. Role conceptions suggest whether a country *sees itself* as, for example, a promoter of human rights and democracy (the Netherlands, the Nordic states, the Czech Republic); as a promoter of the free-market economy and liberalization of the world economy (the UK, Germany, the Netherlands, most Central and Eastern European countries); as an actor that accepts the use of violence and the risks of casualties (France, the UK).

World views and role conceptions play an important function in providing a member state with the conceptual lenses through which foreign policy issues on the international and EU table are framed (see also Aggestam 2004; Hyde-Price 2004). They also provide a general orientation through which to define a national position even if a member state is not interested in the specific matter and has no interests to defend. It is because they are closely related to a country's *identity* that differences in world view and role definition can be considered more serious obstacles in defining EU foreign policy than differences in interests. They are related to the core characteristics of nations by which political leaders and the public identify themselves, and they are difficult to compromise. This points to one of the crucial weaknesses of EU foreign policy: the lack of a sufficiently developed common identity. As Hill and Wallace (1996: 8) remark: 'Effective foreign policy rests upon a shared sense of national identity, of a nation-state's "place in the world", its friends and enemies, its interests and aspirations. These underlying assumptions are embedded in national history and myths, changing slowly over time as political leaders reinterpret them and external and internal developments reshape them.' However, as changes in, for instance, Spain, Italy and Central and Eastern European countries over the last two decades demonstrate, a national role conception and world view can vary over time and can also depend on the political leaders and parties in power.

Strategic culture and political will

Two further immaterial components, 'strategy' and 'will', play a role in shaping the foreign policy and the actual power of an actor. *Strategy* is 'a plan of action designed in order to achieve some end; a purpose together with a system of measures for its accomplishment' (Baylis and Wirtz 2007: 5). Reychler (1994: 11–13) draws attention to the weakly developed strategic culture in Europe, which is in its turn a consequence of 45 years of stability under the East–West 'order'. In the Cold War system, responsibility for military security and external actions largely rested in American hands, with only the UK, France and (in a different way) the neutral countries deviating to some extent from this norm. As Reychler emphasizes, the East–West order allowed many EU countries to adopt a strongly moral–legalistic approach to international politics and to embrace several illusions: the illusion of peace (peace is evident and enduring); the illusion of distance (conflicts and violence happen far away); and the illusion of time (important decisions for our security and welfare can be postponed to a distant future).

It is a major obstacle for EU foreign policy that many member states still lack the strategic culture necessary to resolutely pursue a long-term foreign policy, to determine foreign policy and security goals, to develop and deploy instruments in function of these foreign policy goals and to accept the related costs. Meyer's (2004) study of European strategic culture looks at this issue from yet another angle: the problem is not the lack of strategic culture, the problem is one of too many different national strategic cultures and the absence of a 'common' strategic culture.

Will refers to the degree of determination of the population as well as the political elite to implement a strategy and to accept the costs of this policy (Cline 1980: 22). The 'lack of political will' of member states is one of the most popular explanations for the success or failure of EU foreign policy. 'Political will' is too often prescribed as the magic cure to all the EU's foreign policy ills, while the 'lack of political will' has become a convenient excuse for practitioners and analysts not to further explore what actually lies behind the EU's problems.

Member states' 'lack of political will' might actually mean that they have different interests, or are, quite simply, just not interested at all. It can also point to the different world views or role conceptions which make action on the EU level difficult, even where there are no real disagreements about a specific foreign policy issue *per se*. In this latter case, the so-called 'lack of political will' can be broken down into several dimensions, each of which refers to other obstacles in creating a common foreign policy:

• *A general lack of will to strengthen the EU as an international actor*: in this case, the 'lack of political will' is not related to the issue at hand, but is the result of member states' reluctance or refusal to allow the EU to play a more active role on a particular issue and in foreign policy generally.

• *A lack of political will to play a more active role in foreign policy and to take the lead*: the problem in this case is not the attitude of the member states towards the EU as such, but the fact that member states are unwilling or not used to taking the lead in international politics.

• *A lack of political will to accept costs and risks*: the problem in this case is member states' reluctance to accept the political, moral, budgetary, and other costs linked to a more active and assertive EU foreign policy. The extent to which a member state is sensitive to these costs and to the risk of casualties varies. However, in most member states, there is a limited willingness to accept '*du sang versé*' and '*sacrifice comme prix de l'influence*' (Bourlanges 1996). This lack of political will also results from a lack of strategic culture.

- A *lack of 'common' political will*: even where the will for the EU to undertake assertive external action does exist, it might be focused on different aspects of international politics or different courses of action. For example, in some member states there is significant political will to increase development spending and to strengthen EU development policy as a central instrument of foreign policy. In other member states, there is political will behind using power politics and putting strong pressure on third states to force their compliance with EU demands. And, in yet other member states, there is sufficient political will to intervene militarily, even where this risks casualties. In short: the problem is not the lack of political will, but the fact that there are too many *different* political wills.

- A *lack of 'public' will*: the amount of political will reflects public attitudes in the member states. Public opinion can act as a brake on an assertive EU foreign policy in the context of Western Europe, a continent in which people became accustomed to the peaceful order of the post-World War II period. In Central Europe, the experience of repression is more raw and reflected in a desire to see security and an assertive foreign policy played out in different international settings, and particularly those dominated by the US. This difference between member states also relates to the absence of a European public opinion and a common European identity.

There are yet more dimensions to the 'political will' problem (Keukeleire 2006b). However, the conclusion is clear: the 'lack of political will', which is often considered as one of the main obstacles for an effective and active European foreign policy actually refers to several kinds of obstacles. This also implies that solving the 'lack of political will' problem will be more challenging than just convincing the member states to make EU foreign policy more of a priority.

Europeanization

The relationship and interacting processes of foreign policy on the national level and foreign policy on the EU level are often labelled as *'Europeanization'* – although 'EU-ization' would be a more correct term, given that 'Europe' is not synonymous with the 'EU' (see Chapter 1). 'Europeanization' means different things to different people (see Featherstone and Radaelli 2003; Bulmer and Lequesne 2005; Wong 2005, 2007). Here, the concept refers to the following interrelated processes:

- *national adaptation* to the EU level, implying changes in national policy-making mechanisms, policies, values and identity;
- *national projection* of domestic foreign policy objectives and approaches onto the EU level;
- *increasingly pursuing foreign policy on the EU level* (in general or on specific issues);
- *EU export* of its structures and values beyond its territory and *embedding third countries* within these.

This last dimension is relevant for the analysis of the EU's structural foreign policy, enlargement process (Grabbe 2003) and crisis management policy (Coppieters *et al.* 2004) (see Chapter 10). In the rest of this section we will focus on the first three 'Europeanization' processes outlined above as well as the related phenomenon of 'socialization'.

National adaptation – or modernization?

The process of national adaptation to the EU level involves changes first in national policy-making structures and processes, second in national foreign policies themselves, and third in the world view and identity which lie at the core of these national policies. The nature of each of these three dimensions is different in each member state, hence Europeanization is not a uniform process throughout the Union.

National foreign policy structures and processes adapt to the EU context on both a political and bureaucratic level. Formal procedures, organizational practices and coordination mechanisms grow out of the need to continuously formulate 'national' positions as input into EU meetings and to react to the endless stream of policy documents. The balance of power and interaction between national players change as a result of the EU foreign policy context. Examples of this include the growing role of Heads of State and Government and 'domestic' ministers and ministries for civilian crisis-management operations, as discussed above.

Europeanization implies gradual changes in a national actor's world view, values and norms, role conception and identity. As Tonra (2001: 225) argues, there is a 'significant change in the context of policy formation and a consequent internalization of norms and expectations arising from a complex system of collective European policy making'. We should not overestimate this process as such immaterial dimensions are deeply rooted. Nevertheless, gradual changes in member states' norms, world views and role conceptions have been induced as well as facilitated by EU membership. This has been clear in the development of ESDP, which could only come about because of gradual rapprochement of the world views and role definitions of the three largest member states and the neutral countries.

The actual contents of national policies change as a result of consultation, coordination and joint policy-making at the EU level. To a greater or lesser extent, member states do take common views and policies into account in domestic foreign policy positioning. Europeanization also leads to member states developing a foreign policy on issues or countries on which they had no previous policy. For example, Tonra (1997: 190) explains in his study of Danish foreign policy that through EU membership, Danes suddenly had a foreign policy on South East Asia and were, for the first time, involved in Central America. The same stands true for most member states – in terms of both geographical coverage and specific foreign policy issues or approaches (such as 'civilian crisis management'). At the time of their accession, most member states that joined the EU in 2004 and 2007 had no real development policy. But, as a result of membership and their incorporation within the broad context of EU development policy, they have gradually started to explore and develop this new policy domain.

Europeanization has offered a way for former colonial powers, traditionally neutral countries and countries which historically have had to take into account specific sensitivities (such as Germany in view of World Wars I and II and the Holocaust) to overcome the legacy of constraining national foreign policies (Manners and Whitman 2000c: 246–9). Europeanization has helped governments overcome both domestic and external resistance to change. It has allowed member states to transport problematic topics from the national arena to Brussels in order to play down a particular national line or set of bilateral relations (for example, with former colonies). It has also given member states an opportunity to either hide or adopt policies that do not fit within the traditional contours of national foreign policy, such as the military dimensions of ESDP for the neutral countries.

It is in this sense that Europeanization can often be understood as modernization, allowing or forcing member states to update their foreign policy. This involves developing a foreign policy beyond geographically adjacent countries or historically well-established patterns towards a foreign policy adapted to new challenges, requirements and with the policy tools of a globalized world. In this sense, for many member states, Europeanization has also amounted to a 'European rescue of national foreign policy' (Allen 1996: 290).

National projection

The EU foreign policy context also strengthens national foreign policies as it allows member states to project national foreign policy objectives, priorities and approaches to the EU level. Europeanization allows member states to pursue and even expand foreign policy objectives (in specific regions, or with regard to specific themes) beyond those attainable with domestic capabilities. In so doing, a state has the added bonus of obtaining support (budgetary, diplomatically and economically) from the EU institutions and from other member states to pursue objectives more intensively and with a heightened potential impact.

Using the EU as a conduit for national foreign policy has also meant member states could develop a structural foreign policy which would have been beyond national reach. Germany in Central and Eastern Europe in the late 1980s and 1990s, and Spain in the Mediterranean through the Barcelona Process in the second half of the 1990s, are examples, both of which have allowed these member states to punch above their weight. The EU's new member states in 2004 also lobbied for the countries of the South Caucasus to be included in the nascent European Neighbourhood Policy reflecting their specific concerns about stability in their region. However, member states are not always successful in projecting their foreign policy objectives to the EU level or in obtaining a fully fledged operational EU foreign policy instead of a merely declaratory policy. This also explains the frustration of member states, and their subsequent attempts to find other fora or networks through which to project their foreign policy goals.

In short, Europeanization can amplify national power and national foreign policy (Manners and Whitman 2000c). Hence, national foreign policy is not in retreat, but has rather found new opportunities through the EU. This explains one of the basic arguments of Chapter 1 – that the relationship between national and EU foreign policy can be a positive-sum game, with EU foreign policy complementing and even strengthening national foreign policies.

Europeanization and multilateralization

'Europeanization' is used to label the process in which foreign policy is increasingly pursued at the EU level and not, or not only, at a national level. Manners and Whitman (2000c: 243) argue that it now seems 'appropriate to suggest that the Member States conduct all but the most limited foreign policies objectives inside an EU context'. However, this needs some qualification.

Crucial issues such as the Iraq crisis and the Iraq war in 2003–04 are not Europeanized at all. Moreover, while most foreign policy objectives may indeed be pursued in an EU context, the subsequent policy achieved within this framework often does not go beyond the level of declaratory policy or of contractual relations. In these cases, operational foreign policies are to be found in other international fora. Indeed, although most foreign policy objectives are pursued in an EU context, this is often in addition to pursuing these national policies in other fora. EU foreign policy is indeed only one part of a broader multilocation foreign policy (see Chapter 1). Understood from this perspective, Europeanization is only one dimension of a broader process of *multilateralization* which today characterizes member state foreign policies. National foreign policy structures and mechanisms have not adapted to EU procedures, practices and norms alone. These same processes have occurred *vis-à-vis* other international organizations and fora such as NATO, the OSCE, the UN or the G7/G8.

Europeanization and socialization

Often associated with the Europeanization of national foreign policies is the phenomenon of socialization, which was already a characteristic of European Political Cooperation in the 1970s and 1980s. Socialization refers to a process through which national officials attached to EU institutions in Brussels or that are closely involved in EU policy-making increasingly think in European rather than (solely) in national terms. National civil servants in Brussels and even national diplomacies have become more European, which translates into a growing coordination reflex in foreign policy-making. Socialization between ministers, diplomats and civil servants has been seen as playing a major role in identity reconstruction, in shaping and changing not only the practices and perceptions, but also the interests, values and identity of policy-makers (Manners and Whitman 2000b: 8; Wong 2005: 138).

However, the 'socialization effect' of Europeanization tends to be exaggerated. Firstly, the EPC period was different to the current context. With its club-like atmosphere facilitating an informal exchange of views and information flowing between merely 9 or 12 member states the potential impact of socialization was higher (see Nuttall 1992: 313). The formalization of EU foreign policy-making under CFSP, the increasing involvement of first pillar actors and procedures and the growing number of member states has made relying on the socialization effect more problematic. As the EU enlarged to 15 and later on to 25 and 27 member states, socialization became more difficult with diplomats and civil servants from countries with different foreign policy cultures fitting sometimes rather uncomfortably into the fold.

Secondly, the impact of socialization is different in the various member states. With their larger administrations, their elaborate network of bilateral relations and their more active role in other international organizations, the impact of socialization is felt less strongly in France, Britain and Germany.

Thirdly, there is a clear difference in the socialization effect on, on the one hand CFSP insiders and diplomats whose business is (or is closely related to) EU policy-making, and, on the other hand, the many diplomats and departments within a Foreign Ministry with more limited or no involvement in EU networks and with a dominant focus on bilateral relations or on other multilateral fora. Moreover, each multilateral department in a Foreign Ministry is 'emotionally as well as bureaucratically attached to its multilateral client. Each serve[s] to feed back the views and interests of the client organization and of the nations which composed it into the national bureaucracy where they [compete] with the views and interests of the unilateralists and of other multilateralists' (Jørgensen 1997: 176).

Conclusion

Within each of the policy-making regimes analysed in Chapter 4, national foreign policy actors are seen to play an important, though varying role as one level in the EU's multilevel foreign policy system. The methods of policy-making within the member states, coupled with the extent to which they possess more or less of the ingredients of power, are important indicators of their importance in EU foreign policy-making. Hence, particularly Britain, France and, although to a lesser extent, Germany, play a dominant role. This goes both ways – the largest member states provide crucial apparatus and relationships to make EU foreign policy operational, but if they do not agree to a particular course of action, it is unlikely that this will ever see the light of day. The smaller member states play a more prominent role when they can draw upon specific areas of expertise and relationships with third countries. The increasing segmentation of EU foreign policy, itself a pragmatic response to managing member states' different interests, provides space for smaller member states to have an impact in specific dossiers. This also indicates that the Europeanization process is interactive, with the member states 'uploading' their policies to the EU level, and the EU influencing member states' foreign policies.

Chapter 6

The Common Foreign and Security Policy (CFSP)

Why was the Common Foreign and Security Policy (CFSP) created? How do the various EU actors perceive CFSP, and what do they expect from it? Chapter 2 argued that different and even conflicting motivations lay at the root of CFSP's creation in a separate second pillar by the 1991 Maastricht Treaty. As had been the case with European Political Cooperation (EPC) in the early 1970s, the decision to create CFSP stemmed as much from member states' interrelational, integration and identity objectives as their external objectives. For some member states, transforming the EU into a strong foreign policy actor was essential to counter the disappearance of the old East–West 'order' and consequent instability in the external environment. However, for many member states, the main rationale was to allow the EU to manage interstate and inter-institutional dynamics within the Union and not, or not in the first place, to tackle the outside world. It is thus not surprising that whilst member states could agree to create a CFSP at Maastricht, they had no intention of providing it with the necessary actors and instruments to turn it into a robust foreign policy tool. It was only from the late 1990s onwards that the majority of member states, and particularly the largest, started to consider the CFSP framework useful to pursue external objectives. This has led to the development since the late 1990s of both common actors (see Chapter 3) and new instruments (see Chapter 7), making the initially rather empty CFSP shell an increasingly useful operational entity.

This chapter provides a critical assessment of the formal set-up of the CFSP as outlined in the TEU and juxtaposes this treaty image against the reality. It then turns to one of the most important, although often overlooked, elements of second pillar foreign policy – systematic cooperation – before finally considering the scope and thematic priorities of CFSP.

Formal characteristics

CFSP: what's in a name?

According to Article 11 TEU, 'The Union shall define and implement a common foreign and security policy covering all areas of foreign and security policy'. The very name *common foreign and security policy*, as well as this opening sentence to the treaty provisions on CFSP, created major expectations. The name explicitly indicated that CFSP was a '*common*' policy. This gave the impression that it was on a par with the common policies of the EU's first pillar, such as the common agricultural policy and common commercial policy. But, the Maastricht Treaty did not provide for the common actors, common instruments or common budget that would have been necessary to develop a *common* policy. Moreover, in the EC context, the term 'common' denotes policy domains in which the EC has exclusive or quasi-exclusive competence. In contrast, foreign and security policy is a kind of parallel competence, with competences remaining largely in member state hands.

The word '*policy*' suggested that the CFSP was qualitatively different from the 'cooperation' between member states which had characterized the CFSP's less ambitious predecessor: EPC. In fact, cooperation between member states in the conduct of their national foreign policy remains of crucial importance to CFSP.

As far as the range of foreign policy areas was concerned, the CFSP label pointed to a '*foreign and security*' policy, with the Articles 11(1) and 17(1) of the Treaty on European Union explicitly stating that CFSP was to cover '*all* areas of foreign and security policy' and should 'include *all questions related to the security of the Union*, including the eventual framing of a common defence policy, which might lead to a common defence, should the European Council so decide' (our emphasis). Both of these assertions are misleading. CFSP is not all-encompassing, does not cover 'all areas of foreign and security policy' and does not 'include all questions related to the security of the Union'. The territorial defence of member states is not covered by CFSP, for example, and for many member states NATO remains the major forum for security policy.

Developments from the late 1990s did somewhat change this picture: common bodies and actors were established, operational capabilities and a limited CFSP budget were created and the scope of policies was significantly broadened to include some military dimensions of security. Nevertheless, 15 years after its creation, CFSP is still not exclusive, all-encompassing or completely common. The misleading label 'common foreign and security policy' has been one of the factors behind what Hill famously termed in 1993 the EU's 'capability–expectations gap'. At its inception, CFSP held out the promise of a fully fledged foreign and security policy, but has struggled to keep up with this rather grand rhetoric (for the genesis of CFSP, see Nuttall 2000).

The binding effect of CFSP

The Treaty's opening article on CFSP generated expectations that member states had entered into a higher level of commitment (Art. 11(2) TEU):

> The Member States shall support the Union's external and security policy actively and unreservedly in a spirit of loyalty and mutual solidarity.
> The Member States shall work together to enhance and develop their mutual political solidarity. They shall refrain from any action which is contrary to the interests of the Union or likely to impair its effectiveness as a cohesive force in international relations.
> The Council shall ensure that these principles are complied with.

From a legal perspective, this provision, and particularly the use of the word 'shall', is significant as it indicates that CFSP is legally binding (Wessel 1999). However, from a political perspective this is no more than a highly *conditional* binding power – the member states' active and unreserved support and 'loyalty' towards CFSP depends on the degree to which specific policies have actually been developed within the CFSP framework, the degree to which 'the interests of the Union' have been specified, and the degree to which the EU is indeed acting efficiently 'as a cohesive force in international relations' in this matter. When these conditions are not met, the treaty provisions imply that the member states can go their own way – as they clearly have done on many occasions.

In CFSP, the Council is responsible for ensuring that the above-mentioned commitments and principles are observed – and not the Commission and the Court of Justice, as is the case in the first pillar. Since the member states are not renowned for their ability to control each other, this clearly contributes to the limitations of CFSP's binding effect. The Council has not developed any enforcement mechanisms and the Council Secretariat has no systematic record of whether member states have complied with CFSP engagements. The largest member states in particular have a tendency to divert from the EU-line, citing their other 'responsibilities' in international fora (UN Security Council, G8 or 'special relationships') as an excuse.

However, where a well-elaborated and unambiguous policy has been developed towards a specific foreign policy issue, it becomes politically more problematic for member states to fall out of line. Peer pressure amongst member states and a degree of socialization does have its impact. Ultimately, the main problem for CFSP is not member states' deliberately embarking on policies which run counter to those developed within the EU, but rather their apathy, their lack of active support both for the CFSP in general as well as for many of its specific policy initiatives.

CFSP objectives

CFSP's objectives are listed formally in Art. 11(1) TEU as being:

- to safeguard the common values, fundamental interests, independence and integrity of the Union in conformity with the principles of the UN Charter;
- to strengthen the security of the Union in all ways;
- to preserve peace and strengthen international security, in accordance with the principles of the UN Charter, as well as the principles of the Helsinki Final Act and the objectives of the Paris Charter, including those on external borders;
- to promote international cooperation;
- to develop and consolidate democracy and the rule of law, and respect for human rights and fundamental freedoms.

How can we assess these noble general objectives? The first objective may sound quite straightforward, but in fact is not. It necessitates that member states are in agreement on what their common values and fundamental interests actually are. More fundamentally, questions can be raised about the reference to safeguarding the Union's 'independence and integrity'. This is linked to the second objective, which is very misleading. For many member states, the objective of CFSP is far from being 'to strengthen the security of the Union *in all ways*' (our emphasis). For the majority of member states, the military 'way' of strengthening the Union's security is the preserve of NATO and/or national forces. These same considerations apply to the reference to OSCE commitments (through the Paris Charter) on external borders and to the objective to 'safeguard the . . . independence and integrity of the Union'.

A more positive assessment can be given to the last three objectives, which are indeed central to the EU's foreign policy towards other parts of the world. Preserving peace, strengthening international security, and promoting international cooperation, democracy and other values are consistently evident in the CFSP's policy declarations and actions. Moreover, the references to the UN and the OSCE (Helsinki Final Act and Paris Charter) are not entirely rhetorical. Indeed, many CFSP actions have aimed at strengthening, supporting or complementing UN and OSCE actions as part of a multilocation foreign policy. Some critical comments are however useful.

First, rather then being precise goals that provide guidance for concrete foreign policy actions, the treaty provisions are general principles to which member states could easily subscribe, but that leave scope for very different views on what concrete action might be undertaken to pursue these goals. The cleavage among EU member states on the war against Iraq in 2003 is illustrative. For some countries, a military operation was necessary to 'strengthen international security', while others actually considered a military operation as undermining international security; for some member states, UN resolutions provided a firm basis for military actions, while for others they were insufficient to legitimize the use of violence. The Iraq crisis was an extreme case, but similar divergent views on how to operationalize the EU's basic principles and objectives characterize the EU's internal discussions on many foreign policy issues.

Secondly, self-evident and generally accepted as the CFSP's objectives may be, in practice they are not always compatible. For instance, CFSP initiatives to promote human rights and democracy in China or Russia may actually impede international cooperation with these countries to tackle specific international crises (such as Darfur, North Korea or Iran).

Thirdly, and referring to the categorization of objectives in Chapter 1: CFSP's five objectives are rather more identity objectives and interrelational objectives than external objectives. The ritual repetition of these consensus-generating objectives in declarations on all possible foreign policy issues serves both to mask disagreements between member states on their actual operationalization and to underscore the EU's self-comfortingly superior moral identity.

Instruments

Article 12 TEU states that the EU shall pursue the CFSP's objectives by:

- defining the principles of and general guidelines for the CFSP;
- deciding on common strategies;
- adopting joint actions;
- adopting common positions;
- strengthening systematic cooperation between member states in the conduct of policy.

These are often referred to as the instruments of CFSP. This set of instruments to pursue CFSP objectives appears logical. The CFSP's highest political authority (the European Council) defines the principles, general guidelines and common strategies. The Council of Ministers then adopts decisions to further develop and implement policy, through joint actions when operational action is required and through common positions when the EU approach is to be defined. And, to complement all this, member states strengthen their foreign policy cooperation. Strengthening systematic cooperation is a continuation of the method used since the start of EPC in the early 1970s. Common strategies, joint actions and common positions are binding legal instruments and their use is published as a legal act of the Council in the 'Legislation' section of the Official Journal.

However, what might look reasonable, solid and useful for diplomats during Intergovernmental Conferences can seem ambiguous, unwieldy or outright unworkable for diplomats that have to shape EU foreign policy. The result is that, in practice, the satisfying logic of the treaty has not been followed and the instruments used in CFSP are more diffuse than this neat categorization indicates. These legal instruments have been used less widely than expected or, in the case of common strategies, have been dropped entirely. Instead, many other kinds of instruments have been used and developed on an ad hoc basis: that is, decisions, action plans, strategies and other instruments that do not fit within the formal categories outlined in Article 12 TEU.

The instruments detailed above can be understood as a method of organizing and formulating EU foreign policy within the EU machinery. However, CFSP is also vested with the standard diplomatic instruments with which to carry out foreign policy: declarations, diplomatic demarches, high-level visits and meetings, participation in international conferences, informal talks and telephone calls, mediation, sending observers, and so on – in order to consult, confirm, support, show solidarity, suggest solutions or options, demand, protest, disapprove, accuse, reject, deter, sanction, and so on. With the development of ESDP, a range of civilian and military crisis management and peace-building instruments were added to this list. In addition, CFSP can call on first pillar instruments that are politically steered through the CFSP framework (such as sanctions) or that are brought in through EC mechanisms (such as financial support). Member states can also make national instruments available to support CFSP.

Common strategies, joint actions and common positions

Common strategies

While the EU has adopted on an ad hoc basis many strategies and strategy documents (such as the *European Security Strategy* or the EU Strategy for Africa) these are distinct from 'common strategies' as a legal instrument. At first sight, the common strategies instrument, created by the 1997 Treaty of Amsterdam, provides an appropriate framework for devising a comprehensive strategic policy *vis-à-vis* specific regions, countries or policy issues. According to the TEU, the European Council decides on 'common strategies to be implemented by the Union in areas where the Member States have important interests in common'. Decisions on common strategies set out the objectives, duration and the means to be made available by both the Union and the Member States (Art. 13(2)). A major contribution of the common strategies instrument was that it would allow the EU to use relevant instruments from across the three EU pillars as well as from the member states in one comprehensive strategy. This would thus increase both the vertical and horizontal consistency of the EU's foreign policy.

A further innovative feature was that once a common strategy had been adopted by unanimity, its implementation through joint actions, common positions and other decisions could be adopted by qualified majority vote (QMV). This new instrument thus seemed impressive as it could guarantee three important aspects of effective foreign policy: high-level strategic guidance, coherence of policies and a voting procedure that allowed for smooth implementation.

However, a short overview of both the genesis and the use of common strategies paints quite a different picture. The 'common strategies' instrument was not launched because member states wanted to strengthen the effectiveness and cohesion of EU foreign policy, but because in the negotiations leading to the Amsterdam Treaty, it appeared to be an essential device to bridge the gap between those countries that wanted majority voting in CFSP matters and those that were vigorously opposed (Nuttall 1997b; Haukkala 2001: 34–7).

The problematic nature of this new foreign policy instrument became clear in the preparation and implementation of the first, and only, three common strategies: on Russia and Ukraine in 1999 (see Haukkala and Medvedev 2001) and on the Mediterranean in 2000 (see Biscop 2003). Less than two years after the first common strategy was adopted, Javier Solana presented to the European Council his scathing *Common Strategies Report* (Secretary General/High Representative 2000). This led to the virtual burial of common strategies as an instrument of EU foreign policy.

Common strategies had indeed failed on nearly all points. They constituted little more than a continuation of the broad (and largely first pillar) policies that had existed prior to the Amsterdam Treaty. They did not cover new ground and offered no added value, particularly as the anticipated stronger CFSP input and improved synergies with member states' instruments did not materialize. QMV was never actually used to implement the strategies, and thus they did not facilitate CFSP decision-making. And, although they were comprehensive, the Union did not use them as an opportunity to address key issues. In the Common Strategy with Russia, for example, the situation in Chechnya did not even earn a mention. Most importantly, they failed to offer a *strategy*. The Common Strategies were the object of such intense negotiation amongst the member states that they contained no real priorities and became little more than inventories of existing policies and activities. Written with their publication in mind, they lacked the sharpness needed to make them a truly useful internal strategy (ibid.).

It was clear from the outset that this new instrument was not suitable for the EU's most crucial foreign policy domain where a real strategy was needed: the Balkans. Consequently, the Stabilisation and Association Process (SAP) for South East Europe was developed outside the framework of a Common Strategy. No new common strategies were adopted after 2000, and the Common Strategies on Ukraine and Russia were not extended beyond their expiry date of 2004, while the Common Strategy on the Mediterranean was extended only once, until January 2006.

Joint actions and common positions

Whereas common strategies quickly fell from grace, joint actions and common positions have become part of the standard CFSP mechanism, although they play a less dominant and less structuring role than initially envisaged. A closer examination of these instruments is useful particularly because it is informative about the nature of CFSP and the prudence required when reading treaty texts (see also Denza 2002; Eeckhout 2004: 398–405).

Following the treaties, joint actions might well appear to be the most important instrument of EU foreign policy. Article 14 TEU, dedicated to joint actions, is indeed the longest article of the whole CFSP chapter. Two paragraphs of the article summarize their main features:

> Joint actions shall address specific situations where operational action by the Union is deemed to be required. They shall

lay down their objectives, scope, the means to be made available to the Union, if necessary their duration, and the conditions for their implementation.

Joint actions shall commit the Member States in the positions they adopt and in the conduct of their activity. (Art. 14(1 and 3) TEU)

Remarkably, four of the seven subparagraphs articulate what is expected from the member states. Joint actions commit the member states in their positions and the conduct of their activities. Whenever they plan to adopt a national position or take national action pursuant to a joint action, they shall provide information in time to allow, if necessary, for prior consultations within the Council (except if measures are merely a transposition of Council decisions). Should there be any major difficulties in implementing a joint action, a member state has to refer them to the Council which shall seek an appropriate solution. In the case of urgent need arising from changes in a situation and failing a Council decision, member states may take the necessary measures as a matter of urgency and inform the Council immediately.

In practice, however, the story is rather different. After trying to assess what their practical use might be (see Holland 1997; Regelsberger *et al.* 1997; Denza 2002), from mid-2000 on, joint actions have been mainly used for the limited number of CFSP/ESDP actions that are financed through the CFSP budget and need to be adopted through a legal act. These consist mainly of three categories of decisions:

- the appointment of EU Special Representatives and the extension of their mandate;
- civilian crisis management operations within the ESDP framework;
- support for actions in the fields of non-proliferation, disarmament and the fight against the spread of light weapons by the International Atomic Energy Agency, UN and other organizations.

We can draw two conclusions from this. Firstly, the fields of application and the added value of the joint action instrument are limited. This is because many operational actions that could have been undertaken through a joint action are often more effectively undertaken through the first pillar. It is the EC that possesses the necessary budgets, procedures, expertise and contractual relations with third countries to undertake the kind of actions that could also have been implemented using joint actions. Election monitoring is one such example. In fact, some of the civilian crisis management operations and support for initiatives in the field of non-proliferation and the fight against the spread of small arms and light weapons could just as easily have been adopted through the EC. The limited added value of joint actions also relates to the measly contributions many member states are willing to provide to joint actions, which brings us to the next point.

The second conclusion is that the fields covered by joint actions do not require any particular additional commitment from the member states. This is even true for those joint actions relating to civilian crisis management operations – the member states have to put national personnel at the EU's disposal, but their participation is voluntary. This implies that from a set of treaty provisions which seemed to require clear national commitment and support for CFSP interventions, the member states reorientated the nature of the joint actions to issues that did not require much commitment from them. Thus, the treaty's detailed provisions on member state obligations are rather irrelevant. This is characteristic of CFSP's overall evolution – member states accept the development of CFSP on the condition that the impact on their national foreign policy is limited.

Similar conclusions also apply to common positions. This legal instrument is described briefly in Article 15 TEU: 'Common positions shall define the approach of the Union to a particular matter of a geographical or thematic nature. Member states have to ensure that their national policies conform to the common positions'. In practice, instead of becoming a useful tool to gradually define an EU approach towards foreign policy issues, the use of common positions has been largely restricted to a very narrow field: the adoption of sanctions and restrictive measures against unsavoury regimes and key individuals from the countries concerned (through arms embargos, travel bans, freezing of funds and economic resources, etc.). Moreover, most of these sanctions merely implement decisions adopted at the UN. For the sanctions to actually come into effect requires first pillar intervention, implying that the added value of this second pillar instrument is limited, except that it enables member states to retain their intergovernmental control.

There are exceptions in which common positions have been adopted to define the EU's approach to an issue. Examples include the common positions on EU support for the International Criminal Tribunal for the former Yugoslavia (ICTY), on the 2005 Review Conference of the Parties to the Treaty on the Non-proliferation of Nuclear Weapons, on the International Criminal Court, and on the prevention, management and resolution of conflicts in Africa.

In conclusion, the fields of application, the added value and the binding effect on member states of these two instruments has been more limited than initially foreseen. As a result, CFSP actions and positions are often adopted or shaped outside the formal framework of these two legal instruments through ordinary decisions of the Council (on the basis of Art. 13(3) TEU), through decisions adopted via the silence or simplified written procedure (see Chapter 3), or via systematic cooperation between member states.

Systematic cooperation between member states

'Strengthening systematic cooperation between Member States in the conduct of policy' is the last instrument mentioned in Art. 12 TEU to pursue CFSP objectives. It is probably one of the most important instruments, as well as one of the most overlooked. It is often ignored by analysts of EU foreign policy because it is less visible than other CFSP instruments and because it does not fit comfortably within the notion of a common policy. The fact that Art. 12 TEU speaks about 'strengthening' systematic cooperation already testifies to this ambiguity, signifying as it does that systematic cooperation should not be taken for granted. Strengthening systematic cooperation between national diplomacies, which was at the heart of EPC, remains the backbone of CFSP mechanisms and output. This brings us to a fundamental point on CFSP – that despite its expanding set of common actors and instruments, national foreign policies and diplomacies maintain a central position.

A number of other Treaty provisions provide additional information about the nature of systematic cooperation. Member states 'shall *inform* and *consult* one another within the Council on any matter of foreign and security policy of general interest in order to ensure that the Union's influence is exerted as effectively as possible by means of *concerted and convergent action*'. In parallel, member states' embassies and Commission delegations in third countries and to international organizations 'shall step up *cooperation* by exchanging information and carrying out joint assessments' (Arts 16 and 20 TEU, our emphasis). Systematic cooperation also carries treaty obligations regarding coordination, dialogue and information exchange in international organizations and conferences, including those fora in which not all member states are represented (Art. 19 TEU) (see Chapter 11).

Systematic cooperation between national diplomacies is a generic term incorporating different levels of cooperation: information exchange, consultation and convergent action. It is based on continuous interaction between national foreign ministries, their representatives in Brussels, their embassies in third countries and the CFSP's central actors which can facilitate this process. The continuous exchange at all political, diplomatic and administrative levels led to what has been labelled the 'consultation reflex': if something happens in the world, member states automatically first consult each other through the CFSP framework before reacting to events and before taking initiatives of their own. Exchanging information and consulting each other can contribute to member states at least basing their national policy positions on similar information and assessments of external developments and to developing a common thinking on the issue at hand. This consultation also contributes to the interrelational objectives of EU foreign policy: it facilitates member states' understanding of the position of other member states and it helps to avoid external events leading to misunderstandings between them.

Shared information, consultation and common views can – but do not necessarily – lead to 'concerted and convergent action'. Member states can agree on a course of action towards a specific policy issue, which they then pursue through national foreign policy instruments and actions. Hence, while the tone may differ, all member states convey the same basic message. 'Concerted and convergent action' can be further strengthened through CFSP declarations or through confidential CFSP demarches by the Presidency or the troika, or by all Heads of Mission in the capital of the third country concerned. How can we evaluate the record of systematic cooperation? Overall, systematic cooperation has been strengthened over the last 15 years, with member states accepting it as a familiar part of national foreign policy-making. By and large, exchanges of information and consultations occur more intensively and more automatically than in the past. However, this dynamic has not been felt in all policy issues or by all parts of national foreign policy bureaucracies. A consultation reflex clearly exists among Brussels-based national diplomats and those capital-based diplomats involved in the EU's main foreign policy issues. But, it is not as strong, and in some cases is absent, among the many capital-based diplomats responsible for their countries' bilateral relations with third countries or relations with other organizations. This means that the 'consultation reflex' is much less widespread or intensive than is often suggested.

This critical remark on the reach of systematic cooperation is valid for both the small number of foreign policy issues at the top of the international agenda (the 'CNN issues') and the larger number of issues lower down the international agenda. On many 'CNN issues', there is no full exchange of information and no systematic consultation between member states. This can be because member states diverge in their position, because other international actors are their main interlocutors, or because these issues are considered too sensitive to share information with all EU member states. Examples of such policy issues include the wars in Iraq and Afghanistan and, to some extent, the crisis with Iran or the relationship with Russia.

Systematic cooperation does not always occur on foreign policy issues that are lower on the international agenda because these matters only tend to be of interest to some member states, because the EU is not seen as the most relevant setting for cooperation on that particular issue, or because a member state simply does not have the specialized desk officer or the embassy in a specific third country to allow them to be involved in intensive consultation. Thus, a 'consultation reflex' or a 'cooperation reflex' might exist, but it might not be to consult all EU member states, and it is just as feasible that the consultation and cooperation reflex will be played out in different fora and with other states.

Scope and substance

Having analysed the CFSP's general features, its instruments and methods to develop policies, in this section we turn to its substance. It is important to recall that assessing CFSP in isolation from the EU's general foreign policy and particularly the first pillar is somewhat artificial. Chapters 10 and 11 thus take a more holistic approach to the EU's foreign policy *vis-à-vis* the main geographic arenas and structural powers.

The scope and reach of CFSP has widened greatly in the last 15 years. Policy matters and regions of the world that were in the past beyond the reach of EPC and CFSP are now familiar points on the CFSP agenda and subject to systematic cooperation and concerted or common action. The so-called '*domaines réservés/chasse gardée*' policy issues or regions of the world that were considered to 'belong' to a specific member state have decreased. Developments in member states' former colonies in Africa, for example, were for a long time deemed too sensitive or too important nationally to feature in the EU's political deliberations. In the past, the problem was that countries wanted to shield their '*domaines réservés*' from EU-level deliberations, which acted as a major constraint on EU foreign policy. Now, the problem is often rather the opposite: member states want these national foreign policy priorities to be 'Europeanized', but are faced with the difficult task of selling this to the other member states (see Chapter 4).

The expanding reach of CFSP becomes evident if we look at some clearly visible indicators (Council 2006a and 2007c). In 2006, besides the thousands of messages touching on all parts of the world exchanged through the COREU network, there were approximately:

- 150 CFSP declarations directed towards around 60 countries;
- 220 *démarches* (protests and messages through diplomatic channels) towards almost all countries in the world;
- 320 reports from Heads of Mission (of EU member states and the Commission) in the capitals of approximately 100 third countries;
- 155 'political dialogue' meetings (on Head of State/ Government, Ministerial or senior official levels) with 50

third countries and with the member states of 20 regional organizations;
● joint actions, common positions and other decisions covering dozens of countries (Council 2007c).

The main focus of CFSP is Eastern Europe and the Southern Caucasus, the Balkans, the Mediterranean, the Middle East and Africa (see Chapter 10). But, there are marked differences across even these regions in terms of the intensity of CFSP attention they receive. A low level of attention can indicate that the issue at hand is not prioritized by the EU or that there are major disagreements between member states and hence they neglect these issues. For instance, in the Mediterranean, it is remarkable how little attention is given to specific individual countries and conflicts, such as Algeria and the conflict in Western Sahara. More dramatically, from late 2003 to early 2004, Iraq did not even feature on the agenda of CFSP meetings and was not the subject of any CFSP instruments or initiatives, even though the issue was hotly debated in the member states, in the UN, and in bilateral contacts.

Declaratory foreign policy

CFSP has a wide scope, but this alone tells us little about its substance, added value and operationalization. When scrutinizing CFSP's output in more detail, it becomes clear that this is often limited to general principles and objectives – a routine repetition of CFSP objectives such as peaceful resolution of conflicts, rejection of the use of violence or criticizing violations of human rights. Member states' views can be easily accommodated as long as CFSP output remains uncontroversial and limits itself to general goals. The EU's identity objectives (its specific values) dominate over the EU's external objectives (influencing the international environment). This explains the dominance of a declaratory foreign policy in which activities are often rather routine and in which the policy position adopted is more about common sense than common policy.

It is important to nuance this argument. Continuously indicating where you stand in the world and *vis-à-vis* the constant stream of events is a basic function of diplomacy. Declaratory foreign policy is therefore a standard part of CFSP. It is important for the

EU to project its identity and promote its values in international politics and even relatively anodyne declarations and demarches can have some impact. However, in most cases, to make a difference on the international scene, a policy must go beyond routine declaratory foreign policy.

Operational foreign policy

On many complex foreign policy issues, the EU has only a limited or no operational foreign policy. When operational action is required, CFSP outputs are often of limited or no use because they are too vague and general. To have an operational foreign policy, the EU's representatives (Presidency, High Representative and his staff, and European diplomats in third countries) need to have the mandate, the flexibility and the instruments to intervene actively in a specific foreign policy issue. The EU must be able to react on a daily basis in a flexible and detailed way to the demands, reactions, proposals, counterproposals and often tough dilemmas that characterize international politics.

Seen from this perspective, the CFSP's output is much less substantial than it might at first appear. On many complex foreign policy issues, the EU actually has no, or only a limited, operational foreign policy. This is even the case when EU actors appear to be involved in an issue. Chris Patten (2005: 164), former Commissioner for External Relations, is cynical: 'We were consistent about one thing at least in Brussels. When we did not have a policy, we would go on a visit, or send Javier Solana, or both him and me, or the so-called Troika . . . An active presence on the ground was too often an alternative to having anything very useful to say or do once we had got there.' There are, however, a number of priority areas where CFSP has produced a significant operational foreign policy, albeit with varying levels of intensity, consistency and success (see Chapter 10). Examples include the Balkans, successful mediation in the Orange Revolution in Ukraine, Moldova/Transnistria, the Palestinian Territories, Iran, the DRC and Aceh/Indonesia.

Several factors, related to qualitative changes to CFSP since the late 1990s, help to explain both the gradual widening of the EU's operational radius and the number of successful operational foreign policy actions. The development of permanent CFSP actors in the form of the High Representative, his team and EU

Special Representatives have significantly upgraded the EU's capacity to develop, implement and sustain foreign policy initiatives. The development of new ESDP civilian and military crisis-management instruments means EU diplomatic actors can offer new kinds of concrete EU contributions in response to demands. The EU can now go beyond supporting the peaceful resolution of a conflict in words to also offering to deploy (limited) military and civilian capabilities.

Thematic priorities

This last section discusses the main thematic priorities of CFSP: human rights, non-proliferation, the export of arms, crisis management, conflict prevention, counter-terrorism and support for the International Criminal Court (Council 2006a, 2006b, 2007c, 2007d). Although EU policy on these priority areas is also analysed elsewhere in this book (particularly Chapter 8 for first pillar policies and Chapter 9 for counter-terrorism), this short assessment provides some answers to questions of the scope, reach and substance of CFSP specifically.

Human rights

In terms of visible output, human rights are traditionally at the top of CFSP priorities. Indeed the main bulk of CFSP declarations and diplomatic demarches are devoted to human rights issues. This dimension is prominent in CFSP common positions, most of which are dedicated to putting in place restrictive measures against authoritarian regimes. Human rights issues are also a major component of political dialogue with third countries and regions. Specific human rights dialogues and consultations have been established with problematic but important countries such as Russia, China and Iran.

Much of the human rights-related CFSP output fits within the declaratory foreign policy of the EU. However, CFSP has shifted up a gear with regard to some third countries and some dimensions of human rights, supplementing declarations with a broader set of negative and/or positive actions. In most cases, this also requires the involvement of first pillar instruments and actors (see Chapter 8).

Since 1998, the Council has adopted six 'EU human rights guidelines' highlighting dimensions in which to intensify initiatives in international fora and through bilateral contacts. These include the death penalty; torture and other cruel, inhuman or degrading treatment or punishment; children and armed conflict; the protection of human-rights defenders in third countries; the promotion of international humanitarian law; and human rights dialogues with third countries. These dimensions have been the subject of more intensive lobbying campaigns conducted by the Presidency, Brussels-based CFSP actors and the EU Heads of Mission in third countries and international organizations. To further support these efforts, the role of Personal Representative of the Secretary General/High Representative for Human Rights was created in early 2005.

Several critical comments can be formulated with regard to the focus on human rights in CFSP (see also Chapter 8). There is a remarkable difference in the approach adopted by CFSP and by the Commission, EP and first pillar in general. Whereas in the first pillar 'democracy, rule of law and human rights' are generally treated as a package, CFSP focuses on human rights with the promotion and defence of democracy and the rule of law receiving much less emphasis (K. Smith 2003: 140). Even the choice of human rights dimensions is illustrative in this regard. The EU has manifested itself clearly as a normative power in relation to issues such as the death penalty (Manners 2002; Lerch and Schwellnus 2006). However, the death penalty has received more attention from CFSP actors than, for instance, the defence of minority rights, which even in some EU member states remains a sensitive issue. As Sjursen (2006: 178) points out, 'while the EU's policy on the death penalty seems to support the concept of the EU as "normative" power on all levels, its position on minority protection offers a different picture'.

The strong focus on human rights can in some cases also be interpreted as a diversion from a harsher reality. It can function as a façade to mask the inability of member states to agree within the CFSP framework on more fundamental problems which have a more profound effect on the life of individuals in the countries concerned. This also puts the death penalty campaign into perspective: it is quite obvious that in many of those countries targeted (such as Sudan, the DRC, Iraq or Afghanistan), the main danger individuals face is war, chaos and poverty – and not the death penalty.

Non-proliferation and weapons of mass destruction (WMD)

Non-proliferation is one of the long-standing policy priorities of CFSP – one of the first joint actions adopted under the CFSP regime in 1994 was related to the Non-Proliferation Treaty (NPT). This was followed two years later by a joint action in support of KEDO, the Korean Peninsula Energy Development Organization, created as part of a tentative solution to North Korea's nuclear ambitions (Cornish *et al.* 1996).

However, from the outset the EU's non-proliferation policy suffered from member states' widely diverging views about the role of nuclear deterrence, with the UK and France as nuclear powers on one side and the rest of the member states on the other. This divergence was further strengthened from 1995 onwards with the accession of neutral countries to the EU, with France conducting a series of eight nuclear tests in French Polynesia (from September 1995 to January 1996) and with the French proposal for 'concerted deterrence' in 1995. This nuclear 'crisis' added to a growing cleavage within the EU, in which the Nordic countries actively countered London and Paris in international fora, and to a weakening of the EU's non-proliferation policy (Grand 2000). The result was that during the following Review Conferences of the Parties to the NPT the EU was only able to adopt a common position on part of the agenda and had no common stance on aspects of the discussion which touched on the position of London and Paris. The EU's non-proliferation policy thus increasingly amounted to useful initiatives such as supporting the physical security of nuclear installations in the former Soviet Union, but that nevertheless were at the margins of the fundamental debate on nuclear proliferation.

The 2001 terrorist attacks against the US and subsequent concern about the nuclear capabilities/ambitions of Iraq, Iran and North Korea again brought the non-proliferation issue to the heart of CFSP debates. The results of this have been mixed: the question of how to tackle concrete non-proliferation challenges led to the deepest crisis CFSP had ever suffered (with regard to Iraq) and to one of the most dynamic diplomatic efforts ever undertaken under the leadership of the three largest EU member states and the High Representative (with regard to Iran) (Borda 2005; Peimani 2006). The North Korean issue has generally gained much less CFSP attention even though this issue is indirectly threatening for Europe through the potential sale of nuclear technology to terrorist groups or radical regimes in the Middle East (see Wulf 2006).

The new priority given to non-proliferation post-2001 also took the form of an *EU Strategy against the Proliferation of Weapons of Mass Destruction*, adopted by the European Council in December 2003 as a complement to the *European Security Strategy* (European Council 2003b). The EU Strategy and related Action Plan are at the basis of an extensive operational foreign policy which includes a whole range of initiatives and concrete steps to strengthen the international non-proliferation system with regard to nuclear, biological, toxin and chemical weapons and ballistic missiles. It is clear from this extensive set of actions, including Javier Solana's appointment of a Personal Representative on non-proliferation of WMD, that the EU has passed the level of a merely declaratory foreign policy. In fact, the European strategy makes a real contribution to the fight against the proliferation of WMD and to reducing the risk of diversion (Alvarez-Verdugo 2006).

Nevertheless, the new dynamic could not conceal the enduring differences of opinion between the member states on nuclear issues. The gap between the EU's nuclear powers and other member states has even grown as, quietly, London and particularly France started to rethink their nuclear doctrine and no longer assume nuclear weapons would only be weapons of last resort. The EU and the EU3 (France, the UK and Germany) faced a serious credibility issue as they pressured third countries to sign and respect the NPT, to renounce their nuclear ambitions and to accept the non-proliferation provisions in their contractual relations with the EU, while remaining adamant that they should not give up their own nuclear privileges. But perhaps the most important weakness the EU and its nuclear powers face in terms of power politics is that, unlike the US, they are unable to provide a credible and longstanding security guarantee to third countries, which often pursue nuclear capability as an answer to their precarious security situation (see also Sauer 2004; Pullinger 2006b) .

Arms exports and combating the spread of small arms

Arms exports and the arms trade has featured on the CFSP agenda since its early days. The first initiative was the 1994 joint action on the control of exports of dual-use goods, which also involved the Commission given its external trade competence (Emiliou 1996). In 1998, the Council adopted the European Union *Code of Conduct on Arms Exports* – the beginning of a common approach to arms exports by EU member states. This Code of Conduct has been further developed and refined, but is consistently criticized for a lack of transparency and for insufficiently rigorous minimum standards for arms exports (see Bauer 2004).

Learning in part from the experience of the Balkans where arms trafficking has remained a major source of instability, with negative spillover for member states' internal security, CFSP gradually broadened its sphere of action to include the spread of small arms and light weapons (SALW). After the adoption of first joint actions supporting the collection and destruction of SALW in Albania and South East Europe, the EU broadened the geographic reach and intensity of this policy. The European Council in December 2005 adopted an *EU Strategy to Combat Illicit Accumulation and Trafficking of Small Arms and Light Weapons (SALW) and their Ammunition* (Council 2006c). Financial support was provided to projects developed by international organizations such as the OSCE and the UN in, for example, Ukraine, Cambodia and Africa. The EU also worked to develop international rules, including support for ongoing negotiations on the establishment of a legally binding international instrument on marking and tracing SALW.

Although this attention did demonstrate the EU's acknowledgement of the SALW problematic, EU policy was also criticized. Several CFSP joint actions received very limited financial resources, making them more symbolic than substantive. And, for some member states, taking a stand on SALW policy was more about inter-institutional struggles with the Commission, which considered this policy (at least with regard to Africa) as falling under EC competence. Most fundamentally, these policies only really scratched the surface, ignoring as they did the fact that EU countries are among the largest weapons producers and exporters worldwide (SIPRI 2004: 390). The *Code of Conduct on Arms Exports* may have had some positive effect, but it has not fundamentally altered the fact that a significant proportion of illicitly gathered and trafficked weapons are 'Made in the EU'.

Conflict prevention, crisis management and peacebuilding

Conflict prevention, crisis management and peacebuilding have cast a long shadow over CFSP since its inception, with the debacle in the former Yugoslavia reflecting CFSP's impotence even before its formal establishment. A major part of joint actions, common positions and other CFSP decisions have been related to crisis management and peacebuilding efforts in the Balkans (and to sanctions against the warring parties), with the administration of the Bosnian city of Mostar being one of its most important achievements.

CFSP activities in the Balkans were not part of a broader second pillar policy on conflict prevention, crisis management or peace-building. This remained the case until the Swedish Presidency of 2001, at which point conflict prevention moved up the CFSP agenda – itself a good example of the 'Europeanization' of national foreign policy priorities. The Göteborg European Council in 2001 endorsed the *EU Programme for the Prevention of Violent Conflicts*. This rather short document largely mirrored the contents of the more elaborate *Communication on Conflict Prevention* which had been presented just previously by the Commission (see Chapter 8). Like the Commission's Communication, the Council's Programme emphasized the need to address the root causes of conflicts and the distinction between 'instruments for structural long-term and direct short-term preventive actions'. The Council foresaw a yearly follow-up to its programme, including annual *Reports on the Implementation of the EU Programme for the Prevention of Violent Conflict*. Initially, the development of this priority within CFSP suffered from major constraints: the instruments for conflict prevention mostly fell under the first pillar (see Chapter 8) and the various instruments foreseen under the fledgling ESDP had not yet materialized. Moreover, it was clear that not all member states considered conflict prevention and crisis management a priority (for a detailed analysis, see Wouters and Kronenberger 2004).

CFSP's attention in this area increasingly focussed on Africa, as reflected in the 2005 common position concerning 'Conflict Prevention, Management and Resolution in Africa' and the establishment in 2006 of a 'European Concept for Strengthening African Capabilities for the Management and Prevention of Conflicts' (Council 2005a, 2006d). In its approach, CFSP prioritized strengthening African ownership in this field and supporting the development of the African Union and other African organizations' conflict prevention, management and resolution capabilities. This also aims at shifting the responsibility, burden and risks to the Africans themselves.

Combined, the emerging ESDP, the growing role of the second pillar's common actors and the support of key member states in particular foreign policy dossiers allowed the EU to enhance its activity, credibility and relevance in various crises in the world. Examples of major conflict prevention, crisis management and peace-building activities are the CFSP actions in the Balkans (which were particularly successful in FYROM) (Piana 2002), the DRC (Faria 2004; Ehrhart 2007), and Aceh/Indonesia (Braud and Grevi 2005). The EU-EU3 policy towards Iran 2004–05 can also be seen as a major (if unsuccessful) crisis-management initiative (Borda 2005). Nevertheless, as Schroeder (2006: 4) argues, the 'institutional divorce' of crisis management capacity into Council and Commission tasks has led to overlaps and tensions, and has hindered the development of a coherent cross-pillar strategy.

The fight against terrorism

The fight against terrorism is among the most all-encompassing and pillar-spanning policies of the EU as is seen clearly in the *EU Counter-Terrorism Strategy* and related Action Plan adopted by the European Council in December 2005. This policy is mainly analysed in Chapter 9. It is sufficient here to point towards some of the priorities which have been identified in the field of CFSP: the promotion of the EU's 'Radicalisation and Recruitment Strategy' in meetings with partner countries; coordination of efforts to integrate initiatives against radicalization and recruitment in wider assistance programmes; work to address terrorist propaganda; the initiation of reflection on ways to engage with non-violent Islamic organizations; delivery of technical assistance to third countries with a view to strengthening their counter-terrorism capacity;

and, negotiations in the UN on developing a comprehensive Convention against International Terrorism and attaining consensus on a UN Counter-Terrorism Strategy (for a detailed analysis, see Mahncke and Monar 2006).

Support for the International Criminal Court

The preceding overview of the CFSP's main priorities focused on broad foreign policy domains. However, CFSP has also been used for more narrowly defined policy issues which sometimes only require close attention for a couple of years. One of the most successful examples of such a CFSP priority has been the active promotion of the International Criminal Court (ICC) since the adoption of a common position on the ICC in June 2001 and an Action Plan in early 2004. The EU's activist diplomacy has been important in two respects. Firstly, the EU has been a strong and systematic lobby for the ICC through all possible CFSP actors, channels and instruments. Through negotiations and political dialogue with third countries and regions as well as diplomatic demarches and statements, the EU promoted the widest possible ratification, acceptance, approval, accession to and implementation of the Rome Statute of the ICC. In this way, the EU played a major role in securing the necessary number of states to ratify it. Secondly, through its financial assistance the EU contributed to the initial period of the Court's functioning which has since been translated into a more structured support through the signing in April 2006 of the *Agreement between the ICC and the EU on Cooperation and Assistance*. Interestingly, the EU concluded this agreement on the basis of Art. 24 TEU (which is part of the Treaty's Title V on CFSP) and not on the basis of an article from the EC Treaty.

The CFSP approach towards the ICC is probably the best example of the second pillar reflecting a structural foreign policy approach, through the promotion of a rules-based international order with an institutional and legal structure to sustain it. CFSP activism on the ICC was all the more remarkable because it pitched the EU against the United States and required that EU member states actively counter the diplomatic offensive against the ICC that Washington started through its bilateral agreements with third countries, often dependent on US support. However, it is also an example of the EU's inability to convince its most important strategic partner to change its mind on crucial issues (see also Groenleer and van Schaik 2005).

Conclusion

At the particular juncture of 1990–91, establishing the CFSP was considered a necessary diplomatic tool to create a politically stronger Union which could embed a unified Germany into a stronger European entity. And to balance this strengthened EU, placing CFSP in quarantine in a separate intergovernmental pillar was considered by most member states essential to retain full control over EU foreign policy, to avoid creeping communitarization, and particularly to counter the Commission's increasingly active and self-assured involvement in foreign policy matters. For some member states, creating a CFSP was as much about interrelational and identity goals as achieving external goals. CFSP's limited toolbox, and the fact that it was formally separated from the EU's strongest external powers organized under the first pillar, made this apparent. Nevertheless, particularly since the early 2000s, the increasing institutionalization of CFSP and the support of member states on several key dossiers have lifted CFSP from a purely declaratory machine to also undertaking operational foreign policies. In this process, the new opportunities for civilian and military intervention provided by ESDP, and discussed in the next chapter, has been critical.

Chapter 7

The European Security and Defence Policy (ESDP)

In the European integration project, security and defence have traditionally been taboo. The successive failures of the French 1950 attempt to create a European Defence Community, and the Fouchet Plans of the early 1960s, resulted in defence issues being taken off the menu. From this point onwards, whilst a vast array of policies was coordinated within the European Community, European cooperation in the field of defence was organized in NATO. This was not to change until the early 1990s, when the more integrationist-minded member states won some grand statements in the Treaty of Maastricht on 'the eventual framing of a common defence policy, which might in time lead to a common defence' (Art. J.4(1)).

However, it was not until exogenous pressure, and particularly that of the conflicts in the Balkans, that member states were forced to re-evaluate the status quo ante. Tony Blair and Jacques Chirac's 1998 Saint Malo Declaration, itself a product of its particular geopolitical context (see Chapter 2), marked a change of course. Since, the EU has incrementally sought to create an operational military and civilian crisis management capacity. By the time the TEU was being reviewed at Nice in 2000, the member states announced:

> The common foreign and security policy shall include all questions relating to the security of the Union, including the *progressive* framing of a common defence policy, which might lead to a common defence, *should the European Council so decide*. (Art. 17(1) TEU, our emphasis)

In practice, the Heads of State or Government had already taken the political decision to establish a European Security and Defence Policy during their meetings in Cologne and Helsinki in

1999. But reflecting their eagerness to avoid legally binding commitments in this policy domain, they recoiled from the idea of including the new ESDP engagements in the Treaty.

Article 17(1) and the naming of the policy as a 'European Security and Defence Policy' were somewhat misrepresentative of the actual policy being developed. ESDP is not about 'defence', and there are no 'European' forces. Nevertheless, developments in ESDP have occurred with surprising alacrity, particularly apparent when compared to the slow pace at which CFSP has developed and even more so when considering that security and defence is a touchstone of national sovereignty. This chapter provides an overview of the four main elements to ESDP – the military, civilian, industrial and technological, and political dimensions (for a comprehensive analysis of ESDP, see Howorth 2007).

The military dimension

The December 1998 Franco-British *Saint Malo Declaration*, which marked the first major step towards an ESDP, was less a meeting of vision than a compromise between two opposing views on European security. The French had traditionally promoted the idea of a European military capability autonomous of the US and NATO. This position had been juxtaposed against that of the UK, which focussed first and foremost on the primacy of the US and NATO in European security. That Britain and France moved beyond these positions towards a common ground was the fundamental prerequisite for the start-up of ESDP. In their 'Joint Declaration on European Defence', adopted during their summit meeting at Saint Malo, Blair and Chirac agreed that 'the Union must have the capacity for autonomous action, backed up by credible military forces, the means to decide to use them, and a readiness to do so, in order to respond to international crises'. In so doing, it was emphasized that Europe would be 'contributing to the vitality of a modernised Atlantic Alliance which is the foundation of the collective defence of its members' (Rutten 2001: 8–9). This paved the way for the formal adoption of the goal to establish an ESDP by the European Council in Cologne in June 1999, which in its declaration on ESDP practically repeated verbatim these crucial parts of the Saint Malo Declaration. With agreement reached in principle that the EU should be able to conduct military operations, the debate concentrated on how to actually organize this – through national assets, NATO assets or new common European assets.

Berlin Plus

The Clinton Administration's calls for increased European military efforts meant that despite historic opposition to the Europeans developing autonomous military capabilities, the US had little option but to accept ESDP. However, this was on condition that the EU guaranteed to avoid the 'three Ds' as formulated by the then Secretary of State Madeleine Albright: no decoupling (of ESDP from NATO); no duplication (of capabilities); and no discrimination (of non-EU NATO members) (Rutten 2001: 10–12). The solution finally accepted in mid-December 2002 was termed the 'Berlin Plus' arrangements, which govern the relations between the EU and NATO in crisis management. Under these arrangements, the EU can either conduct an operation autonomously or make use of NATO assets and capabilities. If it opts for the second alternative, NATO guarantees that the EU has access to its planning facilities, can request NATO to make available a NATO European command option for an EU-led military operation, and can request the use of NATO assets and capabilities. The finalization of these arrangements was an essential precursor to allowing the EU to take over the NATO operation 'Allied Harmony' in Macedonia in January 2003 and the Stabilisation Force in Bosnia and Herzegovina (SFOR) in Bosnia in 2004.

Berlin Plus is both pragmatic (Europeans alone lack core equipment and logistics necessary for military operations) and symbolic (it institutionalizes what is for many member states and the US an essential interlinking of NATO and the EU institutions). However, it is also one of the devices Washington has used to gain control over EDSP. As Gnesotto has put it: 'Both on the military and the political level, the United States therefore made its acceptance of the ESDP conditional on the Europeans not crossing a very clear red line, ruling out anything that might encourage the autonomy and, above all, the strategic independence of the Union' (2004: 24).

Soldiers and capabilities

A mere six months after its decision in Cologne to establish ESDP, the Helsinki European Council of December 1999 adopted decisions on ESDP's institutional set-up and military capabilities. The latter was translated into the *Helsinki Headline Goal*: 'cooperating voluntarily in EU-led operations, Member States must be able, by 2003, to deploy within 60 days and sustain for at least 1 year military forces of up to 50,000–60,000 persons capable of the full range of Petersberg tasks' (European Council 1999). These Petersberg Tasks, elaborated at a 1992 WEU conference, were incorporated into the TEU by the Amsterdam Treaty: Article 17.2 identifies these as 'humanitarian and rescue tasks, peacekeeping tasks and tasks of combat forces in crisis management, including peace-making'.

Although there seemed to be little difficulty providing the requisite troops, qualitative shortfalls proved much more difficult. In 2000, member states took part in a Capabilities Commitment Conference and set out their pledges in terms of military personnel and hardware in a Helsinki Forces Catalogue. This conference was the beginning of a long process to reinforce military capabilities and meet collective capability goals (see Schmitt 2004). To meet the qualitative shortfalls, a European Capabilities Action Plan (ECAP) was agreed to address shortfalls in a wide range of issues, including: air-to-air refuelling; nuclear, biological and chemical protection; special operations forces; theatre ballistic missile defence; attack and support helicopters; and intelligence and surveillance.

In May 2003, the Council agreed that the EU had operational capability across the full range of Petersberg Tasks. However, this was limited by recognized shortfalls which constrained capability in terms of deployment time and implied that risks might arise in higher intensity operations. These shortfalls concerned both forces (availability, deployability, sustainability and interoperability of forces and military equipment) and strategic capabilities (command, control and communications; intelligence; and air and naval transport capabilities). For this reason, the EU established a Capability Development Mechanism to strengthen the follow-up and evaluation of military capabilities objectives and commitments, and to ensure the coherent development of capabilities across the EU and NATO.

Whereas the 1999 Helsinki Headline Goal was largely determined by the war in Kosovo, the new *Headline Goal 2010* (HG2010) reflected the security context after the 2001 terrorist attacks against the US and the wars in Afghanistan and Iraq which followed. Endorsed by the European Council of June 2004, it focused on building a response to new, unconventional threats. In procedural terms, the member states committed themselves by 2010 to being able 'to respond with rapid and decisive action applying a fully coherent approach to the whole spectrum of crisis management operations covered by the Treaty on European Union'. Forces were to be deployable no later than ten days after the EU's decision to launch the operation. Headline Goal 2010 extended the remit of operations in which the EU might participate beyond the Petersberg Tasks to joint disarmament operations and to supporting third countries in combating terrorism and security sector reform (European Council 2004b).

Within Headline Goal 2010, member states also identified a list of specific milestones. The higher level of ambition in the Headline Goal 2010 was evidence of a qualitative leap forwards compared to the Helsinki Headline Goal. The list of high profile initiatives included: the creation of a Civilian Military Cell with the capability to set up an operation centre for a particular operation; the establishment of a European Defence Agency (EDA) in 2004; achieving by 2010 capacity and efficiency in strategic lift; the development by 2007 of rapidly deployable battlegroups; the availability of an aircraft carrier by 2008; networked linkage and compatibility of all terrestrial and space communications equipment; and quantifiable standards in deployability and multinational training for troops committed to the EU.

In terms of soldiers, attention shifted from the Helsinki Headline Goal (the capacity to deploy 50–60,000 troops) to the Battlegroup Concept. This idea originated in a trilateral proposal from France, the UK and Germany in February 2004, which was approved by the EU's Council of Ministers in April 2004. After a short transitional period, the EU Battlegroup Concept has been at full operational capability since January 2007 (EU Council Secretariat 2007b; Lindstrom 2007). EU member states have remained faithful to the basic principle of ESDP: European military capabilities are not achieved by creating permanent European forces, and even less by establishing a permanent

European army, but are based on the voluntary and temporary contribution of member states to Battlegroups.

For the EU, a Battlegroup is 1,500 troops (with appropriate support) at a high state of readiness (deployable within 15 days) and highly militarily effective (capable of high-intensity operations). The EU aims to be able to concurrently deploy two Battlegroups for a period of 30 days and up to 120 days if resupplied appropriately. Battlegroups can be formed by one nation or a group of nations and are capable of stand-alone operations or of being used for the initial phase of larger operations (for instance, of the UN). Two groups of countries take responsibility for a six-month standby period. For instance, a Nordic Battlegroup made up by Sweden, Finland, Estonia and non-EU country Norway and a second from Spain, Germany, France and Portugal are to be on standby in the first half of 2008. In the second half of the year, responsibility passes to a Battlegroup from the UK and a second made up by Germany, France, Belgium, Luxembourg and Spain.

Whether the EU Battlegroup concept proves useful or effective will only be borne out by practice. Hurdles that will need to be overcome include the operational challenges of the half-yearly rotation system, questions about the EU Battlegroups' relationship with other forces (such as the NATO Response Force and UN forces) and doubts about the rapidity of the political decision-making process. The fact that the EU Battlegroups on standby in 2006 were not used for the 2006 ESDP mission in the DRC, or for supporting the 2006 UN mission in Lebanon, already indicates that the initiative might prove insufficiently flexible for real-life conflicts (Mölling 200 6; Lindstrom 2007: 57–61).

Headquarters

Parallel to its military capabilities, ESDP requires structures to make the policy operational. On a political level, and institutionally located in the Council as part of Solana's staff, the EU Military Committee (EUMC) and EU Military Staff (EUMS) provide the requisite expertise. The EUMC, which is composed of the member states' Chiefs of Defence, is responsible for giving advice and recommendations to the Political and Security Committee (PSC) and the Council of Ministers. The EUMS provides expertise for the ESDP, particularly in the conduct of a military crisis-management operation. It is also responsible for early warning, evaluation and strategic planning for ESDP missions.

There are three options for actually undertaking an ESDP operation. The first option, under the Berlin Plus arrangements, is to make use of NATO's Operational Headquarters located in Belgium at SHAPE (Supreme Headquarters Allied Powers Europe) – with NATO's Deputy SACEUR (Supreme Allied Commander Europe) then being the Operation Commander. This option was used for Operation Concordia in the FYROM and for Operation Althea in Bosnia-Herzegovina.

The second option, for 'autonomous' ESDP operations, is to use facilities provided by one of the Operational Headquarters made available by five EU member states (France, the UK, Germany, Italy and Greece), which are then 'multinationalized' for the EU operation. In this case, the Operational Commander is also provided by the member state providing the headquarters. This option was chosen for Operations Artemis in the DRC (using the French headquarters) and EUFOR DRC (using the German headquarters).

The third option is to command missions and operations from Brussels through the EU Operations Centre (OpsCen) within the EU Military Staff under the command of a designated Operation Commander. This option, which has been available since January 2007, is particularly designed for situations where a joint civil–military response is envisaged and where no national headquarters is chosen. The EU Operations Centre is not a standing headquarters, but can be activated by a Council joint action for operations of up to 2,000 troops and civilian experts. In mid-2007, this third option had yet to be used.

This quite ambiguous third option merits special attention as its genesis is illustrative of just how laborious the institutionalization of ESDP can be. In early 2003 it was foreseen that the EU would rely on national or NATO headquarters for operations. But, some member states considered that the EU required a military planning cell or headquarters within its own institutional structures. During a meeting in April 2003, the Heads of State or Government of Belgium, France, Germany and Luxembourg proposed setting up an autonomous military headquarters for planning and conducting EU military operations without recourse to NATO assets (the Tervuren Initiative) (Missiroli 2003: 76–80). Launched in the wake of the Iraq War, this initiative provoked strong reactions in other European capitals, and in Washington, and reignited the familiar tensions of Atlantic solidarity vs European integration. London, in particular, objected fiercely to the possibility of EU institutions being able to plan and lead military actions autonomously. Nevertheless, France, Germany and Britain undertook difficult negotiations, leading to a delicate and fragile compromise, which was subsequently presented to the other EU member states on a 'take it or leave it' basis (see also Giegerich 2006).

The compromise reached, which was confirmed by the European Council in December 2003, was that the main option for conducting autonomous EU military operations would remain national headquarters, but that a small joint Civilian–Military Cell (also known as a Civ–Mil Cell) would be established within the EUMS with a capacity to rapidly set up an integrated civil–military Operations Centre (OpsCen) for a particular operation (European Council 2003a). An EU Operations Centre would consist mainly of 'double hatted' personnel from the EUMS and from member states, implying that virtually no extra personnel would be provided to the EU. As such, in its final genesis, the Civilian–Military Cell was far from the military headquarters originally proposed in the Tervuren Initiative, but did provide for limited autonomous action by the EU's institutions, thereby going beyond London's original position. This compromise stemmed from both the need to placate the sensibilities of the US and pro-Atlanticists, as well as from operational experiences, particularly in the Balkans, which emphasized the need to build further synergies between civilian and military interventions (Orsini 2006: 10; Pullinger 2006b: 14).

The civilian dimension

The development of a civilian dimension to the ESDP was originally a Swedish–Finnish initiative. For the EU's traditionally neutral states, the development of civilian crisis management capabilities was a necessary complement to the development of military capabilities. They succeeded in convincing the other member states of the validity of their approach as experience in the Balkans made it clear that for longer term stabilization, 'winning the war' was insufficient, and that special efforts were needed for 'winning the peace' (Ojanen 2000).

The Feira European Council of June 2000 defined four priority areas for the EU to develop civilian capabilities: police, strengthening the rule of law, civil administration and civil protection. It committed member states to creating, by 2003, a pool of 5,000 police officers; a pool of judges, prosecutors and civilian administration experts; as well as both assessment and intervention teams for deployment at short notice. The EU then embarked on a process of setting quantitative targets and holding pledging conferences during which member states committed national experts. Progress was rapid: by January 2003 the EU had taken over from the UN's International Police Task Force (IPTF) in Bosnia-Herzegovina (BiH) and has since clocked up an impressive number of operations.

In mid-2004, it was agreed that the range of expertise required should be broadened to reflect the multifaceted tasks being faced. This indicated that the EU was learning the lessons of its own operational experience, and that of other actors (Gourlay 2005). Two new priority areas were defined: developing capability in monitoring missions, and generic support capabilities to support EU Special Representatives or to be included in multifunctional missions. In addition, the EU was to develop the capacity to deploy multifunctional Civilian Response Teams, which could draw upon the full spectrum of expertise and be tailor made to the needs of the context.

The methodology employed to generate capabilities on the military side of ESDP was also adopted for the civilian dimension. A first Civilian Capability Commitment Conference was held in 2004 to assess member states' (voluntary) contributions against requirements, and a *Civilian Headline Goal 2008* (CHG2008) was adopted with clear objectives for the six agreed priority areas: police, rule of law, civilian administration, civil protection, monitoring capabilities and generic support capabilities. In quantitative terms, member states managed substantially to exceed their targets. However, shortfalls were identified on issues such as mission and planning support capability, adequate financing, the ability to deploy at short notice, procurement and capability requirements (forensic specialists, judges and administrative staff with financial expertise). The EU's civilian capacity was less integrated than expected and the capacity goals for 2008 in fact seemed to be unattainable (Viggo Jakobsen 2006). In late 2006, a second Civilian Capability Commitment Conference again focused on these shortfalls.

A brief overview of the six priority areas provides a snapshot of the EU's ambitions with regard to civilian crisis management capabilities. In terms of *police* capabilities, the EU aims to be capable of carrying out any police operation from strengthening missions (advisory, assistance and training tasks) to substitution missions (where the international force acts as a substitute for local police forces). Of a pool of more than 5,000 police officers, 1,400 are to be deployable in less than 30 days. The Police Action Plan prioritized the planning of operations, including developing the capability to establish rapidly operational headquarters and assemble Integrated Police Units (IPUs). Independent of the IPUs, France, Italy, Spain, Portugal and the Netherlands have also developed a European Gendarmerie Force to be made available first and foremost to the EU, but also to other organizations such as the UN or OSCE.

To meet its ambitions in the *rule of law*, a Rule of Law Commitment Conference was held during which member states committed officials, some of whom were to be deployable within 30 days. Rule of law missions, similar to police missions, are to be capable of both strengthening and temporarily substituting for the local judiciary/legal system. Under the *civilian administration* rubric, a pool of more than 500 experts has been created capable of carrying out civilian administration missions to provide basic services that the national or local administration is unable to offer. This covers a broad range of tasks such as elections, taxation or social services. In *civil protection*, the EU has also achieved its objective of developing assessment and/or coordination teams of ten experts which could be dispatched within seven hours as well as intervention teams of up to 2,000 people and additional specialized services. More than 500 experts have been committed for the establishment of a *monitoring capability*. Tasks of monitoring missions could include, for example, border monitoring, human rights monitoring or observing the general political situation. This capability has been designed to improve the EU's presence at all stages of conflict intervention. Finally, the EU has identified areas of expertise which could be useful as *generic support capabilities* to support the work of EU Special Representatives or form part of multifaceted ESDP missions. The pool of 400 personnel includes experts in the field of human rights, political affairs, security sector reform (SSR), mediation, border control, disarmament, demobilization and reintegration (DDR) and media policy (on the EU strategy for SSR, see Helly 2006a, 2006b).

To operationalize and lead civilian crisis management, the EU has developed structures at both the political and operational level. The Committee for Civilian Aspects of Crisis Management (CIVCOM), established in 2001, works at the political level, providing information, giving advice to the PSC and COREPER, and assuring follow-up with regard to civilian crisis management capabilities and operations. On an operational level, the joint Civilian–Military Cell (discussed above) provides the locus for launching civilian crisis management operations. In institutional terms, the civilian side of ESDP is markedly smaller than its military counterpart. Whilst there are around 200 people in the EUMS, there are 40 people working in the Council Secretariat on civilian crisis management. Furthermore, whilst the military dimension has the luxury of recourse to NATO or national headquarters for planning and operational control, EU staff working on civilian operations do not have the potential back-up of external planning entities. The EU can also rely on the civilian crisis management instruments of the first pillar (see Chapter 8). However, these partially complementary, partially overlapping, competences of the EC give rise to turf battles between ESDP actors and the Commission, as well as risking undermining the consistency and effectiveness of the EU's crisis management policy.

The development and deployment of civilian capabilities does come with another particular set of challenges in terms of consistency and inter-actor coordination. Civilian crisis management implicates a wider set of national actors within foreign policy. In addition to Foreign or Defence Ministers, ministries of interior affairs, justice, policing and others are involved, each with its own bureaucracy, procedures and cultures. Moreover, establishing and deploying civilian capabilities cannot be treated in the same way as the military. Two factors are relevant here. Firstly, difficulties in extracting civilian experts from their domestic duties, and in providing sufficient incentives for them to undertake foreign missions, implies that the pool of potential personnel must be large. Problems also result from the different personnel statutes of on the one hand soldiers and on the other civilian personnel – working abroad is normal for the former, whereas extracting judges or policemen from domestic duties and asking them to leave on short notice is more complex and more expensive. Secondly, contributing governments can also be rather reluctant to part with certain resources, particularly where these are in relatively short supply at the national level. Forensics experts and narcotics police, for example, are expensive, and prized domestic resources (see Hansen 2004: 177–80).

Civilian and military operations

Considering that ESDP was only launched in 1999, the time lag between the rhetoric and the reality of civilian and military operations has been relatively slight. In the Laeken Declaration of December 2001, ESDP was declared operational. Although stretching the truth at that time, a year later this statement stood. By June 2007, the EU had undertaken four military operations in the Balkans and the DRC, 13 civilian operations in the Balkans, the DRC, Georgia, Iraq, Aceh/Indonesia and Afghanistan, and one civilian–military operation to support the African Union in Darfur (Sudan). Table 7.1 provides an overview of operations launched up to June 2007.

Before analysing ESDP operations, it is important to recall that EU member states also engage in military operations outside the ESDP framework. For example, with more than 7,000 troops EU member states provided around half of the personnel and the operational command for the UN mission in Lebanon (UNIFIL-II), following the Israel–Lebanon crisis of July 2006. Even though the political decision to contribute was adopted by the member states during the External Relations Council of August 2006, the member states rejected the involvement of the Council Secretariat's military and security apparatus, including Solana, and the contribution did not take the form of an ESDP operation (Pirozzi 2006a; Dembinski 2007).

Given that civilian and military operations are being launched in rapid succession, it is useful to identify criteria through which operations, both past and future, can be understood. In this light,

Table 7.1 Overview of ESDP operations

Operation	Objective	Type of mission	Scope
MILITARY			
Operation Concordia (FYROM, 2003)	To ensure a stable, secure environment to facilitate the implementation of the Ohrid Framework Agreement	Berlin Plus	400 forces
Operation Artemis (DRC, 2003)	Stabilization of security conditions and the improvement of the humanitarian situation in Bunia, North-East DRC	Autonomous (EU OHQ in France)	1,700 forces
EUFOR Althea (BiH, 2004–)	To contribute to a secure environment with objective of signing the EU AA	Berlin Plus	7,000 forces; reduced to 2,500 in 2007
EUFOR DR CONGO (DRC, 2006)	Securing the region during elections, in cooperation with the Congolese authorities (in support of the MONUC)	Autonomous (EU OHQ in Germany)	Over 1,000 forces; rapid force available
CIVILIAN			
EUPM (BiH, 2003–07)	Support local police capacity including to develop independence and accountability; fight organized crime; create institutions	Police	495 police officers and 59 additional staff
Operation Proxima (FYROM, 2003–05)	To consolidate law and order; reform of the Interior Ministry; promoting integrated border management; confidence building	Police	200 police experts

EUPOL KINSHASA (DRC 2005–07)	To monitor, mentor and advise the IPU until national elections	Police	Approx 30 staff members
EUJUST THEMIS (Georgia, 2004–05)	To support reform of criminal justice system	Rule of law	10 international civilian experts
EUJUST LEX (Iraq, 2005–2007)	Support to criminal justice system through training of judges, magistrates, senior police, etc., training in the EU and liaison office in Baghdad	Rule of law	800 judges and police officers
Aceh Monitoring Mission (AMM) (Aceh, 2005–06)	Monitors the implementation of aspects of the peace agreement signed by Indonesia and the Free Aceh Movement on 15 August 2005	Monitoring mission	Approx 80 unarmed personnel
EUPAT (FYROM 2005–06)	Follows termination of Proxima. To support the development of an efficient and professional police service	Police	30 police advisors
EUPOL COPPS (Palestinian Territories 2005–08)	To provide enhanced support to the Palestinian Authority in establishing sustainable and effective policing arrangements	Police	Approx 33 unarmed police and civilian experts
EUBAM RAFAH (Palestinian Territories 2005–08)	To monitor (third party presence) the operations of the border crossing point at Rafah (Gaza)	Border assistance mission	Approx 55 police officers, increased to 75

CIVILIAN

Table 7.1 Continued

	Operation	Objective	Type of mission	Scope
CIVILIAN	EUSEC DR CONGO (DRC, 2005–06)	An EU advisory and assistance mission for security sector reform	Security sector reform	8 experts
	Border Assistance Mission to Moldova and Ukraine (Moldova/Ukraine, 2005–07)	The mission helps to prevent smuggling, trafficking and customs fraud by providing advice and training	Border assistance mission	69 experts and 50 local support staff
	EUPOL AFGHANISTAN (Afghanistan, 2007–10)	The mission will help to develop a self-sustaining capacity to build and maintain a civil police service	Police	160 police and justice sector experts
	EUPT for Kosovo (Kosovo, 2006–)	To prepare for a possible future operation in Kosovo	Rule of law Police	45 officials
CIV/MIL	EU support to Amis II (Darfur) (Sudan, 2005–)	To support the African Union and its political, military and police efforts to address the crisis in the Darfur region of Sudan	Civilian–military	31 police officers, 17 military experts and 10 military observers

Note: Situation as at June 2007.
Source: Council (2007e).

the following six questions indicate some principal axes along which operations can be analysed.

The role of an ESDP operation in the international response to a crisis varies considerably. The first key question is: *Does the EU have the main role or is it an understudy?* For example, the EU is a major actor in ensuring peace in Bosnia-Herzegovina through its EUFOR Althea which took over from NATO's SFOR in 2004 (see Juncos 2006). In the DRC, on the other hand, the EU is a small cog in a much larger wheel. The scope of the EU's contributions in both its military and civilian operations in the DRC has been very limited when compared to the size of the international presence there – the UN's MONUC has more than 16,000 uniformed personnel, including 15,000 troops, with 50 countries contributing military forces (including ten EU member states) and police coming from 25 countries (including two EU member states) (see Faria 2004; Ulriksen *et al.* 2004). It is not a criticism to argue that the EU is the understudy. ESDP operations are one of the primary ways in which the EU can demonstrate its commitment to 'effective multilateralism' (see Chapter 11).

The second key question is: *what is the added value of a given operation?* The scope of operations, in terms of duration, numbers of people involved and so on can mask the added value of an initiative. For example, Operation Artemis had a mandate of only three months and the scope of its deployment was extremely limited (Bunia town and up to 15 km outside). It nevertheless fulfilled a crucial stop-gap function before the deployment of further UN forces, providing short-term stabilization in a high intensity environment at a time when no other international actor was willing or able to provide this capacity (Faria 2004: 52). In undertaking the Aceh Monitoring Mission, again relatively small in scope, the EU had high added value. Indeed, it was the only organization which both parties in Aceh would accept to undertake this mission (see Braud and Grevi 2005; Pirozzi 2006b). At the other end of the spectrum, EUFOR Althea in Bosnia-Herzegovina comprises more than 7,000 troops, no time limits have been set on its duration and the scope of the mission is broad (Osland 2004). However, NATO continues to play an important role in controlling the operation. Given that it had earned a solid reputation in the region whilst the Europeans were still remembered for their dithering during the 1990s, the military added value of this specifically ESDP mission is less clear.

Although decisions to launch an ESDP operation are not easily reached, they can mask a lack of agreement as to the EU's overarching policy goals. The third key question is thus: *to what extent is an operation backed up by a coherent use of instruments?* The extent to which coherence is ensured even across ESDP operations in a given country varies. The EUPM in Bosnia-Herzegovina focused on building the capacity of local police to tackle organized crime and stressed local ownership. However, this was undermined by EUFOR's Integrated Police Unit which conducted high profile anti-organized crime operations, but did not even inform local police (Orsini 2006: 10). Related to this is the scope of follow-up to an ESDP operation and the extent to which the rest of the EU's foreign policy toolbox is used, and used coherently. In some cases, this has worked well. The Commission's long-term engagement with the Palestinian Authorities created the conditions necessary to deploy ESDP missions. In Aceh, the Commission had been involved in the peace process from the outset supporting negotiations and providing aid to support demobilization, disarmament and reintegration through the Rapid Reaction Mechanism (see Chapter 8). The use of these first pillar policies made an important contribution to the effectiveness of the ESDP Monitoring Mission. And, ahead of the planned 2007 rule of law mission in Kosovo, High Representative Solana and Commissioner for Enlargement Olli Rehn have presented joint papers outlining their joint approach (Zehetner 2007: 5). But of course the picture is not all rosy. The priorities of the Commission in implementing longer-term assistance programmes and establishing contractual relations are not always the same as the Council's political priorities, as has been particularly evident in the Balkans. In other cases, it is not clear how Community projects will support the short-term impact of ESDP operations.

The issue of political convergence also relates to levels of interest in a given country or operation. The fourth key question is: *is an operation an EU priority or a member state pet project?* Even if all EU operations nominally have the support of all member states through the Council, not all operations are of equal importance for all member states. It is clear that the driving force behind operations in the DRC comes from Belgium and France; operations in Iraq predominantly from the UK, Italy and Poland; and the Aceh mission from the Nordic member states and the

Netherlands. In contrast, operations in the Balkans are prioritized by all member states, even if this does not always translate
into providing the resources that missions require. Related to this
point is the question: *how 'common' is an operation?* This can
often be deduced from quantitative contributions from particular member states (France provided nearly all the troops for
Artemis), the involvement of other international actors (take
NATO in Bosnia-Herzegovina, for example) and also the extent
of participation from non-EU states (in Aceh, 130 personnel
were from the EU with the remaining 100 being provided by
ASEAN countries).

The objectives laid out on paper for a given ESDP operation
can conceal other objectives. The sixth and final key question is
thus: *what are the objectives behind an operation?* An operation
may be as important for domestic political consumption within
member states as its impact on a third country. For example, a
target country may be of particular historical significance for a
member state's population (for example Belgium and the DRC)
or, conversely, action at EU level may offer legitimation for a
national action which has received a weak reception domestically (for example the UK, the Netherlands, Poland and Italy *vis-
à-vis* EUJUST LEX in Iraq). The EU may deem it advantageous
to be involved in a particular country to demonstrate its commitment, irrespective of the size of a given operation. For example,
the decision to launch a very small rule of law mission with only
ten experts in Georgia in 2004 (EUJUST THEMIS) was an
important symbolic gesture, as well as an effective mission, at a
delicate time in Georgia's reform process (see Kurowska 2006).
Sometimes it is enough for the EU just to be doing something,
irrespective of whether the impact is particularly far-reaching or
the operation could have been carried out by other actors. Of
course, an operation may also fulfil a particular goal with regard
to a third party, for example an international organization or
state, rather than being focused on the country subject to the
ESDP operation. In this light, we could understand EUJUST LEX
in Iraq as being developed because of the member states' desire to
improve US–EU relations after the re-election of George Bush in
2004. And, the ESDP mission in Darfur can be understood as an
attempt by France and other member states to counterbalance
the fact that NATO has begun to play a role in Africa (see also
Gourlay and Monaco 2005).

The industrial and technological dimension

The EU suffers from serious shortfalls in military capabilities which impact on its capacity to undertake operations. The EU is attempting to remedy these through the Headline Goal 2010 process, but its efforts are undermined by three issues: insufficient defence budgets, a fragmented defence market and uncoordinated spending patterns.

The US has long lambasted its European partners for the size of their defence budgets – in 2005 EU member states' annual defence budget was €193 billion whilst that of the US was around €406 billion (EDA 2006a: 2). However, on paper €193 billion should be ample to meet European defence ambitions. The stumbling block is as much the fragmentation of expenditure as the total amounts being spent. It is also a question of how expenditure is directed. For example, too much is concentrated on conscript troops and outdated equipment which are irrelevant for foreign missions.

Defence related industries have largely been left outside the regulatory framework governing the EU internal market, which in part accounts for their fragmented nature. According to Article 296 TEC, any member state can 'take such measures as it considers necessary for the protection of the essential interests of its security which are connected with the production of or trade in arms, munitions and war material'. Although subject to certain conditions, this clause has been used as a carte blanche to exclude defence procurement from Community rules (Schmitt 2005: 7). Defence markets in the EU are dominated by France, the UK and, to a much lesser extent, Germany. The fragmented nature of these markets implies a lack of competition which drives up prices and negatively impacts on innovation.

All of these problems are amplified by the uncoordinated nature of defence spending. For example, in 2005 only 12.4 per cent of defence R&T (Research and Technology) expenditure was spent collectively (EDA 2006b: 9). Member states do not have the budget to bankroll individually large-scale procurement or research projects, and by failing to coordinate expenditure, major shortfalls at the EU level are not addressed. This has a negative impact on the extent to which European defence spending actually translates into operational capability. Furthermore, since the EU does not have its 'own' forces but draws on member state capabilities, interoperability is also a prerequisite for effective ESDP operations. In practice, this can result in countries being excluded from operations because their participation would be just too complicated. The first area of the EU's response to these challenges is in research. More research and development of weapons systems at a European level is essential to ensure interoperability of member states' armed forces and to meet high costs. Cooperating and coordinating research efforts has been targeted by the Commission as an area in which Community level action can add value, even if in formal terms the Commission can only support civilian rather than defence research. Under the 6th Framework Programme (2002–06), aeronautics and space were allocated €1,075 million. The Commission has thus supported dual-use research which has some benefits for ESDP. It is attempting to increase its role through the 7th Research Framework Programme (2007–10) in which it has developed a European Security Research Programme. On the intergovernmental level, one of the European Defence Agency's four functions is to promote European defence-relevant R&T. This involves pursuing collaborative use of national defence R&T budgets to meet priorities set at the EU level.

The second area of response has been to address the fragmentation of the European market in defence equipment. In July 2006, 22 member states implemented a voluntary defence procurement regime. This works on the basis of a Code of Conduct under which defence contract opportunities worth at least €1 million and which fall under the scope of Article 296 TEC (exempting them from EC Public Procurement Directives) are to be advertised. Defence Ministers must evaluate all bids from companies based across the 22 participating nations on the basis of clearly stated criteria. By thus launching a European Defence Equipment Market (EDEM), the EU hopes to increase competition and transparency in defence procurement. However, the regime is voluntary and there are no enforcement mechanisms. The EDA will monitor and report on its implementation, but it remains to be seen whether national governments will hand juicy defence procurement contracts to foreign companies if this risks negatively impacting the national defence industry. Meanwhile, the Commission (2004e) is continuing work which started with its 2004 Green Paper on those defence procurement issues not covered by the Article 296 exemption and hence subject to normal EU regulation.

Finally, in terms of joint procurement initiatives, there has been significant cooperation between member states, but generally outside the EU framework. Specific joint ventures include the production of fighter jets such as Eurofighter (Germany, Italy, Spain, the UK) and the Swedish–British Gripen. Several fora also exist for armaments cooperation including the Western European Armaments Group/Organization (WEAG/O), the Organisation for Joint Armaments Cooperation (OCCAR) and the Letter of Intent (LoI) Framework Agreement between Britain, France, Germany, Italy, Spain and Sweden. However, such cooperative ventures have both run into difficulty (Eurofighter jets arrived ten years after their original target date and massively over budget) and failed to have an overarching positive impact on the European market. Indeed, Schmitt argues the situation has been aggravated by the complex institutional and industrial settings as well as the creation of ad hoc structures for each project (Schmitt 2003: 10–11).

The logic behind establishing a European Defence Agency, proposed by Blair and Chirac at the Le Touquet summit of February 2003, was to address exactly these kinds of issues. The EDA, established through a June 2004 Council Joint Action, is mandated 'to support the Member States and the Council in their effort to improve defence capabilities in the field of crisis management and to sustain the European Security and Defence Policy as it stands now and develops in the future' (Council 2004b: 18). It is headed by the CFSP's High Representative, although it is a separate agency rather than part of any EU institution. Its four functions are: defence capabilities development; armaments cooperation; the European Defence, Technological and Industrial Base (EDTIB) and EDEM; and research and technology. The logic is that by providing one agency with an overview of these different agendas, it should be able to realize the potential synergies between the different areas and develop combined proposals.

A final dimension of the industrial side to ESDP is the development of self-sufficiency in strategic space technology and an autonomous space capability. Under the second pillar, the EU created by a Council Joint Action in 2004 the European Union Satellite Centre (EUSC) in Torrejon, Spain. Dedicated to the exploitation and production of information derived from analysing earth observation space imagery, it has a role feeding into ESDP. However, the most important player in the development of Europe's space ambitions is the European Space Agency (ESA), which is responsible for drawing up and carrying out the European Space Programme in association with the EU (and particularly the European Commission), the member states, national agencies and industry. Burzykowska (2006: 37) argues that:

> ESA's capabilities are indispensable in shaping the European security and defence dimension. Such capabilities are guaranteeing independent access to space, developing industrial infrastructure, operational platforms and ground infrastructure, and many other key technologies and services for effective data gathering, and processing and dissemination. These are fundamental to all forms of security operations.

ESA has oversight of the development of Ariane satellite launchers and testing facilities, which provide the strategic components of a European autonomous space capability – in effect Europe's guaranteed and independent access to space (Braunschvig *et al.* 2003). In 2000, ESA and the European Commission launched two key strategic flagship projects: the Galileo satellite radio navigation system and the Global Monitoring for Environment and Security (GMES) programme. Unlike its US counterpart the Global Positioning System (GPS), Galileo is designed specifically for civilian and commercial use and is under civilian management. It also provides an interesting dimension to the EU's geostrategic toolbox as Russia, China, India and Israel, among others, have signed a cooperation agreement with the Galileo programme. While it is designed for civilian use, it could in the future have ramifications for ESDP projects, making it possible to locate land mines or direct missiles, for example. Similarly, while the civilian side of GMES is emphasized, it is clear that in the future it might provide crucial tools to support surveillance of borders, critical sites and installations.

The developments analysed above testify to the growing role of the industrial and technological dimension of ESDP in the drive towards EU 'martial potency' (Manners 2006: 182). As Manners emphasizes, the gradual but pervasive securitization and militarization of EU policies is not only an answer to the challenges which the international environment throws up. It is also the result of what he labels the European 'military–industrial simplex': 'the way in which both the military–armaments lobby and the technology–industrial lobby have worked at the EU level to create a simple but compelling relationship between the need for forces capable of robust intervention [and] the technological and industrial benefits of defence and aerospace research' (2006: 193) (see also Mörth 2003; Mawdsley *et al.* 2004). This also indicates that the involvement of powerful but barely visible non-state actors may be a crucial factor in explaining the remarkably swift growth and operationalization of ESDP.

The political dimension

Three interlinking issues of the political dimension to ESDP are discussed here: legitimacy, political leadership and ESDP without a European foreign policy.

There are two levels to the legitimacy issue – legitimacy in terms of parliamentary oversight and legitimacy in terms of the visibility of ESDP and public support. Whether there is indeed a legitimacy problem at the heart of ESDP is largely open to interpretation (see also Wagner 2006). The European Parliament is certainly sidelined, implying that the flag bearers of the EP as the key to democratic legitimacy and oversight within EU activities are rather critical. Given that voting in the Council is governed by unanimity, arguably the democratically elected national executives participating in decision-making guarantee the requisite legitimacy. However, whether national parliaments are able to effectively scrutinize their executives through the corridors of Brussels is questionable. Rightly or wrongly, parliaments do tend to be sidelined in foreign policy anyway and we tend to concern ourselves rather less with the democratic accountability of executives in foreign policy-making in institutions such as the UN and NATO.

The EU also faces a publicity problem in ESDP. Operations tend to be about conflict prevention and peacekeeping, implying that there is little to report back to the average citizen – 'no war today' is not an eye-catching newspaper headline. National presses tend to focus on major international conflicts and crises, where the EU is often absent, or on those countries, regions or issues prioritized by that member state, where the EU is generally inactive and where national initiatives receive more column space anyway. Combined, this implies that the public literally does not see (on television or in newspapers) that there is an EU foreign policy or an ESDP. This is problematic for the EU as public opinion polls demonstrate that foreign and security policy is one of the domains in which the public wants an active EU, with 75 per cent of the EU population being in favour of a common defence and security policy (and 68 per cent in favour of a common foreign policy) (Commission 2006a: 22–7; see also Höse and Oppermann 2007).

To date, operations have run smoothly. But, this may not always be the case, which brings us to the second point – the question of where the ultimate political responsibility for ESDP operations lies. The European Council is at the apex of ESDP. This, of course, brings its own challenges – in a crisis situation, decision-making by committee is not ideal. However, if an ESDP operation runs into real trouble – a major violent escalation and geographic spread of a conflict, including a high number of casualties, for example – it is not clear where political leadership and responsibility might lie. The ultimate political responsibility for soldiers on the ground lies in the hands of their respective national governments and parliaments, which, in times of crises, can decide to withdraw their troops, potentially leaving the operation in limbo.

This is related to the third point – the risks inherent in an ever more enhanced ESDP without a sufficiently developed European foreign policy. This potential obstacle to ESDP tends to be neglected. Developing ESDP and undertaking military and civilian crisis management operations has not been paralleled by the same level of developments in a common foreign policy. ESDP operations can be misleading, giving the impression that the EU has an agreed, coherent and comprehensive foreign policy towards the issue at hand. A common foreign policy on a specific issue may exist in terms of general objectives and in terms of supporting peace efforts initiated by others, but often there is not actually a substantive or deep agreement on how to deal with an issue (see Chapter 6). Agreeing to ESDP operations risks becoming a surrogate for a comprehensive and detailed common foreign policy towards specific issues, particularly since ESDP operations are often based on preliminary political solutions provided by other actors (such as the UN, mediators like Martti Ahtisaari in Aceh, or the Contact Group and particularly the US in the Balkans). Central Africa and particularly the Middle East are prime examples of areas where EU member states can agree to ESDP operations, but where political disagreement could very easily emerge on foreign policy *vis-à-vis* these regions, and hence the course to be followed in case of escalation.

Conclusion

This chapter has explored the current status of the EU's attempts to move beyond the political, diplomatic and economic realm which historically defines the Union's foreign policy into the sphere of conventional foreign policy. The speed of change in ESDP is rather impressive when considering both the sensitive nature of the policy field and the various structural impediments discussed. Below the surface of the ESDP dynamic of the EU as a whole lies the much more decisive new dynamic between the UK, France and Germany. ESDP has been able to move forward as it has been increasingly perceived by the member states as a positive-sum game in which the added value of ESDP as a military actor – as compared to acting unilaterally and/or the interventions of international organizations and the US – has been recognized.

Chapter 8

EU Foreign Policy beyond CFSP

This chapter analyses policy fields developed under the Community framework but which in many cases represent the lynchpin of the EU's foreign policy – trade, association and cooperation agreements; development; crisis management and conflict prevention; and the promotion of human rights and democracy. These Community policies have shaped the form of EU foreign policy; are in some cases foreign policy in and of themselves; provide the major instruments of EU foreign policy; yet can also hinder the achievement of EU foreign policy objectives.

We are not interested here in the EU's external relations, but in the EU's foreign policy. The difference is not semantic. As becomes clear in the sections which follow, the vast network of relations the EU has with practically all countries and regions of the world do not alone constitute foreign policy. Rather, we are looking at the manner in which the EU uses these relations and Community instruments to pursue a foreign policy, what this foreign policy actually looks like and how effective it is. In this context it is useful to question the dominant perspectives of foreign policy and to use the concept of structural foreign policy (see Chapter 1). Structural foreign policy provides an analytical perspective allowing us to broaden and update our view of foreign policy without falling into the pitfall of portraying all external relations as foreign policy. This concept makes it easier to recognize the – actual or potential – foreign policy dimension of policies and instruments that are traditionally considered as being only within the realm of 'external relations' or 'external policy'.

Trade

Trade power with foreign policy fallout

The EU accounts for approximately one fifth of world trade: it is the world's leading exporter and second biggest importer. The EU's only direct trading competitor is the US. The EU has a larger market than the US (a population of 490 million compared to the America's 300 million). But this pales in comparison to the growing economies of China and India with their populations of 1,300 million and 1,100 million respectively. With growth rates far outstripping the EU and the US, China and India are key economic competitors, and increasing market access to fast growing markets is essential for the EU to maintain its trade dominance.

The Common Commercial Policy (CCP) (Art. 133 TEC) is at the origin of the EU as an international actor. Trade policy forced the EU to define its relations with the rest of the world and also created expectations in third countries that the EU was a major power (see Redmond 1992). This gradually entailed foreign policy related choices. The EU quietly became an international actor and then also a foreign policy actor even though such a role had not initially been foreseen or supported by all member states. Or, to use the concepts launched by Sjøstedt (1977) and Allen and Smith (1990) and further developed by Bretherton and Vogler (2006), the 'presence' of the EU in the world was so significant that it was also compelled to develop further its 'actorness'.

In terms of its representation to the external environment, the EU's trade and foreign policies are inextricably linked. On the one hand, trade policy provides essential instruments for foreign policy, including through sanctions, embargoes and support measures. On the other hand, the EU's trade and agricultural policies can undermine foreign and development policy objectives, including poverty reduction. Trade is not 'just' an external policy. The type of trade policy conducted by the EU, both in multilateral fora and *vis-à-vis* specific third countries, can affect their economies and, indirectly, their political systems, societies and the welfare of individuals. This impact – positive or negative in terms of human security, societal security and political stability (see Chapter 1) – also determines the international security context in which the EU is embedded and in which it operates as a foreign policy actor.

Trade has never been apolitical, but the furore surrounding WTO meetings, including the vehement protests lead by anti-globalization protestors since Seattle, is testimony to its increasingly political nature. The most recent round of multilateral liberalization was formally suspended by the WTO in July 2006. The so-called 'Doha Development Round' collapsed amid highly vocal mutual recriminations between the EU, the US and developing countries. These tensions revolved around agriculture (developing countries sought increased developed-world market access for their agricultural products and reductions in agricultural production and export subsidies) and non-agricultural market access (the US and EU sought increased market access to emerging economies like China, Brazil and India for their industrial goods through a reduction in industrial tariffs). The EU had also been pushing for services liberalization, reflecting the fact that services represent over 70 per cent of its economy, and other behind-the-border measures: investment, competition policy, government procurement and trade facilitation (the so-called 'Singapore issues') (see Woolcock 2005).

While the EU's rhetoric is all about international trade liberalization, its practice does not bear this out across the board. As Meunier and Nicolaïdis put it, 'the issue is not only how much liberalisation, but also what kind of liberalisation and for whose benefit' (2005: 260). The EU's determination to defend its Common Agricultural Policy (CAP), which also soaks up 40 per cent of its budget, has a serious negative impact on its capacity to achieve goals in international trade negotiations, as well as foreign policy goals such as poverty eradication. Agriculture makes up a small proportion of the EU economy, but it is the mainstay of many developing countries' economies, especially the poorest, accounting for 40 per cent of GDP, 35 per cent of exports and 50–70 per cent of total employment (DEFRA and HM Treasury 2005: 51).

Measures have been taken to reform the CAP. 'De-coupling', replacing a system which linked payments with the volume of production with a 'single farm payment', has reduced pressure to overproduce, thus decreasing dumping of agricultural produce on the world market and distortions of local markets. And, agreement was reached at WTO negotiations in Hong Kong in

December 2005 to phase out export subsidies by 2013. However, market price support reforms, which rely on high import tariffs to maintain artificially high prices, have not been sufficiently far-reaching to have a substantial positive impact on external competitors (DEFRA and HM Treasury 2005). Meanwhile, tariffs and non-tariff barriers (administrative procedures or health and safety standards, for example) on agricultural goods entering the EU market effectively limit imports and protect domestic producers.

In its decision-making, the EU often disregards the political dimension and the broader external impact of its trade policy. Core EU foreign policy objectives, including its commitment to 'effective multilateralism' and the integration of developing countries into the world economy, are fragile when pitched against the realpolitik of protecting Europe's farmers. Where trade objectives are weighed against development or foreign policy objectives, the trade perspective indeed tends to dominate.

Through its 'Everything but Arms' (EBA) initiative adopted in February 2001, the EU tried to mitigate the negative side effects of its trade and agricultural policies on developing countries. The initiative provides for the 49 countries belonging to the Least Developed Countries (LDC) group to be granted duty-free access for all exports to the EU market (except arms and munitions) without any quantitative restrictions. But, imports of bananas, rice and sugar (key markets for many LDCs) were not fully liberalized immediately given their sensitivity to EU producers. Proponents argue this is an important development tool. Others are more cynical, arguing these countries are so removed from competing in the international economy that they have virtually nothing to trade anyway, which makes the initiative quite 'cheap' for the EU (see Page and Hewitt 2002; Yu and Jensen 2005).

The EC's dominance in trade and the fact that it led the EU to develop an international role, and then a foreign policy, has meant that trade has been influential in shaping the nature and form of EU foreign policy. It is unlikely that EU foreign policy would rely so heavily on contractual agreements, through which the EU provides preferential access to the internal market as well as financial and technical aid, if it were not such a strong actor in trade. The decision to conclude a trade agreement with a third country/regional organization, as well as the depth and scope of this agreement, is to a large extent foreign policy. The EU also attempts to use trade agreements to pursue specific foreign policy objectives, for example seeking to incorporate environmental and labour standards in WTO agreements. The EU's attempts to expand its regulatory practice and values have been resisted by developing countries, which perceive such moves as yet another form of protectionism (Bretherton and Vogler 2006: 86).

While the Common Commercial Policy makes trade in goods (which dominated the international trade agenda in 1957) an exclusive EC competence, today other issues such as services and intellectual property, which are areas of shared competence, are at least as important. The Commission's fight against this erosion of its competence has so far proved unsuccessful. However, in practice the EU continues to negotiate as a block on all issues, with the Commission acting as the member states' mouthpiece. Although the EU is largely a 'single' actor in international trade, this does not make it a monolith. Member states not only differ in their economic interests in third countries or regions, but also the extent to which trade-related interests should dominate foreign policy interests. Clearly, third countries can and do make use of such points of divergence within the EU and use their contacts with 'friendly' EU member states to promote their cause (see Bretherton and Vogler 2006: 78–80; Kerremans 2004, 2007).

Sanctions

Sanctions or restrictive measures are a frequently used policy instrument, with the objective of bringing about change in the activities or policies of third states, individuals from third states or non-state entities such as terrorist groups. Measures undertaken include specific or general trade restrictions and, beyond trade, also suspension of cooperation with a third country, arms embargoes, interruption or reduction of diplomatic relations and travel or visa bans. The link between the first pillar and CFSP is particularly important in the realm of sanctions (see Chapter 6). This is the only domain in which an explicit and legally binding second pillar decision is needed for a Community measure to be taken. The political decision to implement sanctions is taken through a common position under the CFSP. If this calls for Community action to implement some or all of the measures involved, the European Commission presents a proposal for a Council

Regulation to the Council of Ministers, in accordance with Articles 60 and 301 TEC.

Sanctions can be either autonomous EU sanctions or (more often) common positions which implement UN Security Council Resolutions (see Eeckhout 2004: 422–53). By nature reactive, these tools generally respond to the use of violence by third states and violations of human rights, international law, the rule of law and democratic principles. The challenge with imposing trade sanctions or embargoes is that as a blanket ban, they cannot be fine-tuned to ensure they only affect their targets. Indeed, the effectiveness of economic sanctions is highly questioned. As Koutrakos argues, 'they are ineffective in terms of both the objectives they seek to achieve and the cost their imposition entails' (2001: 50). Risking high humanitarian and economic costs, trade sanctions are now used only in limited cases, with non-trade sanctions such as targeted financial restrictions (for example freezing funds) and travel and visa bans now being more common.

Association and cooperation agreements

The nature of agreements

Association and cooperation agreements are based on economic instruments such as access to the internal market and the provision of aid. However, these agreements have become increasingly political over the last decades and are today a key component of the EU's foreign policy beyond CFSP. There are three types of agreements:

- pure trade agreements (Art. 133 TEC);
- trade and economic cooperation agreements (Art. 133 TEC and normally Art. 300 TEC) (they can also incorporate Art. 181 TEC if there is a development component or Art. 181a TEC for non-development focused economic, financial and technical cooperation);
- association agreements (Art. 310 TEC).

Normally they will not actually be called 'trade and economic cooperation agreement' or 'association agreement' – they are given a name such as a Stabilisation and Association Agreement, a Partnership and Cooperation Agreement, or the Cotonou

Agreement. In practice, most of these agreements are 'mixed agreements' and will thus be based on several treaty articles. This is because, in addition to issues which fall under the EC's exclusive competence, agreements will generally incorporate other areas where competence is shared with the member states (see Chapter 4).

Scope, contents and motivation

The EU has some form of trade, association or cooperation agreement with nearly every country in the world. In terms of geographical scope, this network of formalized relations is more extensive than the bilateral network of any member state alone. This implies each member state can maintain some form of relationship and foreign policy *vis-à-vis* third countries/regions at minimal cost.

It is the EU's economic power that first and foremost makes it an attractive partner for third countries. However, the EU uses this economic allure to build leverage on political issues. The issues covered in agreements vary substantially. In terms of market access, the level of preference accorded is highly variable. For example, the EU's agreement with Turkey extends its customs union, the Euro-Med agreements include the goal of creating a free trade area with the Mediterranean, while the relationship with Malaysia does not provide for bilateral preferential trade arrangements at all. Agreements also provide the structure through which the EU channels financial and technical aid. Agreements provide for cooperation in various socio-economic fields and in a host of other areas of interest including, for example, migration, justice and home affairs issues, CFSP, drugs, science, culture or the environment. They can also provide for support to the political structures of a country or region (for example capacity building of state institutions, good governance and rule of law). The scope and depth of issues subject to cooperation varies depending on several factors: geographic location relative to the EU, prospect of membership, level and nature of political relations, and (a)symmetry of the relationship between the EU and the third country. A further factor is when the agreement was concluded: as the scope of policy issues deliberated in the EU framework has increased over time, so has the breadth of issues incorporated into agreements.

This last point relates to one of the pitfalls of the EU's continuously expanding relations with third countries and regions. With each new round of negotiations, there is a tendency to broaden the range of issues in the agreements, and to upgrade the text and label given to the relationship to demonstrate the importance attached to the process (from 'Partnership' to 'Strategic Partnership', for example). However, enhancing the terminology and broadening the issues covered by the agreement is often not matched by concrete improvements or increased budgets. Moreover, broadening the scope of agreements often mirrors the continuously expanding competences of the EU rather than reflecting new opportunities for substantive cooperation or real new commitments from the EU or the partners involved. Combined, these factors contribute to the EU's famous 'capability–expectations gap' (Hill 1993).

Concluding, or refusing to conclude, agreements with third states has been a trump card for the EU. As will be discussed in Chapter 10, association and cooperation agreements were used strategically prior to and following the fall of communist regimes in Central and Eastern Europe in 1989. Trade and Cooperation Agreements, and later Association Agreements, were used to support structural changes in the most reform-minded governments, first in Poland and Hungary and later also in other countries. Likewise, the EU's decision to conclude in 1997 an interim Association Agreement with the Palestinian Authority was part of its broader strategy in the Middle East peace process and was also used to send a political message at a moment when the peace process was stalling. More recently, following the terrorist attacks of September 11th 2001, the EU concluded agreements with the Central Asian Republics, which have grown in strategic importance. For example, a Trade and Cooperation Agreement between the EU and Tajikistan had been frozen because of the political situation in that country, but was revived after September 11th, on the Commission's initiative. A Partnership and Cooperation Agreement was duly signed in October 2004. In this case, the strategic importance attributed to Tajikistan is prioritized above its lack of good democratic credentials or human rights record.

The EU can also decide to conclude an agreement as a reward for 'good behaviour'. Examples are agreements with South Africa at the end of apartheid, and with Libya, which was invited to at least partially join the Barcelona process after it dismantled its weapons of mass destruction and after issues such as the bombing of a Pan Am flight over Lockerbie in 1988 were resolved. The prospect of an agreement is also used as an incentive to effect desired changes within a country. And conversely, by rejecting an agreement with a third country, or rejecting the inclusion of issues that are advantageous for that country, the EU can pressurise or sanction a country. For example, the prospect of concluding an agreement with the EU was a primary instrument in attempts by the EU3 in 2004–05 to discourage Iran from pursuing its nuclear ambitions. This was also a cause of displeasure amongst some member states since the UK, France and Germany promised Iran something that was not in their, but rather the EU's, competence to provide.

The examples given above indicate that the agreements concluded by the EU can be an instrument of both conventional and structural foreign policy. Agreements are used as part of the EU toolbox to react to specific conflicts or crises, allowing the EU to reward, sanction or put pressure on third states. And, in view of their longer time perspective and the broad scope of policy fields involved, cooperation and association agreements, at least on paper, can provide a firm basis for a structural foreign policy. They can be instrumental in supporting or inducing structural reforms, or in strengthening existing political, legal and socio-economic structures in third countries and regions – with conditionality and political dialogue instruments, both discussed below, providing further support to this dynamic.

Conditionality

In this context, conditionality refers to the practice of making the conclusion and implementation of agreements, cooperation and assistance dependent on certain conditions being met. Conditionality takes several forms – positive and negative, political and economic, *ex ante* and *ex post*. It holds out the prospect of economic or political gain if conditions are met, and the cessation or reduction of this if conditions are not met.

Ex ante conditionality refers to conditions which must be met *before* an agreement will be concluded. As Fierro argues in relation to EU candidate countries, '*ex ante* conditionality represents the most sophisticated form of conditionality because when it applies to European countries, conditions are spelled out with great detail. They are also periodically examined and regularly monitored' (2003: 377–8). However, where *ex ante* conditionality is applied to non-European countries, it becomes a less sophisticated instrument with monitoring being much more superficial (ibid.: 378).

Ex post conditionality, which is more common, refers to conditions or 'essential elements' which must be met *after* an agreement has been concluded. Since 1995, almost all EU agreements contain at least a human rights clause and often provisions to make the respect for democratic principles and the rule of law essential elements of the agreement (see Eeckhout 2004: 475–81). Since 2004, the EU has also pressured its partners into accepting the inclusion of a non-proliferation clause which makes the fight against the proliferation of WMD an essential element of the agreement. If either party to the agreement does not respect one of its essential elements then the agreement, and thus the cooperation and aid arrangements for which it provides, can be suspended in whole or in part. This would normally follow a period of consultations in which parties attempt to find a mutually acceptable solution.

Because of the difficulty of applying its measures, Fierro argues that *ex post* conditionality 'tends to be static rather than dynamic and symbolic rather than substantial' (2003: 377–8). The EU has made much greater use of conditionality provisions in the EU–ACP Cotonou Agreement than in its relations with Asia, Latin America, the Middle East or the Mediterranean (see Chapter 10). However, as Mbangu (2005) argues, even in EU–ACP relations, conditionality has tended to be a reactive instrument, only invoked where the violation of an essential element was so blatant that it was quasi-impossible to ignore. The negative image of the 'essential elements' clauses that prevails in some ACP countries has made the EU reluctant to even open consultations at an early stage where respect for democracy and human rights is deteriorating. For countries subject to it, 'conditionality' is an ugly and unwelcome practice. The EU's extensive use of terms like 'essential elements' or 'political dialogue' can be understood as a way of avoiding the word 'conditionality', which is not acceptable to many third states.

It is difficult to generalize as to whether the EU's use of conditionality is effective. However, it is interesting to note that the landscape is changing. The West does not have a monopoly on donorship or on buying African exports, particularly oil and commodities. Donors such as China are proving willing to provide aid, but particularly to trade, without the constraints of Western-style conditionality and without asking annoying question about human rights and democracy (see Chapter 11).

Political dialogue

The provisions for political dialogue in agreements are particularly important from a foreign policy perspective. The EU now incorporates political dialogue into its agreements as a matter of course. Generally, agreements establish political dialogue on ministerial, senior official and expert levels. Although the precise aims of political dialogue vary, generally they incorporate some of the following aspects: increasing convergence of positions on international issues of mutual concern; cooperation on matters pertaining to the strengthening of stability and security in Europe and the region in question; and reinforcing democracy and the respect and promotion of human rights, including minority rights and the rule of law.

Each cooperation and association agreement creates a foreign policy machinery through the provisions for 'institutions of the agreement' as well as the regular meetings foreseen for political dialogue. For example, the Euro-Med Association Agreement with Morocco provides for an Association Council (Ministerial level) and an Association Committee (official level), supplemented by six subcommittees (including one on human rights, democratization and governance). The creation of this bilateral apparatus deepens the level of cooperation between the EU and the third country/region. Contacts touch on all sectors of the economy and government, and thus also include meetings of specialized ministers, civil servants and, in some agreements, also members of parliament.

By forming joint institutions, a potentially powerful instrument for foreign policy is created. However, this can also be counterproductive. The high frequency of meetings at Ministerial level adds to an already overburdened agenda and the modus operandi of meetings often precludes a true dialogue. As Chris Patten noted in 2005, recalling his experiences as Commissioner for External Relations: 'Meetings can easily degenerate into the reading of speaking notes to people who are not listening, with occasional allegedly informal exchanges of view that turn too easily into *café du commerce*' (Patten 2005: 162). Furthermore, the EU is invariably eager to formulate positive joint statements and nice declarations following meetings to give the appearance of a positive result of 'foreign policy'. Sensitive foreign policy issues – such as the abuse of human rights or the involvement of a third country in a violent conflict – are therefore often just mentioned as a passing formality, or are not mentioned at all if the 'partner' is too powerful (as with the case of Chechnya in meetings with Russia). Moreover, EU representatives (but also member states' representatives) often prioritize trade and cooperation issues and do not want to disturb negotiations on these issues by tough talks on problematic foreign policy issues. The result is that political dialogue is not exercised to its full foreign policy potential, and cases where it is used as leverage to promote and obtain concrete EU foreign policy goals are limited.

Development policy

The EU as a development world power

The EU (EC and member states) is the largest donor of humanitarian aid and Overseas Development Aid (ODA), providing over 50 per cent of all ODA. The EC itself is the third largest donor of ODA. At the Council of Ministers meeting of May 2005, member states undertook to achieve a target of giving 0.7 per cent of their Gross National Income (GNI) as ODA by 2015, whilst member states which joined the EU after 2002 will 'strive to increase' by 2015 their ODA/GNI ratio to 0.33 per cent. Even this relatively low figure compares rather favourably with the US which committed just 0.22 per cent of GNI to ODA in 2005 (Commission and OECD 2006).

Article 177(1–2) TEC gives development policy the following objectives:

1. Community policy in the sphere of development cooperation, which shall be complementary to the policies pursued by the Member States, shall foster:

- the sustainable economic and social development of the developing countries, and more particularly the most disadvantaged among them,
- the smooth and gradual integration of the developing countries into the world economy,
- the campaign against poverty in the developing countries.

2. Community policy in this area shall contribute to the general objective of developing and consolidating democracy and the rule of law, and to that of respecting human rights and fundamental freedoms.

From a foreign policy perspective, several points are worth noting from the start (see also Holland 2002; Arts and Dickson 2004a). By virtue of its position as the largest international donor, the EU should theoretically be able to use development cooperation to effect changes within third countries in line with its world view, and to promote specific foreign policy objectives – such as conflict prevention, dialogue and cooperation between countries in conflict, good governance and democracy, the rule of law and respect for human rights.

The EU's development objectives, including the goal of poverty reduction, can be understood from a foreign policy angle. Poverty reduction improves welfare and stability and assists in the integration of developing countries into the international system. Indirectly, this contributes to core foreign policy objectives. As the 2003 *European Security Strategy* emphasized: '[t]rade and development policies can be powerful tools for promoting reform. A world seen as offering justice and opportunity for everyone will be more secure for the European Union and its citizens' (European Council 2003b: 10). Improving individuals' human security is also an important element of avoiding a situation in which alternative actors or structures gain power and legitimacy because, in the absence of a well-functioning state, it is these alternative actors and structures which step in to provide financial and food support, education, health care, or at least a minimum of 'order' at a grassroots level. There have been several examples of such shifts in recent years including Hamas in the Palestinian Territories, Hezbollah in Lebanon and Islamic Courts in Somalia.

EU development policy is a complementary or parallel competence – it sits beside member states' own development policies. It also sits within a large international framework which ranges from policy-making within the UN system, IMF and World Bank, to specific initiatives such as the Paris Club which coordinates responses to developing countries' debt problems. In development policy, '[t]he Community and the Member States shall comply with the commitments and take account of the objectives they have approved in the context of the United Nations and other competent international organisations' (Art. 177(3)). The most important of the current initiatives are the UN Millennium Development Goals (MDGs). The eight MDGs, which were agreed to by all countries and leading development institutions in 2000, range from halving extreme poverty to halting the spread of HIV/AIDS and providing universal primary education, all by 2015.

The treaty brings to the fore the importance of the '3Cs' principle: coherence of EC policies; coordination between Community and member state action; complementarity between policies and programmes of the Community and member states (see Commission 2005a; EP, Council and Commission 2006b). However, translating the 3Cs principle into practice is quite a challenge. Even if we only focus on the objectives of development policy as outlined in Article 177, it is clear that there is a risk of incompatibility or at least competing objectives. When foreign policy goals (developing democracy, for example) are added into the mix, their compatibility with pure development objectives and the fight against poverty is not always clear cut. For instance, to what extent should the EC fight poverty in countries where there is no possibility that it will be able to promote democracy and where the human rights situation is appalling?

The problem of coherence and complementarity is even more difficult when the EC's other policies enter the equation. The Treaty's chapter on development cooperation indicates that the Community 'shall take account of the objectives referred to in Article 177 in the policies that it implements which are likely to affect developing countries' (Art. 178 TEC). In practice, this is not straightforward. For example, how compatible is the objective of fostering the integration of developing countries into the world economy with the EC's agricultural and trade policies which, understandably, promote and protect the EU's own economic interests? The EU's stance during the Doha negotiations demonstrates that, despite some concessions, it was not prepared to sacrifice its own economic interests to support reforming the structure of the world economy to the advantage of developing countries.

Since development policy is a parallel and not an exclusive competence, ensuring vertical consistency is as important as ensuring horizontal consistency. The treaty provisions on development cooperation therefore pay considerable attention to mutual consultation, coordination and cooperation between the EC and the member states. However, in practice, levels of coordination between member states and the Community tend to be low, with progress proving rather difficult. Member states prefer to keep their hands free in their national development policies, which are also considered a useful tool to raise the national flag around the world.

The shifting sands of development policy priorities

EU development policy can be conceptualized as a two-dimensional patchwork in terms of its geographical coverage and its policy priorities.

Geographical priorities

With the exception of a handful of budget lines such as the European Instrument for Democracy and Human Rights or the EU Water Initiative, the EU has a dual-track approach to development policy – the ACP (African, Caribbean and Pacific) countries on the one hand, and the rest of the world on the other.

Development cooperation with the ACP countries began with the conclusion of the Yaoundé Agreement in 1963, replaced by a succession of Lomé agreements and today managed through the Cotonou Agreement (see also Chapter 10). With each agreement, the scope of cooperation has broadened and, since Lomé III and IV, become increasingly political and conditional. In institutional terms, the European Commission's DG Development manages the EU's relations with ACP countries, DG RELEX manages the EU's relations with developing countries in the rest of the world, and projects are managed by EuropeAid. Development cooperation with the ACP countries is financed through the European Development Fund (EDF). The EDF does not fall under the general Community budget, although this issue was hotly debated in the run up to the 2007–13 financial perspectives. It is funded by member states which set its budget in the Council, has its own financial rules, and is managed by its own committee (the EDF Committee). The EDF allocation for the five year period 2008–13 is €22.7 billion. Historically, non-reciprocal highly preferential market access, including specific protocols guaranteeing import prices for a range of commodities such as sugar and rice, has also been at the heart of the EU–ACP 'special relationship'.

Development cooperation with the rest of the world's developing countries is rather different, and much less tangible. Firstly, in institutional terms, development policy towards these countries is not managed by DG Development but rather by DG RELEX. This is somewhat confusing. The EU's development policy is supposed to focus on poverty reduction and two thirds of the world's poor live in Asia (dealt with by DG RELEX). Are we to understand then that the EU–ACP relationship is primarily about development (and poverty reduction) whereas the EU's relations with regions such as Asia is primarily about other issues that fall under the more political remit of DG RELEX? Secondly, there is no specific development fund for these countries equivalent to the EDF. Rather, funding comes from the annual EC Budget which covers cooperation with developing countries in all geographic regions – the Development Cooperation Instrument. For the 2007–13 period, €16.9 billion has been allotted to this instrument. Thirdly, although non-ACP countries gain some degree of preferential access to the EU market through the Generalised System of Preferences (GSP), this is much less favourable than trade terms granted to ACP countries. The EU's approach to development is thus different depending on the region. This is probably a good thing. However, the difference in approach does not appear to grow out of an understanding of the different challenges each region faces, but rather out of the different tools and types of agreements (internally defined) that the EU employs.

The ACP states have historically been prioritized by the EU's development policy. However, this has gradually changed. The Cotonou Agreement marked the end of the ACP place at the apex of the EU's pyramid of trade preferences with non-reciprocal preferential market access only retained through the EBA initiative, which is open to all LDCs, not just ACP states (see Holland 2002: 225–32). This to some extent normalizes EU relations with the poorest developing countries and moves these relations beyond previous historical preferences. EU aid is significantly more evenly spread across the globe than that of other donors. For example, 55 countries receive more than 50 per cent of their total ODA from the EU, while America's ODA is concentrated on the Middle East and that of Japan on Asia. Hence, although EU development aid is to some extent directed by strategic foreign policy objectives (particularly the stabilization of its neighbourhood), this is less the case than with other actors (Commission and OECD 2006: 13, 27).

Policy priorities

In the evolution of EU development policy from the early 1960s to today, several trends are apparent. In the 1960s and 1970s, there was a notable distinction between EC development policy and that of other actors. Lomé was conceived on a basis of aid not trade; grants not loans; and non-reciprocal preferential market access rather than a 'normal' trade relationship. However, the reality has not stood up to the intentions: 'Lomé has not been replicated, and its mixed results have initiated a process of rethinking the concepts underlying ACP–EU relations and the instruments available to shape them' (Arts and Dickson 2004b: 2). The result was a gradual and partial shift from aid to trade, which was also reflected in the Cotonou Agreement and in the objective to conclude 'Economic Partnership Agreements' with the ACP countries (see Chapter 10).

One of the main principles of policy through Yaoundé, Lomé I and Lomé II was neutrality, which also differentiated EC development policy from that of other actors. However, in its development discourse and activities, the EU has increasingly linked development with specific foreign policy concerns aiming to promote specific norms and objectives – such as human rights, democracy, respect for the rule of law, good governance, and the fight against WMD. As Karagiannis (2004: 14) argues, this 'meant definitely breaking with the tradition of neutrality'. The promotion of these issues or 'values' appears in the provisions of new agreements with developing countries, in political dialogue, as well as in specific projects established and funded through EU development policy (see also Bonaglia *et al.* 2006).

Another major feature of EU–ACP relations was 'partnership'. If this relationship can be understood as a partnership, it is a heavily unequal one. It is not the ACP countries that create or discontinue their relationship with the EU, nor that provide the terms of reference in the evolution of this relationship. The ACP countries had little option but to accept that the development component of their relationship be complemented and sometimes superseded by a range of other objectives (such as anti-terrorism, migration, WMD). ACP countries have also had to accept that there has been significantly greater use of conditionality in their relationship with the EU than in the EU's relations with Latin America, Asia, the Mediterranean or the Middle East.

The EU also increasingly links development with security, as was confirmed in the 2003 *European Security Strategy*: 'security is a precondition of development' (European Council 2003b: 2; see also Schroeder 2006; Hadfield 2007). This reflects the EU's growing attention to conflict prevention and peace-building in development policy, a tendency which was initiated much earlier by the Commission, starting with its pioneering Communication on *The EU and the Issue of Conflicts in Africa: Peacebuilding, Conflict Prevention and Beyond* (Commission 1996). In this context, although the above analysis tends to suggest that ACP countries are becoming less prioritized in strict development terms, Africa is becoming increasingly important in foreign policy terms. Africa is an important element of the EU's aspirations to develop a global foreign policy presence, and security took a prominent place in both the 2005 EU Strategy for Africa and the Cotonou Agreement (see Chapter 10).

Crisis management, conflict prevention and peace-building

Developing crisis management capabilities has, since the late 1990s, particularly centred on the development of military and civilian capabilities under the ESDP (see Chapter 7). However, crisis management, conflict prevention and peace-building have a longer history in the first pillar and are still to a large extent based on EC instruments. This appeared clearly in the two major policy documents of 2001 that both shaped and reflected the EU's emerging conflict prevention and peace-building policy: the

Commission's *Communication on Conflict Prevention* (2001a) and the Council's *EU Programme for the Prevention of Violent Conflicts* adopted in 2001 at the end of the Swedish Presidency (for a detailed analysis of this policy, see Wouters and Kronenberger, 2004).

Long-term conflict prevention and peace-building

European integration can itself be conceptualized as a long-term conflict prevention and peace-building project. The EC/EU's own experience and the challenges it has faced in the Balkans explain the EU's strong emphasis on the need for a comprehensive approach to conflict prevention and peace-building. From the outset, the EU emphasized the need to take a genuinely long-term and integrated approach which promotes an environment conducive to peace, addresses all aspects of structural (in)stability in countries at risk, and tackles the root causes of conflict. This appeared clearly in key documents on the subject. The section on long-term conflict prevention in the 2001 *Communication on Conflict Prevention* deals with issues ranging from strengthening regional cooperation and building trade links to reforming the security sector and managing access to natural resources. This approach demonstrated a strong focus on shaping the political, legal, socio-economic and security structures in other regions and countries, with attention to the individual and societal level as well as the state and interstate level. It therefore adopts the structural foreign policy approach outlined in Chapter 1, which was reflected in the Council (2002: 5) labelling the EU's approach as 'structural conflict prevention' (see Keukeleire 2004).

This approach also emerged in the EC instruments listed as directly or indirectly relevant to the prevention of conflict: development cooperation and external assistance, economic cooperation and trade policy instruments, humanitarian aid, social and environmental policies, and economic and other sanctions. The most powerful instruments at the Community's disposal are its agreements and cooperation programmes with other countries and regions in the world. However, the EC has also developed several specialized sectoral assistance instruments for long-term peace-building, such as programmes for aid to uprooted people, the EIDHR, action against anti-personnel mines, and the programme on rehabilitation and reconstruction.

Strengthening government, regional and subregional organizations' capacity for conflict prevention and working with international organizations is another important component of the long-term strategy. The EU has sought to build and support international regimes *vis-à-vis* specific conflict related issues, such as the International Criminal Court (ICC) and the Kimberley Process (which aims at ending a source of revenue to rebel groups by establishing an international control regime for trade in rough diamonds).

Given this breadth of instruments, 'mainstreaming' conflict prevention (integrating conflict prevention/peace-building considerations into *all* policies towards fragile/conflict-prone states) becomes a critical factor. The main tools to operationalize this are the Country Strategy Papers and the Country Conflict Assessments produced by desk officers and delegations for each country receiving EC assistance.

It is difficult to assess the impact of the EC's approach, but we can make some general observations. Firstly, focussing on the need for a comprehensive and integrated approach to conflict prevention and peace-building is both a strength and a weakness. It reflects the reality that there are no quick and easy solutions for conflicts and that measures other than diplomatic or military interventions are essential for sustainable peace-building. However, this approach requires an enormous amount of financial resources and of political, diplomatic and bureaucratic time and energy. It also necessitates that all EU actors involved do deliberately prioritize the objective of conflict prevention in their policy towards the country or region concerned, and thus accept concessions in terms of other policy objectives. It is clear that this scale of involvement can only be expected and afforded for the limited number of countries or regions that are at the heart of the EU's strategic interests and objectives – currently only the Balkans. The EU's long-term conflict prevention and peace-building efforts in the Balkans are therefore also by far the most comprehensive, integrated and successful, albeit only developed in the wake of seven years of deadly conflict.

Secondly, the effectiveness of EU intervention depends on its ability to succeed in the very difficult task of achieving the right policy mix and, related to this, to avoid conflict prevention initiatives being undermined by trade, agriculture and in some cases development policy itself. Although regularly referred to, 'mainstreaming' conflict prevention is notoriously difficult to achieve in practice. Yet, mainstreaming, even where it is successful, is not the panacea. As Hill argues, 'it is not inherently constructive to load the tasks of conflict prevention onto every aspect of the EU's external relations, especially those which are already functioning with difficulty' (2001: 332).

Thirdly, the EU tends to rely excessively on positive spillover of cooperation programmes, democracy promotion, development policy and so on to achieve conditions for peace without sufficiently considering what the relationship between the different variables might be. Karen Smith makes this point clearly: democratization can 'unleash extreme nationalism and political instability, especially if new parties reflect ethnic divisions'; development or economic assistance and trade concessions can 'create or exacerbate inequalities among different identity groups', which can be a source of conflict; and regional cooperation can 'have disintegrative effects' (K. Smith 2003: 146).

Finally, the fact that the EU has an impressive array of conflict prevention instruments at its disposal does not automatically imply that the EU is an effective conflict prevention actor, even when it does use these instruments. Long-term conflict prevention efforts can fail because they are not sufficiently supported by diplomatic and/or military security efforts. Conflict prevention initiatives by the EU alone are unlikely to have a substantial impact quite simply because one actor alone is unlikely to be able to tackle a conflict. This points to the importance of EU conflict prevention efforts being part of a wider multilocation foreign policy effort, involving other international organizations and states. This is also one of the reasons why the EU's main peace-building effort, in the Balkans, is quite successful, as it is embedded in a broader international effort.

Short-term conflict prevention and crisis management

Some components of the EC's mainstream long-term programmes managed by the Commission can be employed as short-term tools. As the Commission itself has argued (2003a: 9–12), EC development and cooperation assistance can support, for example, political and diplomatic initiatives to defuse a crisis; provide incentives to the parties to a conflict to resolve disputes; provide humanitarian assistance and transitional relief; and foster stability during periods of political transition. The various geographic financial instruments (such as the European Neighbourhood and Partnership Instrument) include funds that can be focused on or reprioritized to conflict prevention. The advantage of these instruments is that they have significant means at their disposal. Their disadvantage, however, is their limited flexibility, their cumbersome procedures and the fact that they are not adapted to situations of crises and conflicts. For this reason, within the first pillar, several more flexible tools for conflict prevention and crisis management have been created.

The main tool is the Instrument for Stability (IFS), launched in January 2007 to strengthen the EU's capacity to provide an effective response to situations of crisis and instability in third countries and to address global and transregional challenges with a security or stability dimension. The IFS is considered complementary to the geographically orientated instruments, providing a basis for interventions when circumstances in a third country/region would make cooperation under the normal geographic or thematic instruments impossible. The IFS, which is managed by the Commission's DG RELEX, particularly aims to (re-)establish the conditions necessary to use the normal regional instruments. Possible actions include support for: mediation initiatives; interim administrations and institution building; international criminal tribunals; demobilization and reintegration programmes for former combatants; mine detection and clearance; and the promotion of human rights, democracy and the rule of law. In addition to these crisis management activities, the EU can use the IFS to provide assistance in two specific security challenges: threats to critical infrastructure, public health and law and order (including the fight against terrorism); and risk mitigation and preparedness relating to chemical, biological and nuclear materials (EP and Council 2006a).

The IFS brings together in one single financial instrument domains that until 2006 were spread over an array of different financial instruments. For example, it replaced the Rapid Reaction Mechanism (RRM) which had allowed the EC to respond in a rapid and flexible manner to situations of urgency or to the emergence of crisis. Briefly considering some of the actions funded through the RRM gives an indication of the type of foreign policy action we can expect the IFS to support. From its creation in 2001 to the end of 2006, around 50 projects of a civilian nature had been launched using the RRM in 25 countries or regions, amounting to a total provision of around €120 million. Projects undertaken included: financing mediation and the monitoring of peace agreements or ceasefire agreements (Liberia, Ivory Coast, Sudan, Indonesia/Aceh, Sri Lanka and East Timor); support to the demobilization and reintegration of former combatants (Indonesia/Aceh); support for the rule of law or civilian administration (DRC/Bunia, Afghanistan and Georgia); and electoral support and election monitoring (Georgia, Kyrgyzstan, Ukraine and Iraq) (Commission 2007d; see also Rummel 2004: 80–4).

Characteristic of these projects was that they supported activities being initiated and implemented by other actors. Although in financial terms the RRM's contribution tended to be limited, its special value was that it cut through the EC's bureaucratic redtape and saved time at critical moments, such as during a ceasefire negotiation or the initial phase of a peace process (International Crisis Group 2005: 40). At these critical moments, it is often less important that the EU itself intervenes or that enormous amounts of money are provided, but rather that the existing momentum be maintained and the relevant actors and structures have the means to achieve results. To give one example, the RRM provided the necessary financial support for former Finnish President Martti Ahtisaari to conduct the peace negotiations which ended the conflict in Aceh/Indonesia early 2005, making use of the political momentum in the aftermath of the tsunami. It also provided Ahtisaari with a lever that was an essential part of the dispute settlement: the possibility of providing immediate financial assistance to 5,000 fighters of the 'Free Aceh Movement' in the framework of their demobilization and reintegration. After the peace agreement had been signed, ESDP played an important role in monitoring the agreement through its Aceh Monitoring Mission. But, to forge the peace agreement in the first place, it was the EC and not CFSP/ESDP that played a role (see Braud and Grevi 2005; Pirozzi and Helly 2005).

Another important tool for crisis management is the African Peace Facility (APF). This instrument came into effect in 2004 and is designed to provide the African Union (AU) and other African regional organizations with the resources to mount effective peacemaking and peacekeeping operations. The APF was allocated €250 million for the 2004–07 period and a further €300 million for 2008–10 (Council 2006e). Interestingly, the APF is financed through the European Development Fund – the EU adopted the unusual, and also criticized, approach of using development money for military security issues. A justification for this approach was however found in the *European Security Strategy*'s claim that 'security is a precondition for development', in the initiative for the APF being taken by African leaders and in the fact that the APF was based on the principle of African ownership.

The APF can be used for all aspects of peacekeeping operations, except military equipment, salaries and military training for soldiers. On its first outings, the APF provided €192 million for the AU mission in Darfur (AMIS – African Mission in Sudan), €20 million for the peace support operation in the Central African Republic (launched by the Central African Economic and Monetary Community), and €6 million for capacity building of the AU. In early 2007 the Commission released €15 million to support the deployment of an AU peacekeeping force in Somalia (Commission 2007e).

The APF and the IFS (and previously also the RRM) gave the Commission a degree of autonomy, which was essential to ensure the effectiveness of the instruments. To the Commission's credit, it has frequently reacted more swiftly to new opportunities or crises than CFSP actors, and supports peace processes in countries that receive scant attention in the CFSP (as was the case with the peace talks in Indonesia/Aceh before the tsunami brought Aceh to the second pillar's attention). These financial instruments have allowed the Commission to develop foreign policy initiatives with regard to crises and conflicts which member states regarded as clearly falling within the remit of the second pillar. This has led to sharp conflicts between the Commission and Council, particularly when the Commission used these instruments for initiatives that were in clear competition with CFSP/ESDP (such as its rule of law package for Georgia in parallel with the ESDP rule of law operation 'EUJUST Themis') or, worse, that conflicted with CFSP positions (for instance with regard to the conflicts in Sudan) (Kurowska 2006). Such turf battles over competence have strengthened the feeling in several national capitals that the locus of EU conflict prevention efforts should be moved to the second pillar, and particularly the EDSP.

There now risks being too much focus on second pillar instruments, with the potential of the first pillar's integrated and long-term approach, and the link with the EU's other policy instruments, being too readily overlooked.

Human rights and democracy

Objectives and challenges

The promotion of human rights, democracy and the rule of law is both one of the major objectives of EU foreign policy and one of the constitutive elements of the EU as a values-driven international actor. Promoting these objectives and values has increasingly permeated not only CFSP, but also most aspects of EU foreign policy beyond CFSP. As Balfour (2006: 127) demonstrates, the EU, more than any other international actor, has formalized the principles of democracy and human rights in the structures and policies of its foreign relations and has matched its commitments by creating tools for promoting these values. This is reflected in the incorporation of political conditionality and the provisions on political dialogue in association and cooperation agreements, in the inclusion of the explicit goals of respect for human rights and democracy in development policy, and in the creation of specific instruments to promote democracy and human rights. This final section evaluates the nature of the EC as a normative power in promoting these objectives and highlights some of the obstacles and ambiguities in EU policy (for discussion of second pillar interventions, see Chapter 6; for an in-depth analysis of the EU as a normative power, see Lucarelli and Manners 2006; Sjursen 2006).

Promoting human rights, democracy and the rule of law is not only important as an external objective but also as an identity objective. The goal is not just to further human rights and democracy outside the EU's borders, but also to shape a distinct international identity for the EU as a values-driven normative power (see also Panebianco 2006). The EU faces a myriad of challenges in trying to translate its democracy and human rights discourse into concrete actions and results. Both principles are open to interpretation. Democracy is not enshrined as a principle in international law which makes it harder to legitimize intervening in third countries to promote the democracy cause (see K. Smith 2003: 123). This is less problematic for human rights where there exists a relatively well-established international framework of (more or less enforceable) universal principles. Nevertheless, the legitimacy of the EU's emphasis on human rights has been contested. For example, a key stumbling block in EU–ASEAN relations and Asia–Europe Meetings (ASEM) has been that Asian countries believe the EU overemphasizes human rights issues, to the detriment of objectives that they consider to be important, such as stability and human security. As Asian countries are less dependent on European aid and cooperation than African countries, they have more freedom to reject the EU's normative agenda.

The EU also faces the challenge of trying to achieve sustainable results in terms of democracy and human rights. It is not sufficient to provide support for establishing democratic and rule-of-law structures in third countries – the main challenge is to make these norms part of the mental structures of elites and the population in the third country. Sustainable results not only require the potential for clear gain on the part of the third country (as is the case with candidate countries to the EU) but also a sufficiently strong endogenous basis to make long-term structural changes and an internalization of norms and values possible (see Matlary 2004: 149). This is also one of the reasons that in its policy towards the developing world, the EU has aimed 'to encourage a socialization of identities around a positive adherence to democratic norms, while directing political aid towards strengthening the broad socio-economic foundations of sustainable democracy rather than particular institutional patterns' (Youngs 2001: 353).

The EU's ability to maintain the normative high ground is damaged by the inconsistency with which it applies conditionality and human rights and democracy standards. Some examples will illustrate this. Whilst the EU refuses to negotiate an agreement with Cuba until the one-party communist political situation changes, there is a 1985 Trade and Economic Cooperation Agreement and a continued dialogue with (one-party communist) China on human rights (Fierro 2003: 378–9). In a similar vein, the EU has been rather vehement in its reaction to Palestine's Hamas government, Iran and Libya (in the past), but has little problem developing contractual relations with countries from the Gulf Cooperation Council even though countries such as Saudi Arabia are among the least democratic in the world and even though their commitment to human rights is questionable. Although other factors have contributed to determining the EU's position towards Iran and Hamas, it is not surprising that influential Arab satellite broadcasting stations, such as Al Jazeera and Al Arabia, brand the US and the EU as the 'axis of double standards'. That the EU refused to cooperate with Hamas after it won democratic elections in the Palestinian Territories in 2006 can in this sense be understood as a serious blow for both the EU's credibility as a normative actor and for the status of 'democracy' as a value in and of itself (rather than an instrument to promote European and American interests).

Approach

It is difficult to give an overall picture of the approach to promoting democracy, human rights and other prioritized values. Despite some common denominators, such as the important role of political dialogue and conditionality embedded in agreements the EU concludes with third countries, the EU's approach varies substantially across different cases and across different regions in the world. This is also true for the countries in the immediate neighbourhood of the EU, as Balfour (2006) demonstrates in her comparison of the EU's human rights and democracy policy towards the countries in Central and Eastern Europe, South Eastern Europe and the Mediterranean. As Youngs (2004: 415–16) emphasizes in his assessment of the relationship between normative dynamics and strategic interests, human rights policy 'represents not so much a monolithic policy as a broad framework within which a variety of operational and policy-making dynamics might prevail'. This is reflected in the variations in strategies employed to pursue human rights and democracy objectives and in the varying viewpoints on the utility of incorporating these norms in the EU's foreign policy. Consequently, what Fierro (2003: 377) observes with regard to human rights conditionality is also valid for the EU's human rights policy as a whole, 'the EU's approach in any individual case is the result of an inexact equation, which balances the interests of the parties, the EU's subjective assessments and, finally, economic, strategic and political factors'.

Given the limitations of conditionality and the EU's eagerness to present itself as a cooperative normative power, it generally prefers to adopt a 'positive approach' in promoting democracy and human rights. An important instrument in this respect has been the EC's very active policy with regard to election assistance and monitoring and its funding of both reforms in third countries and specific projects through NGOs. Funding has been provided through the various regular instruments of financial and technical cooperation with third countries and regions as well as through the European Instrument/Initiative for Democracy and Human Rights (EIDHR).

In using the Community's external assistance and cooperation instruments (including geographic funding instruments such as ENPI and EDF) to promote human rights, democracy and the rule of law, the EU faces advantages and disadvantages. On the positive side these instruments include considerable funding for long-term reforms of political and legal structures and for specific projects to promote human rights, the rule of law and democracy. However, they also lack flexibility and the third country's government must consent to these programmes because they negotiate the long-term cooperation agreements with the EU. This implies that human rights and democracy promotion becomes impossible in precisely those countries where it is needed most.

The EIDHR budget line, created in 1994 on the European Parliament's initiative, has provided more flexibility by allowing the EC to bypass governments and work directly with other partners (such as NGOs and international organizations) including in countries where regular EC programmes are not available (for instance, because they have been suspended). The EIDHR budget, with an annual allocation of approximately €150 million, has supported: the activities of international criminal tribunals and the ICC, as well as a large number of normally rather small projects centred around democracy, good governance and the rule of law; the abolition of the death penalty; torture prevention; and minority protection. This support has been channelled primarily through NGOs.

Adopting such a 'grass-roots' approach has been understood as valuable in terms of strengthening an indigenous basis for democracy and human rights promotion in third countries. However, given that the scope of projects has generally been too limited to strengthen the grass-roots momentum for change in the countries concerned, this approach has at times made EU policy look more symbolic than substantive and more aimed at identity objectives than external objectives. The decision not to support NGOs and opposition groups that adopt a too confrontational approach has implied that the EIDHR could not function as a lever at critical moments (such as in the people-power revolutions of Ukraine and Georgia, where US funding for opposition movements was essential). As one evaluation of the EIDHR concludes, the result has been 'disappointment that the degree of spill-over from support for relatively apolitical NGOs to broader human rights and democratic reform has in many cases been more limited than hoped' (IMD 2005: 18).

More fundamentally, the EU has often lacked the backbone to take direct action and adopt clear punitive measures against governments and regimes renowned for their human rights abuses, blatant discrimination against minorities, and rejection of democratic principles. This is not necessarily the consequence of member states failing to prioritize human rights and democracy issues. It can also arise from one general feature of EU foreign policy: the reluctance of the EU to use its power to further concrete goals. In this sense, the question is not just whether the EU can be labelled as a civilian, civilizing or normative power, but as a 'power' at all (see Chapter 1).

It is on this particular point that the accession of the Central and Eastern European countries influenced the debate in the EU. The new member states have increased pressure on the EU to make more assertive use of its potential power and to move the EU more towards a US model of funding pro-democracy movements and organizations. For the new member states, this approach should include more flexible, focused and large-scale impact-orientated support for movements that can make a difference in third countries. Their pressure, and the experience of revolutions in Georgia and Ukraine in 2003 and 2004 respectively, contributed to the decision to create a new European *Instrument* for Democracy and Human Rights (EIDHR), which in January 2007 replaced the old European *Initiative* for Democracy and Human Rights (EP and Council 2006b). The new EIDHR aims to provide the EU with a higher degree of flexibility to respond to changing situations in human rights and democracy processes, while at the same time ensuring a smoother and simpler delivery procedure. Whether this renewed instrument will be more than a change of label, and will be sufficient to also change the practice of EU democracy and human rights promotion policies, remains to be seen, as such a change depends on the future willingness of all member states to indeed prioritize human rights and democracy above other strategic objectives.

Conclusion

Consolidating respect for human rights and fundamental freedoms, the rule of law, democracy and peaceful resolution of conflicts within the EC/EU and then promoting these values externally are defining elements of the EU's identity. Yet, the EU also has narrower strategic and trade interests to protect, which in many cases prevail over, and undermine, its stated foreign policy goals. The first pillar policies discussed in this chapter provide the backbone of the EU's structural foreign policy, including its ability to enter into long-term contractual agreements, to offer trade concessions, to support development, democracy and respect for human rights. However, with the exception of the CEECs and the Balkans, these policies have often not been steered sufficiently strategically or backed up with enough resources actually to shape the political, legal, socio-economic, security and mental structures of third countries/ regions: in short, to have a structural foreign policy effect.

Chapter 9

The Foreign Policy Dimension of Internal Policies

In Chapter 1 we argued that the European Union functions as a shield, and an agent, of globalization, seeking to contain, manage and order this process. Member state governments acting alone are unable to protect themselves from the consequences of globalization, or to steer its direction. The EU, and particularly the Community, has been vested with competences in a range of 'internal' policies to try to shape external developments which affect Europe. The development of policies such as economic and monetary integration, health, the environment, energy, common agricultural policy, space and technology policy, demography, cooperation in the area of freedom, security and justice and protection of critical infrastructure can be understood in this perspective.

This chapter draws upon internal policy fields to stress the blurring of the inside/outside divide in today's political environment. The advent of EMU and its impact on the EU's policy in international financial institutions will be discussed in Chapter 11. The role of trade and the common agricultural policy in undermining specific EU foreign policy objectives, particularly development, has been discussed in Chapter 8. Whilst we could convincingly argue that all EU internal policies have some form of external ramification, this chapter can only highlight a few of these: security and justice, terrorism, energy, the environment, health and demographics. When looking at these policy fields, it is useful to recall the 'other dimensions' of foreign policy analysed in Chapter 1. Not only do these policies go beyond the usual areas, actors, interests, capabilities and approaches of foreign policy, they often also have fundamentally different goals.

Freedom, security and justice

Member states have been involved in a loose form of cooperation on internal security since the early 1970s. However, it was implementing the Schengen zone which provided the major catalyst to heighten cooperation, as dismantling national borders necessitated 'compensatory measures' in border-related issues such as migration, asylum and organized crime. Cooperation has been gradually formalized and institutionalized. The fall of the Iron Curtain and popular concerns about a wave of immigration and organized crime provided the context in which the Maastricht Treaty created an intergovernmental third pillar through which to develop cooperation in *justice and home affairs* (JHA). In the context of the enlargement to the east, conflict in the Balkans and increasing frustration with difficult third pillar decision-making processes, the Amsterdam Treaty called for the development of *an area of freedom, security and justice* (AFSJ). While retaining internal security measures involving *police and judicial cooperation in criminal matters* in the intergovernmental third pillar (Title VI TEU), the Amsterdam Treaty brought measures aimed at facilitating the free movement of persons (asylum, immigration, etc.) under a new Title IV of the EC Treaty.

Schengen and border controls

Prior to the 2004 enlargement, the Central and Eastern European Countries (CEECs) acted as a buffer zone between the EU and the rest of the world. JHA issues were prioritized by the EU in its relations with the CEECs: 10 per cent of funding under the PHARE programme was set aside to JHA, of which half was used for border security (Guiraudon 2004: 174). The 2004 and 2007 enlargements also provided the impetus behind launching a range of new measures, legislation and mechanisms. For example, the accession of new member states to the Schengen *acquis* led to the upgrading of the Schengen Information System – a system through which participating member states could alert each other to, inter alia, people who had been refused admission, were wanted for arrest, extradition or to testify in court, or were fugitives.

In 2005, a European Agency for the Management of Operational Cooperation at the External Borders (Frontex) became operational. Frontex supports national authorities with training, technical support and risk-assessment in border control. It is a first pillar agency, yet its effective cooperation with second and third pillar organizations, including Europol, is essential. Such cooperation has also proved problematic. For example, Frontex's migration risk analysis following the Israeli-Lebanon conflict in 2006 would have benefited from second pillar SitCen's intelligence on Lebanon, yet this input was not forthcoming (Donoghue *et al.* 2006).

The task facing Frontex is daunting. The EU has faced in recent years a highly visible and growing immigration crisis on its Mediterranean border. In 2006, it was estimated that more than 30,000 African migrants landed by boat in the Canary Islands, six times more than in 2005, while thousands are believed to have been lost at sea. Frontex has undertaken operations patrolling the Mediterranean coastal area (operation Nautilus) to stem the influx of illegal immigrants crossing from North Africa to Europe during the summer months. Frontex operations have also included patrolling the shores of Mauritania, Senegal and Cape Verde to try to stop immigration at source. However, JHA Commissioner Franco Frattini has criticized member states' willingness to turn their political commitment into concrete action, in June 2007 lamenting the fact that only one tenth of the boats, helicopters and planes promised to Frontex had been delivered (BBC 2007).

Frontex's operations do risk contributing to an ever growing securitization of the EU's borders. There is indeed a difficult balance to be found between internal security threats and larger foreign policy goals. As such, developing rigorous external border controls is deemed essential for internal 'security' (to prevent widespread immigration or organized crime), yet enhancing the stability of the circle of states surrounding the EU is essential to broader foreign policy goals. This latter goal can be negatively affected by EU border controls. As Apap argued in 2001, as the Soviet bloc dissolved, a 'unique area of liberalised movement of persons emerged in Central Europe' thanks to an open-border policy, which 'significantly contributed to efforts to overcome the historical legacy of mutual prejudice, stereotypes and resentment' (Apap *et al.* 2001: 2). With accession, and the adoption of the Schengen system by the CEECs, this disappeared.

Guiraudon (2004: 174–5) gives the Poland–Ukraine example. Prior to enlargement, 2.5 million Ukrainian migrant workers and small traders entered Poland annually. In addition to economic development, this served important goals of promoting Ukrainian stability, acting as a counterbalance to Russian influence in Ukraine and supporting the activities of the Ukrainian democratic opposition, which operated largely out of Poland. The example of Romania and Moldova illustrates the point too. Because of EU accession, at the beginning of 2007 Romania had to introduce visas for Moldovans who previously could have travelled into Romania with only a simple identity card. The new visa requirements have created significant tensions between two countries which had shared a close historical, social and economic past. Likewise, the introduction of Schengen border controls had an adverse effect on national minorities, such as Hungarians living in Slovakia, Romania, Ukraine and Serbia. This gives rise to an interesting paradox: under the Copenhagen Criteria, the protection of minorities is a prerequisite for accession. Yet, by forcing the accession states to adopt the Schengen *acquis*, and imposing its borders further East, the EU effectively endangered this.

Immigration and asylum

The EU's response to the perceived need to tackle immigration and asylum has included the adoption of a range of remote-control (beyond its borders) policies. The aim of such policies is to prevent migrants reaching the EU in the first place. There are two different approaches in remote-control policies. Firstly, 'forms of cooperation that essentially externalize traditional tools of domestic or EU migration control' (Boswell 2003: 619) using primarily restrictive tools such as border controls, visa policy and facilitating return through readmission agreements. Secondly, adopting a 'preventive' approach, which uses 'measures designed to change the factors which influence people's decisions to move, or their chosen destinations' (ibid.: 620). This relates to issues such as the causes of migration flows and providing protection for refugees nearer to their country of origin. With its stress on the need to develop partnerships with third countries of origin and transit, and focus on issues such as border controls and readmission, the 2004 Hague Programme which set the course for the EU's action in AFSJ for the 2005–09 period, the EU appeared to reaffirm its position in the first camp.

This was re-emphasized in the development of the EU's 'blacklist' of countries for which visits for a period of three months or less require a Schengen visa, which is not straightforward to obtain. In theory, there are supposed to be criteria for the inclusion of countries on the blacklist, but, in practice, member states lobby for the inclusion of specific countries from which they fear large-scale immigration, hence the EU blacklist is longer than any of the previous national lists (Guiraudon 2004: 177). It is indicative of the EU's overall approach to immigration/asylum and other related JHA issues that although there is a burgeoning body of measures to combat illegal immigration, legal migration and the rights of third country nationals has been one of the slowest moving areas (House of Lords 2005a: para. 25).

Third countries which fail to cooperate with the EU's immigration agenda risk sanction. In 2002, the UK and Spain went so far as to propose that development aid should be conditional on third country cooperation in migration control. The final text adopted at the Seville European Council did not go quite this far, but did threaten third countries that had 'shown an unjustified lack of cooperation in joint management of migration flows' with the adoption of 'measures or positions under the Common Foreign and Security Policy and other European Union policies, while honouring the Union's contractual commitments and not jeopardising development cooperation objectives' (European Council 2002: 12). A positive spin framed the same sentiment in the 2005 *Strategy for the External Dimension of JHA* which stated that countries 'should be aware that the nature of their relationship with the EU will be positively affected by their level of co-operation [on JHA issues]' (Council 2005b: 5).

For policy-makers, the balance has been to meet growing popular concerns, particularly relating to immigration, whilst not building the regulatory equivalent of the Berlin Wall. In any case, two points are quite clear. First, the area of freedom, security and justice has been developed first and foremost for EU citizens and, although achieving internal AFSJ goals requires external action, there is little evidence that the freedom, security and justice of third country citizens has been of major concern. Obviously, this sheds quite a different light on the EU as a normative power. Second, the EU's approach has been criticized for a one-sided emphasis on 'security' at the expense of the elements of 'justice' and 'freedom'. This 'securitization' process, which had been evident since the mid-1980s and particularly in the late 1990s, occurred in a broad spectrum of issues, some of which (immigration or asylum, for example) were clearly not a security threat per se but were nonetheless framed as fitting within the security agenda (Anderson and Apap 2002; see also Huysmans 2000, 2006). One consequence of this has been that AFSJ issues increasingly interfere with foreign and security issues, and thus also affect the EU's foreign policy.

Agreements

The EU can incorporate AFSJ issues into its cooperation and association agreements with third countries, and can also conclude specific AFSJ agreements with third countries/organizations. These are the main operational instruments of foreign policy-making in AFSJ. Indeed, the EU has deemed working with third countries essential to responding to terrorism, organized crime, corruption and drugs and managing migration. In 2005, the Council argued that the 'EU should therefore make JHA a central priority in its external relations and ensure a co-ordinated and coherent approach' (Council 2005b: 2).

Within the EU's first pillar (under Title IV TEC), the EU can negotiate readmission agreements with third countries which provide for the return of illegal residents to their country of origin or transit and also visa facilitation agreements. The Community is also party to international legal instruments and is developing closer relations with international organizations working in this domain.

Within the EU's third pillar (under Title VI TEU) the EU can conclude agreements with third states and international organizations on police and judicial cooperation in criminal matters (Art. 38 TEU). Examples of these are the 2003 agreements with the US on extradition and on mutual legal assistance. There is also a slightly different category of agreements between agencies created under Title VI TEU, such as the European Police Office (Europol) and Judicial Cooperation Unit (Eurojust), which have legal personality and can conclude agreements with third countries and international organizations. Europol has, for instance, concluded agreements with the US on the exchange of information, including personal data (Commission 2005b). Europol agreements have proved controversial, particularly because of the lower data protection standards in the US and lack of parliamentary control to provide a framework for accountability.

The inclusion of AFSJ issues in agreements with third countries has become a particular priority for the EU's neighbourhood (Council 2005b: 6). In concrete terms, the EU's policy takes several forms ranging from incorporation of AFSJ issues in political dialogue to the development and implementation of specific projects financed by the EU. In the Balkans, the EU supported through its CARDS programme (Community Assistance for Reconstruction, Development and Stabilisation) the development of four priority areas – police and organized crime, integrated border management, judicial reform, and asylum and migration. AFSJ issues are also a priority in relations with the Mediterranean. On a bilateral level, through the MEDA programme, the EU has supported projects on migration, the judiciary and law enforcement cooperation in several countries, and increasingly prioritized JHA issues in interregional dialogue (Commission 2005b: 10). For example, agreement on a (vague) code of conduct to fight terrorism and a five-year work programme in the areas of security and illegal migration were among the few results of the tenth anniversary meeting of the Euro-Mediterranean partnership, celebrated *en mineur* in Barcelona, in November 2005.

From a foreign policy perspective, this strong emphasis on AFSJ issues in the EU's relationship with its neighbourhood has had major implications. Adopting a comprehensive approach towards the 'human dimension' in relations with neighbouring countries, aimed at promoting fundamental structural changes, has been abandoned in favour of a much narrower focus on internal security and migration issues. The AFSJ approach has thus to some extent hijacked and undermined the structural foreign policy approach that had inspired relations a decade previously. And, since the EU relies on these countries' cooperation to achieve its AFSJ priorities, the EU has also weakened its leverage with regard to human rights and democratization issues. For political leaders and public opinion, tackling AFSJ concerns has become more urgent than foreign policy objectives which, particularly in the case of the Mediterranean, had in any case minimal prospect of success (see also Chapter 10).

Terrorism

Nowhere is the blurring of the inside/outside divide more pronounced than in the terrorist threat, and the policy response it has evoked. Although in the wake of the terrorist attacks against the US in September 2001 the EU treated terrorism more as an international problem, the Madrid (2004) and London (2005) bombings were an abrupt realization that 'home-grown' terrorism was equally on the agenda. The existence of 'sleeper cells' within the EU, composed of EU citizens or legal residents but trained abroad and belonging to loose international terrorist networks, threw up a new array of challenges relating to issues as diverse as the integration of immigrant communities and foreign policy choices. It was immediately clear, however, that it was the member states rather than the EU that possessed the majority of instruments that would be needed for countering terrorism. Indeed, protecting its population is one of the core *raisons d'être* of the state, and tools to handle the terrorist threat, including intelligence, judicial and law enforcement systems, go to the very heart of national sovereignty.

The 2001 attacks on the US precipitated a frenetic burst of activity at the EU level with agreement being reached on issues where divergence had previously proved insurmountable. Bombings in Madrid and London had a similarly catalytic effect (for a detailed analysis, see Mahncke and Monar 2006). Concrete developments were achieved in terms of institutions and policy. At the institutional level, the Council set up the Council Working Party on Terrorism (COTER); in the third pillar a counterterrorism taskforce was established within Europol, which was also given extra resources; Eurojust was to be used to facilitate cooperation between national magistrates on cross-border investigations; while the position of Counter-Terrorism Coordinator was created and institutionally located within the High Representative's staff.

In terms of policy, in 2001 EU governments agreed an EU Action Plan on combating terrorism detailing around 200 measures across a wide range of policy areas from infrastructure protection in the event of attack to money laundering legislation. This was revised and updated into an *EU Plan of Action on Combating Terrorism*, adopted by the European Council in 2004 along with a *Declaration on Combating Terrorism* (Council

2004a; European Council 2004a). As Thieux (2004: 63) argues, neither of these documents were particularly innovative. Rather, they emphasized the necessity of strengthening the measures already adopted, the implementation of which had proved patchy. In fact, many of these initiatives had been initially agreed on at the European Council meeting in Tampere in October 1999.

In 2005, the EU adopted a *Counter-Terrorism Strategy* composed of four strands: prevention (tackling the factors or root causes which can lead to radicalization and recruitment); protection (protecting citizens and infrastructure and reducing vulnerability, including through heightened border controls and security measures); pursue (pursuing, investigating and prosecuting terrorists transnationally and impeding terrorist attack by disrupting support networks, funding sources, travel, etc.); and respond (managing and minimizing the consequences of terrorist attack) (Council 2005d). From a legislative perspective, member states adopted a wide range of new measures including a common definition of terrorism, a list of terrorist organizations, an EU-wide arrest warrant, rules for joint operations between national police forces, and legislation on money laundering and asset seizing.

As the list above indicates, the largest part of the EU's response to terrorism has been internal. Even the role envisaged for ESDP (normally an instrument of foreign policy) is in this case largely responding to the consequences of terrorist attack *within* the Union. However, counterterrorism has also become a strategic priority of EU foreign policy and is incorporated across the whole gamut of the EU's relations with third parties (see also Chapter 6).

The EU has prioritized cooperation with the US in fighting terrorism, concluding a number of agreements including on extradition, mutual legal assistance and passenger-name records (see Rees 2006). In attempting to build a broader international consensus, and in line with its professed 'choice of multilateralism', the EU has also actively sought to develop cooperation in international fora. In particular, it has thrown its weight behind the adoption of the 2005 UN Convention against Nuclear Terrorism and the 2006 UN Counter-Terrorism Strategy. It has encouraged third countries to ratify and implement the existing 16 anti-terrorism related UN conventions and protocols. Beyond the UN, the EU also cooperates with other relevant international initiatives, including the OECD's Financial Action Task Force, and supports the non-proliferation activities of the International Atomic Energy Agency (IAEA).

The EU has attempted to mainstream cooperation against terrorism in its foreign policy. Hence, it systematically includes a counterterrorism clause in its agreements with third countries, and has initiated political dialogues on counter-terrorism with the USA, Russia, India, Pakistan, Australia and Japan. The seventh objective of the EU's *Plan of Action on Combating Terrorism* is to 'target actions under EU external relations towards priority Third Countries where counter-terrorist capacity or commitment to combating terrorism needs to be enhanced'. In this vein, beyond its broader programmes on democracy, good governance and the rule of law, the EU has pledged to support third countries in the fight against terrorism, through capacity building and financing specific counterterrorism interventions. Under this rubric, the EU has initiated counterterrorism capacity-building initiatives, including with Algeria, Indonesia and Morocco. The Commission uses various financial instruments to increase capacity-building assistance to third countries. An example is the recourse to the Rapid Reaction Mechanism to fund a programme in Pakistan assessing the state of the education system, with particular emphasis on the religious schools (madaris), which have in some cases become a breeding ground for extremism and terrorism (see B. Smith 2002). However, Keohane is critical of the impact of such projects, quoting EU officials as admitting that programmes in Pakistan, Indonesia and the Philippines have so far had 'mixed results' (2006: 76).

Brokering agreements with countries which gained new strategic significance with the beginning of the so-called 'war on terror' has been a policy choice particularly of the US; but the EU has also proved willing to engage in such realpolitik. It signed in November 2001 a cooperation agreement with Pakistan, despite the fact that previously Pakistan had been the subject of sanctions and President Musharaff, who after all came to power through a military coup, had been systematically criticized. A similar pattern has been repeated with several Central Asian Republics. In 2006 and 2007, for example, several member states sought to roll back sanctions with Uzbekistan, in part because of its geostrategic importance in the fight against terrorism (including NATO's anti-Taliban operation in Afghanistan) (Rees 2006: 133).

That the EU has clearly been prepared to sweep to one side considerations about the health of certain regimes, including their respect for democracy, human rights and the rule of law in these instances does nuance the convictions of proponents of the EU as a normative power. Thieux is highly critical of the EU's confused priorities. While building democracy and respect for human rights is now understood as critical to the fight against terrorism, this has never been prioritized in the EU's relations with the Maghreb and the Middle East, and the EU 'has implicitly supported the authoritarian regimes', a tendency which was 'strengthened when the political ascent of the Islamist movements began to challenge them in the 1980s' (Thieux 2004: 68).

It would be unwise in this context to attempt to measure the impact of the EU's initiatives on the likelihood of future terrorist attack within Europe, or on 'Western' interests abroad. But, a couple of points are worth noting. From an internal perspective, member states' continued failure to implement agreed anti-terrorism legislation in a timely or accurate manner is highly problematic. They have also struggled to cooperate on critical areas such as sharing intelligence. Although they do increasingly provide 'sanitized' intelligence data to Europol and other EU collaborative bodies, sharing sensitive intelligence on terrorism will normally only occur at the bilateral or trilateral level (Wilkinson 2005: 35) and not through the infamously 'leaky' EU.

Coordinating efforts, particularly from an institutional perspective, further frustrates the EU's efforts. Hence, whilst member states created the Counter-Terrorism Coordinator, they failed to provide this role with sufficient resources or a robust mandate. They thus risked adding little more to the counterterrorism fight than a further layer of institutional complexity. While clarity of roles and responsibilities is critical in such a sensitive and strategic policy field, there is 'a multiplicity of groups, some within the Second Pillar, some within the Third Pillar, some outside the pillared structure altogether. Some have a policy focus, some an intelligence focus and others an operational focus' (House of Lords 2005b: 27).

To conclude, it seems a truism to argue that member states would demonstrate high levels of mutual solidarity in the face of external terrorist attack. But this question of solidarity is less clear cut than it might at first appear. At least in the domain of foreign policy, there are examples to the contrary, including the quickly forgotten Leila/Perejil crisis of July 2002 (see Monar 2002). Countries might not only be reluctant to demonstrate solidarity, but also to *accept* acts of solidarity. Discussions on this issue within the EU immediately after the terrorist attacks in Madrid 2004 and London 2005 were quite remarkable. After the attacks in Madrid, EU member states expressed themselves in a joint declaration of solidarity. However, one year later, the British government in the aftermath of suicide bombings in London made it clear that it did not want a similar declaration of solidarity from the EU. For the British, the Atlantic Alliance, not the EU, was the context in which the European partners were to express their solidarity.

Energy

Energy security is a hotly debated topic in the EU, but it is not a new issue. It has been widely discussed at least since the 1973–74 Arab oil embargo, which triggered one of the first major foreign policy actions of the fledgling EPC (see Chapter 2). However, as was the case then, the looming threat to energy security has not automatically led to member states developing a genuine 'common' energy policy. And, as in the 1970s, the inclusion of energy security objectives in EU foreign policy has been problematic. It was not until June 2007 that the European Council confirmed that energy policy would get a legal basis in the Lisbon/Reform Treaty, with ensuring 'security of energy supply in the Union' becoming one of the objectives.

The challenges

The EU faces a number of pressing challenges in the energy field. A first challenge is the EU's growing import dependence. In the next 20 to 30 years, around 70 per cent of the Union's energy requirements, compared to around 50 per cent today, will be met by imported products (Commission 2006b: 3). In 2004, the EU25 energy dependence rate (EDR) was at 53.8 per cent, although this picture varied considerably across the member states. Denmark is a net energy exporter and the UK only became a net importer for the first time in 2004. All other member states are sizeable importers with EDRs of 64.6 per cent in Germany, 54.3 per cent in France, 87.7 per cent in Italy and 81 per cent in Spain (Gikas and Keenan 2006: 1). These varying dependence rates have an impact on the way member states position themselves both in terms of a future common energy policy and in the EU's foreign policy towards Russia or the Middle East. Consequently, energy should not only be understood as a subject of foreign policy. It also provides one explanation for member states' positions on different foreign policy issues and for the EU's (in)ability to define and implement a common foreign and security policy.

A second challenge is that many of the main energy producers are in unstable regions such as the Middle East, or are countries with which the EU has a difficult relationship, such as Russia. In 2004, Russia provided 27 per cent of the EU's oil consumption, the Middle East 19 per cent and North Africa 12 per cent. The natural gas supply situation was more comfortable with nearly 60 per cent covered by domestic production or by Norway, although 24 per cent was still imported from Russia and 10 per cent from Algeria (Commission and Secretary General/High Representative 2006). Russia and its largest energy monopoly, Gazprom, have made clear that they are prepared to exploit their energy dominance, which could have serious consequences. For example, in 2006 and 2007, Russia flexed its energy muscles, hiking up prices for Moldova, Georgia and the Ukraine, and temporarily cutting off supplies to Ukraine and Belarus. When Russia turned off the tap it also led to shortages of gas and oil within the EU, with some member states experiencing a fall of Russian energy supply of between one third and one quarter.

A quick glance at a map of oil and gas reserves indicates that the future is unlikely to be any easier. Countries with significant reserves include: Venezuela, Kazakhstan, Russia, Iran, Iraq, Kuwait, Saudi Arabia, Qatar, Libya and Nigeria (BP 2005: 4, 22). Taking into account that additional production capacity will be indispensable to cover higher global consumption and replace declining oil and gas reserves, this simple list of countries clearly demonstrates the daunting foreign policy challenges ahead (for a detailed analysis of energy supply security and geopolitics, see CIEP 2004).

This is related to the third challenge: growing international demand for energy. China, India and other rapidly industrializing states are increasingly competing for global energy resources, while energy consumption in developed countries, including the US and the EU's member states, continues to rise, albeit at a slower rate. World energy demand is expected to rise by 60 per cent by 2030 (Commission 2006b: 3). China in particular is developing a very proactive foreign policy in which guaranteeing future energy supplies plays a central role. This increasingly thwarts EU foreign policy with regard to Africa, human rights and democracy.

The foreign policy response

The European Commission in 2000 presented its Green Paper *Towards a European Strategy for the Security of Energy Supply* (2000) even before the major upheavals of the first years of the millennium forced member states and the Council to take the issue more seriously. With this Green Paper, the Commission appeared as a strategic actor defining Europe's interests, future challenges and possible responses. In so doing, the Commission emphasized just how poorly equipped the EU was to face the potential problems, not least since there was no explicit mandate for a European energy policy in the treaties. The EU lacked the means to negotiate and exert pressure on third countries, and suffered from having no competence and no Community cohesion in energy matters. The member states largely turned a blind eye to the Commission's proposals and did not adopt any major concrete initiatives on energy security within the Council, although energy policy does gain a stronger treaty basis in the Lisbon/Reform Treaty (IGC 2007).

In the context of instability in Iraq, Iran's nuclear ambitions, China's growing energy demands and Russia's newly assertive energy policies, the Commission launched a new Green Paper on *A European Strategy for Sustainable, Competitive and Secure Energy* in 2006. Although it largely elaborated old proposals, the core of this new document was 'whether there is agreement on the need to develop a new, common European strategy for energy' (Commission 2006b: 4). The question was quickly answered when, some weeks later, the 2006 Spring European Council called for an 'Energy Policy for Europe' – and not for a 'Common Energy Policy', even if the member states' Heads of State and Government agreed on basic principles and launched a process of intensified deliberation on strengthening cooperation in energy policy. There is clear agreement at the European level that the current situation in terms of energy supply and transit is problematic. Yet, reaching agreement on how and what to do about this is rather more complex, with member states proving extremely reluctant to hand responsibility over to 'Brussels'. This was confirmed in a rush of new initiatives adopted in the following year, including during the European Council's 'Energy Summit' in March 2007 (2007a). Moreover, certain topics, and notably the role of nuclear power in meeting EU energy needs, remain highly controversial.

From a foreign policy perspective, there are a number of interesting issues, of which the following are discussed here: the development of critical infrastructure, securing and diversifying energy supplies, and developing relationships with the main energy suppliers.

The development of critical infrastructure revolves around identifying priorities for upgrading and constructing new infrastructure to ensure supply security. This includes, for example, the Nabucco gas pipeline project, aimed at constructing a 3,400 km pipeline across South East Europe to the end of Anatolia, to facilitate the transit of Caspian oil supplies to the EU (Hoogeveen and Perlot 2005: 139). This project is supported both politically and (to a limited extent) financially by the Commission. However, the notion of developing a common approach has been overtaken by member states' realpolitik and attempts to develop privileged bilateral contacts and contracts with energy suppliers. A case in point is the German–Russian endeavour to construct a pipeline through the Baltic Sea without involving Poland or the Baltic member states – undermining not only the common external policy approach towards energy supply but also the objective of developing energy transit routes which bypass Russia.

The second issue at stake is diversifying energy sources, the main objective being to reduce dependence on Russia (gas) and the Middle East (oil). The Nabucco gas pipeline project, which would allow countries such as Iran, Azerbaijan and Turkmenistan to supply the EU with gas, is one example. However, none of these countries are without their own problems (ibid.: 138–9). Ensuring the political and economic stability of these and other producer countries would make a major contribution to uninterrupted energy supply. But, as the significant diplomatic energy the EU expended on Iran demonstrates, this will not be easily achieved. We can also understand the European Neighbourhood Policy in this context. The promotion of 'a ring of well governed countries to the East of the European Union and on the borders of the Mediterranean with whom we can enjoy close and cooperative relations' (European Council 2003b: 9) is positive for an array of reasons, but is also important for stabilizing the EU's energy supply.

The need to secure and diversify energy sources might in the future imply looking to different regions, such as Africa's oil producing states (Sudan, Angola, Libya, Nigeria and Egypt). This will bring to the fore questions of how to prioritize foreign policy objectives. For example, is the EU prepared to buy oil from Sudan even though the government in Khartoum is accused of supporting the systematic eradication of its population in Darfur? For the EU we might think this would be difficult. For other countries, such as China, the prioritizing of pure strategic interests above more normative or values-driven goals so far seems to be less of a concern. However, the question of which of its major foreign policy goals the EU might be prepared to sacrifice to improve access to energy is probably less difficult than at first sight. The EU was heavily criticized in 2006 for negotiating a trade agreement with Turkmenistan, a process under which human rights concerns were largely put to one side in favour of European companies' access to Turkmenistan's huge gas reserves. The EU has also maintained a relationship with Saudi Arabia to guarantee oil access despite this country's poor human rights record and lack of democracy. The EU thus seems to be just as determined to prioritize pure strategic interests above values-driven goals.

Furthering energy dialogues with the main energy suppliers appears as an objective in most recent EU texts on energy security. Energy dialogues have been inserted as part of agreements with a large number of third countries and regional organizations, and the EU is holding out the promise of heightened cooperation with other 'strategic partners' such as Turkey, Ukraine and the Caspian and Mediterranean countries. However, the effectiveness of this dialogue is dubious – particularly with regard to Moscow. The EU and Russia already in 2000 launched an Energy Dialogue which also covered security of supply and infrastructure. Although this has resulted in regular meetings of experts and high-level political discussions at annual EU–Russia summits, the result has been of a more symbolic than substantive nature. There is continued disagreement on many fundamental issues such as pipelines, gas supply contracts and nuclear fuel supplies (Grant and Barysch 2003). Russia not only holds most of the bargaining chips, but the EU and Russia also play by different rules of the game. As Emerson points out: 'The EU is all about supranational rules of economic and political conduct and dispute settlement by ordered legal procedures, whereas Russia is showing itself to be all about raw power, with little or no regard for any overarching international legal framework' (2006). EU foreign policy is struggling to internalize this reality, which does not fit within its 'civilized' and rules-based approach to foreign policy. As argued in Chapter 1, discussions about the EU's power are not just about whether the EU needs military instruments to back up its civilian power, but also about whether the EU actually has, or is able to use, its (civilian) power.

The EU's failure to 'speak with one voice' does limit its potential to effect change in the high geopolitics of energy. But, this is not to argue that the EU is impotent. Economically powerful, the EU is a large consumer and a large trading partner, particularly for Russia, which depends on EU investment to improve its energy infrastructure, but also for other energy supplying countries. Whether the EU's developing foreign policy will equip it to just react to crises, or to proactively influence the structures and rules of the game that will determine the following decades, will be pivotal to its future energy security.

Environment

From a foreign policy perspective, EU environmental policy provides an interesting case. This policy has demonstrated the EU's potential to act as a structural power on the international scene and has played an important role in asserting and shaping its international identity. In terms of the treaty basis for EC external action in this field, Title XIX on 'Environment' (Art. 174 TEC) explicitly defines 'promoting measures at international level to deal with regional or worldwide environmental problems' as one of the four objectives to which EU policy should contribute. To this end, the treaty foresees that the EC and member states shall cooperate with third countries and competent international organizations, including entering into agreements between the EC and relevant third parties as long as this does not prejudice member states' own competence to negotiate in international bodies and to conclude international agreements.

The EU does not have a *common* environmental policy comparable to the common agricultural policy or the common commercial policy – it has 'a policy in the sphere of the environment' (Art. 3 TEC), which has important ramifications for external representation and hence ability to influence and negotiate at the international level. Moreover, as Bretherton and Vogler (2006: 91) emphasize, environmental policy has been incrementally pieced together internally, which is reflected in the lack of clear lines of responsibility externally. These constraining factors aside, external environmental policy has been an important feather in the EU's foreign policy cap and, referring to the concepts presented in Chapter 1, environmental policy is one of the most significant fields in which the EU seeks to pursue milieu goals and global public goods.

Leadership in global environmental governance

As the US gradually abdicated from its leadership in international environmental policy, the EU happily stepped up to fill the vacant seat, and today regularly claims leadership in global environmental governance (Vogler 2005: 835–7). The EU has indeed played an important role contributing to multilateral environmental agreements. The best and most visible example of this was during climate change negotiations and the ratification of the Kyoto Protocol, discussed below. However, the EU has also been active on other fronts. For example, it assumed a leadership role in strengthening the Montreal Protocol on Substances that Deplete the Ozone Layer, and it was at the forefront of negotiations on the cross-border movement of hazardous chemicals and on attempts to provide a regulatory framework for GMOs (Bretherton and Vogler 2006: 105).

The EU has also contributed to the dissemination of environmental practices and standards. This has been most evident with the Union's enlargement. By virtue of the transposition of the *acquis* into the national law of new member states, an extensive corpus of environmental legislation has gradually spread over European countries. In the words of the Commission (2001b: 13): '[t]he enlargement of the European Union may in fact be the biggest single contribution to global sustainable development that the EU can make'.

EU agreements with third countries generally incorporate environmental clauses and third countries have to meet certain environmental standards to trade with the EU. Regionally, the EU is an important environmental actor both *vis-à-vis* Russia and the ex-Soviet countries (through Partnership and Cooperation Agreements and the ENP) and the Mediterranean (through the Euro-Mediterranean Policy and the ENP). In both regions, the EU is active in raising environmental standards using dialogue, technical expertise and (most importantly) funding. This should not come as a surprise – as Vogler points out, among its neighbours, the Union has had 'a deeply self-interested concern to use financial instruments to minimize the possibility of transboundary and particularly nuclear contamination' (2005: 842). For the EU, regional environmental cooperation is a question of far-sighted self-interest.

Environment and relational power

International environmental agreements are one example of a genre of long-term rules-based international relations which fits comfortably with the EU's structural power. However, exerting relational power has also been essential for the EU to achieve its environmental goals internationally. This has been particularly evident with regard to the 1997 Kyoto Protocol to the UN Framework Convention on Climate Change (UN FCCC), which sets legally binding limits on emissions.

In 2001, George W. Bush announced that the US would not ratify the Kyoto Protocol, threatening its coming into force. This rejection reflected a more general reluctance to see American policy bound by international rules. It also mirrored a fundamentally different environmental policy ethos, with the US leaning more towards market-led approaches and to a *'use-with-risk* strategy', which ran in contrast to the EU's tendency towards 'a more cautious, risk *aversion* strategy' (Baker 2006: 91–2).

Despite its privileged partnership with the US and intensive transatlantic dialogue, the EU proved incapable of influencing the American position, a clear example of the absence of relational power *vis-à-vis* the US (see Chapter 11).

The EU's policy towards Russia tells quite a different story, in which the EU has been ready to use other policy instruments to achieve environmental goals. Following the US decision to pull out of the Kyoto Protocol, and in the face of ambivalence from Australia, Canada and Japan, Russia's ratification became crucial for the Protocol – it had to be ratified by 55 countries, accounting for at least 55 per cent of developed-world greenhouse-gas emissions, before it could come into force. The EU hinged its support for Russia's admission to the WTO on its agreement to ratify Kyoto, which was finally achieved in 2004 (Bretherton and Vogler 2006: 109).

The EU's use of an active and coordinated diplomacy to achieve this did, as ever, come in competition with other foreign policy objectives. Prioritizing ratification of the Kyoto Protocol implied that in its diplomatic contacts with Russia, the EU and its largest member states had to choose between its various foreign policy priorities. In 2003–04, in addition to Kyoto, these priorities included gaining support from Moscow for the EU3 efforts on Iran; for France and Germany gaining support from Moscow for their views on Iraq; Russian agreement on the 'Four Spaces'; Chechnya; and the deteriorating human rights and freedom of speech situation in Russia.

Kyoto, and the EU's environmental leadership more broadly, should be understood as a major identity goal of the EU. Environmental foreign policy is used as an instrument to demonstrate international leadership where there is diplomatic space for it to assume such a role, and which happily coincides with real concerns of the EU's population. To some extent, this compensates for the fact that the EU can deliver less in the traditional foreign policy domain. In this sense, succeeding on the Kyoto issue was seen as crucial, even at the expense of other foreign policy goals. Indeed, we could argue that Kyoto gradually became more important as an identity goal than as a policy goal, which we might also conclude from the difficulties EU member states' had in the national ratification process and in complying with Kyoto targets themselves.

Health and demography

The threats faced by European populations today are not only about external factors but also about internal factors such as terrorism, environmental degradation, communicable disease or demographic change. These issues have not historically been strictly related to foreign policy. Yet, in the future, they may well be the foreign policy and security issues splashed all over CNN. This chapter finishes by looking briefly at health and the impact of demographic change on the EU.

Health

In the last decade, health has grown in importance on the international agenda, and is increasingly framed as a security risk. Disease figures as a 'global challenge' in the *European Security Strategy*: 'In much of the developing world, poverty and disease cause untold suffering and give rise to pressing security concerns . . . AIDS is now one of the most devastating pandemics in human history and contributes to the breakdown of societies. New diseases can spread rapidly and become global threats' (European Council 2003b: 2). There are two dimensions to the intersection between health and foreign/security policy: firstly, using foreign policy to protect against health threats to the domestic population; and, secondly, using foreign policy to promote global public health.

Using foreign policy to protect the domestic population from health threats refers particularly to vulnerability to transnational health risks. One of the many side-effects of globalization is that population movements and wide-scale access to international travel mean infectious disease can now spread quickly across the globe. Severe acute respiratory syndrome (SARS) and avian influenza are among the more recent cases. In the EU, this issue has been treated first and foremost as an internal issue, with minimal foreign policy relevance.

The spread of infectious disease can also be the result of bioterrorist attack. The EU is vulnerable to the deliberate release of biological/chemical agents with the potential to cause widespread harm. The small-scale incidents involving anthrax spores in the US in the aftermath of September 11 and the discovery in early 2003 of Ricin (a potentially fatal toxic substance) in a building in London, were sharp reminders of Europe's vulnerability. As the 2003 *European Security Strategy* acknowledged, '[a]dvances in the biological sciences may increase the potency of biological weapons in the coming years; attacks with chemical and radiological materials are also a serious possibility' (European Council 2003b: 3). In the context of the *European Strategy against the Proliferation of Weapons of Mass Destruction* (Council, 2003), the EU has supported initiatives to strengthen and promote international regimes such as the Biological and Toxin Weapons Convention and has taken other initiatives to prevent unauthorized access to, and risks of diversion of, lethal biological products.

Beyond the obvious counterterrorist dimension, there are further important areas of foreign policy concern. For example, in the global rush to obtain key vaccines, these have been left in short supply, in turn resulting in foreign policy tensions over the hoarding of essential drugs by the US (McInnes and Lee 2006: 14). In the EU, this core issue of the availability of vaccines has not been answered through a common response, as had been proposed by the Commission. Instead, member states have resisted stockpiling at the EU level, prioritizing purely national measures. This clearly runs counter to declared commitments of solidarity, reflecting the broader solidarity problematic of the EU's foreign, security and defence policy. Member states' refusal to stockpile at the EU level is also illustrative of their response to many new threats: they provoke intense cooperation between member states and the EU institutions, but, on crucial points, the member states recoil from formulating a genuinely *common* policy.

The second dimension to the health–foreign/security policy intersection is focused on pursuing milieu goals – the promotion of global public health. This is both a question of solidarity and compassion as well as of far-reaching self-interest. As McInnes and Lee argue (2006: 16), we can understand the promotion of global health as being in an actor's own interests if we agree that poor health is destabilizing because it undermines state economic and social structures, and because tools to maintain state order (security forces) are particularly prone to sexually transmitted diseases, including HIV/AIDS. In this context, it is clear that the chance of foreign policy initiatives succeeding in stabilizing the countries of Southern Africa – where, for example, HIV infection rates stand at a staggering 20 per cent in Zimbabwe, 24 per cent in Botswana and 33 per cent in Swaziland – is critically hampered by the devastating impact of this pandemic (UNAIDS/WHO 2006).

The EU promotes global public health through its development policy, and also through particular trade initiatives. For example, it played an active role in negotiating amendments to the World Trade Organisation's Agreement on Intellectual Property (TRIPS) to improve access to medicines by allowing poor countries without manufacturing capacities in the pharmaceutical sector to import generic medicines for humanitarian purposes. However, global public health scarcely features on Foreign Ministers' agendas. In their analysis of the relationship between health, security and foreign policy, McInnes and Lee (2006: 22) argue convincingly that:

> [t]he relationship between the two policy communities [global public health and foreign/security] tends to be unidirectional, namely how selected health issues may create risks for (inter)national security or economic growth, and how therefore they might be issues of concern to foreign and security policy. The agenda is not one of how foreign and security policy can promote global public health.

This point is highly pertinent, relating as it does to questions formulated in Chapter 1 about which issues are considered to lie within the foreign policy remit and which goals structure foreign policy. For example, why is it that democratic elections or free speech are firmly on the foreign policy agenda and are clear objectives of EU foreign policy when this is not the case with public health issues even though on an individual basis, health is clearly of more vital and pressing concern than the ballot box? This is also linked to the West's conceptual fixation with human rights, and its neglect of wider human security issues (see Chapter 1).

Taking a non-Western centric view of health also puts the EU's focus on bio-terrorism and terrorism more generally into perspective. Globally speaking, in quantitative terms, the threat to life from biological weapons is probably rather small. But, terrorism is, and is seen to be, a threat to the West. The level of response is thus a function of perspective rather than level of objective global threat. In its 2006 Human Development Report, the United Nations Development Programme (UNDP) states that some 1.8 million children die annually as a result of diarrhoea – 4,900 deaths each day. The Report continues, 'Deaths from diarrhoea in 2004 were some six times greater than the average annual deaths in armed conflict for the 1990s' (UNDP 2006: 6). Yet diarrhoea is yet to figure on the foreign policy agenda. Bioterrorism is not the only way that disease can be used as an instrument of aggression. Another example is the use of rape as a weapon of war. Above and beyond the psychological, social and physical harm of victims, this plays a role in the spread of HIV/AIDS, has a long-term disruptive effect on societies and undermines efforts to pursue post-conflict stabilization. Rape has been systematically used as a weapon of war in, for example, Bosnia, Sudan and the DRC (Amnesty International 2004). Yet, this dimension of 'bio-terrorism' is not emphasized in EU foreign policy.

Demography

The change in Europe's demographics ranks alongside climate change and energy security as a major preoccupation for Europe in the decades to come. Faithful to its responsibility to act in the general interests of the EU, the European Commission is increasingly drawing attention to the dramatic demographic challenges facing the EU – in sharp contrast to the silence of the Council on this issue. In its Green Paper, *Confronting Demographic Change*, the Commission (2005c) highlights two major demographic issues.

The first is falling birth rates. The fertility rate required to renew Europe's population is around 2.1 children per woman. However, in many member states, the birth rate has fallen below 1.5 children per woman and immigration has become essential to population growth. Demography is not a foreign policy issue per se. However, shrinking populations do constitute a threat to a nation's vital interests and to its societal security. Combined with the relative increasing demographic size of other regions, the consequence of demographic patterns in Europe is that the share of the EU-25 of world population between 2000–30 is likely to fall from 12 per cent to 6 per cent (Commission 2005c: 16). This evolution, together with its budgetary implications, is likely to have a significant impact on the EU's international weight.

The second major issue is changes to Europe's demographic structure and particularly its ageing population. The decrease in size of the EU's population is much more pronounced when we consider only the population of working age. In its study on *The Impact of Ageing on Public Expenditure* (2006c) the Commission estimates that:

> Starting already from 2010, the working age population (15–64) is projected to fall by 48 million (or 16 per cent) by 2050. In contrast, the elderly population aged 65+ will rise sharply, by 58 million (or 77 per cent) by 2050 . . . Europe will go from having four people of working age for every elderly citizen currently to a ratio of two to one by 2050.

These evolving dependency ratios in turn have a major impact on competitiveness (decrease in number of persons employed, decline in GDP growth) and the European social model (increases in public spending for pensions, health care and long-term care). Changes in EU demography thus imply a growing fiscal burden. Whether the societal model of EU member states, based on a socially corrected market economy, is sustainable in financial and 'personnel' terms is questionable in this context of demographic change. In addition to the risk of societal survival, this implies foreign policy related choices. For example, should the EU expedite Turkey's accession because its younger population could help redress Europe's demographic imbalance? In a similar vein, the EU will have to decide whether despite popular concerns regarding immigration, EU countries should in fact be increasing immigration both over the short-term (to bolster the work force) and the long-term (to have an impact on dependency ratios).

Conclusion

In steering change in the policy fields considered here – freedom, security and justice, terrorism, energy, the environment, health and demographics – a number of themes recur, which are the subject of this conclusion. In the majority of policy fields discussed, the Commission has presented itself as both a strategic actor and one which was able to design comprehensive long-term programmes to tackle the challenges it had recognized and to further common interests therein.

In most of these dossiers, member states within the Council have only reluctantly accepted the formulation of common policies, the transfer of new competences to the EU level and the operational involvement of central EU actors in new policy fields. It is understandable that member states have often been reluctant, or have outright refused, to transfer competences to the EU level. Yet, it remains paradoxical since the ability of nation states to tackle the risks and challenges invoked in this chapter is often limited. Perhaps unsurprisingly, advances have often only been possible in the aftermath of dramatic events (such as terrorist attacks in the US, London and Madrid) or sudden crises which demonstrated the EU's vulnerability (such as gas shortages when Moscow cut off supplies to Ukraine and Belarus).

Finally, characteristic of each policy field mentioned here is that other institutional actors on both the EU and national level play a role in developing new policies, with Ministers, ministries, DGs and civil servants responsible for justice, counterterrorism, the environment, energy and health being central. The blurring inside/outside divide in policy is thus paralleled by a blurring of the traditional picture of foreign policy actors responsible for managing relations with the outside world.

Chapter 10

The Main Arenas of EU Foreign Policy

This chapter analyses in brief the main arenas of EU foreign policy – Central and Eastern Europe, the Balkans, the Commonwealth of Independent States, the Mediterranean, the Middle East and Africa. For each arena discussed, we assess the extent to which the EU has gone beyond trade and contractual relations towards developing a conventional foreign policy and a structural foreign policy (see Chapter 1). As such, we are concerned with whether the EU has successfully influenced the political, socio-economic, security and mental structures of the region and whether the EU has also tackled conflicts and crises and changed the behaviour of third states. It is not possible to evaluate all dimensions of the EU's structural foreign policy as outlined in Chapter 1, nor the EU's stance towards all crises, conflicts and problematic states. Rather, we are selective, and explore only the main features and patterns of EU policy. Asia and Latin America are not analysed here, as the EU's foreign policy towards these continents is less developed, focusing mainly on trade and contractual relations and the promotion of interregionalism (see Oudjani 2004; Ribó Labastida 2004). A detailed analysis of the EU's promotion of interregionalism is provided by Aggarwal and Fogarty (2004), Söderbaum and Van Langenhove (2006), and Telo (2001). The EU's relations with the US, Russia and China are the topic of Chapter 11.

The arenas discussed here fall under three categories:

- The EU's foreign policy towards Central and Eastern Europe, the Balkans and Turkey is or was developed within the framework of their *(potential) membership*. This provides the EU with a unique leverage and set of carrots and sticks that it cannot use *vis-à-vis* other regions.

- Since 2004, the EU's relations with the Commonwealth of Independent States (CIS, the former Soviet republics), the countries of the Mediterranean and the Middle East are structured through the *European Neighbourhood Policy* (ENP). The EU's decision to develop this new policy field reflects its vital interest in the economic development, stability and governance of its neighbourhood. The ENP was designed to prevent the emergence of new dividing lines between the enlarged EU and its neighbours; to offer them the chance to gain a stake in the internal market and participate in certain Community programmes and CFSP/ESDP activities; to help with economic modernization and liberalization; and to strengthen democracy, good governance, the rule of law and human rights as well as 'stability, security and well-being for all concerned' (Commission 2004f: 3). In the ENP Action Plans negotiated with each country, to obtain the 'carrot' of deepened cooperation and dialogue, countries must achieve agreed targets, though without the incentive of accession (see K. Smith 2005; Dannreuther 2006).
- The EU's foreign policy towards Africa is quite distinct from the other arenas. Foreign policy here is closely intertwined with development policy while the shadow of member states' old colonial ties, and the leverage and 'responsibilities' these entail, remain pertinent.

Central and Eastern Europe

Since the EU's enlargements of 2004 and 2007, the Central and Eastern European countries (CEECs) are no longer objects of EU foreign policy but rather subject to the normal dynamics of mutual and supranational control that characterize all EU member states. Nevertheless, analysing two decades of EC/EU foreign policy towards this region is insightful – it is the most important (and most underestimated) success of EU foreign policy and it is often used as a (misleading) point of reference for the EU's policy towards other regions.

Structural foreign policy

That the CEECs are peaceful, stable, democratic and adhere to human rights and the rule of law is now taken for granted.

However, given the state of these countries 20 years previously and comparing their journey to that of the Balkans in the 1990s and several former Soviet-republics now, this progression was far from inevitable. With the end of the Cold War and the sudden disappearance in 1989–90 of the Moscow-led communist structures that had ordered political, economic and societal life within and between the CEECs for 40 years, there was a real risk of instability. By implementing a comprehensive and sustained structural foreign policy, the EU played a major role in restructuring and stabilizing the CEECs. And in so doing, the EC and its member states contributed to the peaceful character of the end of the East–West divide. They were also instrumental in avoiding a destabilizing power vacuum in the EU's Eastern neighbourhood and in the fact that the CEECs did not exchange communist structures for new authoritarian regimes. In contrast to what is often asserted, the EU's policy towards the East did not start with the 1993 Copenhagen criteria that initiated the enlargement process. Prior to the fall of the Berlin Wall and the Iron Curtain in late 1989, the EC was already supporting and promoting structural reforms in Central and Eastern Europe, despite US doubts about whether these reforms should be taken seriously (Keukeleire 1993).

In a strong expression of both positive and negative conditionality *avant la lettre*, the EC developed an active policy from the moment some of the CEECs began to question their decaying communist structures and adopt reform measures. In 1988–89, the EC concluded its first wide-ranging trade and cooperation agreements with the reform-minded governments in Warsaw and Budapest, while conservative Czechoslovakia was to content itself with a less advantageous trade agreement, and Romania saw negotiations broken off because of its failure to respect human rights. And, from mid-1989 onwards, the Commission began coordinating Western aid to Poland and Hungary through its PHARE programme. When, in November–December 1989, revolts broke out in Eastern Germany, Czechoslovakia, Bulgaria and Romania, the EC already had firmly installed signposts towards alternative political, economic and societal structures – including a whole set of incentives and 'carrots' to encourage these countries to follow. The EC also offered the elites and population the perspective of a new post-communist identity at the moment the old gown was thrown off.

In the years which followed the fall of the communist regimes, the EC continued its policy of systematically strengthening interaction and aid with the most ambitious countries (Poland, Hungary and Czechoslovakia) and reducing aid and contacts with those governments that were moving in a more authoritarian direction (Romania and later on Slovakia). In 1991 the first Association Agreements, known as *Europe Agreements*, were signed with Warsaw, Prague and Budapest – with the other CEECs signing Agreements in the years that followed. Europe Agreements structured relations in the format the EC had developed from the Helsinki negotiations of the early 1970s – politics, economics and social/cultural/human issues (see Chapter 2). The aim of the Agreements was to provide a framework for political dialogue; to promote the expansion of trade and economic relations between the EC and CEECs; to provide a basis for financial and technical assistance and for the gradual integration of the CEECs into a wide range of Community policies; and to promote cooperation in cultural and human matters.

The EU was successfully conducting a structural foreign policy in the region which, from 1993 onwards, was to step up a gear. The Copenhagen European Council of 1993 agreed that those associated CEECs that wished to become members of the EU could do so if they fulfilled the so-called *Copenhagen criteria*:

- stability of institutions guaranteeing democracy, the rule of law, human rights and respect for and protection of minorities;
- the existence of a functioning market economy as well as the capacity to cope with competitive pressure and market forces within the Union;
- the ability to take on the obligations of membership including adherence to the aims of political, economic and monetary union.

In 1995, the Madrid European Council added a fourth condition: that administrative and institutional structures would have to be adjusted to guarantee effective implementation of the *acquis* (the body of EU legislation that is binding on all member states). The European Council of December 1997 decided that accession negotiations should be opened on 31 March 1998 with the six countries recommended by the Commission: the Czech Republic, Estonia, Hungary, Poland, Slovenia and Cyprus. By thus dividing the CEECs into two groups, the vanguard and the laggards, the EU laid down the gauntlet for the laggards to improve their performance. A year later, the EU decided to also initiate negotiations with Latvia, Lithuania, Malta, Slovakia, Bulgaria and Romania.

The candidate countries were confronted with a highly detailed list of conditions in nearly every policy domain that had to be fulfilled. The EU was exporting its structures and values beyond its territory and embedding the CEECs within its own structures, policies and beliefs. This reflected a deep 'governance by conditionality' on the part of the EU and led to the gradual socialization and Europeanization of the CEECs (see Schimmelfennig and Sedelmeier 2005; Grabbe 2006; Schimmelfennig *et al.* 2006). As Grabbe argues, through the accession process and the resulting Europeanization of the CEECs, the EU influenced the development of governance in these countries in ways that went well beyond its official competences in the current member states (2001: 1013). After a long process of adaptation, eight of the CEECs (together with Malta and Cyprus) joined the EU in May 2004, with Romania and Bulgaria following in January 2007. Their accession marked an end, at least for the time being, of what Zielonka has labelled 'an impressive exercise in empire-building' (2006: 20).

The successful transformation, democratization, stabilization and incorporation of ten neighbouring countries concluded one of the most geostrategically significant foreign policy achievements of the EU, and indeed of the 'West' more globally. Not surprisingly, the approach adopted towards the Eastern neighbours was and is often taken as a model for developing the EU's policy towards other regions of the world. However, using this as a point of reference is misleading, for four reasons.

Firstly, despite obvious ambiguities and hesitations, the EU developed a long-term and comprehensive policy that tackled the political, legal, socio-economic and other structures on all relevant levels. And crucially, the member states agreed to provide the necessary sustained budgetary support for this policy. The only structure that the EU could not tackle alone – the military security structure – was taken care of by NATO and the US. It is clear that this long-term, comprehensive effort and such budgetary dedication could not be generated for all regions of the world.

Secondly, in most CEECs the EU's policy was facilitated by existing endogenous dynamics and preferences. Although the EU has been criticized for not sufficiently taking into consideration domestic actors and sensitivities, in general terms, the elites and the population of most CEECs shared the values and wanted the transformations and structures the EU was promoting. This also explains why the new values and rules of the game were quite easily internalized and gradually became part of the mental structures of the population and elites. The EU strengthened and channelled the existing reformist dynamic, alleviated some of the pain of reforms, and helped bring countries back on the right track when they diverted from the reformist course or slackened in their efforts. Evidently, such positive endogenous forces do not always exist in other regions where the EU promotes similar structural changes.

Thirdly, the EU was able to successfully pursue its long-term structural foreign policy objectives because these goals were not overshadowed by manifest military security threats or other conventional foreign policy concerns. This is also a major difference with, for instance, the EU's policy towards the Mediterranean area where the Middle East conflict undermines a more structural foreign policy approach.

Finally, in its policy towards its Eastern neighbours, the EU was seen by both the member states and other international actors (such as the US and initially also the USSR/Russia) as a useful actor that provided clear added value, was complementary in its approach, and in general posed no threat to their own interests. Again, this is not the case for EU interventions in many areas of the world.

Conventional foreign policy

With the crumbling of the Soviet Union and the disappearance of the old order in the early 1990s, the CEECs faced a range of conventional foreign policy problems that could have easily escalated tensions. These included general tensions between the Baltic countries and Russia, sensitive minority problems (such as the Hungarian minorities in Romania and Slovakia, and the Russian minorities in the Baltic states), tensions within Czechoslovakia (that in 1993 led to the divorce between the Czech Republic and Slovakia), and specific bilateral conflicts such as between Slovakia and Hungary on the Gabcikovo Dam. These areas of contention did not lead to violence, a fact which is often taken for granted, but is not self-evident.

In conjunction with other actors, the EC/EU contributed to the de-escalation and desecuritization of most of these areas of contention. It did not generally intervene with conventional foreign policy measures and CFSP played only a limited role. Rather, the EC/EU addressed these issues first and foremost through a structural foreign policy approach. The EU used its leverage from the conditionality built into agreements to make the tackling of conflictual issues a prerequisite for deepening relations with the EU including, ultimately, accession. The EU's structural foreign policy towards the CEECs also fundamentally altered the context and priorities of these countries and their populations. New priorities such as economic growth and EU membership implied that issues which had previously defined the national psyche, such as minority problems, were to some extent overshadowed and de-dramatized by new prerogatives. This is not to imply that the issues of contention within and between the CEECs were entirely resolved, with old antagonisms miraculously swept aside. But, conflictual areas were situated within an EU framework which downplayed their importance and provided for a more rational and organized debate. Finally, by anchoring the CEECs firmly within the EU framework, they had been largely shielded from negative developments within Russia, up to the mid-2000s at least (see Chapter 11).

The Balkans and Turkey

Interaction with the Balkans has had the most defining impact on the image, nature and development of the EU's second pillar. Throughout the 1990s, the Balkans was the site of European foreign policy's most resounding failure, with neither EPC nor CFSP able to stop the wars in its immediate backyard that resulted in more than 100,000 casualties and around 2 million people displaced. Since the early 2000s, the Balkans has become the site of the EU's most comprehensive structural foreign policy and has emerged as the main testing ground of EU leadership and of an increasingly robust CFSP/ESDP. The case of the Balkans also demonstrates clearly that EU foreign policy is embedded within a wider multilocation foreign policy, including NATO, the UN, the OSCE and the Contact Group for the Balkans. The EU wields the full spectrum of its policy toolbox in the region, reflecting its position as the de facto leader of the international community's stabilization efforts. By 'Balkans' we refer to the countries of the former Yugoslavia and Albania, also known as the 'Western Balkans' or 'South East Europe' – Albania, Bosnia and Herzegovina (BiH), Croatia, the former Yugoslav Republic of Macedonia (FYROM), Montenegro, Serbia and Kosovo (as defined by UNSCR 1244). At the end of this section, we also briefly discuss Turkey – not a Balkan country *per se*, but a candidate country with a long and difficult accession history, and one which shares many of the challenges faced by the Balkans.

Conventional foreign policy at its rock bottom

Before focusing on current policies, it is useful to reflect on Europe's abject failures at the start of the Yugoslav War and to point to some paradoxes therein (De Gucht and Keukeleire 1991: 64–76). It is important to bear in mind that as the Yugoslav War was starting in mid-1991, EPC was in its final stages and the member states were embroiled in negotiations for the TEU (Maastricht Treaty) which, along with its new provisions for a CFSP, would come into force two years later.

A first paradox is that although EPC/EC demonstrably failed to prevent escalation in the Balkans, in the first stages of the crisis it did assume responsibility and was highly innovative (see details in Ginsberg 2001: 57–104). With an unprecedented swiftness and flexibility, in June–July 1991 the member states took new initiatives and added new instruments to the European foreign policy toolbox. They mandated the Ministers of Foreign Affairs of the EC's Troika to mediate in person between the warring parties; they appointed Lord Carrington as their Special Representative to facilitate negotiations; they convened a peace conference, leading to the July 1991 Brioni Agreement that brought war in Slovenia to an end; and they sent unarmed EC observers to monitor the ceasefire agreement. Interestingly, while the civilian power (EC/EPC) willingly became involved in this military conflict, the traditional military powers and military security providers (the US and NATO) stayed resolutely on the sidelines for three years and even obstructed efforts of the

Europeans and the UN. However, EPC/EC efforts did not bear fruit in the conflicts in Croatia and later Bosnia-Herzegovina not only because of their greater complexity but also because of the inability of the EC/EPC in August–September 1991 to back up its intensive diplomatic efforts with the necessary military instruments to monitor ceasefires or take up positions in buffer zones.

This is related to a second paradox: countries such as the UK that were most critical of the EPC/EC failure to tackle conflict in the Balkans, were also the most fiercely opposed to endowing the EPC with military crisis-management instruments. The British rejection of various proposals to dispatch military observers or peacekeeping forces through the WEU was not only based on legitimate concerns about their operational feasibility. Within the context of the final negotiations on the Maastricht Treaty, it also reflected London's basic principle that NATO should remain the only setting for military cooperation, despite the fact that NATO refused to intervene. In this sense, the British refusal to consider the use of military crisis management tools in the early stage of the Yugoslav War was probably more damaging to EPC/CFSP's effectiveness and the subsequent dramatic developments in the Yugoslav conflict than the more publicized German recognition of Croatia and Slovenia (when Berlin implemented too early the decision adopted by all EPC/EC member states to recognize those two states).

The third paradox relates to the highly ambivalent attitude of the US. On the one hand, Washington repeatedly let it be known that the Yugoslav question was a European problem. On the other hand, it brought considerable pressure to bear on various member states to prevent the Maastricht Treaty turning the EU into an international actor with autonomous military capabilities. In other words, the Europeans were to somehow do their duty, but without equipping themselves with the necessary instruments. Indeed, the Maastricht Treaty did not lead to a strengthening of the EU's crisis management capabilities (see Chapters 2 and 6). And, unsurprisingly, during the subsequent Bosnian and Kosovo wars, CFSP was no better able to perform than EPC had been.

Interestingly – and this is a last paradox – the EU's first pillar to some extent compensated for CFSP's weakness. As Michael Smith (1997: 284) points out, at a moment of EU diplomatic resignation, the Commission was effectively taking on the non-military aspects of the Yugoslav War through economic sanctions, administration of the Bosnian city of Mostar, humanitarian assistance and organizing large-scale reconstruction programmes (for a detailed discussion, see Ginsberg 2001: 57–104).

Conventional foreign policy at its height

The demands of conflict in the Balkans became a lever to breathe life into CFSP and create ESDP. The Kosovo debacle influenced in 1999 the EU's choice of the first High Representative of the CFSP – then NATO Secretary General Javier Solana, who had extensive experience in the Balkans and had led NATO through the Kosovo War. As the member states were determined that the EU should now succeed in the Balkans, they gave the High Representative the necessary freedom of manoeuvre to develop a highly intensive diplomacy in the region, particularly evident during the successful conflict prevention campaign in FYROM in 2002–03 and the equally successful mediation between Serbia and Montenegro (Piana 2002; Friis 2007).

The EU Special Representatives (EUSR) in the Balkans also play an important role in improving the EU's operational capacity there. The EU currently has three EUSRs in the region: for the *Stability Pact for South Eastern Europe* (now officially called 'Special Coordinator'), for Bosnia-Herzegovina, and for FYROM. In mid-2007, as part of the future arrangements for Kosovo, the EU was planning to appoint an EUSR that would also be the head of the International Civilian Office to Kosovo. Since late 2005, the EUSR for FYROM is also Head of the European Commission delegation – which was an unprecedented and for the EU a unique institutional innovation. The most powerful of the three is the EUSR for Bosnia-Herzegovina. This position is double hatted, with the EUSR also being the UN mandated High Representative – a position endowing him with far-reaching powers as the 'final authority' regarding interpretation of the Agreement on the Civilian Implementation of the Dayton Agreement.

The EU's diplomacy in the Balkans is supported by a whole array of legal and other instruments from both its first and second pillars. These range from restrictive measures such as visa bans and the freezing of funds to positive measures such as support for the peaceful separation of Serbia and Montenegro. The most innovative instruments were those provided under the ESDP framework. Since its inception in 2003 up to mid-2007 the EU has undertaken several ESDP operations in the Balkans – with a civilian crisis management operation in Kosovo in the pipeline in June 2007 (see also Chapter 7):

- The *EU Police Mission in Bosnia-Herzegovina*, the EU's first ever civilian ESDP operation, took over from the UN International Police Task Force in January 2003 and acted as the lead agency for police reform in the country (until December 2005).
- *Operation Concordia*, the EU's first ever military operation and the first operation to make use of the Berlin Plus arrangements with NATO, involved 400 troops and took over from NATO in March 2003. Its mandate was to ensure a stable, secure environment in FYROM to facilitate the implementation of the Ohrid Framework Agreement.
- *Operation Proxima*, the EU police mission (of 200 police advisors), took over from Concordia in FYROM in December 2003. The aim of the Operation was to support the reform process within the Macedonian police service – a role which in late 2005 was taken over by *EUPAT*, the much smaller EU Police Advisory Team.
- *Operation EUFOR-Althea*, the EU's largest military operation, in December 2004 took over from the NATO-led multilateral stabilization force in Bosnia-Herzegovina (SFOR). With 7,000 troops, in a context of continued interethnic tensions and weak state institutions, its objective is to provide a safe environment for the population, to ensure compliance with the peace agreements and to support the international and local authorities.

In the Balkans, we see an ESDP coming of age as the scope and size of missions increase. The use of ESDP clearly demonstrated the EU's potential as a post-crisis stabilization force able to conduct mutually reinforcing military and civilian operations. ESDP operations also played a role in shaping the security structures in the Balkans, indicating that these civilian-military instruments are also a component of the EU's structural foreign policy in the region.

Structural foreign policy

The foreign policy efforts of the international community in the Balkans intertwine conventional and structural foreign policy, relational and structural power, hard and soft power. After the peace agreements at the end of the Bosnian and Kosovo wars it was clear that the continued presence of extensive military forces would not alone achieve sustainable peace. To achieve sustainable peace would require a fundamental transformation of the region in order to gradually desecuritize interstate and intersocietal relations.

It is in this transformation process that the EU's role has been key. From a position of impotence in the 1990s, it has evolved into a key actor in the region, employing the full range of instruments at its disposal. The EU is undertaking its most comprehensive and challenging structural foreign policy, which works on the majority of structures (political, legal, socio-economic, security) and levels (individual, societal, intrastate, interstate, intersociety, regional). The EU's structural foreign policy towards the Balkans is, however, only successful because its actions have been complemented by NATO's strong conventional foreign policy in the region. And, while the EU is gradually replacing other actors, particularly the UN and NATO, the Balkan countries still consider the US as the only actor able to provide the ultimate security guarantee in case things go wrong.

The cornerstone of the EU's policy is the *Stabilization and Association Process* (SAP) (see Grabar-Kitarović 2007). Launched in 1999, the SAP is based on a progressive partnership with each country, in which the EU offers a mixture of trade concessions, economic and financial assistance (through the Instrument for Pre-Accession, which in 2007 replaced the CARDS Programme) and contractual relationships (through *Stabilization and Association Agreements* (SAAs)) which govern the political, trade and economic relations of the EU with the Balkan countries. SAAs cover areas such as the four freedoms, including the creation of a free trade area; the approximation of legislation to the EU *acquis*; political dialogue; and cooperation in all areas of EU policies, including in the area of freedom, security and justice. Similar to the Europe Agreements with the CEECs, they provide the contractual framework for relations between the EU and the individual Balkan countries until their accession to the

EU. Large sums of financial assistance aside, it is indeed the prospect of accession that again gives the EU its greatest leverage.

Differentiating between the countries of the Western Balkans – rewarding 'good' behaviour and punishing lack of compliance – has underpinned the EU's policy. In this process, the EU has gone beyond the common elements of conditionality that governed its relations with the CEECs pre-accession (democracy, rule of law, human rights and market economy reforms) and has added further conditions related to the Balkans' specific post-war situation and the need to overcome regional tension. These conditions include a commitment to good neighbourly relations and a readiness to engage in cross-border cooperation with neighbouring countries; compliance with obligations under the various peace agreements and with the International Criminal Tribunal for the former Yugoslavia (ICTY) in The Hague; and commitments on protecting minorities and on facilitating the return of displaced people.

In mid-2007, the EU's relations are most developed with Croatia and FYROM: SAAs entered into force in 2005, both countries have been granted candidate-country status and accession negotiations opened in late 2005. An SAA was signed with Albania in June 2006, but awaits ratification. In November 2005, negotiations on an SAA began with Bosnia-Herzegovina, Montenegro and Serbia. Negotiations with Serbia were however overshadowed by concerns over Belgrade's cooperation with the ICTY and, particularly, by uncertainty over Kosovo's final status. Following a decision on its status, responsibility to support Kosovo in its process of state-building and stabilization will largely move from the UN to the EU (see ISIS Europe 2006; Greiçevci *et al.* 2007).

The EU is increasingly effective in fostering structural change in the Balkans. However, a range of factors within both the EU and the region indicates this transformation will continue to be a difficult process. Irrespective of how often the EU repeats that 'the future of the Western Balkans lies in the EU', the EU's increasing concern with its own 'absorption capacity' risks weakening its trump card. The question of the EU's receptiveness aside, the Balkan countries face a number of challenges before their accession seems plausible. As Batt (2004) argues, EU accession presupposes a functioning state, with undisputed and secure borders. Apart from Croatia, these fundamental characteristics are missing in all Balkan countries. Levels of interstate and intrastate animosity remain high, and, while restoring war damaged infrastructure is relatively straightforward, rebuilding economic structures and particularly repairing the societal and psychological damage of war is far from it. In conjunction with 45 years of communist rule which only ended in 1991, it is clear that the adaptation of mental structures and interiorization of the new rules of the game, essential elements of an effective structural foreign policy, are a very real challenge in this region.

Discussions on the prospective membership of the Balkans have been closely linked to that of Turkey, and in both cases EU enlargement has been seen in the first place through a foreign policy prism. Holding out the carrot of accession has been viewed as essential to trigger structural changes in these countries, to smooth tensions and conflicts, and to gradually embark on a process of reidentification. However, Turkey has a longer experience of the trials and tribulations of seeking EU membership. That Turkey could accede to the EC/EU was first established by the 1963 Ankara Agreement, and it formally applied for membership in 1987, prior to any of the countries that have joined the EU in its successive enlargement waves since 1995. In December 2004, the EU finally decided to begin the Turkish accession process, opening membership negotiations in October 2005. However, since then, the support of EU member states for Turkish membership has waned and the pace of reform within Turkey has slowed.

Meanwhile, the EU failed to use accession to solve one of the major problems in EU–Turkey relations: the conflict over Cyprus, an island divided into Greek and Turkish parts. When in April 2004, on the eve of their accession to the EU, the population of Southern Cyprus rejected the UN plan on Cyprus's unification, but were allowed to join the EU anyway, the EU lost its leverage to tackle the conflict. The Cyprus conflict has thus been allowed to continue to paralyse various EU policies, not least relations with Turkey.

Turkey, like all countries, has to meet the Copenhagen Criteria to join. As is the case with the Balkans, further areas of conditionality have also been specifically designed for Turkey (see Redmond 2007: 310). The EU's main concerns, in addition to the dispute over Cyprus, can be summarized in four points. The first is the political situation, and more concretely the state of democracy, the role of the military and respect for human rights, the rule of law, minority rights (particularly the Kurds) and fundamental freedoms, including freedom of speech, the press and assembly. The second relates to the state of the Turkish economy. Despite undergoing substantial reform, Turkish per capita GDP remains below that of any EU member state. The third and fourth concerns are more complex and related to matters of identity for both Turkey and the EU – that Turkey is a Muslim, if secular, state, and that its credentials as a 'European' country have been questioned.

However, the EU potentially has much to gain from Turkish membership. Turkish accession could be a counterweight to the 'clash of civilizations' thesis, ending the image of the EU as a Christian club, and helping to redefine its relationship with the Muslim world. As a Muslim country embracing Western structures of democracy, respect for human rights and fundamental freedoms, Turkey has the potential to act as a positive model for other Muslim states worldwide. Its accession could also make a concrete contribution to the difficult relations between EU member states and their Muslim populations (see Chapter 11). With its young and growing population, immigration from Turkey could help counter the demographic time bomb EU member states face. And, the EU could take advantage of Turkey's valuable geostrategic position, not only in terms of its potential to improve energy-supply security as a transit route for oil and gas (see Chapter 9) but also to augment the EU's potential to make its voice heard in the Middle East and the Southern Caucasus, with Iran, Iraq, Syria, Georgia and Armenia becoming its new neighbours. This also implies that, parallel to Turkish membership, the EU would have to seriously upgrade its foreign policy towards these new neighbouring countries.

The carrot of EU membership has brought about wide-ranging reforms on all levels within Turkey. However, in failing to offer resolute support to its membership, the EU has undermined the willingness of Turkey to make painful, and often politically costly reform *ad infinitum,* and levels of popular support for EU membership within Turkey have waned. If the EU is not careful, it risks missing what is, from a foreign policy perspective, an invaluable geostrategic opportunity.

The Commonwealth of Independent States (CIS)

The EU's enlargement to incorporate the CEECs had a profound impact on its eastern flank. Enlargement turned Belarus, Ukraine and Moldova into immediate neighbours, and brought distant conflicts and authoritarian regimes closer to home. It fuelled new hopes and aspirations, increased pressure on neighbouring countries, but also prompted new dividing lines and areas of tension. As Casier (2007) argues, by drastically redrawing the European map, the EU and the Russian Federation became potential direct competitors, leading to a 'clash of integration processes'.

In this region, the EU's main emphasis is on developing contractual relations, which only to some extent constitute a basis for a structural foreign policy. Only recently has the EU also undertaken some elements of a conventional foreign policy, a development which has been limited by Moscow's influence over the former Soviet republics and its global strategic importance (for a detailed analysis of EU–CIS–Russia relations, see Malfliet *et al.* 2007).

Contractual relations or structural foreign policy?

Rapidly normalizing relations with the Soviet Union from 1988 onwards, the EC tried to use economic power to support the political and economic reforms initiated by the then Soviet leader Mikhail Gorbachev. However, with the fall of the Berlin Wall in 1989 and the demise of the Soviet Union in 1991 the EU focussed on the CEECs and relations with Russia itself, thereby largely neglecting the newly independent states in Eastern Europe (Ukraine, Belarus, Moldova) the Southern Caucasus (Armenia, Azerbaijan, Georgia) and Central Asia (Kazakhstan, Kyrgyzstan, Uzbekistan, Tajikistan and Turkmenistan). As the 2004 enlargement grew closer, the EU was compelled to tackle this blind spot and define a policy towards what would become its new neighbourhood. Currently, the main tools of EU cooperation with the post-Soviet states are: bilateral Partnership and Cooperation Agreements (PCAs) concluded with all former Soviet republics; the four 'Common Spaces' between the EU and Russia; the European Neighbourhood Policy (ENP) with the countries in Eastern Europe and the Southern Caucasus (but not Central Asia); and various financial instruments to support these policies.

Partnership and Cooperation Agreements constitute the legal framework for the political, economic and trade relations between the EU and its partner countries. PCAs were concluded in the late 1990s for a period of ten years with all countries in the region, although some of these have not been ratified or have been suspended because of problems with human rights and democracy. The contents of the PCAs vary considerably – those with the Eastern European CIS countries are more elaborate and extensive than those with the CIS countries of Central Asia and the Caucasus, for example. However, they all contain the classical ingredients of the EU's contractual relations with third countries including: supporting efforts to consolidate democracy and economic development; promoting trade and investment and harmonious economic relations; creating the conditions for the future establishment of a free trade area; cooperating in economic, social, financial, technological and cultural fields; and providing a framework for political dialogue.

Launched in 2004, the *European Neighbourhood Policy* (ENP) complements rather than supersedes the PCAs. The major advantage of the ENP Action Plans is that they allow for a more tailor-made approach for each country and, if the partner countries meet the objectives set, for intensified cooperation and involvement in specific EU policies. Like the PCAs, ENP Action plans rest on a shared commitment to 'common values' and aim to support structural changes or consolidation in the direction of democracy, rule of law, good governance, respect for human rights and market economy principles. In this sense, the ENP has the potential to provide an alternative or complementary institutional context to the predominant context of Russian influence and of inward-looking authoritarian regimes. As of June 2007, Action Plans had been adopted for Ukraine, Moldova, Georgia, Armenia and Azerbaijan. Belarus is excluded because of its authoritarian regime. The implementation of the Action Plans and the PCAs is supported financially through the new European Neighbourhood and Partnership Instrument (ENPI), which replaced the TACIS programme in 2007.

The ENP has sought to assuage the aspirations of Georgia and Ukraine towards EU accession following democratic revolutions in 2003–04. Whereas Georgia and Ukraine saw EU membership as a strategic priority, the majority of EU member states considered this as politically and economically out of the question –

despite the insistent support of the Baltic countries and Poland. Hence, whilst the ENP carries the potential to support structural reforms, it does so without the major incentive of accession. By defining it as distinct from the enlargement process, rather than the gateway to EU membership, the ENP in practice also limits its own potential to inspire reforms. However, as Casier (2007: 89) argues, if a partner country were to make full use of the potential of ENP Action Plans, it would become difficult to keep membership off the table, particularly for unambiguously 'European' countries such as Ukraine (see also Hillion 2007).

The European Commission's (2006d, 2006e) first evaluation of the implementation of the ENP Action Plans with Ukraine and Moldova indicates that they have made the Action Plans a major point of reference in their domestic reform strategies. However, the Commission also points to three areas in which the partner countries have been disappointed by the ENP process: too limited efforts to resolve conflicts in the region, a failure to improve access to the EU market for the products most important to them, and the lack of progress on improving the movement of citizens from partner countries to the EU. These disappointments are symptomatic of a major flaw in the EU's structural foreign policy towards the region. While it wants far-reaching structural change within these states, the EU refuses to make the internal changes necessary to achieve this. By refusing to consider the ENP as a preparation for EU membership, and by rejecting the free movement of their products and their population, the EU has made clear that it will not structurally reform the political, economic and human patterns that define its relations with its ENP partners.

Beyond its relations with the CIS of Eastern Europe and the South Caucasus, the EU's capacity to influence is more limited. In particular, the EU struggles with the question of how to deal with the Central Asian countries, staggering between upholding its own values and yielding to the enticements of realpolitik given the strategic importance of this region (in the supply of energy, the 'war on terrorism' and as a transit area for European troops to Afghanistan).

Conventional foreign policy

The EU and Russia have managed to defuse a range of potentially highly conflictual conventional foreign policy issues in the

CIS region. For example, they succeeded in reaching agreement in 2002 on the difficult problem of the Russian enclave Kaliningrad. That issues could be tackled within a framework of contractual relations and political dialogue contributed to gradually diminishing their prominence. However, the problems surrounding Russian minorities in the Baltics which appeared to have de-escalated, if not been resolved, have flared up again since the mid-2000s.

With enlargement imminent, from 2003 onwards the EU began to use its second pillar toolbox to develop policy towards the post-Soviet states' various conflicts and crises (see Coppieters *et al.* 2004). The results have been varied, including successes (Ukraine), increased involvement (Moldova), mixed performance (Georgia) and utter neglect (Chechnya). The EU's main diplomatic success has been the way it handled the political revolutions in Georgia and particularly Ukraine during the Orange Revolution in late 2004. In the midst of the crisis, High Representative Javier Solana, Polish President Aleksander Kwasniewski and the Lithuanian President Valdas Adamkus worked in Kiev to negotiate the contours of a democratic solution between the rival interests. The EU's constant scrutiny and diplomatic pressure on the Yanukovych government in the run-up to and aftermath of presidential elections in Ukraine in 2004 has been seen as contributing to the peaceful revolution (Karatnycky 2005).

The Council has appointed EU Special Representatives for Moldova, for the South Caucasus and for Central Asia, and embarked on a number of ESDP missions in the region. In 2004–05, the EU undertook its first modest rule of law mission in Georgia (EUJUST THEMIS). The EU provides some limited support to a Joint Control Mission in the South Ossetia conflict. And in late 2005, the EU initiated its first and more ambitious Border Assistance Mission (BAM) along the 800 km Ukraine–Moldova border. In so doing, the EU supports Ukraine and Moldova in countering the secessionist leaders of Transinistra, which are in turn supported by Moscow.

Increasing its involvement in local hotspots has inevitably risked bringing the EU into collision with Russia's policies in the region (Aliboni 2005: 16) and with the EU's other strategic objectives. It is from this perspective that Moscow's use of its control over energy resources in 2006 was of major significance – and can also be considered as having been rather effective (see Chapter 9). Moscow has been able to force EU member states into deciding where their real priorities lie: maintaining a good relationship with a strategically important Russia, or strengthening the EU as an increasingly active regional power in Russia's backyard, even though this carries the risk of alienating the Russian leadership. This conundrum also partially explains why despite its growing interest in the region, the EU is reluctant to become more actively involved in conflict resolution mechanisms and peacekeeping efforts in other flashpoints of regional instability. These include the Nagorno-Karabakh conflict between Armenia and Azerbaijan and the conflicts between Russia and Georgia in Abkhazia and South Ossetia.

The Mediterranean region

The Mediterranean was projected to the centre of EU foreign policy in the mid-1990s, when the EU sought to balance its dominant policy towards the East with a new comprehensive policy towards its Mediterranean neighbours. The area which is covered by the EU's Euro-Mediterranean Partnership (Barcelona Process) and ENP comprises Algeria, Egypt, Israel, Jordan, Lebanon, Morocco, the Palestinian Authorities, Syria and Tunisia, with Libya as an observer. As such, what the EU classifies as the Mediterranean also includes many countries normally understood as located in the Middle East. To some extent, we follow this pattern in this chapter. Under 'The Mediterranean', we discuss the Barcelona Process and the ENP, included as they affect countries like Lebanon, Israel and Palestine. In the subsequent 'The Middle East' section, we focus almost exclusively on the Israeli-Palestinian conflict.

Structural foreign policy: the Barcelona Process and the ENP

The 1993 Oslo Agreement between Israel and the Palestinians provided a window of opportunity for structural changes in the Mediterranean, as it appeared that with this agreement the major conventional foreign policy issue – which had served as a convenient alibi to block reforms – was finally resolved. Within this new context, the EU wanted to apply to its relations with the Mediterranean the objectives and methodology that had proved so successful with its Eastern neighbours. The EU envisaged fundamental changes in the political, legal, economic and societal structures within the individual Mediterranean countries, in their mutual relations and in their relations with the EU. However, in this case the EU could not play its trump card – the prospect of accession (for a comparison of the EU's Eastern and Mediterranean policies, see Maresceau and Lannon 2001).

The ground-breaking Euro-Mediterranean Conference of November 1995 in Barcelona for the first time brought together Foreign Ministers of the EU member states with their colleagues from the Maghreb, the Middle East and Cyprus, Malta and Turkey. The Barcelona Conference established the *Euro-Mediterranean Partnership* (EMP) and laid the foundations of a process (the 'Barcelona Process') designed to build a comprehensive multilateral framework for dialogue and cooperation in the three dimensions of the partnership: the political and security partnership; the economic and financial partnership; and the partnership in social, cultural and human affairs.

The EMP established a detailed Working Programme, created an institutional mechanism with regular meetings of a wide range of actors (ministers, officials, parliamentarians, regional and local authorities, social partners, civil society organizations), and provided for considerable budgetary resources through loans from the European Investment Bank and through the new financial instrument 'MEDA' (the Mediterranean counterpart of 'PHARE' and 'TACIS'). The multilateral approach of the EMP was complemented by a new set of bilateral agreements which allowed the EU to differentiate its policy *vis-à-vis* its different partners. It gradually replaced cooperation agreements with more ambitious Association Agreements, which also included stronger conditionality (see also Biscop 2003; Gomez 2003).

Despite limitations and ambiguities, the EMP looked promising: it focused on genuine structural reforms, was comprehensive in nature and could rely on a wide set of policy instruments. However, despite the intrinsic value of this unique institutionalized framework for Euro-Mediterranean dialogue and cooperation, a decade later disappointment overshadowed the tenth anniversary of the Barcelona Process. Although the structural foreign policy dimension was strong in both intent and the set-up of the EMP, it was weak in terms of output and effects. A short overview of the objectives formulated for the three 'partnerships' and of the actual achievements makes clear why.

The 'Political and security partnership', aimed at 'establishing a common area of peace and stability', included engagements with regard to both interstate relations and states' internal organization. The participants undertook to settle their disputes by peaceful means, respect territorial integrity, consider confidence and security-building measures, etc. They also agreed to 'pursue a mutually and effectively verifiable Middle East Zone free of weapons of mass destruction'. With regard to their internal organization, the Declaration pointed out that the signatory states 'undertake to' develop the rule of law and democracy in their political systems, respect human rights and fundamental freedoms and respect pluralism in their societies.

Ten years later, the overall picture of this political dimension is negative. In many countries the most that has been achieved is the 'modernisation of authoritarianism' (Aliboni 2004: 12) or the development of authoritarian pluralism. In 1995, the EU had readily embraced the delusion that the (majority of) undemocratic Mediterranean regimes would suddenly be willing to engage in political reforms that could endanger their very survival. The refusal of many of these governments to respect their engagements was paralleled by the reluctance of the EU to use the Barcelona provisions to exert pressure on the states that failed to observe these principles. The EU also proved to be a fair-weather friend to democracy in the region, unwilling to support democratic processes if elections resulted in victory for Islamic parties (see also Youngs 2002).

The failure is even more striking in terms of the security dimension. Despite the deteriorating peace process in the Middle East, diplomats from all EMP countries found consensus on a draft Euro-Mediterranean Charter for Peace and Stability which included a set of confidence-building measures. However, the total collapse of the peace process in late 2000 blocked their adoption on a political level and thereafter obstructed any further serious negotiations. The Arab countries also increasingly distrusted the EU countries, which they blamed for not clearly condemning Israel (for its nuclear policy and its policy towards the Palestinians) but at the same time promoting confidence-building measures which they saw as undermining their defence capabilities (Biscop 2003: 33–63).

The 'Economic and financial partnership', aimed at 'creating an area of shared prosperity', was to be realized through the creation of a free trade area by 2010 and through the development of cooperation in a wide range of fields (industry, environment, energy, etc.). The free trade area was to be established through the new Association Agreements between the EU and the Mediterranean countries, as well as by free trade agreements to be concluded between the Mediterranean countries themselves. The primary purpose was to lay down the methodology by which the EU's framework of neoliberal economic governance would be extended to the Mediterranean region (Gomez 2003: 81). At first glance, the economic chapter of the EMP seemed to be its most successful. This was not surprising as it was based on the comprehensive set of instruments available in the EU's first pillar, with the European Commission steering the process. The Working Programme led to cooperation and exchanges in a wide range of economic sectors, and Association Agreements were signed with eight partner countries. Through these agreements and the EMP, the Mediterranean countries were pushed forward in the process of economic liberalization, with the EU in essence supporting the structural adjustment programmes of the IMF.

However, in terms of practical effects, the results were less impressive and in some cases even negative. The impact of cooperation remained very limited. The goal of establishing a free trade area by 2010 proved unattainable, and the anticipated rise in intra-Mediterranean trade did not materialize. Moreover, the EU's policy was ambiguous, with its neoliberal trade policy conveying a different message from its migration and agricultural policies. In a large number of Mediterranean countries the overall economic situation has actually deteriorated since the start of the Barcelona Process (see EUROMED 2006). This has also had negative effects in terms of human security, societal security and political stability. The EMP cannot shoulder all the blame for this decline. However, although the medium- and long-term impacts of the structural reform programmes may be positive, the EU has failed to acknowledge that in the short term, the socio-economic impact of liberalization can be negative, particularly for the weaker strata of society (which is also the largest part of the population in the Mediterranean countries) (Khader

2001: 280). In conjunction with other factors, this deteriorating socio-economic situation contributed to the rising popularity of 'fundamentalist' Islamic movements, perceived as both more legitimate and more effective in fulfilling the basic needs of the population (see Chapter 11).

The 'Partnership in social, cultural and human affairs' aimed at 'developing human resources, promoting understanding between cultures and exchanges between civil societies'. This chapter emphasized the importance of dialogue and exchanges as essential factors 'in bringing their people closer, promoting understanding between them and improving their perception of each other'. The EMP participants undertook to promote people-to-people contacts among all types of civil society groups. The Barcelona Process failed completely in this dimension and the situation is now worse than it was in 1995. The anticipated gradual process of socialization of the Mediterranean partners did not happen. And, the EMP has not been able to act as a counterforce to growing distrust between the West and the Muslim world.

The regimes in the Mediterranean countries sought to retain control over exchanges between civil societies, to ensure the Euro-Mediterranean dialogue would not have a 'destabilizing' impact on their societies and political system. The EU member states shifted priorities too, from promoting exchanges between societies to a more narrow focus on their own immediate interests: migration, anti-terrorism and other internal security issues. This shift in priorities weakened the EU's lever on human rights and democratization issues, as the EU needed the help of the Mediterranean regimes to achieve its internal security objectives (see Chapter 9).

The results of the three dimensions of the Euro-Mediterranean Partnership are disappointing and the Barcelona Process has not acted as a motor for far-reaching structural change. This failure was a hard lesson for the EU: that pursuing a long-term and comprehensive structural foreign policy, without being able to provide an answer to the conventional foreign policy challenge of the Middle East peace process, was impossible. As the peace process faltered from 1996 onwards, so vanished the hope that Arab elites and populations would now refocus on internal reforms and on strengthening their relations with each other and with Europe. Furthermore, the EU's structural foreign policy was never going to be effective because its objectives were not sufficiently supported by endogenous forces and actors. The reformist movements that existed in several Mediterranean countries had not reached the required critical mass among the population and elites to generate a sufficiently strong reformist dynamic and overcome the unavoidable hurdles linked to structural reforms. But, the Europeans also failed to pay sufficient attention to the immaterial dimension of foreign policy, to other-regarding interests and to the societal and human security dimension in the Mediterranean area. In a growing number of countries, the attractiveness of the structures the EU was promoting paled in comparison to those promoted by Islamist movements and parties, which paid more attention to both the immediate basic material needs and the immaterial and identity related longings of the population (see Chapter 11). Without the prospect of accession, the EU could not offer the Mediterranean's populations a new and attractive context or identity to replace the lamentable state of affairs in a major part of the Arab world (see UNDP 2002–06).

These explanations for the failure of the Barcelona Process are relevant to evaluating the EU's attempts to upgrade and 'rescue' the Euro-Mediterranean Partnership through the ENP. The ENP does not supersede the Barcelona Process (although its financing instrument MEDA was replaced in 2007 by the ENPI). Rather, the EU asserts that it will 'reinvigorate' the process, strengthen the Barcelona objectives and provide new benchmarks and incentives to improve their implementation. The Association Agreements remain, but these are supplemented by ENP Action Plans which provide for a deeper and wider partnership.

It is too early to give a definitive assessment of the ENP, particularly as the structural changes it promotes can only bear fruit over the longer term. Nevertheless, we can make some initial observations. The EU has been criticized for reacting to the Barcelona Process' failure by merely reasserting its objectives and instruments more strongly rather than deeply revising its strategy (see Aliboni 2004: 12). For instance, the inclusion of new areas of cooperation in the ENP mainly mirrored the EU's expanding policy competences and widening policy agenda since the 1995 Barcelona Conference and since the original Association Agreements were agreed, rather than symbolizing a considered policy development. The EU's strategy was paradoxically becoming more inward looking.

On the other hand, in its first progress reports of the six ENP Action Plans adopted in 2004, the European Commission (2006d, 2006e) emphasized that the Action Plans were closely linked to the internal reform programmes and priorities of Mediterranean countries such as Jordan and particularly Morocco. For the latter, which has made modernization and the linkage to Europe its strategic priorities, the ENP Action Plan serves as an anchor for internal political and economic reforms. This indicates that the ENP is not merely about the EU imposing its values and rules onto its partner countries. Furthermore, the Commission's reports also point to the difficulty of translating commitments to structural reform into concrete progress. This is normal to the extent that structural reforms inevitably take time to have an impact. Many of the political, economic and human costs of the very ambitious reform programme that the EU seeks are upfront, while these reforms will often only come to fruition later, and while the incentives given by the EU are perceived by the partner countries as too limited. With few exceptions, poverty and unemployment, poor economic performance, corruption, bleak prospects for the population, weak or undemocratic government, as well as open and 'frozen' conflicts remain major challenges in the Mediterranean (see also the assessment of the ENP in this chapter's section on the CIS).

Even if endogenous support for structural change exists among the political and economic elites of some Mediterranean countries, this support is not the case for all ENP partners. Also, in the handful of countries with a (moderately) reformist leadership, endogenous public support for modernization, liberalization and 'Western' reforms appears to be fading among some sections of society, with support for the competing Islamic structures increasing. The evolution in the Palestinian Territories was most illustrative of this trend, but it is also one of the reasons why a country such as Egypt remains quite suspicious of the ENP endeavour. A problem for the sustainability and legitimacy of the EU's ENP strategy is that the EU has once again disregarded the immaterial dimension of foreign policy, to the societal and human security dimension, and to the interests of its partners (see also Bicchi 2006).

Conventional foreign policy

The failure of the EU's structural foreign policy towards the Mediterranean has also had negative repercussions for tackling conventional foreign policy issues. The EU was unable to provide a more rule-based setting to approach conflicts, nor to create a fundamentally new context that would have made old conflicts and areas of tensions less relevant. Its record in tackling the conventional foreign policy challenges through its second pillar instruments have proved yet more problematic. The EU at least had the ambition of having a structural impact on the Mediterranean area. It has not even tried to develop a common policy towards several conflicts in the region. This is most blatant *vis-à-vis* conflicts in Northern Africa – the EU's most immediate Mediterranean neighbourhood – on which there have been nearly no joint actions, common positions or ESDP operations (for the Middle East, see the next section). Two examples can illustrate this.

In Algeria, although violence has reduced since the early 2000s, conflict between Islamist rebels and government forces from 1992 caused more than 100,000 deaths. As Gomez (2003: 162) argues, 'Instead of leading by example, the Union stood back and watched human rights abuses occurring on a breathtaking scale'. Despite the magnitude and vicinity of this bloody conflict, Algeria seldom figured at the top of the CFSP agenda. The EU made little concerted effort to mediate, to press for negotiations between the regime and the opposition parties, or to press for substantial democratic reform. Its non-performance can be partially explained by the complexity of tackling an internal conflict in a third country. However, it is also the result of diverging views among the member states and of the important position of Algeria as a major supplier of gas (Gomez 2003: 147–63).

Diverging views and EU member states' bilateral relationships also explain the EU's inaction regarding conflict in the Western Sahara between Morocco (which administers this area) and Algeria (which supports the exiled Polisario Front). Again, the EU failed to define a clear position towards the crisis, let alone to offer active mediation services to solve the conflict. And again, the Barcelona Process and the ENP have not been used as leverage to pursue a negotiated settlement.

The Middle East

This section evaluates EU foreign policy towards the major and most long-standing issue in the Middle East: the Israeli-Palestinian conflict. This issue merits extensive attention since it has featured on the European agenda since the start of EPC in the early 1970s and as the Europeans have played a major role in advancing the fight for self-determination of the Palestinian people. The EU's role and impact in this area can be evaluated from three perspectives: in terms of agenda-setting, the Europeans played a crucial role in putting the Palestinian case on the international agenda; from a structural foreign policy perspective, the EU's policy towards the Palestinians is amongst its most active and comprehensive; but, from a conventional foreign policy perspective, the EU has played a limited role in diplomatic negotiations and tackling crises (see also Ginsberg 2001: 105–80). The EU's relations with Israel and Palestine in the framework of the Barcelona Process and ENP have been discussed above.

Agenda setting

The EU was probably at its most successful in framing the terms of the debate. From the outset, the EC/EU recognized Israel's right to exist within secure and internationally recognized borders. From 1973 on, the Europeans also supported the Palestinians' cause, thereby progressively changing the parameters of the international debate. During the Arab-Israeli conflict of 1973, in their first major EPC declaration on the Middle East, the member states recognized 'the legitimate rights of the Palestinians'. The European Council's Venice Declaration of 1980 established 'the right to existence and to security of all States in the region, including Israel, and justice for all the peoples, which implies the recognition of the legitimate rights of the Palestinian people'. The next milestone in the EU's position came in the 1999 Berlin Declaration which introduced the notion of a 'democratic, viable and peaceful sovereign Palestinian State' (see documents in Hill and Smith 2000: 287–316). Following the resumption of violence and the collapse of the Oslo peace process, the June 2002 Seville European Council made explicit the EU's perspective: the goal of a two state solution, implying 'an end to the occupation and the early establishment of a democratic, viable, peaceful and sovereign State of Palestine, on the basis of the 1967 borders, if necessary with minor adjustments agreed by the parties'.

Through its policy, the EC/EPC/EU progressively redefined the terms of the international debate. It played an important role in gradually transforming the Palestinian leader Yasser Arafat into an acceptable interlocutor for the West. As such, it paved the way for the peace negotiations that led to the Oslo and Madrid Agreements between Israel and the Palestinians, which resulted in the creation of the Palestinian Territories and the Palestinian Authority.

Structural foreign policy

The EU was absent from the negotiations that led to the Oslo and Madrid Agreements brokered in 2003–04 by Norway and the US. Nevertheless, it played a pivotal role in the peace process: by shaping the terms of the debate prior to the Oslo agreement and by then developing a comprehensive structural foreign policy to translate the agreements into practice.

The first major component of the EU's structural foreign policy was supporting the creation of Palestinian political, legal, security, administrative and economic structures, which in most cases had to be established from scratch. In financial terms, the EU invested heavily, providing nearly half of all foreign funding. From 1994 to the end of 2002, the EU had committed approximately €1 billion in grants and loans, and a further €500 million in contributions to the UN Relief and Works Agency for Palestine Refugees in the Near East (UNRWA), while bilateral EU Member State assistance amounted to €2.5 billion (Commission 2007f).

EU funding and expertise allowed for the establishment of a Palestinian administration and of local authorities, for the development of an education system, the organization of the first democratic elections, the creation and functioning of Palestinian police forces, and the development of basic economic and transportation structures such as the airport in Rafah (destroyed in 2001, and again in 2006, by Israel). In 1997, the EU and the Palestinians signed an Interim Association Agreement on Trade and Cooperation. However, after the outbreak of the intifada in the Palestinian Territories in 2000, and the imposition by Israel of blockades and curfews within the West Bank and Gaza Strip, implementation of various aspects of the agreement became extremely difficult.

At first sight, the bilateral dimension of the EU's structural foreign policy was quite successful. The various structures that buttressed the new Palestinian Territories were established in a remarkably short time period. And the newly created Palestinian Authority and democratically elected President Arafat could function thanks to the EU's political and financial support. However, judged over the longer term, the EU's policy has clearly failed. The EU only very reluctantly used its leverage over the Palestinian leaders to force them to take the agreed rules of the game seriously – such as respect for the competences of the parliamentary assembly and for the separation between executive and judiciary. In effect, the EU turned a blind eye to increasing authoritarianism, corruption and an uncooperative Palestinian leadership. It failed to ensure that its massive financial aid had positive effects on the standard of living and well-being of the Palestinian people, whose living conditions have deteriorated rapidly in the last decade. The EU also shied away from using its extensive trade, contractual relations and cooperation projects with Israel to compel Tel Aviv to restrict its military operations against civilian targets, halt its settlement policy, and stop its economic and humanitarian sanctions against the Palestinian population in Gaza and the West Bank.

The dramatic deterioration of the human security and societal security situation of the Palestinian population contributed to the growing popularity of the radical Islamic movement Hamas, which moved into the vacuum left by the Palestinian government and the Western powers. This paved the way for its victory in the elections of January 2006 on a programme based on the fight against not only Israel, but also corruption and poverty (see ICG 2006). With Hamas's election, the EU paid the price for its one-sided focus on the state and interstate level, and for its neglect of the impact of policies at the individual and societal level. The victory of the Islamic movement demonstrated the painful gap between the perception of the EU (which put Hamas in 2003 on its list of terrorist organizations) and of the majority of the Palestinian population (that considered Hamas as the best guarantee for their future). The EU's refusal to deal with Hamas after it won the EU-sponsored free elections was not only a slap in the face of the Palestinians: it also undermined the credibility of one of the main rules of the game the EU was trying to promote in the Middle East, namely democracy (see also Tocci 2006).

The second major component of the EU's structural foreign policy was to embed the emerging Israeli-Palestinian peace settlement in a long term process of regional cooperation, including not only Israel and the Palestinian Authorities, but also Lebanon, Syria, Jordan and Egypt. This was seen as essential to fundamentally altering the context and to making peace in the Middle East sustainable. The proposals of the Commission (1993a, 1993b), launched a week before the Oslo Agreement was concluded, reflected strikingly the spirit of Monnet and Schuman and of Europe's own experience after World War II. The Commission suggested that regional cooperation should focus on pooling common capacities and tackling common problems, particularly water, energy and transportation. It proposed establishing the basis for a Middle East economic area with free movement of goods, services, labour and capital; developing common transport and energy infrastructures; and exploiting common resources.

After the Oslo Agreement, the EU had the opportunity to further elaborate its proposals for regional cooperation by playing a leading role in the multilateral working groups established to coordinate and finance economic, infrastructural, energy and other projects in the region. Moreover, the Euro-Mediterranean partnership, launched in Barcelona in 1995, provided a further tool to embed evolving Arab-Israeli relations into an even broader scheme of interregional cooperation. However, the assassination of the Israeli Prime Minister Yitzhak Rabin by an Israeli extremist in late 1995, his succession by a critic of the Oslo Agreements, and the resumption of violence from both sides in 1996 not only gradually undermined the Israeli-Palestinian peace process, but also meant that negotiations on regional cooperation ended before they had even started.

The various countries in the region, as well as the Palestinian Territories, are all part, or are potentially part of, the ENP (see above). Although both aim at shaping and influencing structures, the difference between the ENP and the regional policy proposed by the EU in the mid-1990s is striking. The latter was based on a genuinely regional approach and focused primarily on the issues important for the countries themselves (such as water). The ENP mainly focuses on bilateral relations between the EU and the third country, is based on the EU's own agenda and interests, and mainly aims to export the European order onto other regions. This suggests that the chances of the ENP having a positive impact are rather limited.

Conventional foreign policy

One of the main reasons for the failure of the EU's structural foreign policy in the Middle East is the failure of the peace process which it was meant to complement and convert into sustainable peace, but which faltered from 1996 on and collapsed completely after 2000. In this sense, the failure of the EU's Middle East policy reflected the general failure of all international actors, including the US despite its wide array of conventional foreign policy instruments.

When assessing the EU's policy from a conventional foreign policy perspective, the main reproach is not that the EU was unable to broker peace, but that it initially did not even manage to get a place at the diplomatic negotiation table, despite being the Palestinians' largest donor and the Israelis' main trading partner. During the diplomatic negotiations leading to and following the 1993 Oslo Agreements, the EU was excluded by the US and Israel from the negotiations, although it was expected to pay the bill and help implement the agreement (see Gomez 2003: 124–32). After the collapse of the peace process, the EU shifted its approach and attempted to assume a more proactive role. It did so first in terms of diplomatic activities, then from 2005 onwards also through small-scale initiatives focusing on the military security dimension.

In 2002, the EU joined the UN, the US and the Russian Federation in the 'Middle East Quartet'. The EU was represented by the Council Presidency, the High Representative for the CFSP and sometimes also the Commissioner for External Relations. It was largely responsible for drawing up the 'Roadmap' which was accepted in 2003 as the basis of the Middle East Quartet's intervention. The Roadmap lays out reciprocal steps by both Israel and the Palestinian Authority in political, security, economic, humanitarian and institution-building fields, with a negotiated two-state solution to the conflict at its core. Although the EU still considers the Roadmap as the main point of reference (in addition to relevant UN resolutions) its fate is unclear as the US has failed to put its weight behind the plan or to put pressure on Israel to accept it. Today, the Roadmap no longer seems to fit a conflict that has further escalated.

The EU has increasingly recognized that it would only be taken seriously if it also played a role in tackling the hard security aspects of the conflict. Some first careful steps were taken in 2005, with the small ESDP civilian police mission in the Palestinian Territory (EU COPPS, with around 30 experts) and the border assistance mission at Rafah (EU BAM Rafah, with 70 personnel) (see Sabiote 2006). A major new step was taken in August 2006 in the aftermath of the Israeli-Lebanon crisis. During the specially convened meeting of EU foreign ministers, member states committed up to 7,000 troops to a UN force to oversee the fragile ceasefire. Though not an ESDP operation, European countries provided the backbone of the force and France and Italy are leading this potentially risky mission (see Chapter 7).

However, the EU's potential effectiveness remains undermined by some major flaws. Despite recent initiatives, the EU still lacks the instruments to provide hard security guarantees to actors in the region or to stop an escalation of violence. Furthermore, both the US and the Israelis harbour distrust of an EU perceived as maintaining a pro-Arab bias. This 'legitimacy deficit' (Harpaz 2007) has effectively prevented the EU being seen as an acceptable negotiating partner.

Despite its alleged pro-Arab bias, the EU has proved highly accommodating towards Israel, and has shied away from using either positive or negative conditionality. For instance, since their 1980 Venice Declaration, EU member states have declared that Israeli settlements are illegal under international law. But, in nearly three decades, they have never dared to employ serious sanctions against Israel. Using conditionality or sanctions in EU–Israel relations is one of the strongest taboos in EU foreign policy, even though Tel Aviv's settlement policy, use of violence against civilians, destruction of EU-funded infrastructure, or simply withholding Palestinian tax and customs revenues have given ample reason for sanctions or at least counter-measures. Israel and the EU member states have managed neatly to shield economic and contractual relations from foreign policy issues – despite the fact that the Middle East crisis and Israel's foreign policy are among the most determining factors of Europe's own long-term security (see Tocci 2006).

The problem is not just that the EU is not a credible *military* power in the region – the problem is that it is equally doubtful whether the EU is *a power* at all in the Middle East (see Chapter 1). This reluctance to adopt a more assertive position towards either Israel or the Arab countries is also influenced by the historical links of EU member states with particular countries in the Middle East, or by the shadow of the past (particularly for Germany, in view of the Holocaust). This also explains why particularly during the most sensitive crises, the EU is often not able to take a clear stance, and why the member states have never given the High Representative or the Presidency the same clear mandate and room to manoeuvre as they have in, for instance, the Balkans.

Africa

The EC/EU has maintained highly institutionalized relationships with particular areas of Africa since the very beginning of the European integration process. When, in December 2005, the European Council adopted the Strategy for Africa, it was the first time the EU had developed a comprehensive, integrated and long-term framework for its relations with the continent as a whole. Geographically, it brought an extra layer to the EU's policy, which is subdivided into three distinctive policies towards:

- the Northern African (Mediterranean) countries, organized through the European Neighbourhood Policy and the Barcelona Process (see above)
- sub-Saharan Africa (minus South Africa), organized mainly through the Cotonou Agreement with the African Caribbean and Pacific (ACP) countries and, since 2003, also gradually through the use of second pillar instruments
- South Africa, organized through the bilateral Trade, Development and Cooperation Agreement and partially also the Cotonou Agreement

This section focuses on the EU policy towards sub-Saharan Africa, evaluating the policy changes of the Cotonou Agreement and the Strategy for Africa, and the increasing use of other policy instruments through CFSP and ESDP.

Structural foreign policy – or still development policy?

The Cotonou Agreement between the 77 ACP countries and the EU provides the framework for the EU's contractual relations with Africa. The Cotonou Agreement is made operational through five-year Country Strategy Papers and Regional Strategy Papers. These country and region specific documents, which are negotiated between the Commission and the government of the third country, provide the framework through which the EU's development aid is programmed. The EU structures its financial assistance to Africa through the European Development Fund (EDF), which operates outside the normal EU budget. The EU (EC and member states) provide over 50 per cent of all ODA, and the EU in 2005 agreed to double aid between 2004 and 2010 and to allocate half of this to Africa (see also Chapter 8).

The Cotonou Agreement was hailed as marking a significant departure from the four successive Lomé Agreements which had organized EU–Africa relations since 1975. Signed in March 2000 and entering into force in April 2003, the Cotonou Agreement has a duration of 20 years, with five-year reviews. The objectives of Cotonou are

> to promote and expedite the economic, cultural and social development of the ACP States, with a view to contributing to peace and security and to promoting a stable and democratic political environment. The partnership shall be centred on the objective of reducing and eventually eradicating poverty consistent with the objectives of sustainable development and the gradual integration of the ACP countries into the world economy.

Cotonou brought about three main developments – in trade provisions, broadened participation and political dialogue – leading to what Holland (2002: 219) labelled a 'paradigmatic shift in the focus and direction of EU–ACP relations'. However, these evolutions were more reflective of the changing global context and the EU's own agenda, interests and values, than a response to the demands and concerns of the African 'partners' (see Hurt 2003; Elgström 2005; Farrell 2005).

Arguably, it was Cotonou's trade provisions that marked the most significant break with the preceding four decades of cooperation. Under the Lomé agreements, Africa benefited from non-reciprocal preferential market access arrangements. This trade arrangement ran counter to the WTO's most favoured nation clause. It had also been widely criticized for reinforcing African countries' reliance on primary commodities and contributing little to promoting an increase in higher value manufactured goods (Sourd 2005: 15). Despite African countries' reluctance, economic liberalization prevailed in the Cotonou Agreement which provided for new 'Economic Partnership Agreements' (EPAs) by 2008. EPAs will replace the trade chapters of the Cotonou Agreement, will create free trade agreements between the EU and six subregional groupings of ACP countries, and are also designed to encourage subregional economic integration. The goal of EPAs is to succeed where Lomé failed – to reduce the marginalization of Africa in the international economy. However, there have been significant doubts about the feasibility and potential impact of EPAs given the capacity problems on the African side, the lack of additional financial support to cover the anticipated adjustment costs, and the danger of (subsidized) European agricultural products crowding out local products (Sourd 2005).

A second major development with the Cotonou Agreement was its provision for broadening the participation of civil society, local actors and the private sector in EU–ACP relations and political dialogue. The aim in encouraging a broader participation was to increase the feeling of 'ownership', to encourage the development of civil society and to broaden the EU's interlocutors on the ground. However, in practice this approach is difficult to implement. In countries which already have a vibrant civil society used to participating in political processes, the level of engagement within the Cotonou process is good. However, where chaos and insecurity rule, or where the enabling environment provided by the state is restrictive, civil society struggles to fulfil its role (Saferworld 2005).

A third innovation of the Cotonou agreement relates to a more vigorous promotion of the political elements of the agreement's agenda. These have developed in-line with evolving concerns on the EU's side, and are a stark demonstration that the EU–Africa relationship is only a 'partnership' on paper. Nevertheless, the intention was that political dialogue would become deeper, wider and more dynamic than in the past, covering a broad range of political issues that fall outside traditional development cooperation – such as peace and security, the arms trade, and migration. The objective of political dialogue is to exchange information, to foster mutual understanding, and to facilitate the establishment of agreed priorities and shared agendas.

In addition to increasing the emphasis on political dialogue, Cotonou built on a trend which had already begun under the Lomé agreements of building political conditionality into the agreement (see Chapter 8). While since 1995 including a human rights clause is standard in most EU-third country agreements, in the Cotonou agreement, at the EU's behest, respect for human rights, democracy and the rule of law became 'essential elements' of the agreement. Against the wishes of the ACP states, the agreement also includes a non-execution clause under which the violation of an 'essential element' forms the basis of consultation procedures and the eventual application of 'appropriate measures', a process which potentially leads to the suspension in whole or in part of cooperation and aid. During negotiations in 2000, the EU also pushed for 'good governance' to be an 'essential element' of the agreement. This frustrated the African 'partners' who argued that it was unnecessary given the democracy and rule of law provisions already present. Ultimately, a different procedure was agreed for good governance – it would be a 'fundamental element', meaning that its violation would not constitute a ground for suspension. Reflecting both the EU's own strategic concerns and the extent to which it de facto determines the agenda of this partnership agreement, the revised Cotonou Agreement of 2005 also included new provisions on WMD (through a 'non-proliferation clause' as a new 'essential element') and on the fight against terrorism and support for the ICC (see Hadfield 2007).

Even after the changes introduced by the Cotonou Agreement, EU policy towards Africa was a far cry from the structural foreign policy which it had developed and implemented *vis-à-vis* its neighbouring countries. With the EU's Strategy for Africa, this did seem to move at least in the direction of a genuine structural foreign policy approach. The Africa Strategy of 2005 explains how the EU will channel its resources between 2006 and 2015 to support African efforts to build a 'peaceful, democratic and prosperous future'. The main aims of the Strategy are the achievement of the Millennium Development Goals and the promotion of sustainable development, security and good governance in Africa. According to the Commission (2005d: 2), the EU Strategy for Africa is to provide a 'comprehensive, integrated and long-term framework' for EU–African relations in order to address fragmentation in policy formulation and implementation: between policies and actions of the EU member states and the Commission; between trade and economic development; and between socio-economic development and strategic political priorities. Negotiations started in mid-2006 on translating the unilateral EU strategy into a 'Joint EU/Africa Strategy' and joint Action Plan to be adopted at the EU–Africa Summit planned for December 2007.

This joint strategy will indicate whether the EU's policy towards Africa is evolving into a fully fledged structural foreign policy. This will depend on several factors. Firstly, through the Cotonou Agreement and CFSP/ESDP policies the EU has already developed policy initiatives that, at least on paper, aim at transforming or strengthening the various political, economic and security structures in Africa, both on the regional and pan-African level. The question is whether the joint strategy will manage to further substantiate this new focus and will also direct financial resources to supporting these structural changes.

Secondly, sustainable and viable structural reforms will require that the EU leaves behind what is often perceived as its paternalist or neocolonial attitude, which has seen the EU repeatedly impose its own agenda and solutions on Africa. The main question is whether this 'joint' EU/Africa Strategy will translate the concerns and demands of African countries (such as market access and changes to the EU's agricultural policy) into concrete policy, as much as it reflects the EU's own interests and policies. The question of whether African countries consider the EU–Africa Strategy to be relevant and also to their advantage will contribute to determining whether in the future they will consider the EU as a privileged partner or will increasingly turn to other powers, such as China.

Thirdly, for a structural foreign policy to be effective, individuals and societies must feel the advantages in terms of welfare, security and identity. The generally disappointing results of the EU's development policy, its overall limited involvement and record in providing security and the growing impact of Islamic groups, do not bode well in this regard.

Fourthly, and most importantly, an effective EU policy depends on the extent to which the African countries themselves have both the willingness and (institutional and financial) capacity to take structural reforms seriously and implement the various ambitious reform programmes. As indicated in Chapter 1, an effective structural foreign policy ultimately depends on the cooperation and engagement of the partner countries. Through its structural power, the EU can make this challenge easier or more difficult for the African partners and can widen or restrict the set of choices available to them.

Conventional foreign policy

It is clear that development no longer exclusively dominates the EU–Africa relationship. Not only has development itself become more concerned with issues of conflict, elections, respect for minorities, and so on, but these issues in and of themselves have also become more prominent. This has resulted from three inter-related factors: the EU's growing self-confidence to deal in political currency; the availability of a broader spectrum of instruments (ranging from contractual to diplomatic to military); and, as stated in the 2003 *European Security Strategy*, a recognition that 'security is a precondition for development', which in turn is essential for Europe's own security.

In responding to Africa's conventional foreign policy challenges, the EU uses a broad range of instruments. It generally takes both a bilateral and multilateral route, including interaction with regional groupings such as the African Union (AU) or broader international fora (the UN and its specialized agencies, the IMF, the World Bank). Interestingly, although the EU has used its second pillar instruments in a limited number of cases, it is particularly through the Commission and through the EC's development budget that it contributes most systematically to peace-building and structural stabilization in Africa. Two specific instruments have been created within the first pillar to allow it to respond more rapidly to conflict situations. The African Peace Facility provides support for the African Union and other African regional organizations to mount peacemaking and peacekeeping operations. The Instrument for Stability (and until late 2006 the Rapid Reaction Mechanism (RRM)) allows the EU to make targeted financial contributions to peacekeeping efforts, particularly of the AU. Examples of initiatives funded through the RRM include support to: ceasefire talks in the Horn of Africa; an observer mission to monitor the implementation of ceasefire agreements in Burundi; mediation efforts in the Central African Republic and Ivory Coast; and various peace-building initiatives in the DRC (Commission 2007d) (see also Chapter 8).

However, using 'development money' for security related issues has been controversial both for the EC's development community and among the member states. The latter greeted the prospect of the Commission developing itself as a foreign policy actor in Africa with little enthusiasm. While the Commission is, on paper, the implementing agency for financial support, these 'implementation' decisions often entail political choices, which the Council considered as belonging to its competence. Moreover, in some cases, Commission decisions have not corresponded to the political choices (or lack of choices) within CFSP deliberations – Darfur being a case in point.

Despite their criticism of the Commission, the member states have only gradually accepted the idea of developing a more active second pillar policy to meet foreign policy challenges thrown up by a region in which they have invested heavily over the last four decades. This has led to greater involvement from the Council of Ministers and the High Representative's foreign policy machinery. However, as Kingah (2006: 542) notes, with a conservative CFSP budget, 'the High Representative of the CFSP has very little latitude to dispense limited resources for apparently limitless challenges which the EU faces further afield'.

The only country which has been the subject of a dynamic and comprehensive EU policy has been the DRC (Faria 2004; Martinelli 2006; Ehrhart 2007). Operation Artemis of 2003 was the EU's first 'out of area' and first independent military operation (without recourse to NATO planning and assets). Although limited in scope, the operation succeeded in providing the necessary time for the deployment of additional UN troops and stemmed some of the worst violence in Eastern DRC. In 2005–06 the EU was one of the key players in helping the DRC move towards peace and democracy after a decade of war and chaos. It supported the fragile transition process and the DRC's first democratic elections for 40 years by using the full spectrum of its instruments in a remarkably coherent way: through increased development and macroeconomic support; EC support for judicial and governance reforms; demobilization, disarmament and reintegration projects and security sector reform (both through the EC and ESDP); an ESDP police mission in Kinshasa; an ESDP military operation in support of the UN Mission during the election process (dispatching 1,400 soldiers); the monitoring of, and massive financial and technical support to, the election process; and the sustained diplomatic involvement and interventions of High Representative Solana, Development Commissioner Michel, EU Special Representative for the Great Lakes region Aldo Ajello, and politicians and diplomats from several EU member states. This list already makes it clear that the EU's policy towards the DRC closely linked tackling conventional foreign policy challenges with developing a broader structural foreign policy towards the country.

The conflict in Darfur/Sudan is another area where the EU has gradually strengthened its engagement: through financial, technical and political support for the various peace initiatives, and through the EU civilian-military supporting action for the AU Mission in Darfur (AMIS). In 2005, the Council also appointed an EU Special Representative for Sudan. However, the intensity of the EU's involvement in this conflict has been substantially more limited than in the case of the DRC. This was not only due to the assertiveness of the regime in Khartoum and the complexities of the conflict. The intensity and cohesiveness of the EU's policy was also undermined by competition between first and second pillar actors and between the EU and NATO, which had a divisive effect among member states and which weakened the authority of EU representatives.

In most other conflicts in Africa, the EU has played a very modest role, with interventions from individual member states such as France in Ivory Coast and the UK in Sierra Leone, from a limited number of EU states such as the EU Core Group on Somalia (which includes the UK, Italy, Sweden and the Commission), or with the EU being almost entirely absent (such as in Liberia) (see Youngs 2006). When one considers the multitude of crises and conflicts in Africa, it indeed becomes clear that despite a growing engagement, the scale of the EU's involvement is highly limited both in terms of geographical coverage (the DRC is the only country where the full spectrum of EU instruments has been used) and in terms of scope (for example, the police mission in Kinshasa is composed of only 30 police, whilst the mission in Bosnia-Herzegovina has 495 police officers).

Conclusion

What does this whirlwind tour of the main arenas of EU foreign policy tell us about its impact and nature? Particularly since the beginning of the 2000s, the EU has developed its capabilities as a conventional foreign policy actor. It has developed instruments and institutional capabilities in both the second and first pillars, including the possibility to intervene in conflicts and crises using a range of civilian and military tools. However, outside the rather specific context of the Balkans, and to some extent also the DRC, the EU has rarely used its full range of foreign policy tools to tackle conflicts and crises, not least because, groundbreaking though the new ESDP instruments are, they are also relatively modest. Despite the dynamic generated by the High Representative and the other common actors in both the first and second pillars, their actual impact on most issues that dominate the international agenda has remained limited. The firm political and operational support of member states is critical to effective foreign policy actions, but is not always forthcoming.

Since the late 1980s, the EC/EU has conducted a clear structural foreign policy *vis-à-vis* the CEECs and, from the mid-1990s onwards, the structural foreign policy model has gradually become the mainstay of the EU's relations across the Eurasian and African continents. In contrast to its conventional foreign policy, the EU's structural foreign policy has been perceived by the member states as complementary to their own foreign policy and to that of other international actors (including the US, NATO and the UN). It has also been relatively easy for the EU to develop a structural foreign policy because it could often draw on well-developed first pillar procedures, budgetary resources and the institutional set-up. Because a structural foreign policy does not aim at quick reactions to sudden external changes, but at pursuing long-term goals through comprehensive initiatives, the complexity and slow nature of policy making under the

Community method has not proved to be an obstacle. Since it aims to reorganize and restructure the external environment, it is also of a largely regulatory nature, mirroring patterns of internal EC policy-making. Allowing the Commission to adopt an important role in these policies was deemed acceptable by the member states because political guidance and control was provided by the Council and the second pillar actors, and because the major strategic decisions were adopted by the European Council.

On paper at least, many of the EU's policies towards other regions look rather far-reaching. However, when assessing the EU's structural foreign policy, it is important to differentiate between (a) a structural foreign policy discourse and set of objectives; (b) a structural foreign policy which translates these words and goals into operational measures with budgetary resources; and (c) a structural foreign policy that is also actually having a structural foreign policy effect.

The EU has structural foreign policy discourse and objectives *vis-à-vis* most regions of the world (including regions that have not been discussed here, such as ASEAN and Latin America). It has an operational structural foreign policy (to varying degrees) towards the CEECs, the Balkans, the Mediterranean area, some countries in the CIS and to a lesser degree sub-Saharan Africa. However, for the time being the EU has only had a successful structural foreign policy effect with the CEECs and potentially also the Balkans. In contrast, the impact of policies towards the Mediterranean have been disappointing, and towards Africa have so far failed to effect real positive change, while it is too soon to judge the long-term effects of the European Neighbourhood Policy. It has been with the CEECs and the countries of the Balkans that the EU could play its trump card – the prospect of accession. However, these regions also had other characteristics: the EU was able to take a long-term approach; could tackle all structures in a comprehensive and consistent manner; the structures it was promoting were embedded in endogenous processes; and the conventional foreign policy problems were tackled by other actors and gradually diminished. These other factors meant that the countries of Central and Eastern Europe and the Balkans more or less met the conditions for a successful structural foreign policy in a way that has not been mirrored in the other regions of the world discussed here.

Chapter 11

The EU, Multilateralism and Competition with Structural Powers

This chapter evaluates the EU's policy towards two sets of what we term global 'structural powers': powers that have the capacity to set or influence the organizing principles and rules of the game that other actors have to follow (see Chapter 1). We first consider the main international political and financial institutions. We then turn to the structural power of three states – the United States, Russia and China – then the increasingly influential structures under the umbrella term of 'Islamism'. In addition to assessing the nature of the EU's relationship with, and policy towards, these other powers, this chapter also seeks to answer two further questions: to what extent are the structures shaped or promoted by these other actors similar to or compatible with the structures promoted by the EU? And, to what extent is the EU able to influence, gain support from or, if necessary, counter these other powers? In so doing, we explore how the EU copes with the strategic opportunities and challenges emanating from the (manifest or potential) structural power of the other major players on the world scene.

The EU and multilateral organizations

The existence of major political, economic and financial international organizations, such as the UN, the WTO, the IMF and the World Bank, are to a large extent the result of the US's use of its impressive structural power since World War II. Through its comprehensive structural foreign policy, Washington not only established these international organizations, but also shaped and promoted various regimes and organizing principles (such as 'democracy' and 'free market economy'). Although the US still has a major impact on these international organizations and related organizing principles, these organizations have obtained a dynamic of their own and, to different degrees, have grown into structural powers in their own right.

Organizations such as the WTO, the IMF and the World Bank define, shape and influence the structures which countries must adopt or to which they must adapt. These structures affect states, non-state actors, societies and individuals worldwide. Within a context of globalization and technological progress, organizing principles such as 'free-market economy' led to a process in which power was no longer solely or even mainly situated in the hands of states or international organizations. Structural power is increasingly located in, or emerging from, transnational economic and financial groups, networks, markets and 'flows' of capital, technology, ideas and information (see Castells 2000). Structural power emanating from international organizations and from these other groups, networks, markets and flows have an impact on European welfare and security, provide opportunities and challenges for EU foreign policy, and also influence the parameters within which EU foreign policy operates.

The EU's choice of effective multilateralism

The EU's stance towards international political and financial organizations seems at first sight to be one of unequivocal support. The EU is generally understood to be one of the main supporters and proponents of a global order based on international organizations and rules – itself an external reflection of the EU's internal endeavour to base interstate relations on common rules and institutions.

This position is reflected in three basic EU documents. The TEU points explicitly to the need to pursue foreign and security policy objectives in accordance with the principles of the UN Charter and of the OSCE (Art. 11 TEU). The EU's commitment to multilateralism as both a defining principle and objective of foreign policy is also prominent in its *European Security Strategy*. One of the three strategic objectives defined in this Strategy is an 'international order based on effective multilateralism'. The EU's approach is to develop 'a stronger international society, well functioning international institutions and a rule-based international order', in particular prioritizing the UN

Table 11.1   Ratification of 25 core international treaties

	EU member states	USA	China	Russia
Prevention and Punishment of Genocide (1948)	R (–MT)	R	R	R
Elimination of Racial Discrimination (1966)	R	R	R	R
Economic, Social and Cultural Rights (1966)	R	– (S)	R	R
Civil and Political Rights (1966)	R	R	– (S)	R
Protocol on Civil and Political Rights (1966)	R (–UK)	–	–	R
Abolition of the Death Penalty (1989)	R (–FR,LV,PL)	–	–	–
Elimination of Discrimination Against Women (1979)	R	– (S)	R	R
Elimination of Discrimination Against Women – Optional Protocol (1999)	R (–EE,LV,MT)	–	–	R
Convention Against Torture and Other Cruel Treatment (1984)	R	R	R	R
Rights of the Child (1989)	R	– (S)	R	R
Involvement of Children in Armed Conflict (2000)	R (–CY,EE, HU,IE,NL)	R	– (S)	– (S)
Sale of Children, Child Prostitution and Child Pornography (2000)	R (–CZ,FI, DE, EL,HU,IE, LU,MT,UK)	R	R	–
				→

(European Council 2003b: 9). The Strategy equally emphasizes the importance of 'key institutions in the international system' such as the WTO and the international financial institutions (the IMF and the World Bank), of regional organizations, and of the development of new international law in response to new challenges (with the International Criminal Court being the main example).

The belief in multilateralism, and in the UN as the pivot of the multilateral system, was yet more firmly stated in the Communication *The European Union and the United Nations: The Choice of Multilateralism*, which was adopted some months before the *European Security Strategy* by the Commission (2003b). This document not only included a rhetorical profession

→	EU member states	USA	China	Russia
Protection of Migrant Workers (1990)	–	–	–	–
Safety of UN and Associated Personnel (1994)	R (–LV,MT)	– (S)	R	R
Suppression of Terrorist Bombings (1997)	R	R	R	R
International Criminal Court (1998)	R	– (S)	–	– (S)
Prohibitions on the Use of Certain Conventional Weapons (1980)	R	R	R	R
Prohibitions on the Use of Mines (1996)	R	R	R	R
Prohibition of the Development and Use of Chemical Weapons (1992)	R	R	R	R
Comprehensive Nuclear Test Ban (1996)	R	– (S)	– (S)	R
Prohibition of Anti-Personnel Mines (1997)	R (–FI,PL)	–	–	–
Kyoto Protocol on Climate Change (1997)	R	– (S)	R	R
Biological Diversity (1992)	R	– (S)	R	R
Combat Desertification (1994)	R (–EE)	R	R	R

Notes: This list is the core group of multilateral treaties identified in the context of the UN Millennium Summit by the Secretary General Kofi Annan in his letter of 15 May 2000 to all heads of State or Government (UN 2000). The data are compiled on the basis of the UN Treaty Collection (UN 2007) (situation on 15 March 2007). Abbreviations: 'R': ratified; 'R (–. . .)': ratified by all EU states, except those mentioned between brackets; '–(S)': not ratified (but signed); '–': neither signed nor ratified; CR: Cyprus; CZ: Czech Republic; DE: Germany; EE: Estonia; EL: Greece; FI: Finland; FR: France; IE: Ireland; HU: Hungary; LV: Latvia; LU: Luxembourg; MT: Malta; NL: Netherlands; PL: Poland.
Source: UN (2007).

of faith in multilateralism: it also formulated concrete proposals to strengthen effective multilateralism as well as the EU's own effectiveness within multilateral fora.

That the EU does systematically choose multilateralism is borne out by the findings in previous chapters. EU foreign policy is part of a broader multilocation foreign policy and the EU itself is embedded in a far broader multilateral setting, including international organizations and regimes, in which EU member states also participate. Many of the EU's actions are explicitly adopted alongside or in support of the initiatives of other international organizations. For instance, a sizeable proportion of joint actions adopted within the CFSP context boil down to providing political and financial support to activities of one of the UN agencies, the OSCE or regional organizations such as the African Union. Moreover, if EU foreign policy has been successful in the Balkans over the last decade this is because its actions were undertaken in close cooperation with the actions of the UN, the World Bank, the OSCE, the Council of Europe and NATO.

The EU's choice of multilateralism is clearly demonstrated in Table 11.1. This table shows that the EU's choices, and thus its approach towards defining and codifying norms at the international level, differ from those of the other major global powers. Of the 25 core international treaties identified by UN Secretary General Kofi Annan in 2000, 21 were ratified by all, or nearly all, member states, and most of the exceptions are because the new member states have not yet caught up in the ratification process. Only in a limited number of cases have member states purposefully refused to sign or ratify a treaty (such as the Finnish and Polish refusal to sign the 1997 Treaty on the Prohibition of Anti-Personnel Mines, in view of their border with Russia).

The EU's choice of multilateralism not only appears from its record in ratifying international treaties. It has also played a pivotal role in the development, adoption and implementation of important new multilateral legal instruments, such as the Kyoto Protocol, the ICC and various disarmament regimes and initiatives like the Biological and Toxic Weapons Convention Verification Protocol, the Ottawa Convention banning anti-personnel land mines, and international actions on the fight against small arms and light weapons (Krause 2002). In the case of the Kyoto Protocol, the EU used active diplomacy to encourage a broad set of smaller players as well as a crucial large power – Russia – to follow its path.

The EU's success in promoting new international regimes has largely depended on whether it managed to achieve the necessary vertical and horizontal consistency. The best example of this was the EU's dynamic diplomatic offensive to push through the signing, ratification and accession to the founding Rome Statute of the ICC. The EU used a wide set of instruments from all three pillars including: common positions; diplomatic demarches towards a large number of third countries; political dialogue with third countries; legal instruments from the third pillar; EC support through the European Initiative/Instrument for Democracy and Human Rights to assist third countries in adapting their legal systems; and practical and financial support for the ICC itself (see also Chapter 6).

Remarkably, in the case of both the Kyoto Protocol and the ICC, the EU's relational and structural power prevailed over that of its main partner and rival, the US, even where Washington had developed an active diplomacy against these new international regimes. However, the EU's power was not sufficient to also compel the US to accept the structures which it had managed to forge at the international level – significantly weakening their potential effectiveness in the process.

Painting the EU as an effective multilateral actor of course only tells one part of the story. Only in a limited number of cases do EU member states manage to agree to an activist EU approach. In some cases they are too divided to even agree on a common EU stance, as in the case of the nuclear non-proliferation regime. Whether the EU is itself an effective actor within multilateral organizations is another question.

The EU in international fora: legal status and coordination

The EC's and EU's legal status in international organizations does not augur well for its ability to act as a strong multilateral actor. Both the EU's member states and other third states have proved extremely reluctant to accept the EC or EU as a member of international organizations – a privilege they have sought to retain for themselves (see Govaere *et al.* 2004). The only exceptions to this rule are EC membership, alongside the member states, to the Food and Agriculture Organization (FAO) and the Codex Alimentarius Commission within the UN system, and to the WTO and the European Bank for Reconstruction and Development (EBRD) outside the UN system. The EC has the status of 'Full Participant' in five other UN bodies and of 'Observer' in most other UN bodies. In some of the most powerful multilateral organizations, such as the UN Security Council, the World Bank, the IMF and the International Court of Justice, the EU has no status at all (see the overview in Wouters *et al.* 2006: 402–5; see also Hoffmeister and Kuijper 2006; Hoffmeister 2007). This lesser status or lack of status for the EC/EU undermines the EU's capacity to pursue its objectives in multilateral fora.

As neither the EC nor the EU are actors in their own right within the UN or most other multilateral settings, and as the member states remain central players, effective consultation and coordination are essential to make the EU's voice heard. With regard to CFSP issues, Article 19 TEU includes a set of obligations for member states, which can be summarized as follows:

● member states are to coordinate their action and uphold common positions in international organizations
● where not all the member states participate in an international organization, those which do participate are to uphold common positions and keep the rest informed of any matters of common interest
● member states which are members of the UN Security Council (UNSC) are to 'concert' and keep the other member states fully informed and defend the EU's positions and interests, which with regard to the permanent members of the UNSC is 'without prejudice to their responsibilities under the provisions of the UN Charter'

For Community issues, a wide variety of arrangements has been developed for representation and coordination in international organizations. The formal arrangements will depend on the nature of EC competences, leading to different roles for the Commission, the member states and the Presidency (see Azoulai 2005; Lenaerts and Van Nuffel 2005: 820–5). However, practical arrangements can deviate from formal arrangements and the formal attribution of competences. For instance, the Commission can represent the member states even if the EC has no exclusive competence in the issue on the table; or, a member state might be asked to take the lead in negotiations for the EU as a whole (see examples in Wouters *et al.* 2006). In terms of both formal and actual representation, all this results in a rather confused view for the outside world.

The EU and the UN

The EU plays an important role in sustaining the UN, not only politically but also financially. Combined, the member states provide approximately 40 per cent of its regular budget and 50 per cent of contributions to UN funds and programmes. In political and operational terms, since the early 2000s the EU and the UN have significantly strengthened their consultation and cooperation on a wide range of EC and CFSP/ESDP issues (see the comprehensive overview in Wouters *et al.* 2006). This had particularly been the case in the field of crisis management, where better coordination became imperative given the growing number of ESDP operations complementing UN operations. The EU also took steps to organize itself more effectively within the UN system and to strengthen its internal consultation and cooperation mechanisms on both first and second pillar issues (Luif 2003: 9–19; Farrell 2006).

Laatikainen and Smith (2006: 12) offer an interesting insight into member states' growing convergence in voting behaviour in the UN General Assembly. There is an increasing number of identical votes by EU member states, including on some important and sensitive foreign policy matters such as the Middle East. In the period 1997–2003, the (then 15) EU member states voted identically in between 70 and 80 per cent of votes. This is a remarkable improvement when compared with the overall cohesion score of 50 to 65 per cent in the early 1990s. When looking at the voting behaviour of the individual member states, it appears that 13 of the 15 member states voted in 93 to 99 per cent of the cases with the EU majority. Even before accession, most candidate member states had to a large extent adjusted their positions to that of the EU (Johansson-Nogués 2006). The two countries with a more diverging voting pattern are the UK and France, which voted with the EU majority in 84 to 89 per cent of cases.

More detailed scrutiny paints a less impressive picture of the EU's record in the UN. Laatikainen and Smith concluded from their case studies that the EU does not contribute to more effective UN multilateralism and that, in general, 'the intersection of

EU and UN multilateralisms is dysfunctional' (2006: 21–2). They confirm the European Commission analysis (2003b) that the EU's influence falls well short of its economic and political weight, that the EU gets little return for the 40 per cent it contributes to the UN budget and, surprisingly, that it also expects little from this major contribution.

Although convergence is growing, an overall cohesion score of around 70 to 80 per cent of the votes in the UN General Assembly means that there are still a sizeable number of 'split votes' (with member states voting differently). As these are mostly related to matters falling under the CFSP remit, this undermines the credibility of the EU, and the CFSP in particular. Despite the image given during the Iraq crisis, the major cleavage within the EU is not between the Atlanticists (led by the UK) and Europeanists (led by France) or between 'new' and 'old' Europe, but between these two European permanent members of the UN Security Council and the others. The diverging voting behaviour of London and Paris reflects the cleavage between these two 'great powers' and the other EU countries discussed in Chapter 5 (see also Hill 2006b). Unsurprisingly, the main split votes have related to strategic issues, disarmament and nuclear non-proliferation issues in particular, on which France and Britain are often closer to the US than to their EU partners. The British and French have used the qualification of Article 19 'without prejudice to their responsibilities under the provisions of the UN Charter' as a useful mechanism to uphold their superior position and to keep coordination and information-sharing to a strict minimum (Biscop and Drieskens 2006).

While the EU has developed mechanisms for internal consultation and coordination and for defining and upholding common stances, these are not sufficiently efficient for it to have a systematic impact on negotiations within international organizations. The EU's stance in the various UN fora is generally a reactive one, with the agenda set by other players and the EU not promoting its core objectives actively enough. The EU dedicates most of its energy to reconciling interests between its member states and institutions, leaving insufficient time for what really matters in international diplomacy: nurturing contacts and negotiations with other parties in order to convince them of its views and to build coalitions to support its positions. Moreover, the EU's positions are often too vague or, at the other extreme, too narrowly defined to leave EU representatives with sufficient flexibility to negotiate seriously. As a result, the EU is frequently ineffective in defending its interests and in using its potential structural power within the UN system to shape the international milieu along the lines it favours.

The EU also struggles in relation to the UN reform process. Broadly speaking, it has supported the reforms proposed by the former UN Secretary General Kofi Annan to strengthen the UN. However, there is no common EU position on two of the most pivotal issues. The member states have no common view on what is probably the most important aspect of UN reform: that of the Security Council. With London and Paris firmly holding onto their privileged position as permanent members and with the Germans and Italians competing for their own permanent seats, a common position was clearly impossible, and any talk of one common EU seat merely theoretical (Hill 2006b). EU member states have also proved reluctant to respond positively to the Secretary General's repeated request for them to provide more troops for UN peacekeeping operations in order that they have more well-trained and well-equipped troops. Although their reluctance is understandable in view of previous negative experiences with UN operations, this position makes the declaratory support for a stronger UN role in international security somewhat hypocritical. From this perspective, the European countries' decision in mid-2006 to lead the UN operation in Lebanon has gone some way to repairing an image of Europeans not prepared to get their hands dirty or risk their soldiers' lives in the quest for more effective multilateralism.

The international financial institutions

The EU demonstrates a systematic neglect of multilateralism in its attitude towards international financial institutions (IFIs) and fora such as the IMF, the World Bank and the G8. Whereas in trade the EU speaks with one voice, and in the UN it at least tries to get its act together, the EU has demonstrated no such activity *vis-à-vis* the international financial architecture. And hence, although it has achieved the status of a heavy weight in global trade, it has not managed to translate its common currency into the status of a heavy weight in global finance (Henning and Meunier 2005).

As McNamara and Meunier (2002: 850) point out, the challenges of international monetary and financial management in fora such as the G8, the IMF and the World Bank are met with a cacophony of voices on the part of European states. This reflects the internal ambiguities and divisions regarding EMU: not all member states have adopted the euro, and the relationship between the European Central Bank, the ECOFIN Council (Ministers of Economics and Finance of all EU countries) and the Eurogroup (including only the ministers from the eurozone) is difficult. However, it mainly reflects the member states' desire to retain national representation and reluctance to abdicate from their privileged positions, despite the single currency.

The UK, Germany, France and Italy are members of the G8, while the EU is represented by the country that holds the presidency of the Eurogroup, assisted by the Commission. In the Bretton Woods institutions, however, the member states have not established a format for EU representation. Although the aggregate voting power of all EU member states in the IMF amounts to around 32 per cent (compared to 17 per cent for the US), the EU is unable to defend or even define its interests. While the EU and its member states have failed to recognize or take into account the tremendous foreign policy impact of the IFIs, since the 1940s the US has shaped and used these institutions as a crucial component of its foreign policy toolbox and as the backbone of American structural foreign policy.

The EU is largely absent from the important ideological discussions on economic strategy developed by the World Bank and the IMF. There is no coordinated European stance on issues such as IMF country programmes, rescue packages for third countries or the far-reaching conditionality that the IMF imposes (Hunter Wade 2002; McNamara and Meunier 2002; Bini Smaghi 2004). This is a clear oversight on the EU's part given that the impact of the IFIs' prescriptions extends beyond the economic policy of third countries. Even if, economically, the IFI recipes do have a positive effect over the longer term, they can have a highly negative impact on the societal and human security situation in third countries, on internal political developments and stability, and in some cases also on regional stability and security. It is from this perspective that the IFIs' approach can be understood as one contributory factor to the rise of Islamism in

North Africa and in several Asian countries in the aftermath of the Asian financial crisis of the late 1990s (see Bowles 2002).

This negligence has quite serious implications for the effectiveness of EU foreign policy, particularly since the EU tries to develop its own structural foreign policy towards third countries and regions, without sufficiently acknowledging the far-reaching structural impact of the IFIs' policies. Although the EU works closely with IFIs in specific cases (as in the Balkans), rather than working to shape the overarching strategies of the IMF and World Bank to ensure that these are congruent with the EU's own foreign policy objectives and values, the Commission and the EU more broadly have too readily adopted the IMF and World Bank recipes and integrated them within the EU's own policy. This reflects a broader pattern we have already seen in previous chapters regarding the EU's trade policy – it promotes neoliberal policies and pursues free trade agreements with third countries and regions without due regard to their wider foreign policy implications.

As Hunter Wade (2002) argues, the Europeans' failure to assume their responsibility in the IFIs may be one explanation why the Bretton Woods institutions have historically not been able to rely on a wider variety of possible free market recipes as part of their toolbox – with frequent mismanagement of crises as a consequence. In practice, the IFIs have systematically used the Anglo-Saxon model of capitalism with its focus on the predominance of the market, the withdrawal of the state and the subordination of societal objectives and values to the principles of the free market as the norm for their external interventions. This approach can be appropriate in some contexts, but it clearly does not work across the board.

It is in this respect that the Europeans might have played a constructive role, given the variety of models that exist in Europe itself in terms of organizing a free market economy and reconciling state, society and market in line with the domestic preferences and values of their countries (see Cerny 1990). In European countries, the free market economy has been combined with a larger role for the state and civil society actors, as well as with greater provision of safety nets and public services for the population. This is not to advocate that the models used by European countries could be simply transplanted on to other countries in the world either. But, they could have provided a source of inspiration for developing strategies of global governance that take into account the possibility of different models of state-society-market balance which are sensitive to domestic preferences and values. Unfortunately, the Europeans have almost entirely failed to promote a diversity of models or transpose their own sensitivity to domestic societal preferences into the policies of the IFIs.

The other structural powers: the US, Russia, China and Islamism

In addition to international organizations, other actors also promote political, economic, societal and security structures which shape the international context in which the EU operates and influence the prospects of EU structural foreign policies being successful. The three states discussed here are all nuclear powers and permanent members of the UN Security Council: the United States (undisputedly the most influential structural power since World War II), Russia (the main competing structural power until the fall of communism in the late 1980s) and China (potentially the most important competing structural power for the US in the medium to long term). In order to avoid a one-sided focus on states and clear-cut 'actors' in the analysis of international relations, we also consider the set of increasingly influential structures understood under the label of 'Islamism'.

The United States: the awkward strategic partner

The United States is the actor with the most extensive structural power in today's international system. Following World War II, the US defined the main international (though originally 'Western') structures which are still largely predominant: democracy, the rule of law, free market economy and international organizations such as the IMF and the WTO that organize this economy on a global scale. While the US is the EU's most important partner on the international stage, this is also a relationship which the EU manages with difficulty, and with mixed results. The transatlantic relationship spans an incredibly diverse range of issues and policy fields and, irrespective of events such as the high profile clash over Iraq in 2003, the vast majority of this business continues without episode. The EU and US economies are highly interdependent and together account for approximately 40 per cent of world trade and over 60 per cent of world GDP. The US and the EU share many common domestic features and international goals. However, these similarities can be deceptive, in the same way that the occasional highly publicized disagreements over foreign policy issues mask a more complex reality.

It is worth recalling that the European integration process is a construct of a US structural foreign policy made operational through its post-World War II Marshall Plan (see Chapter 2). The continued expansion of the European integration project has remained an objective of US foreign policy until the present day – assertive support for Turkey's accession to the EU being a case in point. The institutional relationship between the EC and the US was formalized for the first time by the November 1990 Transatlantic Declaration. This Declaration also brought into being annual EU–US Summits of the President of the US, the Commission President, the Head of State or Government of the EU member state holding the Presidency and the Secretary General/High Representative for the CFSP. These supplement the more informal and operational ad hoc contacts which have gradually developed between the EU and the US.

At their 1995 summit in Madrid, the EU and US signed the 'New Transatlantic Agenda' which provided for joint action in four fields: promoting global peace, stability, democracy and development; responding to global challenges; contributing to the expansion of world trade and closer economic relations; and building bridges across the Atlantic. In response to the terrorist attacks on the US in 2001, Madrid in 2004 and London in 2005 and the subsequent 'war on terror', transatlantic cooperation in broader justice and security issues has grown markedly. Agreements have been concluded, including on extradition and mutual legal assistance, in the field of transport on the transfer of passenger name records (PNR) and on sharing intelligence and personal data between Europol and US law enforcement agencies.

Where there is clear EC competence, such as in trade, the US deals directly with the EC. However, in the majority of other cases, the US prefers to structure its relations bilaterally, where it can more easily apply pressure or rely on like-minded countries. This preference to deal with member states bilaterally gives further weight to the 'Atlantic factor' in EU foreign policy-making. Member states are split along a spectrum of the importance they attribute to the 'what would the Americans think?' test. The division between the group of 'Europeanist' member states led by France and the group of 'Atlanticist' member states led by the UK is the most commonly discussed: while France views the development of the EU as an effective actor on the international stage as a prospective counterweight to US *hyper-puissance*, for the UK building EU foreign policy capability is to make the EU a more effective partner for the US. As European countries debated the merits or otherwise of the planned US invasion of Iraq in 2003, the then US Defence Secretary Donald Rumsfeld was quick to lambast 'old' Europe's defiance of American plans and to herald 'new' Europe, in the form of the then eight Central and Eastern European candidate countries, for their support. Crude though this labelling might well have been, it does symbolize a very real distinction between the 'old' member states for whom military threat from a third country is a relatively distant memory and the 'new' member states for whom memories of the Soviet military threat and the fear of a renewed Russian display of strength are vivid. This explains why the CEECs are more sensitive to the continued relevance of the US security umbrella and hence keener to keep the US happy.

On one level, the EU and US share many features and common goals. Domestically, they share the same values of democracy, rule of law, human rights and individual freedoms, free market economies, and so on. On the trade front, both parties support a global free market economy, prioritizing stability and trade growth to ensure their continued economic prosperity. Together, the EU and US regulate the global economy. They also face similar challenges – increasing energy import dependency and competition from the emerging economies of China and India. Common concerns and goals are shared on both sides of the Atlantic in terms of declining natural resources; fighting international terrorism and international crime; resolving conflict, including in the Middle East; and promoting functioning democratic government. The EU and its member states were quick to demonstrate their solidarity with the US following the terrorist attacks of September 11. Invoking Article V of the North

Atlantic Treaty for the first time, and supporting military intervention in Afghanistan, the mood of the moment was encapsulated by the headline of left-leaning French daily newspaper *Le Monde*: 'We are all Americans now' (Garden 2004: 2).

However, beyond these broad brushstrokes, there lies a remarkable array of divergences which go to the very core of the EU and the US and which are played out both in the different global structures the two powers promote and in their approach to multilateralism. Table 11.1 demonstrates a stark contrast between the EU and the US in terms of support for the major international treaties. While EU member states have, with very few exceptions, signed up to nearly all 25 of the core international treaties, the US has either not ratified or not signed up to over half of these, including treaties on the abolition of the death penalty, the ICC, the Kyoto Protocol, the Comprehensive Nuclear Test Ban, the prohibition of anti-personnel mines, biological diversity, economic social and cultural rights, civil and political rights, elimination of discrimination against women, the rights of the child, the status of refugees, and the safety of UN and associated personnel. While the EU and US are systematically lumped together as 'the West', the differences in their voting patterns on these treaties are greater than the differences between the EU and either China or Russia (although this in and of itself is no guarantee of either China or Russia adopting EU-style behaviour).

This data is evidence of a broader phenomenon which is a fundamentally different approach to global governance (see also Kagan 2003; Malone and Khong 2003; Schori 2005). While the EU tries to regulate world order in the same way that it manages its business internally, the US also attempts to structure the external world in line with its internal arrangements. Hence, the importance Europeans attribute to regulating international society reflects the societal and political importance attached to safeguards for individuals and to avoiding the negative effects of unbounded freedom – implying that state intervention and the limitation of individuals' freedom is seen in a positive light. In a similar vein, the highly conflictual transatlantic debate prior to the invasion of Iraq in 2003 exposed a range of transatlantic divergences, including on the use of pre-emptive force and the use of military force rather than 'softer' ways forward. In the same way that within the US domestically the individual is

largely seen as responsible for his own fate, in international politics the US understands itself as responsible for its own fate – and
if it perceives the need to use violence to ensure its own security,
then it will consider it legitimate to do so.

This example is also instructive of the different values that US
and European governments attribute to the multilateral system
and the international rule of law. In the debate over whether an
explicit UN Security Council Resolution was required to autho-
rize the invasion of Iraq in 2003, the US wanted to intervene
regardless, the UK wanted clear UN authority to do so, while
Germany and France wanted more time for weapons inspectors
to ascertain whether Saddam Hussein actually did have weapons
of mass destruction. In general terms, the EU promotes a rules-
based international order while the US tends to be highly suspicious of multilateralism, international rules and frameworks
where these restrain its ability to act autonomously. However,
this does vary depending on the issue at hand (for example the
US sought China's cooperation in dealing with North Korea) and
the administration in power (for example the Clinton administration adopted a less hostile approach to international institutions such as the UN than did the Bush administration). Most
importantly, the existing multilateral architecture is to a large
extent the result of American initiatives. Moreover, where the US
has deemed it to be in its own interest, it has been significantly
more effective than the EU in using multilateral structures such
as the IMF and the World Bank to promote its objectives. In
terms of choosing multilateralism, the US is thus highly effective,
if highly selective (see Patrick and Forman 2002).

The EU has proved reluctant to criticize and unable to sanction the US even where American policy has run counter to the
EU's own fundamental values. If the US were any other country,
concern over its record on human rights protection, lack of
respect for international law, the death penalty, extraordinary
rendition, Guantanamo Bay and trials by military tribunal
would in all likelihood trigger EU sanctions and a policy of
concerted non-cooperation. However, the EU and EU member
states are rarely willing to openly criticize the US, and never dare
actually to use the sticks at their disposal to add weight to their
concerns.

In addition, the EU has been a poor publicist of, or advocate
for, its own foreign policy approach. A report by the UK House

of Lords in 2003 concluded that there is a sore lack of understanding in the US about what the EU is and what it does. It reported, for example, a lack of awareness that EU member states provide significantly more overseas development aid than the US. This is coupled with a lack of concern about the EU's perspective. Having returned from a trip to Washington, this House of Lords delegation concluded: 'we left the US capital with the impression that the US attitude to the EU was "if you agree with us, fine – if you don't then get out of our way"'(House of Lords 2003: 10).

Russia

Global competition between structures promoted by the USSR and by the United States defined international relations from the end of World War II until the late 1980s. The end of the Cold War, the fading away of the communist structures exported internationally by Russia, and internal upheaval across the former Soviet bloc forced Moscow's global influence – and potential to shape the rules of the game – into rapid decline. Russia's position changed from being the main competing structural power in the four decades following the Second World War, to integrating within predominant 'Western' structures in the 1990s. However, since the mid-2000s, there has been a resurgence in Russian assertiveness on the international stage, even if Russia is not (yet) competing as a global structural power beyond its near abroad. Interestingly, Russia's increasing strength has occurred almost in tandem with the gradual deterioration domestically of 'Western' structures of democracy, free speech, respect for human rights and the rule of law and separation of the state and the economy.

The EU's relations with Russia are structured through a Partnership and Cooperation Agreement (PCA) and the development of 'Common Spaces'. The 1997 EU–Russia PCA sets the principal common objectives, establishes the institutional framework for bilateral contacts, and provides for cooperation in a broad range of policy fields. While on paper the PCA provides for a broad relationship, in practice its political dimension is diluted and the EU has been unable to use this agreement as a political instrument to exert influence over Russia. For example, while the PCAs with the other ex-Soviet republics include a reference to respect for minority rights, such a reference does not appear in the PCA with Russia because of Moscow's insistence that this was an internal matter of no relevance to the EU. Moscow also declined the EU's invitation to participate in the European Neighbourhood Policy (ENP), considering the positive and negative conditionalities therein unacceptable. This refusal to be treated as just another third country or as an 'object' of EU policy has marked the development of EU–Russian relations since the late 1990s, and also explains Moscow's earlier dismissal of the EU's 1999 Common Strategy on Russia (see Chapter 6).

As an alternative to the Common Strategy and the ENP framework, in 2003 the EU and Russia agreed to centre cooperation on the long-term creation of four jointly agreed Common Spaces in the framework of the PCA: a Common economic space; a Common space of freedom, security and justice; a Common space of external security; and a Common space of research, education and cultural aspects. These Common Spaces were further elaborated in 2005 through the adoption of a detailed Road Map, including short- and medium-term instruments for their implementation. The difficulties in elaborating this Road Map were a clear demonstration of the nature of the EU–Russia power relationship. Moscow refuses to accept that the EU should be involved in determining the rules of the game internally, while the EU has failed to assert its values and norms in the development of the four spaces, leading to a virtual absence of political conditionality (Vahl 2007: 129).

As Russia's international power position has evolved over the last decade, so has it sought to see this mirrored in the EU–Russia relationship towards one which functions on the basis of equality. It is important to recall that with its enlargements of 2004 and 2007 and growing influence through its ENP with the former Soviet republics, the EU has cut swathes through Russia's sphere of political and economic domination, a fact which is too often overlooked in assessments of EU–Russia relations. From this perspective, Moscow's growing assertiveness and coercive behaviour can be considered a kind of counter-offensive to recover lost ground and avoid further chipping away at Russian influence in its immediate neighbourhood.

Whereas in the late 1990s Moscow had to accept the 'didactic, smug and often patronizing language of the PCA' (Light 2001:

20), half a decade later the situation had changed. Moscow has gradually recovered its old assertiveness and economic strength, attributable in no small part to spiralling gas and oil prices. Moscow has exploited the EU's dependence on Russia as an energy provider, for example disrupting supplies of natural gas to EU countries during a dispute over pricing with Ukraine in 2006 (see Chapter 9). More generally, it has adopted a more confrontational international posture, leading to more clashes with the EU and particularly with the EU countries that once belonged to its zone of influence.

The question of how to handle a newly resurgent Russia has received contradictory answers within the EU. The member states from Central and Eastern Europe have called on the EU to adopt a more assertive attitude towards Moscow and stress the importance of democracy and human rights in foreign policy deliberations. They have also been effective in bringing problems in their bilateral relations with Russia into the EU arena. Poland's decision in 2006 to veto the launch of negotiations on a new EU–Russia treaty because of Russia's embargo on Polish meat imports is one such example, which also contributed to EU–Russia relations reaching a new low in 2007.

However, other member states prioritize the need to gain Moscow's strategic partnership in crucial foreign policy issues, including the fight against terrorism, support for the Kyoto protocol, the EU's negotiations with Iran over its development of nuclear capabilities and support for the EU's position in the Kosovo final status negotiations. In conjunction with growing concerns about the EU's energy dependency, these factors have pushed some member states – particularly Germany and France – to increasingly indulge Russia and restrain any criticisms of developments within that country. For example, the EU has repeatedly chosen not to systematically criticize Moscow's use of excessive violence in Chechnya. The EP did temporarily delay the ratification of the EU–Russia PCA and put TACIS funding on hold in the late 1990s in response to Russia's Chechnya policy. But, particularly since the 2001 terrorist attacks against the US, Russia and the largest EU member states have managed to sideline this issue in EU–Russia relations, turning it into a taboo in their biannual summits and ensuring it does not spoil discussions on what they deem to be strategically more important issues (Hughes 2007). However, in turning a blind eye to developments within Russia, the EU, and particularly its largest member states, have neglected the fact that Europe's long-term strategic interest is in having a neighbouring Russia that shares the EU's fundamental political, economic and societal choices. Clearly, the EU missed the historic opportunity presented by the early 1990s of anchoring post-communist Russia more firmly into a process of wider European integration (Casier 2007: 86).

China

China's massive and rapidly growing economy has been the primary driving force behind its gradual emergence as a global structural power over the last decade. It has succeeded in building this strength by partially adapting itself to, and embedding itself within, the predominant 'global' (but originally US/ Western) structures. This is particularly the case from an economic perspective. China has embraced free market economy principles and undergone a gradual process of economic liberalization, symbolized not least by its joining the WTO in 2001.

China's attitude towards political global structures is less clear cut. On the one hand, in several policy areas, China is gradually adapting to Western-promoted global structures and is adopting a multilateral approach. China is an active participant in international institutions such as the UN, where it is the largest provider of peacekeeping troops among the five permanent members of the UN Security Council. Beijing has also found a peaceful settlement to most of its territorial disputes with other governments – with Taiwan remaining one of the main sore points (Gill and Huang 2006: 21–3). However, it has also refused to sign up to core international treaties, including on civil and political rights, the abolition of the death penalty, the involvement of children in armed conflict, the ICC, the comprehensive nuclear test-ban and the prohibition of anti-personnel mines. China remains a one-party communist state with a dubious record in protecting its citizens' human rights or fundamental freedoms.

From a position of at least partial acceptance of the prevailing global structures, China has already started to export its own structures and rules of the game – a trend that is set to continue. On an economic level, its attractiveness to third countries as a trading partner and investment opportunity has implied that third countries, developed and developing alike, have actively

sought relations with China to a greater or lesser extent following its rules of the game in that relationship (see Nicolas and
O'Callaghan 2007). On a regional level, in the wake of the July
1997 Asian financial crisis, it was China that provided currency
stability and trade concessions supporting the ASEAN
economies at a time when Western powers were largely absent or
offering little more than the prospect of painful IMF-sponsored
reform (Vatikiotis 2006: 30). China could thus freely position
itself as a regional lifesaver, in the process building its structural
power in the region, if not globally. Furthermore, as Gill and
Huang argue (2006: 18), on the societal level, China has actively
promoted the study of the Chinese language worldwide. By late
2005, it had established 32 Confucius Institutes (similar to the
British Council or Goethe Institut) in 23 countries offering
Chinese language and cultural resources and has seen dramatic
growth in foreign student enrolment domestically. On a political
level, China has also taken an activist approach to subregional
and regional institution-building, undermining US influence in
the region in the process – itself a core Chinese foreign policy
goal.

China throws up fundamental foreign policy challenges to the
EU, to which the EU has struggled to form a response. The EU is
China's largest trading partner, ahead of both the US and Japan,
and one of its most important sources of foreign investment
(Casarini 2006: 15). The EU and China also share some common
goals on the international stage. For example, promoting multilateralism is a core objective of both parties, even if the rationale
behind this policy is rather different, with China seeing multilateralism as a vehicle for constraining unbridled US power and
developing what it brands 'the democratisation of international
relations' (Holslag 2006: 564–5) through the development of a
multipolar system.

Many policies pursued by China internationally run directly
counter to core EU foreign policy objectives, as well as the structures that EU foreign policy attempts to promote. China is a
resource-hungry economy, particularly with regard to energy. A
net oil importer since the mid-1990s, its oil import figures in 2000
almost doubled from 36.6m to 70.2m tonnes (Daojiong 2006:
180). Like the EU, China is heavily reliant on the Middle East for
oil imports, but has sought to diversify its sources. In so doing, it
has pursued closer diplomatic relations with, for example,

Zimbabwe's brutal dictator Robert Mugabe, Sudan's government, despite its atrocious human rights record, particularly in the Darfur region, and Iran, despite the international community's concerns over its nuclear ambitions (see also Holslag 2006: 576–7). China thus effectively supports what the EU considers highly dubious regimes and undertakes policies which fly in the face of key 'international community' concerns. It justifies its stance by insisting that 'business is business' (Gill and Huang 2006: 28) – an approach which in fact mirrors that adopted by many EU member states towards China (see below).

China also embodies and promotes a development model alternative to that promoted by the EU – one in which economic liberalization and development need not go hand in hand with political liberalization and development towards Western norms. Gill and Huang argue (2006: 20) that China's economic model is being held up as an attractive alternative to the Western development model, including by former Soviet republics in Central Asia, some countries of South Asia, policy-makers in Latin America, some sections of the Middle East (including Iran) and by authoritarian leaders in Africa. Hence, not only in terms of particular foreign policy dossiers, but also in terms of structures the EU actively promotes, Chinese foreign policy undermines EU foreign policy.

In seeking to respond to the emerging structural power which is China, the EU has adopted a familiar strategy. Since the mid-1990s, it has sought to embed China in international organizations and regimes through a policy of 'constructive engagement'. It has built a strong trading relationship with China, with the dual goal of promoting EU economic interests and attempting to gain political leverage. It has institutionalized this relationship through a Partnership and Cooperation Agreement, which it was agreed at the September 2006 EU–China Summit is to be renewed and deepened. It also conducts a structured dialogue with China on issues deemed to be of particular significance, including, since 1998, a biannual human rights dialogue and a dialogue on Intellectual Property issues. The EU and China have held annual summits since 1998, and since October 2003 have referred to each other as 'strategic partners', although it is less clear what the concrete objectives of this strategic partnership are.

The member states are highly competitive in seeking to build stronger bilateral political relations with China in order to garner favour for national companies seeking lucrative new contracts. This is an approach which Beijing has encouraged, and exploited. Member states also have different positions in terms of the extent to which issues such as respect for human rights should be prioritized in the EU–China relationship. Smaller member states, particularly the Nordic countries, together with the European Parliament, take a more principled approach, while the larger member states, and particularly Germany, France and Britain, are largely responsible for the EU's decreasingly critical attitude (Casarini 2006: 19). The consequence is that the EU's policy on its supposedly core values has been rather weak. While it has held a regular human rights dialogue with China, the list of ongoing concerns – including respect for human rights, political and religious freedoms, Tibet, Taiwan and the 2005 anti-secession law, capital punishment, freedom of press and the Internet – has not appeared to diminish. Moreover, the decision to start a human rights dialogue in 1998 was in itself a quid pro quo for the EU's decision in 1997 to cease its practice, since the Tiananmen Square massacre of 1989, of tabling each year an EU resolution criticizing China's human rights record at the UN Commission on Human Rights.

While the EU's human rights dialogue may have little impact in substantive terms, it is a major source of annoyance for China. The EU thus faces a dilemma over whether it should consistently raise its concerns over human rights and fundamental freedoms, even though this is likely to have little more than a marginal impact and will engender further tensions, or whether to hold its tongue over such sore points and, in so doing, gain more political capital with China in order to pursue key international strategic objectives and, particularly, key economic contracts. The approach that the EU has adopted is an uneasy (and ineffective) mix of the two.

The whole debacle over whether or not to lift the arms embargo imposed by the EU on China following the Tiananmen Square massacre is an interesting example. Motivated primarily by commercial interests and a desire to respond to Chinese concerns, France and Germany first proposed that the embargo be lifted in 2003. This position was opposed in particular by the Nordic countries and the Netherlands, who argued that China's repeated failure to improve its human rights record meant the embargo should remain firmly in place. Ultimately, it was this internal opposition, and intervention from Washington, that has taken this proposal off the agenda, for the time being at least (see Casarini 2006: 30–9).

To sum up, the EU has not developed an encompassing policy to tackle emerging Chinese structural power worldwide. It has failed to develop a forward looking strategy towards China which moves beyond rhetoric and short-term political and economic gain. Despite the fact that the EU is China's largest trading partner, it has been remarkably ineffective in translating this economic capital into political leverage. While China's increasingly active diplomacy in regions prioritized by the EU, including Africa and the Middle East, threatens to thwart EU foreign policy goals and promoted structures, the EU is yet to develop a proper response.

Islamism: challenging the dominant structures

Islamism is a 'power' which does not fit within conventional categories and conceptions of foreign policy. Islamism is multi-faceted, with no clearly defined centre or leadership. It places on an equal footing: grass-roots and societal levels with state and elite levels; networks and flows of ideas and money with clearly structured hierarchical organizations; soft and structural power with hard power; and immaterial elements such as identity and beliefs with material elements such as financial support and social services (see Chapter 1).

Despite its ambiguous character, Islamism can be understood as a formidable structural power in the same league as international organizations, the US, Russia, China and the EU. It has a growing influence in large parts of the world: from Indonesia and Pakistan to the Middle East to half of Africa, many European cities and beyond. It is a competing power which is developing to a large extent both outside and against the dominant structures established and sustained by the West. The main challenge faced by the other global structural powers that we have discussed in this chapter is whether Islamism will remain 'against' the West, leading to an escalation of tension, or whether Islamism and Western structural powers will grow closer and develop a peaceful coexistence. For us to assess the EU's approach towards this structural power, we must first explain what we understand by 'Islamism'.

Common to all manifestations of Islamism is the belief that Islam provides an answer to the political, economic, social, moral and identity crises of Muslim societies and states. It is based on the claim that the teachings of the holy texts can be applied to contemporary society and political life. It is a reaction against the secular state and against 'Western' models and ideologies (such as modernization, nationalism, socialism, communism, capitalism and, particularly, secularism), which have largely failed to provide welfare, security and identity to Muslim people. It is also a reaction against globalization which is perceived as an extension of colonialism and part of the general Western and secular assault (Halliday 2005).

Islam is considered as able to structure all aspects of life, with the Quran and the Sharia playing a central role. The Sharia offers what is believed to be a divinely inspired legal framework which regulates politics, economics, business, banking and finance, family relations, social relations, education, and the day-to-day personal behaviour of Muslims. As Azzam argues, for most Muslims, the Sharia is a fundamentally positive force which, when upheld, will offer security for Muslim citizens against the tyranny of dictators, will counter corruption and other abuses committed by the state, and will counter secular and Western values, which are viewed as mistaken, immoral and corrupting. Hence, 'the issue here is not only secular versus religious; it is also a search for justice versus repression' (Azzam 2006: 1130). This also explains why the Sharia is probably at the heart of one of the major misunderstandings between the West and the Muslim world, with the former seeing the Sharia as a threat and a negative force and the latter seeing it as a solution, relief and positive force.

The political, legal, socio-economic and mental structures that are upheld and promoted by Islamism are thus of a fundamentally different order than those promoted by the West. Generally speaking, structures promoted by Islamism not only question or reject the Western conception of separating religion and politics, but also assert the dominance of religion over politics, of religious answers over non-religious solutions. On a more specific level, they not only provide for different norms or sources of inspiration, but also translate into completely different ways of organizing politics, economics and social relations than in the West. One example is Islamic banking and finance, that allows for transnational economic transactions and capital flows to occur largely outside 'Western' international economic and financial structures (see Kuran 2004; El-Gamal 2006).

Beyond these general features, there are major differences between the many manifestations of Islamism. Islamism is not a monolithic movement, but a complex multifaceted phenomenon that expresses itself through a variety of groups, movements and currents on various levels (for an overview, see Denoeux 2002). Differences relate to questions such as the extent to which a literal reading of the founding religious texts is required, and whether Islamic solutions and structures can be combined with non-Islamic (secular and 'Western') solutions and structures. Divergences also relate to what approaches and instruments are to be employed: the focus can be on *personal behaviour* and issues of morality and faith of the individual Muslim; on *grass-root action* aimed at the regeneration of the individual and the gradual Islamization of society from below; on direct *political action* and the seizure of political power; on bringing about drastic socio-political changes, including through *violent action* within specific national contexts; or on the *holy war* or global 'jihad' against the unfaithful in both the Muslim world and the West (such as the al-Qaeda network).

Several interrelated mechanisms, processes and actors contribute to the growing influence of Islamism. These include: generally increasing religiosity of Muslims; state-controlled (re-)Islamization; financial support for Islamic groups, mosques, Islamic schools and centres worldwide, provided by governments and religious foundations in Iran and particularly Saudi Arabia; and the provision of essential public goods to an often impoverished population and the construction of parallel social and economic structures by organizations, such as Hezbollah in Lebanon, in the absence of a properly functioning state.

The EU has not yet found a way to tackle the unconventional foreign policy challenge posed by Islamism. It has mainly focused on a handful of governmental actors and elites (e.g. Iran, Hamas, Hezbollah), but fails to consider what policy it could develop towards the broader societal and religious changes, grass-root movements and transnational networks that are an intrinsic part of the Islamic resurgence. The EU focuses on the involvement of Islamist actors in violent conflicts, but disregards the soft power that Islamism exerts on major parts of the population, from

Jakarta to Islamabad to London. While focusing predominantly on their armed struggle, the EU neglects the positive contribution actors such as Hamas and Hezbollah have made in tackling some major human and societal security problems of the population (ICG 2003, 2006, 2007). In adopting such a one-sided approach, the EU has undermined its own credibility among the Muslim populations that consider these organizations as positive forces.

The EU seems to be ignoring, or is perhaps paralysed by, the structural power emanating from the rise of Islamism. It is difficult for the West to counter or control Islamism as a structural power, as the conventional instruments of foreign policy are irrelevant to its unconventional actors, instruments, networks and immaterial dimensions. The Islamist assertion in the Muslim world is religious and cultural, and this of course makes it all the more difficult to contend with its growth in security terms (Azzam 2006: 1130). The EU's answer has been to attempt to export Western structures, norms and values to Muslim countries. However, the Euro-Mediterranean Process, for example, launched in 1995, failed to counter either the rise of Islamism or the conditions which provided a fruitful context for its resurgence. As Bicchi (2006: 10) notes, in the implementation of the Euro-Mediterranean Association Agreements 'the EU in fact prefers not to engage with Islamic organizations, regardless of how moderate or how central they are to the social and political scene of Mediterranean Arab countries'. The EU's historic neglect of the Islamic dimension in its policies towards Muslim countries is indicative of the struggle of secular Europeans to understand religious non-Western societies, to take into account non-Western beliefs and cultures, and to respond positively to their desire for recognition.

It is only recently that the EU began to recognize the importance and the potentially positive role of faith groups and religious civil society, and the necessity of engaging with these actors (Council 2005c, 2007f). This is important, as the challenge posed by Islamism is one of the best examples of the blurring inside/outside divide in foreign policy. As Azzam (2006: 1119) emphasizes, the boundaries of the '*umma*', or community of the faithful, have stretched beyond Muslim states to European cities, with a shared sense of belonging to a common faith. According to 2003 statistics, around 16.5 million Muslims live in what is the current EU-27 area, while demographic processes suggest that this figure is likely to increase over the following decades (Savage 2004). From this perspective, it is of vital interest for Europe to develop a comprehensive and sophisticated answer to the multifarious challenges and demands of a growing Islamism and an increasingly 'globalised Islam' (Roy 2004). This is not only important because of the potential threat posed by jihadism, which finds in Europe fertile conditions to prosper (Neumann 2006: 81). It is particularly important to counter a growing feeling of alienation and of societal insecurity among both Muslim and non-Muslim sections of Europe's population.

Conclusion

In mapping the EU's relationship with the main global powers which shape the international system, this chapter sought to respond to two questions. Firstly, we asked to what extent the structures promoted by other actors are similar to, or compatible with, the structures promoted by the EU. From the arguments presented here, we can conclude that on some important issues, the EU is actually relatively isolated on the international stage and occupies a minority position when compared to the other powers. This is even the case when comparing the EU to the US which, although sharing the same basic principles, in some important respects is more distant from the EU than is often anticipated.

Secondly, we asked to what extent the EU can influence and/or gain the support of these other powers to meet its own foreign policy goals. The answer is mixed. In multilateral organizations, the EU increasingly manages to formulate a common position, to make a common position heard and sometimes also to convince other actors. However, this is not the case across the whole gamut of foreign policy issues or in all multilateral organizations. Particularly in the international financial institutions, the EU has failed to define a clear common approach to reflect its foreign policy goals.

Unlike when the EU deals with countries in its neighbourhood, or in unequal power relationships such as with Africa, the EU finds it difficult to identify or to use its carrots and sticks towards the major structural powers when their interests or values diverge. In terms of EU–US relations, this is further complicated by the European–Atlantic divide within the EU, which makes it far from evident to voice a common European view. It has proved yet harder for the EU to influence developments within, or the foreign policies of, Russia or China. Where it has criticized either of these two powers, the result has tended to be their irritation and alienation rather than any substantive policy change. In relation to Islamism, the EU is all but paralysed in the face of this new type of structural power which challenges not only Western structures but also the very conception of how to formulate and implement a foreign policy. However, the EU has played a positive role and, to some extent also been successful, in ensuring that the very notion of a rule-based international order and its multilateral organizations has not lost its relevance. Such an evolution has not been inconceivable given the posturing of the other structural powers. In this sense, it has been quite an achievement for the EU not only to prevail on high profile issues such as Kyoto and the ICC, but also to breathe life into the idea of effective multilateralism, even if the EU itself sometimes struggles to follow the standards it promotes.

Chapter 12

Conclusions: Theorizing EU Foreign Policy

To conclude, we turn to the implications of this book's findings for both International Relations and European integration theories. We cannot provide a systematic overview of the vast corpus of theoretical literature – explanations can be found in the works of, inter alia, Andreatta (2005), Jørgensen (2004), Kelstrup and Williams (2000), S. Smith (2000), Tonra and Christiansen (2004) and Tonra (2006). Neither do we consider interesting approaches, including consociationism (Stavridis 2000), foreign policy analysis (White 1999, 2001), discourse analysis (Larsen 1997, 2004), or other attempts to narrow the 'theoretical capability-expectations gap' (Ginsberg 1999, 2001).

Rather, we combine our conclusions with a brief evaluation of the relevance of some main International Relations (neorealism, neoliberalism), European integration (liberal intergovernmentalism, neofunctionalism, new institutionalism) and constructivist approaches. As these are all large schools of thought, with different subsections, trends and interpretations, the approach taken here is necessarily generalized and selective.

In Chapter 1 we proposed an alternative conceptual framework to guide our analysis of EU foreign policy by developing a 'structural foreign policy–conventional foreign policy' continuum. Here we assess how these concepts link with other theoretical approaches and to what extent these concepts can contribute to our understanding of what is foreign policy. We finish with some critical comments on the field of (EU) foreign policy analysis.

International Relations theories

The very development of EU foreign policy over the last two decades runs counter to the neorealist argument (see Dunne and

Schmidt 2005) that, since foreign, security and defence policy lie at the heart of national sovereignty, states will not integrate in these fields and an international organization itself cannot have a foreign policy. As we have shown in Chapters 3, 4, 6 and 7, the EU today has an extensive foreign policy apparatus, including a complex civilian and even military institutional set-up, and a range of civilian and military instruments. In line with neoliberal perspectives (see Dunne 2005), the EU has proved that it can act as a relatively autonomous force that influences the behaviour of third states and that has a substantive impact on the international environment. As was argued in Chapter 10, it was the EU and not individual member states (even the most powerful) that played the pivotal role in one of the West's major foreign policy successes of the last decades: the sustainable transformation and stabilization of ten Central and Eastern Europe countries and, since the late 1990s, of the Balkan countries (both in conjunction with NATO). Further foreign policy achievements discussed in Chapter 11, including the ICC and the Kyoto Protocol, are testimony to the impact an actor such as the EU can have. These successes were particularly pertinent given the vehement opposition of other major world powers.

However, when the agenda turned to issues of survival and hard military power, neorealist arguments started to look more convincing. EU foreign policy has been thrown into disarray in crises and wars (Iraq), has been partially sidelined by the largest member states (Iran) or has been deafeningly silent (Chechnya). In these cases, the balance of power at the international level and the uneven distribution of capabilities between member states has determined the outcome and the (in)action of the EU. Chapters 1 and 6 demonstrated that at least initially, member states saw the development of a CFSP less as a way to construct a common EU policy than as a national foreign policy tool to achieve interrelational goals by controlling their fellow member states. Although member states gradually agreed to develop military capabilities within the EU framework, they remained averse to renouncing their sovereignty. Many were reluctant to allow the EU to do more in civilian or military crisis management than was useful for, or complementary to, their national policies, NATO and the predominance of the transatlantic security architecture in particular. In a similar vein, we saw in Chapter 11 that while member states were happy for the EU to pronounce its 'choice of multilateralism', they did not give the EU the legal status or representational powers in international fora to actually translate this statement into reality.

But, this was not borne out across the board. Albeit a highly damaging failure for most of the 1990s, EU foreign policy in the Balkans began to contest neorealist assumptions from the late 1990s onwards. As member states handed power to the EU's common actors to intervene in the Balkans, they provided a clear demonstration of neoliberal thought that even in the most pressing foreign policy questions sovereign states would limit their own foreign policy autonomy in favour of a common foreign policy and of common institutional actors.

European integration theories

The development of EU foreign policy is also a matter of discussion among European integration theorists. One of the primary questions revolves around the impact of the various actors on the development and functioning of EU foreign policy. From a liberal intergovernmentalist perspective, EU foreign policy is essentially driven by the member states, by their national interests and by intergovernmental bargains (see Schimmelfennig 2004; Eilstrup-Sangiovanni 2006: 181–303). Member states' ability to reach 'history making decisions' is understood as the key to the development of EU foreign, security and defence policies.

As demonstrated in Chapter 2, this argument can be persuasive if we take a historical overview of the process. Member states' agreements have been crucial in driving EU foreign policy forward – from informal agreements at the outset of European Political Cooperation in the early 1970s to breakthroughs on ESDP since the late 1990s. Reflecting the balance of power between member states, substantive changes in sensitive issues have only proved possible once a preliminary understanding could be reached amongst the three most powerful member states, and between the UK and France in particular (see Chapter 7). The corollary of this equally applies – developing a robust EU foreign policy *vis-à-vis* crucial issues (such as the Middle East and relations with Russia and China) has been impeded by the failure of intergovernmental bargaining to find a consensus.

But, the development of EU foreign policy equally provides examples of 'history-making decisions' and grand bargains being misleading. Thus, while on paper it appeared that the Maastricht Treaty's CFSP was to send the EU down an exciting new foreign policy route, in fact it was the first pillar that, at least initially, remained the policy-makers' main site for foreign policy elaboration. Furthermore, the liberal intergovernmentalists' argument that the need to make concessions with the least compromising governments drives agreements towards the lowest common denominator is contested by the practice of EU foreign policy-making. Both the development of the EU foreign policy mechanism in broad terms and the EU's specific policies towards other regions, countries and issues indeed go much further than a rational assessment of member states' national interests would suggest. As argued in Chapter 4, certain dynamics ensure that even in the largely unanimous second pillar, the limitations of consensus-orientated decision-making can be overcome. One explanation is the dynamic generated by institutional actors and mechanisms, in both the first and second pillar, that pushes EU foreign policy far beyond lowest common denominator bargaining. Another explanation is the partial segmentation of EU foreign policy, with small groups of member states working together with institutional actors to shape policy.

It is in this context that various propositions of neofunctionalism and new institutionalism are interesting (see Eilstrup-Sangiovanni 2006: 89–324). As institutionalist approaches argue, the EU's expanding foreign policy institutional mechanisms clearly matter. Chapter 3 showed that the increasing institutionalization of CFSP and ESDP, through the gradual qualitative and quantitative reinforcement of the common CFSP actors in the Council's Secretariat (the High Representative, Special Representatives, Policy Unit, DG E, ESDP bodies), has led to a new mechanism to define, defend, promote and represent common EU interests, and to develop and implement common policies from this European perspective. Institutions provide an appropriate setting for member states to accept constraints on their behaviour, in order to pursue better their foreign policy interests. Hence, from the late 1990s onwards, the EU member states, including the largest, accepted limits on their Balkans policies in favour of a common EU policy towards the region. EU foreign policy to some extent also supports the new institutionalists' idea that institutions create path dependencies and that historical participation in the EC/EU plays a role in the formation of national objectives. As argued in Chapter 5, participation in EU foreign policy-making leads member states to develop foreign policy objectives on issues and countries on which they previously had no policy. New institutionalists also argue that decisions can evolve in a way that surpasses the original intention. Hence, as argued in Chapter 2, the Commission was able to use its 1957 Rome Treaty powers in the fields of trade and entering into contractual agreements with third countries to develop a fledgling foreign policy, even though this had not been originally foreseen and was not supported by all member states.

Following neofunctional logic, EU foreign policy has at least partially been driven forwards by the internal dynamic of integration. This dynamic is based both on the impulsion provided by activist non-state actors (such as the Commission and the Council Secretariat) and on the mechanism of functional spillover (with measures in one policy field leading to pressure for measures in other policy fields). In terms of the first point, there are clear examples of major foreign policy initiatives which would not have been adopted, or which would not have been discussed in the same way, without the Commission's sound preparatory work and strategic vision. Examples from Chapters 9 and 10 include the EU's long-term strategies towards third countries and regions, including enlargement, and towards 'new' foreign policy challenges, such as energy. Remarkably, although often perceived as an unwelcome intruder in the Council's foreign policy domain, the Commission manifested itself as a useful strategic partner for member states when they wanted to give substance to their latest foreign policy ideas. But, this argument has limits – member states have been careful to establish foreign and defence policy cooperation in a separate unanimity-bound intergovernmental pillar and have happily risked weakening the substance of EU foreign policy output in return for keeping the Community's pretensions at bay.

While the Commission's entrepreneurial role is one explanation for functional spillover, a further reason is that the traditional realm of foreign policy is increasingly intertwined with other policy areas. Chapters 7 to 9 have provided ample illustration of this point: security policy is no longer just about soldiers, but also about training police forces and organizing rule of law missions; development cooperation agreements are no longer just about fighting poverty, but also about de-mining operations, counterterrorism and democracy promotion; technology, health and the environment are no longer just internal policy concerns, but now also foreign policy and security concerns. However, this spillover effect is not an inevitable process, with the EU's pillar structure in particular providing an obvious brake. Functional spillover in foreign policy can also just as easily lead to coordination or cooperation rather than expanding integration, as reflected in the difficult discussions on developing a common energy supply policy.

Constructivism: ideas, values and identity

In contrast to rationalist accounts of EU foreign policy, constructivism focuses on immaterial dimensions such as ideas, values, norms and identity (Jørgensen 1997; Tonra 1997, 2001, 2003; Glarbo 1999; Waever 2000). These are considered not only as influencing EU foreign policy, but also as providing the constitutive elements of EU foreign policy. From this perspective, developing EU foreign policy depends not only, or not in the first place, on the creation of an effective institutional framework, on acquiring foreign policy instruments, or even on defining common interests. Rather, it hinges on the emergence of a shared understanding among EU member states' elites and populations about what should be the EU's role in the world and about what values it should sustain, promote and defend. In Chapter 5 we thus discussed the role of socialization (and related Europeanization processes) even though it was argued that this should not be overstated since member states continue to diverge in terms of their world view, role conception and identity.

In various chapters we have indicated that a shared normative and cognitive framework is being gradually developed within the EU on some issues and is reflected in the values it promotes on the international stage. According to the preamble to the Treaty on European Union, member states are resolved to implement a CFSP, 'thereby reinforcing the European identity'. Throughout this book, it appeared that pursuing identity objectives was just as important as a desire to realize external objectives in the development of EU foreign policy. In Chapters 6 and 8 we learnt that the EU's objectives include promoting international cooperation, developing democracy and the rule of law, and respect for human rights and fundamental freedoms. Consolidating these values within the EC/EU and then promoting them externally are defining elements of the EU's identity.

Analysts of the EU as a normative power – an actor whose foreign policy is driven by identity and values rather than interests – can find ample evidence to support their claims in the growing role of political conditionality in agreements with third countries, in the insertion of social clauses such as labour rights or environmental clauses in multilateral agreements, and in the creation of specific instruments to promote democracy and human rights. However, the picture is not so clear cut (see Lucarelli and Manners 2006; Sjursen 2006). While values are undoubtedly a cornerstone of EU foreign policy, the EU is just as quick to protect its narrower self-interests and geostrategic interests – its policies *vis-à-vis* Russia and China being examples.

The constructivist emphasis on ideas and identities provides some insight into the main successes and failures of EU foreign policy, as discussed in Chapters 10 and 11. EU foreign policy's primary success to date relates to redefining the identity of the Central and Eastern European countries. And, at its core, the EU's current foreign policy priority in the Balkans is to transform the perceptions held by societies and individuals about each other, to change their identity and to alter the norms and values that sustain their actions. From this perspective, EU foreign policy is in essence about transforming the identity of other entities and about shaping ideas held about 'the other'. Arguably, the debate about Turkey's future membership of the EU is first and foremost centred on issues of identity, ideas and values. Interests, power and institutional set-ups are not unimportant, but they nevertheless play second fiddle.

However, nearly four decades of cooperation in the field of foreign policy and the 15-year-old endeavour to construct a common foreign policy have only managed to reshape national foreign policy identities to a limited extent. Despite a strengthened shared normative framework, foreign policy interventions and even some successes, differences in power and in interests remain crucial variables to explaining member states' foreign policy and whether a common EU foreign policy is achievable.

Structural foreign policy

This book presented the 'structural foreign policy–conventional foreign policy' framework as a lens through which to conceptualize foreign policy, including that of the EU. Employing this approach throughout the preceding chapters had several advantages. It allowed us to consider dimensions of the EU's foreign policy which have tended to be overlooked – to go beyond the 'dominant' dimensions of foreign policy by also considering other (often neglected) dimensions of foreign policy (see Table 1.1). The structural foreign policy concept provided the terminology to consider policies such as EU enlargement to the East and policies towards the Balkans since the late 1990s as foreign policy. It offered both a name and an analytical framework to investigate dimensions of foreign policy that are not new (for example American foreign policy towards Western Europe after World War II), but that, in part because of a lack of appropriate terminology and analytical instruments, have not been the main focus of scholars, politicians, the press or public opinion. Structural foreign policy has also provided a vehicle through which to assess developments, processes and structural changes which occur only over the longer term.

The structural foreign policy–conventional foreign policy approach provides some explanations for the success and failure of the EU's foreign policies. We recall here three basic features of the approach. Firstly, structural foreign policy must be complemented by conventional foreign policy and conversely conventional foreign policy must be complemented by structural foreign policy. Hence, EU structural foreign policy towards the CEECs could be a success because the conventional foreign policy issues were being dealt with by NATO. But, if the EU and other international organizations had not provided a structural foreign policy, the results of NATO's successful conventional foreign policy in the Balkans in the 1990s would not have been sustainable. Also the corollary of this proved true: EU structural foreign policy *vis-à-vis* the Mediterranean and Palestinian territories has been a failure because no actor has been able to resolve the conventional foreign policy issues at stake.

Secondly, the extent to which a structural foreign policy also tackles the mental structures of the target country/region's elites and populations, and considers the legitimacy factor, is critical. In Central and Eastern Europe, a large majority of the population and the elite wanted change. While the costs associated with these changes might not have been palatable, they were accepted because the end goal was firmly rooted in the popular consciousness. Without the prospect of enlargement in particular, endogenous processes in the Mediterranean have provided less fertile ground for the EU's structural foreign policy.

Finally, all relevant dimensions of a structural foreign policy must be tackled. As demonstrated in Chapter 10, in the case of the Mediterranean and the Palestinian Territories, the EU's focus has been on the state level to the neglect of the societal level. In contrast, in its more successful policy towards the Balkans, the EU has paid significantly more attention to the pivotal human and societal security dimension.

Using the structural foreign policy–conventional foreign policy framework also throws up its own challenges (see Keukeleire 2008). Because this book could only scrape the surface of the EU's often highly intricate structural foreign policies towards any given country/region, the conclusions drawn have likewise been relatively generalized. This conceptual framework is particularly strong when applied systematically and in detail to a foreign policy and when very specific features of the third party can be brought into the equation. In practical terms, it can be difficult to obtain a sufficiently deep understanding of a foreign policy's impact on the third party. This also relates to the difficulty of observing, measuring and understanding long-term changes and particularly in isolating different variables and establishing causal relations. The difficulties in determining whether a desired change has been the result of an EU policy as distinct from other actors or factors are not inconsequential. The predominantly positivist academic tradition may also explain the reluctance of foreign policy specialists to embrace ambiguous phenomena and dimensions – such as the societal level, human security, structural power or desecuritization – which are more difficult to operationalize and problematic in terms of boundaries and focus.

While this book has been able to discuss dimensions of foreign policy that tend to receive less scrutiny, it has also remained the prisoner of more dominant approaches. For example, with regard to the actors of foreign policy, analysis here has been centred on the member states, on EU institutions and on governmental international organizations, with non-governmental actors, networks and societies gaining much less attention. This is partially the result of the basic objective of this book: to explain the development, functioning and output of EU foreign policy from a European perspective, wherein governmental actors clearly have remained central. Nevertheless, this already indicates a number of challenges for the field of EU foreign policy research.

Structural foreign policy points towards the important role played by various structures (political, legal, socio-economic, security and mental) and levels (from the individual up to the global). This also implies that analysts need to adopt a clearer interdisciplinary approach. A sound understanding of the EU's structural foreign policy means analyses and concepts from other academic fields such as economy, law, history, psychology, sociology or anthropology must be more systematically incorporated. Equally, our understanding would be heightened through greater cooperation with specialized subfields of International Relations and political science, such as globalization studies, security studies, democracy studies, modernization studies and the various area studies. EU foreign policy analysis now too often occurs in isolation from these subfields, without the much needed intellectual cross-fertilization.

(EU) foreign policy analysts must also become more conscious of the impact of what is effectively a Western academic hegemony (see Waever 1998; Aydinli and Mathews 2000). We should question whether our analysis of foreign policy or international relations is actually valid given the very limited input from non-Western scholars. The limited input of Asian, Arab, African or Latin American academics is problematic considering that Western foreign policy is to a large extent directed towards these continents and that, consequently, insights, concepts and approaches developed by these scholars might be indispensable for a serious assessment of Western foreign policy. The generally predominant inside-out analysis thus has to be complemented by an outside-in perspective, in which it is not the EU but the other region or society that is the point of departure for analysing EU foreign policy. This would also help us consider whether the very substance of the structures being promoted by the EU – which have intended and unintended repercussions for people, societies and regions all over the world – should themselves not be questioned.

Bibliography

Adler, E. and Barnett, M. (eds) (1998) *Security Communities*, Cambridge: Cambridge University Press.

Aggarwal, V. K. and Fogarty, E. A. (2004) 'Explaining Trends in EU Interregionalism', in V. K. Aggarwal and E. A. Fogarty (eds), *EU Trade Strategies: Between Regionalism and Globalism*, Basingstoke: Palgrave Macmillan, 207–40.

Aggestam, L. (2000) 'Germany', in I. Manners and R. Whitman (eds), *The Foreign Policies of European Union Member States*, Manchester: Manchester University Press, 64–83.

—— (2004) 'Role Identity and the Europeanisation of Foreign Policy: A Political-cultural Approach', in B. Tonra and T. Christiansen (eds), *Rethinking European Union Foreign Policy*, Manchester: Manchester University Press, 81–98.

Aliboni, R. (2004) *Promoting Democracy in the EMP. Which Political Strategy?*, Lisbon: EuroMeSCo Reports.

—— (2005) 'The Geopolitical Implications of the European Neighbourhood Policy', *European Foreign Affairs Review*, 10(1), 1–16.

Allen, D. (1996) 'Conclusions: The European Rescue of National Foreign Policy', in C. Hill (ed.), *The Actors in European Foreign Policy*, London: Routledge, 288–304.

—— (1998) '"Who Speaks for Europe?" The Search for an Effective and Coherent External Policy', in J. Peterson and H. Sjursen (eds), *A Common Foreign and Security Policy for Europe?*, London: Routledge, 41–58.

Allen, D. and Smith, M. (1990) 'Western Europe's Presence in the Contemporary International Arena', *Review of International Studies*, 16(1), 19–37.

Alvarez-Verdugo, M. (2006) 'Mixing Tools Against Proliferation: The EU's Strategy for Dealing with Weapons of Mass Destruction', *European Foreign Affairs Review*, 11(3), 417–38.

Amnesty International (2004) *Lives Blown Apart: Crimes against Women in Times of Conflict*, www.amnesty.org.

Anderson, M. and Apap, J. (2002) 'Changing Conceptions of Security and their Implication for EU Justice and Home Affairs Cooperation', *CEPS Policy Briefs*, 26.

Andreatta, F. (2005) 'Theory and the European Union's International Relations', in C. Hill and M. Smith (eds), *International Relations and the European Union*, Oxford: Oxford University Press, 18–38.

Apap, J., Boratynski, J., Emerson, M., *et al.* (2001) 'Friendly Schengen Borderland Policy on the New Borders of an Enlarged EU and its Neighbours', *CEPS Policy Briefs*, 7.

Arts, K. and Dickson, A. K. (eds) (2004a) *EU Development Cooperation: From Model to Symbol*, Manchester: Manchester University Press.

—— (2004b) 'EU Development Cooperation: From Model to Symbol?' in K. Arts and A. K. Dickson (eds), *EU Development Cooperation: From Model to Symbol*, Manchester: Manchester University Press, 1–16.

Aydinli, E. and Mathews, J. (2000) 'Are the Core and Periphery Irreconcilable? The Curious World of Publishing in Contemporary International Relations', *International Studies Perspectives*, 1(3), 289–303.

Azoulai, L. (2005) 'The Acquis of the European Union and International Organisations', *European Law Journal*, 11(2), 196–231.

Azzam, M. (2006) 'Islamism Revisited', *International Affairs*, 82(6), 1119–32.

Baker, S. (2006) 'Environmental Values and Climate Change Policy', in S. Lucarelli and I. Manners (eds), *Values and Principles in European Union Foreign Policy*, London: Routledge, 77–98.

Balfour, R. (2006) 'Principles of Democracy and Human Rights', in S. Lucarelli and I. Manners (eds), *Values and Principles in European Union Foreign Policy*, London: Routledge, 114–29.

Barbé, E. (2004) 'The Evolution of CFSP Institutions: Where Does Democratic Accountability Stand?' *International Spectator*, 39(2), 47–60.

Batt, J. (2004) 'Introduction: the Stabilisation/Integration Dilemma', *Chaillot Paper*, EU ISS, 70, 7–20.

Bauer, S. (2004) 'Europe's Arms Export Policies', in K. von Wogau (ed.), *The Path to European Defence*, Antwerpen/Appeldoorn: Maklu, 214–26.

Baylis, J. and Wirtz, J. (2007) 'Introduction', in J. Baylis, J. Wirtz, C. S. Gray and E. Cohen (eds), *Strategy in the Contemporary World*, Oxford: Oxford University Press, 1–15.

BBC News (2007) *EU 'Must Share Burden of Asylum'*, http://news.bbc.co.uk.

Bendiek, A. (2006) 'The Financing of the CFSP/ESDP: "There Is a Democratic Deficit Problem!" ', *CFSP Forum*, 4(6), 8–11.

Bicchi, F. (2006) '"Our Size Fits All": Normative Power Europe and the Mediterranean', *Journal of European Public Policy*, 13(2), 286–303.

Bini Smaghi, L. (2004) 'A Single EU Seat in the IMF?' *Journal of Common Market Studies*, 42(2), 229–48.

Biscop, S. (2003) *Euro-Mediterranean Security. A search for partnership*, Aldershot: Ashgate.

—— (2005) *The European Security Strategy. A Global Agenda for Positive Power*, Hants: Ashgate.

Biscop, S. and Drieskens, E. (2006) 'Effective Multilateralism and Collective Security: Empowering the UN', in K. E. Smith and K. V. Laatikainen (eds), *Intersecting Multilateralisms: The European Union and the United Nations*, Basingstoke: Palgrave Macmillan, 115–32.

Blunden, M. (2000) 'France', in I. Manners and R. Whitman (eds), *The Foreign Policies of European Union Member States*, Manchester: Manchester University Press, 19–43.

Bonaglia, F., Goldstein, A. and Petito, F. (2006) 'Values in European Union Development Cooperation Policy', in S. Lucarelli and I. Manners (eds), *Values and Principles in European Union foreign policy*, London: Routledge, 164–84.

Bono, G. (ed.), (2006) *The Impact of 9/11 on European Foreign and Security Policy*, Brussels: VUB Press.

Borda, A. Z. (2005) 'The Iranian Nuclear Issue and EU3 Negotiations', *FORNET Working Paper*, 1–24.

Boswell, C. (2003) 'The "External Dimension" of EU Immigration and Asylum Policy', *International Affairs*, 79(3), 619–38.

Bourlanges, J.-L. (1996) 'Les européens malades de la PESC', *Politique Internationale*, 74, 207–28.

Bowles, P. (2002) 'Asia's Post-crisis Regionalism: Bringing the State Back in, Keeping the (United) States out', *Review of International Political Economy*, 9(2), 230–56.

Braud, P.-A. and Grevi, G. (2005) 'The EU Mission in Aceh: Implementing Peace', *Occasional Paper*, 61, EU ISS, 37.

Braunschvig, D., Garwin, R. L. and Marwell, J. C. (2003) 'Space Diplomacy', *Foreign Affairs*, 82(4), 156–64.

Bretherton, C. and Vogler, J. (2006) *The European Union as a Global Actor*, London: Routledge.

British Petroleum (2005) *BP Statistical Review of World Energy*, www.bp.com.

Bruter, M. (1999) 'Diplomacy Without a State: The External Delegations of the European Commission', *Journal of European Public Policy*, 6(2), 183–205.

Bulmer, S. and Lequesne, C. (2005) *The Member States of the European Union*, Oxford: Oxford University Press.

Burzykowska, A. (2006) 'ESDP and the Space Sector – Defining the Architecture and Mechanisms for Effective Cooperation', *Space Policy*, 22(1), 35–41.

Buzan, B. (1993) 'Societal Security, State Security and Internationalisation', in O. Waever, B. Buzan, M. Kelstrup and P. Lemaitre (eds), *Identity, Migration and the New Security Agenda in Europe*, London: Pinter Publishers, 41–58.

Buzan, B., Waever, O. and de Wilde, J. (1998) *Security. A New Framework for Analysis*, London: Lynne Rienner Publishers.

Calleo, D. P. (1983) 'Early American Views of NATO: Then and Now', in L. Freedman (ed.), *The Troubled Alliance. Atlantic Relations in the 1980s*, London: Heinemann, 7–27.

—— (1987) *Beyond American Hegemony: The Future of the Western Alliance*, New York: Basic Books.

Caporaso, J. A. and Jupille, J. (1998) 'States, Agency and Rules: The EU in Global Environmental Politics', in C. Rhodes (ed.), *The European Union in the World*, Boulder: Lynne Rienner, 213–31.

Carlsnaes, W. (2002) 'Foreign Policy', in W. Carlsnaes, T. Risse and B. A. Simmons (eds), *Handbook of International Relations*, London: Sage, 331–48.

Casarini, N. (2006) 'The Evolution of the EU–China Relationship: From Constructive Engagement to Strategic Partnership', *Occasional Paper, 64*, EU ISS, 50.

Casier, T. (2007) 'The Clash of Integration Processes? The Shadow Effect of the Enlarged EU on its Eastern Neighbours', in K. Malfliet, L. Verpoest and E. Vinokurov (eds), *The CIS, The EU and Russia. Challenges of Integration*, Basingstoke: Palgrave Macmillan, 73–94.

Castells, M. (2000) *The Information Age: Economy, Society and Culture*, Oxford: Blackwell.

Cerny, P. G. (1990) *The Changing Architecture of Politics*, London: Sage.

Cline, R. S. (1980) *World Power Trends and US Foreign Policy for the 1980s*, Boulder: Westview Press.

Clingendael International Energy Programme (CIEP) (2004) *Study on Energy Supply Security and Geopolitics*, report prepared for DG TREN, The Hague: Clingendael Institute for International Relations.

Cloos, J., Reinesch, G., Vignes, D. and Weyland, J. (1993) *Le Traité de Maastricht. Genèse, analyse, commentaires*, Bruxelles: Ed. Emile Bruylant.

Commission of the European Communities (1993a) *Communication from the Commission – Future Relations and Cooperation between the Community and the Middle East*, COM(1993)375, 8 September.

—— (1993b) *Communication from the Commission – EC Support to the Middle East Peace Process*, COM(1993)458, 29 September.

—— (1996) *Communication – The EU and the Issue of Conflicts in Africa: Peace-building, Conflict Prevention and Beyond*, SEC(1996)332, 6 March.

—— (2000) *Green Paper – Towards a European Strategy for the Security of Energy Supply*, COM(2000)769, 29 November.

—— (2001a) *Communication from the Commission on Conflict Prevention*, COM(2001)211, 11 April.

—— (2001b) *Communication of the Commission – Ten Years after Rio: Preparing for the World Summit on Sustainable Development in 2002*, COM(2001)53, 6 February.

—— (2003a) *Civilian Instruments for EU Crisis Management*, Europa website.

—— (2003b) *The European Union and the United Nations: Choice of Multilateralism*, COM(2003)526, 10 September.

—— (2004a) *Proposal for a Council Regulation Establishing an Instrument for Pre-Accession Assistance (IPA)*, COM(2004)627, 29 September.

—— (2004b) *Proposal for a Regulation of the European Parliament and of the Council Laying Down General Provisions Establishing a European Neighbourhood and Partnership Instrument (ENPI)*, COM(2004)628, 29 September.

—— (2004c) *Proposal for a Regulation of the European Parliament and of the Council Establishing a Financial Instrument for Development Cooperation and Economic Cooperation*, COM(2004)629, 29 September.

—— (2004d) *Proposal for a Regulation of the Council Establishing an Instrument for Stability*, COM(2004)630, 29 September.

—— (2004e) *Green Paper on Defence Procurement*, COM(2004)608, 23 September.

—— (2004f) *Communication from the Commission – European Neighbourhood Policy – Strategy Paper*, COM(2004)373, 12 May.

—— (2005a) *Communication on Policy Coherence for Development: Accelerating Progress towards Attaining the Millennium Development Goals*, COM(2005)134, 12 April.

—— (2005b) *Communication – A Strategy on the External Dimensions of the Area of Freedom, Security and Justice*, COM(2005)491, 12 October.

—— (2005c) *Green Paper – Confronting Demographic Change: A New Solidarity between the Generations*, COM(2005)94, 16 March.

—— (2005d) *Communication – EU Strategy for Africa: Towards a Euro-African Pact to Accelerate Africa's Development*, COM(2005)489, 12 October.

—— (2006a) 'Public Opinion in the European Union', *Eurobarometer*, no. 66, Europa website.

—— (2006b) *Green Paper – A European Strategy for Sustainable, Competitive and Secure Energy*, COM(2006)105/SEC(2006)317/2, 8 March.

—— (2006c) *The Impact of Ageing on Public Expenditure*, Special Report No. 1, Europa website.

—— (2006d) *Communication on Strengthening the European Neighbourhood Policy*, COM(2006)726, 4 December.

—— (2006e) *Commission Staff Working Documents – Accompanying the Communication on Strengthening the European Neighbourhood Policy: Overall Assessment/ENP National Progress Reports/ Sectoral Progress Report*, SEC(2006)1504–1512, 4 December.

—— (2007a) *Financial Programming 2007–2013 (plus Annexes)*, Europa website.

—— (2007b) *General Budget 2007 – Title 19 – External Relations*, Europa website.

—— (2007c) *Europe in Figures. Eurostat Yearbook 2006–07*, Luxembourg: OOPEC.

—— (2007d) *Rapid Reaction Mechanism*, Europa website.

—— (2007e) *African Peace Facility*, Europa website.

—— (2007f) *The EU's Relations with West Bank and Gaza Strip*, Europa website.

Commission of the European Communities and OECD (2006) *EU Donor Atlas 2006 – Volume I: Mapping Official Development Assistance*, Europa website.

Commission of the European Communities and Secretary-General/High Representative (2006) *An External Policy to Serve Europe's Energy Interests – Paper to the European Council*, 15–16 June, Brussels, Europa website.

Conference of the Representatives of the Governments of the Member States (IGC) (2007) *Draft Treaty amending the Treaty on European Union and the Treaty establishing the European Community*, CIG 1/1/07, 5 October, Europa website.

Cook, D. (1989) *Forging the Alliance: NATO, 1945–1950*, London: Secker & Warburg.

Cooper, R. (2003) *The Breaking of Nations: Order and Chaos in the Twenty-first Century*. London: Atlantic Books.

Coppieters, B., Emerson, M., Huysseune, M., *et al.* (2004) *Europeanization and Conflict Resolution: Case Studies from the European Periphery*, Gent: Academia Press.

Corbett, R., Jacobs, F. and Shackleton, M. (2005) *The European Parliament* (6th edn), London: John Harper.

Cornish, P., Van Ham, P. and Krause, J. (1996) 'Europe and the Challenge of Proliferation', *Chaillot paper,* 24, EU ISS.

Corthaut, T. (2005) 'An Effective Remedy for All? Paradoxes and Controversies in Respect of Judicial Protection in the Field of the CFSP under the European Constitution', *Tilburg Foreign Law Review*, 12, 110–44.

Council of the European Union (2002) *Report of the Presidency to the European Council of Sevilla on the Implementation of the EU Programme for the Prevention of Violent Conflict*, 9991/02, 18 June, Europa website.

—— (2003) *Note from the Council to the European Council – Fight against the Proliferation of Weapons of Mass Destruction – EU Strategy against Proliferation of Weapons of Mass Destruction*, 15708/03, 10 December, Europa website.

—— (2004a) *EU Plan of Action on Combating Terrorism*, 10010/3/04, 11 June, Europa website.

—— (2004b) *Council Joint Action 2004/551/CFSP on the Establishment of the European Defence Agency*, OJ L 245/17–28, 17 July.

—— (2005a) *Common Position 2005/304/CFSP Concerning 'Conflict Prevention, Management and Resolution in Africa'*, OJ L 97/57, 15 April.

—— (2005b) *A Strategy for the External Dimension of JHA: Global Freedom, Security and Justice*, 14366/3/05, 30 November, Europa website.

—— (2005c) *The European Union Strategy for Combating Radicalisation and Recruitment to Terrorism*, 14781/1/05, 24 November, Europa website.

—— (2005d) *The European Union Counter-Terrorism Strategy*, 14469/4/05, 30 November, Europa website.

—— (2006a) *CFSP Instruments (Legislative Acts; Declarations, Demarches, Heads of Mission Reports and Political Dialogue Meetings) – 2005*, 7874/06, 28 March, Europa website.

—— (2006b) *Annual Report from the Council to the European Parliament on the Main Aspects and Basic Choices of CFSP, Including the Financial Implications for the General Budget of the European Communities – 2005*, 10314/06, 8 June, Europa website.

—— (2006c) *EU Strategy to Combat Illicit Accumulation and Trafficking of Small Arms and Light Weapons (SALW) and their Ammunition*, 5319/06, 13 January, Europa website.

—— (2006d) *European Concept for Strengthening African Capabilities for the Management and Prevention of Conflicts*, 14556/06, 7 November, Europa website.

—— (2006e) *Council Regulation 617/2007/EC on the Implementation of the 10th European Development Fund*, OJ L 152, 13 June, Europa website.

—— (2007a) *Press Release – 2776th Council Meeting. General Affairs and External Relations – External Relations*, 5463/07, 22 January, Europa website.

—— (2007b) *Presidency Diplomatic Representation in Third Countries – second half of 2007*, 10505/07, 6 June, Europa website.

—— (2007c) *CFSP Instruments (Legislative Acts, Declarations, Demarches, Heads of Mission Reports and Political Dialogue Meetings) – 2006*, 6233/07, 9 February, Europa website.

—— (2007d) *Annual Report from the Council to the European Parliament on the Main Aspects and Basic Choices of the CFSP, Including the Financial Complications for the General Budget of the European Communities – 2006*, 6992/07, 4 April, Europa website.

—— (2007e) *European Security and Defence Policy: Operations*, Europa website.

—— (2007f) *Implementation of the Strategy and Action Plan to Combat Terrorism*, 9666/07, 21 May, Europa website.

Cremona, M. (2003) 'The Draft Constitutional Treaty: External Relations and External Action', *Common Market Law Review*, 40, 1347–66.

Crowe, B. (2005) *Foreign Minister of Europe*, London: The Foreign Policy Centre.

Crum, B. (2006) 'Parliamentarization of the CFSP through Informal Institution-making?', *Journal of European Public Policy*, 13(3), 383–401.

Dannreuther, R. (2006) 'Developing the Alternative to Enlargement: The European Neighbourhood Policy', *European Foreign Affairs Review*, 11(2), 183–201.

Daojiong, Z. (2006) 'China's Energy Security: Domestic and International Issues', *Survival*, 48(1), 179–90.

DEFRA and HM Treasury (2005) *A Vision for the Common Agricultural Policy*, http://www.defra.gov.uk/farm/capreform/vision.htm

De Gucht, K. and Keukeleire, S. (1991) 'The European Security Architecture: The Role of the EC in Shaping a New European Geopolitical Landscape', *Studia Diplomatica*, 44(6), 29–90.

Delpech, T. (2005a) 'Trois européens à Téhéran', *Politique Internationale*, 106, 129–43.

—— (2005b) 'Trois européens à Téhéran (suite et fin?)', *Politique Internationale*, 109, 165–76.

Delreux, T. (2006) 'The European Union in International Environmental Negotiations: A Legal Perspective on the International Decision-making Process', *International Environmental Agreements*, 6(3), 231–48.

Dembinski, M. (2007) 'Europe and the UNIFIL II Mission: Stumbling into the Conflict Zone of the Middle East', *CFSP Forum*, 5(1), 1–4.

Denoeux, G. (2002) 'The Forgotten Swamp: Navigating Political Islam', *Middle East Policy*, 9(2), 56–82.

Denza, E. (2002) *The Intergovernmental Pillars of the European Union*, Oxford: Oxford University Press.

De Ruyt, J. (2005) 'A Minister for a European Foreign Policy', *EUI RSCAS, Policy Papers*, 1–60.

Diedrichs, U. (2004) 'The European Parliament in CFSP', *The Journal of Strategic Studies*, 2, 31–46.

Donoghue, J., Ryan, J. and Vent, A. (2006) *Report on Frontex: The European Union's New Border Security Agency*, Dublin: Institute of European Affairs.

Duchêne, F. (1972) 'Europe's Role in World Peace', in R. Mayne (ed.), *Europe Tomorrow. Sixteen Europeans Look Ahead*, London: Collins, 32–47.

—— (1973) 'The European Community and the Uncertainties of Interdependence', in M. Kohnstamm and W. Hager (eds), *A Nation Writ Large? Foreign-Policy Problems before the European Community*, Basingstoke: Macmillan, 1–21.

—— (1994) *Jean Monnet: The First Statesman of Interdependence*, New York/London: Norton.

Duke, S. (1999) *The Elusive Quest for European Security: From EDC to CFSP*, Basingstoke: Palgrave Macmillan.

—— (2002a) 'CESDP and the EU Response to 11 September: Identifying the Weakest Link', *European Foreign Affairs Review*, 7(2), 153–70.

—— (2002b) 'Preparing for European diplomacy?', *Journal of Common Market Studies*, 40(5), 849–70.

—— (2004) 'The Institutional Dimension of External Action: Innovation in External Action and the Constitution for Europe', *Eipascope*, 3, 30–7.

—— (2005) 'The Linchpin COPS: Assessing the Workings and Institutional Relations of the Political and Security Committee', *European Institute for Public Administration Working Papers*, 5, 35.

—— (2006) 'Areas of Grey: Tensions in EU External Relations Competences', *Eipascope*, 1, 21–7.

Duke, S. and Vanhoonacker, S. (2006) 'Administrative Governance in the CFSP: Development and Practice', *European Foreign Affairs Review*, 11(2), 163–82.

Dunne, T. (2005) 'Liberalism', in J. Baylis and S. Smith (eds), *The Globalization of World Politics: An Introduction to International Relations*, Oxford: Oxford University Press, 185–203.

Dunne, T. and Schmidt, B. C. (2005) 'Realism', in J. Baylis and S. Smith (eds), *The Globalization of World Politics. An Introduction to International Relations*, Oxford: Oxford University Press, 161–183.

Edwards, G. (2006) 'The New Member States and the Making of EU Foreign Policy', *European Foreign Affairs Review*, 11(2), 143–62.

Eeckhout, P. (2004) *External Relations of the European Union – Legal and Constitutional Foundations*, Oxford: Oxford University Press.

Ehrhart, H.-G. (2007) 'EUFOR RD Congo: A Preliminary Assessment', *European Security Review*, 32, 9–12.

Eilstrup-Sangiovanni, M. (2006) *Debates on European Integration*, Basingstoke: Palgrave Macmillan.

El-Gamal, M. A. (2006) *Islamic Finance: Law, Economics, and Practice*, Cambridge: Cambridge University Press.

Elgström, O. (2005) 'The Cotonou Agreement: Asymmetric Negotiations and the Impact of Norms', in O. Elgström and C. Jönsson (eds), *European Union Negotiations. Processes, networks and institutions*, London: Routledge, 183–99.

Emerson, M. (2006) 'What to Do about Gazprom's Monopoly Power?', *CEPS Commentary*.

Emiliou, N. (1996) 'Strategic Export Controls, National Security and the Common Commercial Policy', *European Foreign Affairs Review*, 1(1), 55–78.

EU and USA (2003a) *Agreement on Extradition between the European Union and the United States of America*, OJ L 181/27, 19 July.

—— (2003b) *Agreement on Mutual Legal Assistance between the European Union and the United States of America*, OJ L 181/34, 19 July.

—— (2004) *Agreement on the Processing and Transfer of PNR Data by Air Carriers to the United States Department of Homeland Security, Bureau of Customs and Border Protection* OJ L 183/84, 20 May.

EU Council Secretariat (2007a) *Factsheet – Financing of ESDP Operations*, Europa website .

—— (2007b) *Factsheet – EU Battlegroups*, Europa website

EUROMED (2006) *European Neighbourhood and Partnership Instrument (ENPI) – Regional Strategy Paper (2007–2013) and Regional Indicative Programme (2007–2010) for the Euro-Mediterranean Partnership*, Brussels.

European Convention (2003) *Draft Treaty Establishing a Constitution for Europe*, Luxembourg: OOPEC.

European Council (1999) *Presidency Conclusions – Helsinki Headline Goal*, 10–11 December, Helsinki, Europa website.

—— (2001) *Presidency Conclusions – EU Programme for the Prevention of Violent Conflicts*, 15–16 June, Göteborg, Europa website.

—— (2002) *Presidency Conclusions*, 21–22 June, Seville, Europa website.

—— (2003a) *European Defence: NATO/EU Consultation, Planning and Operations (Annex to the Presidency Conclusions)*, 12–13 December, Brussels, Europa website.

—— (2003b) *European Security Strategy – A Secure Europe in a Better World*, 12 December, Brussels, Europa website.

—— (2004a) *Declaration on Combating Terrorism*, Brussels, 25 March, Europa website.

—— (2004b) *Presidency Conclusions – Headline Goal 2010*, 17–18 June, Brussels, Europa website.

—— (2005) *Presidency Conclusions – The EU and Africa: Towards a Strategic Partnership*, 15–16 December, Brussels, Europa website.

—— (2006) *Presidency Conclusions – Part two: Energy Policy for Europe (EPE)*, 23–24 March, Brussels, Europa website.

—— (2007a) *Presidency Conclusions – European Council Action Plan (2007–09): Energy Policy for Europe (EPE)*, 8–9 March, Brussels, Europa website.

—— (2007b) *Presidency Conclusions – Draft IGC Mandate*, 21–22 June, Brussels, Europa website.

European Defence Agency (2006a) *European–United States Defence Expenditure in 2005*, Europa website.

—— (2006b) *European Defence Expenditure in 2005*, Europa website.

European Parliament and Council of the European Union (2002) *Decision 1513/2002/EC Concerning the Sixth Framework Programme of the European Community for Research, Technological Development and Demonstration Activities, Contributing to the Creation of the European Research Area and to Innovation (2002 to 2006)*, OJ L 232/1-33, 29 August.

—— (2006a) *Regulation 1717/2006/EC on Establishing an Instrument for Stability*, OJ L 327/1-11, 24 November.

—— (2006b) *Regulation 1889/2006/EC on Establishing a Financial Instrument for the Promotion of Democracy and Human Rights Worldwide*, OJ L 386/1-11, 29 December.

European Parliament, Council of the European Union and Commission of the European Communities (2006a) *Interinstitutional Agreement on Budgetary Discipline and Sound Financial Management*, OJ C 139/1-17, 14 June.

—— (2006b) *European Consensus on Development*, OJ C 46/1-19, 24 February.

European Union (2004) *Treaty Establishing a Constitution for Europe*, OJ C 310, 16 December.

—— (2006a) *Treaty Establishing the European Community: Consolidated Version*, OJ C 321 E/37-186, 29 December.

—— (2006b) *Treaty on European Union: Consolidated Version*, OJ 321 E/5-36, 29 December.

Everts, D. and Keohane, D. (2003) 'The European Convention and EU Foreign Policy: Learning from Failure', *Survival*, 45(3), 167–86.

Faria, F. (2004) 'Crisis Management in sub-Saharan Africa: The Role of the European Union', *Occasional Paper*, 55, EU ISS, 87.

Farrell, M. (2005) 'A Triumph of Realism over Idealism? Cooperation between the European Union and Africa', *European Integration,* 27(3), 263–83.

—— (2006) 'EU Representation and Coordination within the United Nations', in K. E. Smith and K. V. Laatikainen (eds), *Intersecting Multilateralisms: The European Union and the United Nations,* Basingstoke: Palgrave Macmillan, 27–46.

Featherstone, K. and Radaelli, C. M. (eds) (2003) *The Politics of Europeanization,* Oxford: Oxford University Press.

Fierro, E. (2003) *The EU's Approach to Human Rights Conditionality in Practice,* The Hague: Martinus Nijhoff.

Forsberg, T. (2004) 'Security and Defense Policy in the New European Constitution: A Critical Assessment', *The Quarterly Journal,* 3(3), 13–27.

Forster, A. (2000) 'Britain', in I. Manners and R. Whitman (eds), *The Foreign Policies of European Union Member States,* Manchester: Manchester University Press, 44–63.

Friis, K. (2007) 'The Referendum in Montenegro: The EU's "Postmodern Diplomacy"', *European Foreign Affairs Review,* 12(1), 67–88.

Fursdon, E. (1980) *The European Defence Community: A History,* London: The Macmillan Press.

Garden, T. (2004) 'The Future of European–American Relations: A Historic Bond', *European Analysis,* www.europeananalysis.com.

Gegout, C. (2002) 'The Quint: Acknowledging the Existence of a Big Four-US *Directoire* at the Heart of the European Union's Foreign Policy Decision-Making Process', *Journal of Common Market Studies,* 40(2), 331–44.

George, A. L. and Keohane, R. O. (1980) 'The Concept of National Interests: Uses and Limitations', in A. L. George (ed.), *Presidential Decisionmaking in Foreign Policy,* Boulder: Westview Press, 217–38.

Giegerich, B. (2006) 'E3 Leadership in Security and Defence Policy', *CFSP Forum,* 4(6), 5–7.

Gikas, A. and Keenan, R. (2006) *Eurostat 2006 – Statistical aspects of the Energy Economy in 2004,* Luxembourg: OOPEC.

Gill, B. and Huang, Y. (2006) 'Sources and Limits of Chinese Soft Power', *Survival,* 48(2), 17–36.

Ginsberg, R. H. (1999) 'Conceptualizing the European Union as an International Actor: Narrowing the Theoretical Capability–Expectations Gap', *Journal of Common Market Studies,* 37(3), 429–54.

—— (2001) *The European Union in International Politics – Baptism by Fire.* New York: Rowman & Littlefield.

Glarbo, K. (1999) 'Wide-awake Diplomacy: Reconstructing the Common Foreign and Security Policy of the European Union', *Journal of European Public Policy,* 6(4), 634–51.

Gnesotto, N. (2004) 'ESDP: Results and Prospects', in N. Gnesotto (ed.), *EU Security and Defence Policy: The First Five Years (1999–2004)*, Paris: EU ISS, 11–31.

Goetz, K. H. and Hix, S. (eds) (2000) *Europeanised Politics? European Integration and National Political Systems*, Illford: Cass.

Goldstein, J. and Keohane, R. O. (eds) (1993) *Ideas and Foreign Policy: Beliefs, Institutions and Political Change*, Ithaca: Cornell University Press.

Gomez, R. (2003) *Negotiating the Euro-Mediterranean Partnership: Strategic Action in EU Foreign Policy*, Aldershot: Ashgate.

Gomez, R. and Peterson, J. (2001) 'The EU's Impossibly Busy Foreign Ministers: "No one is in control"', *European Foreign Affairs Review*, 6(1), 53–74.

Gourlay, C. (2005) 'EU Civilian Crisis Management', *European Security Review*, 25, 5–8.

Gourlay, C. and Monaco, A. (2005) 'Training Civilians and Soldiers to Improve Security in Iraq: An Update of EU and NATO Efforts', *European Security Review*, 25, 1–3.

Govaere, I., Capiau, J. and Vermeersch, A. (2004) 'In-Between Seats: The Participation of the European Union in International Organizations', *European Foreign Affairs Review*, 9(2), 155–87.

Grabar-Kitarović, K. (2007) 'The Stabilization and Association Process: The EU's Soft Power at Its Best', *European Foreign Affairs Review*, 12(2), 121–5.

Grabbe, H. (2001) 'How Does Europeanization Affect CEE Governance? Conditionality, Diffusion and Diversity', *Journal of European Public Policy*, 8(6), 1013–31.

—— (2003) 'Europeanization Goes East: Power and Uncertainty in the EU Accession Process', in K. Featherstone and C. M. Radaelli (eds), *The Politics of Europeanization*, Oxford: Oxford University Press, 303–27.

—— (2006) 'The Impact of the EU's Biggest Enlargement so far', *CFSP Forum*, 3(3), 1–3.

Grand, C. (2000) 'The European Union and the Non-proliferation of Nuclear Weapons', *Chaillot Paper*, 37, EU ISS, 1–67.

Grant, C. and Barysch, K. (2003) 'The EU–Russia Energy Dialogue', *CER Briefing Note*.

Greiçevci, L., Papadimitriou, D. and Petrov, P. (2007) 'To Build a State: Europeanization, EU Actorness and State-Building in Kosovo', *European Foreign Affairs Review*, 12(2), 219–38.

Groenleer, M. L. P. and Van Schaik, L. (2005) 'The EU as an "Intergovernmental" Actor in Foreign Affairs: Case Studies of the International Criminal Court and the Kyoto Protocol', *CEPS Working Document*, 228.

Guiraudon, V. (2004) 'Immigration and Asylum: A High Politics Agenda', in M. G. Cowles and D. Dinan (eds), *Developments in the European Union 2*, Basingstoke: Palgrave Macmillan, 160–80.

Hadfield, A. (2007) 'Janus Advances? An Analysis of EC Development Policy and the 2005 Amended Cotonou Partnership Agreement', *European Foreign Affairs Review*, 12(1), 39–66.

Halliday, F. (2005) *The Middle East in International Relations: Power, Politics and Ideology*, Cambridge: Cambridge University Press.

Hansen, A. S. (2004) 'Security and Defence: The EU Police Mission in Bosnia-Herzegovina', in W. Carlsnaes, H. Sjursen and B. White (eds), *Contemporary European Foreign Policy*, London: SAGE Publishers, 173–85.

Harpaz, G. (2007) 'Normative Power Europe and the Problem of a Legitimacy Deficit: An Israeli Perspective', *European Foreign Affairs Review*, 12(1), 89–109.

Haukkala, H. (2001) 'The Making of the European Union's Common Strategy on Russia', in H. Haukkala and S. Medvedev (eds), *The EU Common Strategy on Russia: Learning the Grammar of CFSP*, Helsinki: Ulkopoliittinen Instituutti, 22–80.

Haukkala, H. and Medvedev, S. (eds) (2001) *The EU Common Strategy and Russia: Learning the Grammar of the CFSP*. Helsinki: Ulkopoliittinen Instituutti.

Held, D. and McGrew, A. (eds) (2000) *The Global Transformations Reader. An Introduction to the Globalization Debate*, Cambridge: Polity Press.

—— (eds) (2002) *Governing Globalization: Power Authority and Global Governance*, Cambridge: Polity Press.

Held, D., McGrew, A., Goldblatt, D. and Perraton, J. (eds) (1999) *Global Transformations: Politics Economics and Culture*, Cambridge: Polity Press.

Helly, D. (2006a) 'Developing an EU strategy for Security Sector Reform', *European Security Review*, 28, 7–9.

—— (2006b) 'Security Sector Reform: From Concept to Practice', *European Security Review*, 31, 11–13.

Henning, C. R. and Meunier, S. (2005) 'United against the United States? The EU's Role in Global Trade and Finance', in N. Jabko and C. Parsons (eds), *The State of the European Union: With US or against US? European Trends in American Perspective*, Oxford: Oxford University Press, 75–102.

Hill, C. (1993) 'The Capability–Expectations Gap, or Conceptualizing Europe's International Role', *Journal of Common Market Studies*, 31(3), 305–28.

—— (ed.) (1996) *The Actors in Europe's Foreign Policy*, London: Routledge.

—— (2001) 'The EU's Capacity for Conflict Prevention', *European Foreign Affairs Review,* 6(3), 315–33.

—— (2003) *The Changing Politics of Foreign Policy,* Basingstoke: Palgrave Macmillan.

—— (2006a) 'The Directoire and the Problem of a Coherent EU Foreign Policy', *CFSP Forum,* 4(6), 1–4.

—— (2006b) 'The European Powers in the Security Council: Differing Interests, Differing Arenas', in K. E. Smith and K. V. Laatikainen (eds), *Intersecting Multilateralisms: The European Union and the United Nations,* Basingstoke: Palgrave Macmillan, 49–69.

Hill, C. and Smith, K. E. (2000) *European Foreign Policy: Key Documents,* London: Routledge.

Hill, C. and Wallace, W. (1996) 'Introduction: Actors and Actions', in C. Hill (ed.), *The Actors in Europe's Foreign Policy,* London: Routledge, 1–18.

Hillion, C. (2007) 'Mapping-Out the New Contractual Relations between the European Union and its Neighbours: Learning from the EU–Ukraine "Enhanced Agreement"', *European Foreign Affairs Review,* 12(2), 169–82.

Hocking, B. (2002a) 'Introduction: Gatekeepers and Boundary-Spanners – Thinking about Foreign Ministries in the European Union', in B. Hocking and D. Spence (eds), *Foreign Ministries in the European Union: Integrating Diplomats,* Basingstoke: Palgrave Macmillan, 1–17.

—— (2002b) 'Conclusion', in B. Hocking and D. Spence (eds), *Foreign Ministries in the European Union: Integrating Diplomats,* Basingstoke: Palgrave Macmillan, 273–86.

Hocking, B. and Spence, D. (eds) (2005) *Foreign Ministries in the European Union: Integrating Diplomats,* Basingstoke: Palgrave Macmillan.

Hoffmeister, F. (2007) 'Outsider or Frontrunner? Recent Developments under International and European Law on the Status of the European Union in International Organizations and Treaty Bodies', *Common Market Law Review,* 44, 41–68.

Hoffmeister, F. and Kuijper, P.-J. (2006) 'The Status of the European Union at the United Nations: Institutional Ambiguities and Political Realities', in J. Wouters, F. Hoffmeister and T. Ruys (eds), *The United Nations and the European Union: An Ever Stronger Partnership,* The Hague: T.M.C. Asser Press, 9–34.

Hogan, M. (1987) *The Marshall Plan: America, Britain and the Reconstruction of Western Europe, 1947–1952,* Cambridge: Cambridge University Press.

Holland, M. (ed.) (1997) *Common Foreign and Security Policy: The Record and Reforms,* London: Pinter.

—— (2002) *The European Union and the Third World*, Basingstoke: Palgrave Macmillan.

Holslag, J. (2006) 'The European Union and China: The Great Disillusion', *European Foreign Affairs Review*, 11(4), 555–80.

Holsti, K. J. (1970) 'National Role Conceptions in the Study of Foreign Policy', *International Studies Quarterly*, 14(3), 233–309.

—— (1995) *International Politics: A Framework for Analysis*, London: Prentice Hall.

Hoogeveen, F. and Perlot, W. (eds) (2005) *Tomorrow's Mores: The International System, Geopolitical Changes and Energy*, The Hague: Clingendael Institute for International Relations.

Höse, A. and Oppermann, K. (2007) 'Public Opninion and the Development of the European Security and Defence Policy', *European Foreign Affairs Review*, 12(2), 149–67.

House of Lords – EU Committee (2003) *A Fractured Relationship? Relations between the European Union and the United States of America*, London: The Stationery Office.

House of Lords – EU Home Affairs Subcommittee (2005a) *The Hague Programme: A Five Year Agenda for EU Justice and Home Affairs*, London: The Stationery Office.

—— (2005b) *After Madrid: The EU's Response to Terrorism*, London: The Stationery Office.

Howorth, J. (2000) 'Britain, France and the European Defence Initiative', *Survival*, 42(2), 22–55.

—— (2001) 'European Defence and the Changing Politics of the European Union: Hanging together or Hanging separately', *Journal of Common Market Studies*, 39(4), 765–89.

—— (2007) *Security and Defence Policy in the European Union*, Basingstoke: Palgrave Macmillan.

Hudson, V. M. (ed.) (1997) *Culture and Foreign Policy*, Boulder: Lynne Rienner.

Hughes, J. (2007) 'EU Relations with Russia: Partnership or Asymmetric Interdependency?', in N. Casarini and C. Musu (eds), *European Foreign Policy in an Evolving International System: The Road towards Convergence*, London: Palgrave, 76–96.

Hunter Wade, R. (2002) 'US Hegemony and the World Bank: The Fight over People and Ideas', *Review of International Political Economy*, 9(2), 201–29.

Hurt, S. R. (2003) 'Co-operation and Coercion? The Cotonou Agreement between the European Union and ACP States and the End of the Lomé Convention', *Third World Quarterly*, 24(1), 161–76.

Huysmans, J. (2000) 'Contested Community: Migration and the Question of the Political in the EU', in M. Kelstrup and M. C. Williams (eds), *International Relations Theory and the Politics of*

European Integration: Power, Security and Community, London: Routledge, 149–70.

—— (2006) *The Politics of Insecurity: Fear, Migration and Asylum in the EU*, London: Routledge.

Hyde-Price, A. (2004) 'Interests, Institutions and Identities in the Study of European Foreign Policy', in B. Tonra and T. Christiansen (eds), *Rethinking European Union Foreign Policy*, Manchester: Manchester University Press, 99–113.

IGC (2007) Conference of the Representatives of the Governments of the Member States (2007) *Draft Treaty amending the Treaty on European Union and the Treaty establishing the European Community*, CIG 1/1/07, 5 October, Europa website.

Institute for Multiparty Democracy (IMD) (2005) *No Lasting Peace and Prosperity without Democracy – Harnessing Debates on the EU's Future Financial Instruments*, www.democracyagenda.org.

International Crisis Group (ICG) (2003) *Islamic Social Welfare Activism in the Occupied Palestinian Territories: A Legitimate Target?*, Amman/Brussels.

—— (2005) *EU Crisis Response Capability Revisited*, Amman/Brussels.

—— (2006) *Enter Hamas: The Challenges of Political Integration*, Amman/Brussels.

—— (2007) *After Mecca: Engaging Hamas*, Amman/Brussels.

International Institute for Strategic Studies (IISS) (2006) 'Europe', in *The Military Balance 2006*, London, 61–134.

ISIS Europe (2006) 'The EU's Changing Role in Kosovo: What Next?', *European Security Review*, 29.

Jaeger, T. (2002) 'Enhanced Cooperation in the Treaty of Nice and Flexibility in the Common Foreign and Security Policy', *European Foreign Affairs Review*, 7(3), 297–316.

Johansson-Nogués, E. (2006) 'Returned to Europe? The Central and East European Member States at the Heart of the European Union', in K. V. Laatikainen and K. E. Smith (eds), *Intersecting Multilateralisms: The European Union and the United Nations*, Basingstoke: Palgrave Macmillan, 92–111.

Jørgensen, K. E. (1997) 'PoCo: The Diplomatic Republic of Europe', in K. E. Jørgensen (ed.), *Reflective Approaches to European Governance*, London: Macmillan, 167–80.

—— (ed.) (1997) *Reflective Approaches to European Governance*, London: Macmillan.

—— (2004) 'European Foreign Policy: Conceptualising the Domain', in W. Carlsnaes, H. Sjursen and B. White (eds), *Contemporary European Foreign Policy*, London: SAGE, 32–56.

Josselin, D. and Wallace, W. (2001) *Non-state Actors in World Politics*, New York: Palgrave.

Juncos, A. E. (2006) 'Bosnia and Herzegovina: A Testing Ground for the ESDP?', *CFSP Forum,* 4(3), 5–8.

Juncos, A. E. and Pomorska, K. (2007) 'The Deadlock that never Happened: The Impact of Enlargement on the Common Foreign and Security Policy Council Working Groups', *European Political Economy Review,* 6, 4–30.

Juncos, A. E. and Reynolds, C. (2007) 'The Political and Security Committee: Governing in the Shadow', *European Foreign Affairs Review,* 12(2), 127–47.

Kagan, R. (2003) *Paradise and Power,* London: Atlantic Books.

Karagiannis, N. (2004) *Avoiding Responsibility: The Politics and Discourse of European Development Policy,* London: Pluto Press.

Karatnycky, A. (2005) 'Ukraine's Orange Revolution', *Foreign Affairs,* 84(2), 35–52.

Katzenstein, P. J. (1996) *The Culture of National Security: Norms and Identity in World Politics,* New York: Colombia University Press.

Kaul, I., Grunberg, I. and Stern, M. A. (eds) (1999) *Global Public Goods: International Cooperation in the 21st Century,* Oxford: Oxford University Press.

Kelstrup, M. and Williams, M. C. (2000) *International Relations Theory and the Politics of European integration: Power, Security and Community,* London: Routledge.

Keohane, D. (2006) 'Implementing the EU's Counter-Terrorism Strategy: Intelligence, Emergencies and Foreign Policy', in D. Mahncke and J. Monar (eds), *International Terrorism – A European Response to A Global Threat?,* Oxford: Peter Lang Verlag, 63–72.

Keohane, R. O. (1984) *After Hegemony: Cooperation and Discord in the World Political Economy,* New Jersey: Princeton University Press.

Kerremans, B. (2004) 'The European Commission and the EU Member States as Actors in the WTO Negotiating Process: Decision Making between Scylla and Charibdis?', in B. Reinalda and B. Verbeek (eds), *Decision Making within International Organizations,* London: Routledge, 45–58.

—— (2007) 'Proactive Policy Entrepreneur or Risk Minimizer? A Principal–Agent Interpretation of the EU's Role in the WTO', in O. Elgström and M. Smith (eds), *The European Union's Roles in International Politics: Concepts and Analysis,* London: Routledge, 172–88.

Keukeleire, S. (1993) 'Ending the Cold War: The USSR–FRG/EC Partnership and the Changing of the Guard over Eastern Europe', *Cahiers Internationale Betrekkingen en Vredesonderzoek,* 36(2), 31.

—— (1998) *Het buitenlands beleid van de Europese Unie,* Deventer: Kluwer.

—— (2001) 'Directorates in the CFSP/CESDP of the European Union: A Plea for "Restricted Crisis Management Groups"', *European Foreign Affairs Rreview*, 6(1), 75–102.

—— (2002) *Reconceptualizing (European) Foreign Policy: Structural Foreign Policy*, paper presented at the 1st Pan-European Conference on European Union Politics, Bordeaux.

—— (2003) 'The European Union as a Diplomatic Actor: Internal, Traditional and Structural Diplomacy', *Diplomacy and Statecraft*, 14(3), 31–56.

—— (2004) 'Structural Foreign Policy and Structural Conflict Prevention', in J. Wouters and V. Kronenberger (eds), *The European Union and Conflict Prevention: Legal and Policy Aspects*, The Hague: T. M. C. Asser Press, 151–72.

—— (2006a) '"EU Core Groups": Specialization and Division of Labour in EU Foreign Policy', *CEPS Working Document*, 20.

—— (2006b) 'EU Foreign Policy and (the lack of) "Political Will"', *CFSP Forum*, 4(5), 11–4.

—— (2008) *Structural Foreign Policy*, IIEB Working Paper, Leuven: Institute for International and European Policy.

Khader, B. (2001) 'The Economic, Social and Political Impact of the Euro-Mediterranean Partnership', in M. Maresceau and E. Lannon (eds), *The EU's Enlargement and Mediterranean Strategies: A Comparative Analysis*, Basingstoke: Palgrave, 269–82.

Kingah, S. S. (2006) 'The European Union's New Africa Strategy: Grounds for Cautious Optimism', *European Foreign Affairs Review*, 11(4), 527–53.

Knodt, M. (2004) 'International Embeddedness of European Multi-level Governance', *Journal of European Public Policy*, 11(4), 701–19.

Koenig-Archibugi, M. (2002) 'The Democratic Deficit of EU Foreign and Security Policy', *International Spectator*, 37(4), 61–73.

Koutrakos, P. (2001) *Trade, Foreign Policy and Defence in EU Constitutional Law: The Legal Regulation of Sanctions, Exports of Dual-use Goods and Armaments*, Oxford: Hart.

Krahmann, E. (2003) *Multilevel Networks in European Foreign Policy*, Hampshire: Ashgate.

Krause, K. (2002) 'Multilateral Diplomacy, Norm Building, and UN Conferences: The Case of Small Arms and Light Weapons', *Global Governance*, 8(2), 247–73.

Kubálková, V. (ed.), (2001) *Foreign Policy in a Constructed World*, New York: M. A. Sharpe.

Kuran, T. (2004) *Islam and Mammon: The Economic Predicaments of Islamism*, New Jersey: Princeton University Press.

Kurowska, X. (2006) 'Beyond the Balkans but Still in Civilian Uniform: EUJUST THEMIS to Georgia', *CFSP Forum*, 4(3), 8–11.

Laatikainen, K. V. and Smith, K. E. (2006) 'Introduction – The European Union at the United Nations: Leader, Partner or Failure?', in K. E. Smith and K. V. Laatikainen (eds), *Intersecting Multilateralisms: The European Union and the United Nations*, Basingstoke: Palgrave Macmillan, 1–23.

Larsen, H. (1997) 'British Discourses on Europe: Sovereignty of Parliament, Instrumentality and the Non-mythical Europe', in K. E. Jørgensen (ed.), *Reflective Approaches to European Governance*, London: Macmillan, 109–15.

—— (2004) 'Discourse Analysis in the Study of European Foreign Policy', in B. Tonra and T. Christiansen (eds), *Rethinking European Union Foreign Policy*, Manchester: Manchester University Press, 62–80.

Latouche, S. (1996) *The Westernization of the World*, Cambridge: Polity Press.

Laursen, F. and Vanhoonacker, S. (eds) (1992) *The Intergovernmental Conference on Political Union: Institutional Reforms, New Policies and International Identity of the European Union*, Maastricht, Dordrecht: EIPA and Martinus Nijhoff.

Leal-Arcas, R. (2001) 'The European Community and Mixed Agreements', *European Foreign Affairs Review,* 6(4), 483–513.

Lenaerts, K. and Van Nuffel, P. (2005) *Constitutional Law of the European Union*, London: Sweet & Maxwell.

Lerch, M. and Schwellnus, G. (2006) 'Normative by Nature? The Role of Coherence in Justifying the EU's External Human Rights Policy', *Journal of European Public Policy,* 13(2), 304–21.

Light, M. (2001) 'The European Union's Russian Foreign Policy', in K. Malfliet and L. Verpoest (eds), *Russia and Europe in a Changing International Environment*, Leuven: Leuven University Press, 13–24.

Lindstrom, G. (2007) 'Enter the EU Battlegroups', *Chaillot Paper,* 97, EU ISS, 1–90.

Lord, C. (2005) 'Accountable and Legitimate? The EU's International Role', in C. Hill and M. Smith (eds), *International Relations and the European Union*, Oxford: Oxford University Press, 113–33.

Lucarelli, S. and Manners, I. (2006) *Values and Principles in European Union Foreign Policy*, London: Routledge.

Luif, P. (2003) 'EU Cohesion in the UN General Assembly', *Occasional Paper,* 49, EU ISS.

Mahncke, D. and Monar, J. (eds) (2006) *International Terrorism – A European Response to a Global Threat?*, Oxford: Peter Lang Verlag.

Malfliet, K., Verpoest, L. and Vinokurov, E. (eds) (2007) *The CIS, The EU and Russia: Challenges of Integration*, Basingstoke: Palgrave Macmillan.

Malone, D. M. and Khong, Y. F. (eds) (2003) *Unilateralism and US Foreign Policy*, Boulder: Lynne Rienner.

Manners, I. (2002) 'Normative Power Europe: A Contradiction in Terms?', *Journal of Common Market Studies*, 40(2), 235–58.

—— (2006) 'Normative Power Europe Reconsidered: Beyond the Crossroads', *Journal of European Public Policy*, 13(2), 182–99.

Manners, I. and Whitman, R. (eds) (2000a) *The Foreign Policies of European Union Member States*, Manchester: Manchester University Press.

—— (2000b) 'Introduction', in I. Manners and R. Whitman (eds), *The Foreign Policies of European Union Member States*, Manchester: Manchester University Press, 1–16.

—— (2000c) 'Conclusion', in I. Manners and R. Whitman (eds), *The Foreign Policies of European Union Member States*, Manchester: Manchester University Press, 243–73.

Maresceau, M. and Lannon, E. (eds) (2001) *The EU's Enlargement and Mediterranean Strategies: A Comparative Analysis*, Basingstoke: Palgrave Macmillan.

Marshall, G.C. (1947) *The Marshall Plan*, http://usinfo.state.gov/usa/infousa/facts/democrac/57.htm

Martinelli, M. (2006) 'Helping Transition: The EU Police Mission in the Democratic Republic of Congo (EUPOL Kinshasa) in the Framework of EU Policies in the Great Lakes', *European Foreign Affairs Review*, 11(3), 379–99.

Matlary, J. H. (2004) 'Human Rights', in W. Carlsnaes, H. Sjursen and B. White (eds), *Contemporary European Foreign Policy*, London: Sage, 141–54.

Maurer, A., Kietz, D. and Völkel, C. (2005) 'Interinstitutional Agreements in the CFSP: Parliamentarization through the Back Door?', *European Foreign Affairs Review*, 10(2), 175–95.

Mawdsley, J., Martinelli, M. and Remacle, E. (eds) (2004) *Europe and the Global Armament Agenda: Security, Trade and Accountability*, Baden-Baden: Nomos.

Mbangu, L. (2005) 'Recent Cases of Article 96 Consultations', *ECDPM Discussion Paper*, 64.

McInnes, C. and Lee, K. (2006) 'Health, Security and Foreign Policy', *Review of International Studies*, 32, 5–23.

McNamara, K. R. and Meunier, S. (2002) 'Between National Sovereignty and International Power: What External Voice for the Euro?', *International Affairs*, 78(4), 849–68.

Meunier, S. and Nicolaïdis, K. (2005) 'The European Union as a Trade Power', in C. Hill and M. Smith (eds), *International Relations and the European Union*, Oxford: Oxford University Press, 247–69.

Meyer, C. O. (2004) 'Theorising European Strategic Culture: Between Convergence and the Persistence of National Diversity', *CEPS Working Document*, 204, 25.

Missiroli, A. (2003a) 'Ploughshares into Swords? Euros for European Defence', *European Foreign Affairs Review,* 8(3), 5–33.

—— (2003b) 'From Copenhagen to Brussels – European defence: Core Documents, Volume IV', *Chaillot Paper,* 67, EU ISS.

Mölling, C. (2006) 'EU Battle Groups 2007: Where Next?', *European Security Review,* 31, 7–10.

Monar, J. (1997) 'The European Union's Foreign Affairs System after the Treaty of Amsterdam: A "Strengthened Capacity for External Action?"', *European Foreign Affairs Review,* 2(4), 413–36.

—— (2002) 'The CFSP and the Leila/Perejil Island Incident: The Nemesis of Solidarity and Leadership', *European Foreign Affairs Review,* 7(3), 251–6.

Monnet, J. (2003) 'A Ferment of Change', in B. F. Nelsen and A. Stubb (eds), *The European Union: Readings on the Theory and Practice of European Integration,* Basingstoke: Palgrave Macmillan, 19–26.

Mörth, U. (2003) *Organizing European Co-operation – The Case of Armaments,* Lanham: Rowman Littlefield.

Müller-Brandeck-Bocquet, G. (2006) *The Future of European Foreign, Security and Defence Policy after Enlargement,* Baden-Baden: Nomos Verlag.

Neumann, P. (2006) 'Europe's Jihadist Dilemma', *Survival,* 48(2), 71–84.

Nicolas, B. and O'Callaghan, A. (2007) 'Complementarity and Rivalry in EU–China Economic Relations in the Twenty-First Century', *European Foreign Affairs Review,* 12(1), 13–38.

Nugent, N. and Saurugger, S. (2002) 'Organizational Structuring: The Case of the European Commission and its External Policy Responsibilities', *Journal of European Public Policy,* 9(3), 345–64.

Nuttall, S. (1992) *European Political Co-operation,* Oxford: Clarendon Press.

—— (1997a) 'Two Decades of EPC Performance', in E. Regelsberger, P. de Schoutheete de Tervarent and W. Wessels (eds), *Foreign Policy of the European Union: From EPC to CFSP and Beyond,* Boulder: Lynne Rienner, 19–39.

—— (1997b) 'The CFSP Provisions of the Amsterdam Treaty', *CFSP Forum,* 3, 1–2.

—— (2000) *European Foreign Policy,* Oxford: Oxford University Press.

—— (2005) 'Coherence and Consistency', in C. Hill and M. Smith (eds), *International Relations and the European Union,* Oxford: Oxford University Press, 91–112.

Nye, J. S., Jr. (2004) *Soft Power: The Means to Success in World Politics,* New York: Public Affairs.

Ojanen, H. (2000) 'Participation and Influence: Finland, Sweden and the post-Amsterdam Development of the CFSP', *Occasional Paper,* 11, EU ISS, 1–26.

Olsen, G. R. and Pilegaard, J. (2005) 'The Costs of Non-Europe? Denmark and the Common Security and Defence Policy', *European Security*, 14(3), 339–60.

Orsini, D. (2006) 'Future of ESDP: Lessons from Bosnia', *European Security Review*, 29, 9–12.

Osland, K. (2004) 'The EU Police Mission in Bosnia and Herzegovina', *International Peacekeeping*, 11(3), 544–61.

Oudjani, R. (2004) 'EU–Asia Relations', in D. Mahncke, A. Ambos and C. Reynolds (eds), *European Foreign Policy: From Rethoric to Reality?*, Oxford: Peter Lang Verlag, 335–55.

Page, S. and Hewitt, A. (2002) 'The New European Trade Preferences: Does "Everything But Arms" (EBA) Help the Poor?', *Development Policy Review*, 20, 91–102.

Panebianco, S. (2006) 'Promoting Human Rights and Democracy in European Union Relations with Russia and China', in S. Lucarelli and I. Manners (eds), *Values and Principles in European Union Foreign Policy*, London: Routledge, 130–46.

Patrick, S. and Forman, S. (eds) (2002) *Multilateralism and US Foreign Policy: Ambivalent Engagement*, Boulder: Lynne Rienner.

Patten, C. (2005) *Not Quite the Diplomat: Home Truths about World Affairs*, London: Allen Lane.

Peimani, H. (2006) 'The EU and US Policies towards Iran: Common Objectives and Different Approaches', in G. Bono (ed.), *The Impact of 9/11 on European Foreign and Security Policy*, Brussels: VUB Press, 231–56.

Piana, C. (2002) 'The EU's Decision-making Process in the Common Foreign and Security Policy: The Case of the Former Yugoslav Republic of Macedonia', *European Foreign Affairs Review*, 7(2), 209–26.

Pijpers, A., Regelsberger, E. and Wessels, W. (eds) (1988) *European Political Cooperation in the 1980s*, Dordrecht: Martinus Nijhoff.

Pirozzi, N. (2006a) 'UN Peacekeeping in Lebanon: Europe's contribution', *European Security Review*, 30, 1–3.

—— (2006b) 'Aceh Peace Process', *European Security Review*, 31, 13–14.

Pirozzi, N. and Helly, D. (2005) 'Aceh Monitoring Mission: A New Challenge for ESDP', *European Security Review*, 27, 3–6.

Pritzel, I. (1998) *National Identity and Foreign Policy: Nationalism and Leadership in Poland, Russia and Ukraine*, Cambridge: Cambridge University Press.

Pullinger, S. (2006a) 'Why Europe Should Care about Britain's Trident', *European Security Review*, 31, 1–4.

—— (ed.) (2006b) *Developing EU Civil Military Co-ordination: The Role of the New Civilian Military Cell*, Brussels: ISIS Europe and CeMiSS.

Quille, G. (2004) 'The European Security Strategy: A Framework for EU Security Interests?', *International Peacekeeping*, 11(3), 422–38.

Redmond, J. (ed.) (1992) *The External Relations of the European Community: The International Response to 1992*, New York: St Martin's Press.

—— (2007) 'Turkey and the European Union: Troubled European or European Trouble?', *International Affairs*, 83(2), 305–17.

Rees, W. (2006) 'International Cooperation in Counter-Terrorism: The Transatlantic Dimension and Beyond', in D. Mahncke and J. Monar (eds), *International Terrorism – A European Response to a Global Threat?*, Oxford: Peter Lang Verlag, 113–28.

Regelsberger, E., de Schoutheete de Tervarent, P. and Wessels, W. (eds) (1997) *Foreign Policy of the European Union: From EPC to CFSP and Beyond*, Boulder: Lynne Rienner.

Representatives of the Governments of the Member States Meeting within the Council (2006) *Internal Agreement on the Financing of Community Aid under the Multiannual Financial Framework for the Period 2008 to 2013 in Accordance with the ACP–EC Partnership Agreement and on the Allocation of Financial Assistance for the Overseas Countries and Territories to which Part Four of the EC Treaty Applies*, OJ L 247/32–45, 9 September.

Reychler, L. (1994) 'The Art of Conflict Prevention: Theory and Practice', in L. Reychler and W. Bauwens (eds), *The Art of Conflict Prevention*, London/New York: Brassey's, 1–21.

Ribó Labastida, A. (2004) 'EU Foreign Policy towards Latin America', in D. Mahncke, A. Ambos and C. Reynolds (eds), *European Foreign Policy: From Rethoric to Reality?*, Oxford: Peter Lang Verlag, 357–70.

Rosamond, B. (2002) *Theories of European Integration*, Basingstoke: Palgrave Macmillan.

Roy, O. (2004) 'Afghanistan: la difficile reconstruction d'un Etat', *Chaillot Paper, 73,* EU ISS.

Rummel, R. (2004) 'The EU's Involvement in Conflict Prevention – Strategy and Practice', in V. Kronenberger and J. Wouters (eds), *The European Union and Conflict Prevention – Policy and Legal Aspects*, The Hague: T.M.C Asser Press, 67–92.

Rutten, M. (2001) 'From St. Malo to Nice: European Defence: Core Documents', *Chaillot paper*, 47, EU ISS, 1–225.

Sabiote, M. A. (2006) 'EU BAM Rafah: A Test for the EU's Role in the Middle East?', *CFSP Forum*, 4(4), 8–11.

Saferworld, InterAfrica Group and Africa Peace Forum (2005) *Strengthening Civil Society Participation and Promoting Conflict Prevention under the Cotonou Partnership Agreement*, Report of a regional meeting on lessons learned in the Horn of Africa, Nairobi: 14–15 November.

Sauer, T. (2004) 'The "Americanization" of EU Nuclear Non-proliferation Policy', *Defence and Security Analysis,* 20(2), 113–31.

Savage, T. M. (2004) 'Europe and Islam: Crescent Waxing, Cultures Clashing', *Washington Quarterly,* 27(3), 25–50.

Scannell, D. (2004) 'Financing ESDP Military Operations', *European Foreign Affairs Review,* 9(4), 529–49.

Schimmelfennig, F. (2004) 'Liberal Intergovernmentalism', in A. Wiener and T. Diez (eds), *European Integration Theory,* Oxford: Oxford University Press, 75–96.

Schimmelfennig, F., Engert, S. and Knobel, H. (2006) *International Socialization in Europe: European Organisations, Political Conditionality and Democratic Change,* Basingstoke: Palgrave Macmillan.

Schimmelfennig, F. and Sedelmeier, U. (eds) (2005) *The Europeanization of Central and Eastern Europe,* Ithaca: Cornell University Press.

Schimmelfennig, F. and Wagner, W. (2004) 'Preface: External Governance in the European Union', *Journal of European Public Policy,* 11(4), 657–60.

Schmitt, B. (2003) 'The European Union and Armaments: Getting a Bigger Bang for the Euro', *Chaillot Paper,* 63, EU ISS, 1–69.

—— (2004) 'European Capabilities: How many Divisions?', in N. Gnesotto (ed.), *EU Security and Defence Policy: The First Five Years (1999–2004),* Paris: EU ISS, 89–110.

—— (2005) *Defence Procurement in the European Union,* Report of an EU ISS Task Force, Paris: EU ISS.

Schori, P. (2005) 'Painful Partnership: The United States, the European Union, and Global Governance', *Global Governance,* 11(3), 273–80.

Schroeder, U. C. (2006) 'Converging Problems – Compartmentalised Solutions: The Security–development Interface in EU Crisis Management', *CFSP Forum,* 4(3), 1–4.

Schuman, R. (1950) *Declaration of 9 May 1950,* Europa website.

Secretary General/High Representative (2000) *Common Strategies Report,* 21 December, Brussels.

Sjøstedt, G. (1977) *The External Role of the European Community,* Farnborough: Saxon House.

Sjursen, H. (ed.) (2006) 'What Kind of Power? European Foreign Policy in Perspective', *Journal of European Public Policy,* 13(2), 167–327.

Smith, B. (2002) *Report of the EC Rapid Reaction Mechanism Assessment Mission: Pakistan Education,* Europa website.

Smith, K. E. (2003) *European Union Foreign Policy in a Changing World,* Cambridge: Polity Press.

—— (2005) 'The Outsiders: The European Neighbourhood Policy', *International Affairs,* 81(4), 757–73.

Smith, M. (1997) 'The Commission and External Relations', in G. Edwards and D. Spence (eds), *The European Commission*, Essex: Longman, 262–302.

Smith, M. E. (2001) 'Diplomacy by Decree: The Legalization of EU Foreign Policy', *Journal of Common Market Studies*, 39(1), 79–104.

—— (2004) *Europe's Foreign and Security Policy*, Cambridge: Cambridge University Press.

Smith, S. (2000) 'International Theory and European Integration', in M. Kelstrup and M. C. Williams (eds), *International Relations Theory and the Politics of European Integration: Power, Security and Community*, London: Routledge, 33–56.

Söderbaum, F. and Van Langenhove, L. (eds) (2006) *The EU as a Global Player: The Politics of Interregionalism*, London: Routledge.

Soetendorp, B. (1999) *Foreign Policy in the European Union*, London: Routledge.

Sourd, R. (2005) 'L'Union et l'Afrique subsaharienne: quel partenariat?', *Occasional Paper*, 58, EU ISS.

Stavridis, S. (2000) 'Confederal Consociation and Foreign Policy: The Case of the CFSP of the EU', *European Integration*, 22(4), 381–408.

Stetter, S. (2004) 'Cross-pillar Politics: Functional Unity and Institutional Fragmentation of EU Foreign Policies', *Journal of European Public Policy*, 11(4), 720–39.

Stockholm International Peace Research Institute (SIPRI) (2002) *SIPRI Yearbook 2002: Armaments, Disarmament and International Security*,Oxford: Oxford University Press.

—— (2004) *SIPRI Yearbook 2004: Armaments, Disarmament and International Security*, Oxford: Oxford University Press.

—— (2006) *The SIPRI Military Expenditure Database*, http://first.sipri.org/.

Strange, S. (1994) *States and Markets*, London: Pinter.

Stubb, A. (2002) *Negotiating Flexibility in the European Union: Amsterdam, Nice and Beyond*, Basingstoke: Palgrave Macmillan.

Télo, M. (ed.) (2001) *European Union and New Regionalism: Regional Actors and Global Governance in a Post Hegemonic Era*, Aldershot: Ashgate.

Thieux, L. (2004) 'European Security and Global Terrorism: The Strategic Aftermath of the Madrid Bombings', *Perspectives: Central European Review of International Affairs*, 22, 59–74.

Thym, D. (2006) 'Beyond Parliament's Reach? The Role of the European Parliament in the CFSP', *European Foreign Affairs Review*, 11(1), 109–27.

Tocci, N. (2006) 'Has the EU Promoted Democracy in Palestine...and Does it still?', *CFSP Forum*, 4(2), 7–10.

Tonra, B. (1997) 'The Impact of Political Cooperation', in K. E. Jørgensen (ed.), *Reflective Approaches to European Governance*, London: Macmillan, 181–98.

—— (2001) *The Europeanisation of National Foreign Policy: Dutch, Danish and Irish Foreign Policy in the European Union*, Aldershot: Ashgate.

—— (2003) 'Constructing the Common Foreign and Security policy: The Utility of a Cognitive Approach', *Journal of Common Market Studies*, 41(4), 731–56.

—— (2006) 'Conceptualizing the European Union's Global Role', in M. Cini and A. K. Bourne (eds), *European Union Studies*, Basingstoke: Palgrave Macmillan, 117–30.

Tonra, B. and Christiansen, T. (2004) *Rethinking European Union Foreign Policy*, Manchester: Manchester University Press.

Ulriksen, S., Mace, C. and Gourlay, C. (2004) 'Operation Artemis: The Shape of the Things to Come?', *International Peacekeeping*, 11(3), 508–26.

UNAIDS and WHO (2006) *Report on the global AIDS epidemic*. www.unaids.org.

UNDP (1994) *Human Development Report 1994: New Dimensions of Human Security*, http://hdr.undp.org.

—— (2006) *Human Development Report 2006 – Beyond Scarcity: Power, Poverty and the Global Water Crisis*, http://hdr.undp.org/.

—— (yearly) *Human Development Report*, http://hdr.undp.org/.

United Nations (2000) *World Leaders Invited to Sign Key Treaties at United Nations Millennium Summit*, http://www.un.org/millennium/media/treaties.htm.

—— (2007) *United Nations Treaty Collection*, http://untreaty.un.org.

Vahl, M. (2007) 'EU–Russia Relations in EU Neighbourhood Policies', in K. Malfliet, L. Verpoest and E. Vinokurov (eds), *The CIS, the EU and Russia*, Basingstoke: Palgrave Macmillan, 121–41.

Van Ham, P. (2004) 'The EU's War over Iraq: The Last Wake-Up Call', in D. Mahncke, A. Ambos and C. Reynolds (eds), *European Foreign Policy: From Rethoric to Reality?*, Oxford: Peter Lang Verlag, 209–26.

Vatikiotis, M. (2006) 'The Architecture of China's Diplomatic Edge', *Brown Journal of World Affairs*, 12(2), 25–37.

Viggo Jakobsen, P. (2006) 'The ESDP and Civilian Rapid Reaction: Adding Value is Harder than Expected', *European Security*, 15(3), 299–322.

Vogler, J. (2005) 'The European Contribution to Global Environmental Governance', *International Affairs*, 81(4), 835–50.

Waever, O. (1993) 'Societal Security: The Concept', in O. Waever, B. Buzan, M. Kelstrup and P. Lemaitre (eds), *Identity, Migration and the New Security Agenda in Europe*, London: Pinter, 17–27.

—— (1995) 'Securitization and Desecuritization', in R. D. Lipschutz (ed.), *On Security*, Columbia: Columbia University Press, 46–86.

—— (1998) 'Insecurity, Security and Asecurity in the West European Non-war Community', in E. Adler and M. Barnett (eds), *Security Communities*, Cambridge: Cambridge University Press, 69–118.

—— (2000) 'The EU as a Security Actor: Reflections from a Pessimistic Constructivist on Post-sovereign Security Orders', in M. Kelstrup and M. C. Williams (eds), *International Relations Theory and the Politics of European Integration: Power, Security and Community*, London: Routledge, 250–94.

Wagner, W. (2006) 'The Democratic Control of Military Power Europe', *Journal of European Public Policy,* 13(2), 200–16.

Wallace, H. (2000) 'The Policy Process: A Moving Pendulum', in H. Wallace and W. Wallace (eds), *Policy-Making in the European Union*, Oxford: Oxford University Press, 39–64.

—— (2005) 'An Institutional Anatomy and Five Policy Modes', in H. Wallace, W. Wallace and M. A. Pollack (eds), *Policy–Making in the European Union*, Oxford: Oxford University Press, 49–90.

Wendt, A. (1999) *Social Theory of International Politics*, Cambridge: Cambridge University Press.

Wessel, R. A. (1999) *The European Union's Foreign and Security Policy: A Legal Institutional Perspective*, The Hague: Kluwer Law International.

White, B. (1999) 'The European Challenge to Foreign Policy Analysis', *European Journal of International Relations,* 5(1), 37–66.

—— (2001) *Understanding European Foreign Policy*, Basingstoke: Palgrave Macmillan.

Whitman, R. (2006) 'Road Map for a Route March? (De–)civilianizing through the EU's Security Strategy', *European Foreign Affairs Review,* 11(1), 1–15.

Wilkinson, P. (2005) 'International Terrorism: The Changing Threat and the EU's Response', *Chaillot Paper,* 84, EU ISS.

Wolfers, A. (1962) *Discord and Collaboration: Essays on International Politics*, Baltimore: The Johns Hopkins Press.

Wong, R. (2005) 'The Europeanization of Foreign Policy', in C. Hill and M. Smith (eds), *International Relations and the European Union*, Oxford: Oxford University Press, 134–53.

—— (2007) 'Foreign Policy', in P. Graziano and M. P. Vink (eds), *Europeanization*, Basingstoke: Palgrave Macmillan, 321–34.

Woolcock, S. (2005) 'Trade Policy', in H. Wallace, W. Wallace and M.A. Pollack (eds), *Policy-Making in the European Union*, Oxford: Oxford University Press, 377–400.

Wouters, J., Hoffmeister, F. and Ruys, T. (eds) (2006) *The United Nations and the European Union: An Ever Stronger Partnership*, The Hague: T. M. C. Asser Press.

Wouters, J. and Kronenberger, V. (eds) (2004) *The European Union and Conflict Prevention – Policy and Legal Aspects*, The Hague: T. M. C. Asser Press.

Wulf, H. (2006) 'Stopping North Korea's Nuclear Programme: An Active Role for the EU', *European Security Review*, 31, 4–7.

Youngs, R. (2001) 'European Union Democracy Promotion Policies: Ten Years on', *European Foreign Affairs Review*, 6(3), 355–73.

—— (2002) *The European Union and the Promotion of Democracy – Europe's Mediterranean and Asian Policies*, Oxford: Oxford University Press.

—— (2004) 'Normative Dynamics and Strategic Interests in the EU's External Identity', *Journal of Common Market Studies*, 42(2), 415–35.

—— (2006) 'The EU and Conflict in West Africa', *European Foreign Affairs Review*, 11(3), 333–52.

Yu, W. and Jensen, T. V. (2005) 'Tariff Preferences, WTO Negotiations and LDCs: The Case of the "Everything But Arms" Initiative', *The World Economy*, 28(3), 375–405.

Zehetner, T. (2007) 'Waiting in the Wings – The Civilian ESDP Mission in Kosovo', *European Security Review*, 33, 4–7.

Zielonka, J. (2006) *Europe as Empire : The Nature of the Enlarged European Union*, Oxford: Oxford University Press.

Index